SMOOTHING THE GROUND
ESSAYS ON NATIVE AMERICAN ORAL LITERATURE

SMOOTHING THE GROUND
ESSAYS ON NATIVE AMERICAN ORAL LITERATURE

edited by BRIAN SWANN

University of California Press
Berkeley, Los Angeles, London

University of California Press
Berkeley and Los Angeles, California
University of California Press, Ltd.
London, England

©1983 by The Regents of the University of California

Library of Congress Cataloging in Publication Data

Main entry under title:

Smoothing the ground.

   I. Indian literature — History and criticism — Addresses,
essays, lectures.   I. Swann, Brian.
PM156.S6   1982   810′.9′897   82-16155
ISBN 0-520-04902-0
ISBN 0-520-04913-6 (pbk.)

Designed and Typeset at
The Cooper Union Center for Design and Typography,
New York City.

An old storyteller would smooth the ground in front of him with his hand and make two marks in it with his right thumb, two with his left, and a double with both thumbs together. Then he would rub his hands, and pass his right hand up his right leg to his waist, and touch his left hand and pass it on up his right arm to his breast. He did the same thing with his left and right hands going up the other side. Then he touched the marks on the ground with both hands and rubbed them together and passed them over his head and all over his body.

[*Cheyenne Memories*, John Stands in Timber & Margot Liberty]

Some of the essays in this book have appeared in journals.

Portions of Kenneth Lincoln's "Native American Literatures" appeared in *The Southwest Review* 60, no. 2 (Spring 1975): 101–116, and the *American Indian Culture and Research Journal* 1, no. 4 (1976): 14–21 and vol. 4, nos. 1–2 (1980): 1–17.

Dennis Tedlock, "On the Translation of Style in Oral Narrative," reproduced by permission of the American Folklore Society from *The Journal of American Folklore* 84 (331): 114–33, 1971.

John Bierhorst, "American Indian Verbal Art and the Role of the Literary Critic," reproduced by permission of the American Folklore Society from *The Journal of American Folklore* 88 (350): 401–08, 1975.

Jeffrey F. Huntsman's essay, "Traditional Native American Literature: the Translation Dilemma," appeared in an earlier version in *Shantih*, 4, no. 2 (Summer-Fall, 1979): 5–9.

Pat Carr's and Willard Gingerich's "The *Vagina Dentata* Motif in Nahuatl and Pueblo Mythic Narratives: A Comparative Study," appeared in *New Scholar* 8, no. 1, (1981).

"Poetry and Culture: the Navajo Example," by Paul G. Zolbrod, appeared in an earlier version in *Shantih* 4, no. 2 (Summer-Fall, 1979): 10–14.

Arnold Krupat's "The Indian Autobiography: Origins, Type, and Function," appeared in *American Literature* 53, no. 1, (March, 1981): 22–42. (Copyright 1981, Duke University Press, Durham, N.C.)

"Indian Sacred Materials: Kroeber, Waters, and Kroeber," by H. David Brumble III, appeared in *The Canadian Review of American Studies* 11, no. 1 (Spring, 1980): 32–48. "Reasoning Together" appeared in the Fall, 1981 issue.

Karl Kroeber's "Poem, Dream, and the Consuming of Culture," appeared in *The Georgia Review* 32, no. 2 (Summer, 1978) : 266–80.

I would like to thank the editors of these journals for permission to reprint, and thanks also to the Summer Institute of Linguistics for permission to use Comanche material in Galen Buller's essay "Comanche and Coyote, the Culture Maker," and to Everett/Edwards, Inc., publishers of the cassette tape, *American Indian Folklore,* ed. Harry Cohen, (1979), where portions of Kenneth Roemer's "Native American Oral Narratives : Context and Continuity," first appeared. We are grateful to The University of New Mexico Press for permission to use section XVI of N. Scott Momaday's *The Way to Rainy Mountain* in Kenneth Roemer's essay.

I would like to thank Kenneth Lincoln, Publications Chairman of the UCLA American Indian Studies Center, for his support and editorial acumen. Thanks also to Campbell Grant whose photograph of Chumash rock art is used for the cover of this book.

I apologize for not having Native American scholars represented in this volume. I contacted all those I knew who were working in the field, but at the time they had nothing appropriate for the book. I regret the omission of such important scholars as Alfonso Ortiz, Ines Talamantez, Vine Deloria, Bea Medicine, N. Scott Momaday, Paula Gunn Allen, Leslie Marmon Silko, and others.

I would like to express my thanks to George Sadek, Director of The Cooper Union Center for Design and Typography, for generously taking on this project, and to Thomas Kluepfel, Designer; Marina Kyprianou, Typographer; and Elizabeth Ginsberg, Typesetter, whose skills saw it through to completion.

Brian Swann: INTRODUCTION

ONE The languages of North America were, and are, various and diverse. Each, in prayer, story, speech, or song, made the Word central in its culture.[1] At the head of this volume, John Stands in Timber describes the sacredness of the word among the Cheyenne, and Chief Buffalo Long Lance has outlined how the mothers of his tribe set large store by correct language usage. Someone who used language without "absolute correctness," he says, was "relegated to an outcast in the tribe," and was never allowed to speak in public.[2] Early visitors to the Iroquois were impressed by the oratorical skills of speakers whom they, unaware of the rhetorical training involved, assumed to be naturally and natively inspired. The Word, in fact, is a sacrament, a vital force, so that, for instance, a hunting song is not just a pleasant aesthetic experience, but possesses an active relationship with the hunting act. "The purpose of the song," writes the contemporary Native American poet Simon Ortiz, "is first of all to do things well, the way that they're supposed to be done, part of it being the singing and performing of a song. And that I receive, again well and properly, the things that are meant to be returned to me. I express myself as well as realize the experience."[3]

It is only natural that a society which carried its past in the spoken word, and incorporated its values in story and song, would invest words with reverence and power. Our own vocabulary is hardly adequate to encompass the phenomena of the Word in Native American literature and life. All too often, our rationalistic bias has been satisfied to describe the word-phenomena in such phrases as 'sympathetic word-magic'. This is probably because we ourselves, having contaminated words, have lost faith in them. In our society, words have been suborned. "Oversold like detergents," they wave "their long tails in public / With their prostitute's exclamations."[4]

Kenneth Rexroth has written: "Poetry and song does not play a vatic role in Native American society, but is itself a numinous thing. The role of art is holy—in Rudolph Otto's sense—an object of supernatural awe, and as such an important instrument in the control of reality on the highest plane."[5] In an Indian context, however, the concept of 'control' does not really obtain. Reality is not 'controlled,' no matter on how high a plane. We would do better to talk about reciprocity, balancing, right acting and right telling in the interests of equilibrium. Power *flowed;* it was not wielded. As often as not, power itself does the choosing, for on the highest level power is a force for common good.[6] In matters of the spirit there was no real hierarchy, since matters of the spirit were simultaneously matters of the mundane. As Lame Deer explained (and Black Elk said the same thing): "We Indians live in a world of symbols and images where the spiritual and the commonplace are one."[7]

If, then, we are to approach Native American literature and take what it offers, we will have to cleanse our own words, and reorient our minds. We will also have to revitalize our religious terminology. Rexroth's phrase "supernatural awe," for example, does not describe the Indian's relationship to *wakan* or *orenda*. *Wakan* is a quality in all things (the translation of 'Wakan Tanka', as 'Great Spirit', is a missionary's misleading interpretation). It is closer to being "the creative force of the universe."[8] "Religious awe" suggests a large element of fear in the "holy" and potential self-abasement. This may be appropriate enough for the white man's understanding of holiness, but not, it is clear, Black Elk's relationship to his Great Vision.

A truly sacramental sense of language means that object and word are so fused that their creation, the 'event,' is itself creative, bringing into this time and place the enduring powers which truly effect that which the event claims, and such action cannot be undone. Its only aim and intent is truth, not manipulation. 'Correct' form, in such a context, is the fundamental moral dimension of the human engagement with words. Lies destroy correct form. They destroy the real relationship between man and the natural order. When an Indian made a treaty, he did so with a formula invoking the growing of grass and the running of waters. He linked the truth of words to the truth of nature.

For the Indian there was great power in words. The story, the 'event,' was often regarded as having a life of its own; an entity existing independent of its narrator, (a phenomenon similar to that described by Edward Sapir where a name exists independent of the bearer). In *Wishram Texts,* Sapir collected a story called, simply, "The Story Concerning Coyote." After performing a deed of self-fellation, Coyote attempted to lock up the story of his deed. Some say he locked it up in a mountain north of the Columbia River, whose name was 'Story'. But the story of Coyote's deed burst out with tremendous force, causing clefts in the mountain. Thus, a story brings about its own consequences. It is a repository of irrepressible truth, and reveals itself spontaneously, despite all efforts to hold it in.[9]

Two

Where do we find these stories? Apart from the living continuing tradition,[10] one place is in the comfortable old green volumes of the 47 Annual Reports of the Bureau of American Anthropology, Department of the Smithsonian, which were published from 1881–1932. The collectors of this 'sacred art' (songs, poems, stories, dramas) were anthropologists, ethnologists, linguists; distinguished scholars such as Boas, Sapir, Kroeber, Radin. They deserve our gratitude, for without their dedication much of great value would have been lost forever. In these green volumes I first began reading Native American literature, and then went on to supplement my reading with material published by the American Ethnological Society, such as Ruth Bunzel's *Zuni Texts,* or William Jones's *Kickapoo Tales,* with its Wıza'kä'ą cycle. I also came across Leonard Bloomfield's *Menomini Texts,* in which there are a score of memorable stories, including my favorite "The Man Who Married a Deer Woman."[11] These series, and others, are, of course, still available in libraries. But what we now need are new versions, or better still, new translations in cheap editions for school and college use; translations with the same fundamental engagement with language as that of the original creators. Dell Hymes has put out a call for new translations which utilize "the perspectives and tools of linguistics" as well as "anthropological philology." In his essay he outlines the need, in addition, for skilled poet translators. "The contemporary reader," he writes, "now has modern translations of Greek drama by Lattimore, Fitzgerald, Grene, Arrowsmith and others that are manifestly poems in a contemporary idiom; but for much Amerindian poetry, he has translations from two poetic generations ago, or more, many of which are not even by intention poetry, but careful prose."[12]

Hymes himself has set about the task, (in this, as in much else, opening the way). In his translations, he utilizes the discovery that behind the plain prose of the texts is a complex poetic structure, and that what, in poetry, appear to be meaningless syllables, under analysis turn out to serve a structural purpose. In addition to Hymes, Dennis Tedlock has probably provided the most exciting translations in his *Finding the Center: Narrative Poetry of the Zuni Indians* (Lincoln, Nebraska, 1977). Here the text is scored for voicing, and a sense of 'total' translation comes over. Then, in addition to this kind of attention, a tradition going back to Longfellow has continued, a tradition of 'versions' and inspirational influence. The names of Yvor Winters, Rexroth, Snyder, Wagoner, Merwin, come immediately to mind, as well as Rothenberg's recastings, which are attempts to get back to the original effect or 'feel' of a performance.[13]

THREE

Sooner or later the question arises: Why have we had to wait so long for attention to be paid? Milman Parry discovered the oral-formulaic structure of Homer about forty years ago. Why has it taken so long for his lead to be followed in America? Is it only in the last few years that racist attitudes have changed to any large degree? Possibly, though a glance at recent events in the Mohawk Nation, the Pacific Northwest, the destruction of Indian lands and people in the Southwest, the northern Great Plains, and elsewhere, plus the various bills in Congress aimed at eliminating the land-base of Indians—e.g. H.R. 9054, H.R. 9951—should cause one to temper one's optimism. Perhaps the reason why Native American oral literature is finally being taken seriously is that, as Harry Levin has suggested, "the Word as spoken or sung, together with the visual image of the speaker or singer," has been regaining its hold through "electrical engineering."[14] A culture based on the written word has undergone change. Pleas have been made by educators for new understanding of 'primary' and 'secondary' orality, since universities are now called upon to teach students from oral backgrounds. "Our students from oral or residually oral cultures," writes Walter J. Ong, SJ, "come not from an unorganized world, but from a world which is differently organized, in ways which can now be at least partially understood."[15]

Moreover, cultural arrogance and attitudes of cultural imperialism, while they have by no means disappeared, have weakened, at least for the moment. The civil rights movement has had much to do with this. Also, the later twentieth century has been an age of contact, of translation, of cross-cultural connections on a large scale, when things thought exclusive or disparate have been brought into fruitful proximity and contact. The old certainties, the assumptions of cultural superiority, which many in the nineteenth century held as gospel, have largely disappeared. We no longer come across such blatant condescension as this from the introduction to *Ojibwa Texts,* published in 1917 by the American Ethnological Society: "Simplicity is a characteristic mode of the narratives throughout: they run along with such an even, quiet pace, that they leave an impression of dull monotony."[16]

The fact is that Western man has at last begun to realize his limitations. His values are being called in question, and the literature of warning, from Commoner to Lasch, points to his "effective loss of cultural traditions."[17] And now, at last, some people are ready to accept the fact that they have a culture and a literature on their own doorstep through which they can begin to relearn values.[18]

For a long time, Native American literature had been treated as tales for children.[19] Native American literature is adult and serious. This does not mean that it is gray and downbeat, or that children cannot enjoy it (in fact, a number of stories are deliberately intended for children—but what an Indian meant by a child and what we mean are hardly the same thing). Quite the contrary. The stories are often funny and bawdy, and always affirm life. The aim, in Cicero's phrase, is to instruct and to delight. The purpose is to tell the truth, even if the truth, as revealed for instance by Melville Jacobs' analyses, is often disturbing and frequently horrific or frightening.[20] As an old Eskimo told Knut Rasmussen: "Our narratives deal with the experiences of man, and these experiences are not always pleasant or pretty. But it is not proper to change our stories to make them more acceptable to our ears, that is if we wish to tell the truth. Words must be the echo of what has happened and cannot be made to conform to the mood and the taste of the listener."[21] It would be hard to find a higher concept of verbal art!

Perhaps it is because our own society is so lacking in balance and authentic symbolism, so void of a concept of *man* as a total being, so lacking in self-confidence, that it has become able to look more humbly on those cultures which before it had sought to destroy.[22] There are attitudes and energies present in Native American society which we look on with envy. For this society has placed the heaviest stress on keeping everything in balance and good order, within what one might call a cosmic framework and reference. This can be seen in the symbolism of the Sioux circular encampment, as well as in the function of their *heyoka,* sacred clowns, "upside-down" men, as Lame Deer called them,[23] who, by destroying the balance of expectations and norms, draw attention to that which they challenge, and so strengthen and reinstate it. This sense of cosmic balance can be seen in the architecture of the Pawnee who orient their structures cosmically,[24] an orientation, incidentally, which was once part of our own civilization, as Vincent Scully has shown.[25] (It is curious how, despite the distance between White and Native American civilizations, so often one comes upon some feature which strikes strange familiar chords, as if we had been there before.)

"I was not born and raised on this land for fun," said the Sioux, Crow Feather.[26] What is revealed in Native American societies is, then, a sense of the seriousness of man's existence. The meaningfulness of life, not its meaninglessness. The stories and poems are a record of vital, vigorous peoples, confident in their achievements and abilities, and proud of their civilizations. As one man said: "What is civilization? Its marks are a noble religion and philosophy, original arts, stirring music, rich story and legend. We had these."[27] Everything in this civilization had a place, and its order was not so much imposed as proven to be good by its being *lived*. Man himself discovers what is best. There is no divine fiat which he is forced to obey. Everything is 'fitted.' This is the point of a story in one of Melville Jacobs' collections, "The Animals Determine Who Will Be Elk," where they all try on the antlers. Jack Rabbit runs off so fast he gets skinny. When they catch him he's all bone and good for nothing. The other animals produce similar results, until Elk puts on the antlers and they suit him perfectly. He couldn't run so fast, and so when he was caught he was still fat.[28]

In short, then, it is about time that we began to study this literature as seriously as we study Faulkner or Hemingway. There is wisdom here that we need to heed. Man is not the conqueror in these stories, for the conqueror role is ultimately self-defeating. Instead, the stories and poems concern themselves with what Aldo Leopold, referring to the biosphere, called "lines of dependence."[29] Man is a triumphant survivor, always adequate to the task, ready to take risks and learn. There is little or no sense of alienation and its attendant figure, irony. The aim is wisdom, not irony, elegant or otherwise.

There are at least two reasons for understanding Native American literature. One, to overcome one's cultural isolation and narcissism by studying a civilization different in many important ways from our own. And two, in order to understand more of ourselves and our own civilization. This entails confronting our own psyche and our history, a history which is still all too often sentimentalized and misrepresented. We still perpetuate myths of how the country was won. As Richard Slotkin has written, "a people unaware of its myths is likely to continue living by them though the world around that people may change and demand changes in their psychology, their world view, and their institutions."[30] It was tragic that we were still living a powerful national myth in Viet Nam, where the enemy became Gooks, descendants of Chingachgook. The United States owes a large part of its national character to the suppression of its Indian past. "The conquest of the Indians made the country uniquely American," as Michael Rogin has noted.[31] And Octavio Paz has remarked that while Mexico is the most Spanish country in Latin America, it is also the most Indian. On the other hand, the Indian element in the

United States is invisible, the reason being that "the Christian horror of 'fallen nature' extends to the natives of America: the United States was founded on a land without a past. The historical memory of Americans is European, not American."[32] The American, then, is always searching for roots, since he refused to graft himself onto the plant already flourishing when he arrived and instead did his best to eradicate it. As Paz notes, one of the most persistent themes in American literature from Melville and Thoreau to Faulkner,[33] from Whitman to William Carlos Williams, has been the search for and invention of American roots. How long can we, in our alienation and loneliness, afford to neglect, ignore, and pervert our *American* past? Who better to tell us about it than the first Americans?

To this end I have assembled the following essays and translations. We are in a renaissance—more properly a *naissance*. But the message has only just begun to trickle into the classrooms. So one of the main aims of this book is to make it possible for teachers to begin including Native American stories and poems in their courses on American literature, or oral literature, or American history, or whatever. Within a few years I would like to see Minabozho as familiar to undergraduates as Billy Budd!

I believe the time is ripe for a collection of essays which outlines the scope and achievements of what is, after all, a new discipline, incorporating anthropology, linguistics, folklore, translation, and criticism into a new and vital field of study. After this book appears, I hope that what Melville Jacobs once claimed will no longer be true: "Except for a small band of professional folklorists, readers of non-Western literature are, I suppose, about as rare as nuclear physicists who read Bulgarian poetry."[34]

New York City, 1980

NOTES

[1]For a discussion of "American Indian languages," see Harry Hoijer et al., *Linguistic Structures of Native America* (Viking Fund Publications in Anthropology, no. 6, 1944).

[2]*Long Lance* (New York, 1929), p. 6. It is interesting to note that Mary Austin had remarked on the compositional method of native orators. "Direct observation," she says, "of Indian speech-making leads the writer to conclude that the aboriginal orator composed his speech in units, the order and arrangements of which were varied to meet the special audience" (*The Cambridge History of American Literature*, ed. Trent, Erskine, Sherman, and Van Doren [New York, 1969], p. 613).

[3]*Sun Tracks,* Spring 1977, p. 10.

[4]Ted Hughes, "Crow Tries the Media," *Crow* (New York, 1971), p. 35. As a result of the deterioration in word-usage we are unable to approach words in their purest form, that is, in poetry. How many people read poetry today? Moreover, the words that survive commercialization (vile word!) or indifference are themselves subject to attack. We have upon us, for example, an influential band of ironists called deconstructivists who march under the banner of Jacques Derrida. We are now being told that the idea of the 'text' has been redefined. To believe that words have

meanings and that texts refer to something beyond themselves is now charmingly naive. To Derrida and his followers, meaning is lost, dead, or hidden. Meaning becomes a form of mystification. Texts must be read *sous rature,* under erasure, so that at once texts mean and do not mean. The explication of a text, a task for the new priesthood, becomes of as much importance as the text itself. We are led into a mad mirror world where symbols refer to symbols and the concept of a real world becomes, to all intents and purposes, pointless. "Life to us is a symbol to be lived," said Lame Deer, (p. 118). But symbols for the deconstructivists are ends in themselves. Right and responsible action has no place in such a world. The outward turn into narrative is rejected for withdrawal into a world of words. The growth of this movement and the consequent decline of mimetic theory is part of the contemporary bankruptcy of humanism, part of our defunct ontology.

[5] "American Indian Songs," *Assays* (New York, 1961), p. 56.

[6] 'Power,' in its most meaningful sense of spiritual power, is a fusion of active and passive. It links past and present in profound conservatism. As an informant told Morris Edward Opler: "It seems that the powers select for themselves. Perhaps you want to be a shaman of a certain kind, but the powers don't speak to you. It seems that, before power wants to work through you, you've got to be just so, as in the original time," *An Apache Life-Way* (New York, 1956), p. 202. All essential time is, then, through power, made into original and eternal time. Our idea of power, on the other hand, is simply to perpetrate individualistic time.

[7] John Fire/Lame Deer and Richard Erdoes, *Lame Deer, Seeker of Visions* (New York, 1972), p. 101.

[8] Raymond J. DeMallie, Jr., and Robert H. Lavenda, "Wakan: Plains Siouan Concepts of Power," in *The Anthropology of Power: Ethnographic Studies from Asia, Oceania, and the New World* (New York, 1977), p. 154.

[9] *Publications of the American Ethnological Society* 2 (Leyden, 1909). Sapir's literally-rendered version of the story is as follows:

THE STORY CONCERNING COYOTE

"And then he went on. He went and went (until) he seated himself. And then Coyote looked all around. Then Coyote sucked himself. Thus he did: he turned up his penis, and bent down his head (so that) he stooped down. Coyote said: 'You have not done me good.' And then Coyote locked up the story (of his obscene act); he did not wish that people should find out about it. So he headed the story off. But then the story loosened itself; they caused it to break out (from its prison).

And then everybody found out what Coyote had done to himself."

Sapir notes:

"The text is obscure. It is said that Coyote requested all things present not to carry off the 'story,' but forgot about the clouds (itká)*, just then sailing above the spot. Not bound by a promise, they tore out the 'story' from its fastness and conveyed it to the people. Thus was explained how all had heard of Coyote's obscenity, though no one had witnessed it, and though he himself did not tell anyone of it. North of the Columbia and opposite Mosier may still be seen a long, high mountain called* Idwô 'tea *or 'Story,' in which Coyote attempted to lock up the 'Story.' Its clefts are due to the sudden force with which*

the 'story' broke out."

[10]A number of scholars have done valuable work on contemporary, living oral narrative. The classic work here is "Poetic Retranslation and the 'Pretty Languages' of Yellowman," by Barre Toelken and Tacheeni Scott, reprinted in *Traditional American Indian Literatures: Texts and Interpretations,* ed. Karl Kroeber (Lincoln, Neb.: 1981).

[11]Note the words "text" and "tale," one denoting a linguistic function, the other a folkloric orientation. It is time to call these "texts" and "tales" what they are: stories, literature, no matter if "literature" presupposes the use of letters and the use of books in the transmission of the imagination.

[12]"Some North Pacific Coast Poems: A Problem in Anthropological Philology," *American Anthropologist* 67, no. 2, (April 1965), p. 335.

[13]This peak of interest is the second in the twentieth century. The first occurred in the early part of the century with the Imagists, and Mary Austin was the spokesman. In 1917, Carl Sandburg noted ironically that "the suspicion arises definitely that the Red Man and his children committed direct plagiarism on the modern imagists and vorticists," *Poetry* 9, no. 5, (February 1917), p. 225.

[14]Preface to Albert B. Lord, *The Singer of Tales* (New York, 1973).

[15]*Profession,* 79 (M.L.A. Publications Center, New York, 1979), p. 5.

[16]*Ojibwa Texts,* collected by William Jones, edited by Truman Michelson, *Publications of the American Ethnological Society,* vol. 2, pt. 1 (Leyden, 1917).

[17]Christopher Lasch, *The Culture of Narcissism* (New York, 1979), p. 261.

[18]The cultures and literatures of China and Japan have long been admired. Now people are able to see that the best traditions of these societies have tantalizing similarities to Native American societies. Black Elk or Lame Deer would have found themselves at home in Tao, for example, with "the notion of one power permeating the universe, instead of emphasizing the Western dualities of spirit and matter, creator and created, animate and inanimate, and human and non-human." For more on Tao, see George Rowley, *Principles of Chinese Painting* (Princeton, 1959). The quote above is from page 5.

[19]It has also been treated as a mine to be exploited. Sounding like an oil driller or a uranium engineer, Mary Austin wrote: "We have here the richest field of unexploited aboriginal literature it is possible to discover anywhere in the world," *Cambridge History of American Literature,* p. 610.

[20]*The Content and Style of an Oral Literature: Clackamas Chinook Myths and Tales* (Chicago, 1959).

[21]Quoted by Stanley Diamond in his Introduction to Paul Radin's *The World of Primitive Man* (New York, 1974), p. xxi.

[22]Claude Lévi-Strauss has devoted his life to recovering for us the wisdom of "the savage mind." As he writes in *The Origin of Table Manners,* tr. John and Doreen Weightman, (New York, 1978), p. 507: "In the present century, when man is actively destroying countless livng forms, after wiping out so many societies whose wealth and diversity had, from time immemorial, constituted the better part of his inheritance, it has probably never been more necessary to proclaim, as do the myths, that sound humanism does not begin with oneself, but puts the world before life, life before man, and respect for others before self-interest."

[23]*Lame Deer*, p. 13. See also Chapter 7, "The Clown's Way," in *Teachings From the American Earth*, ed. Dennis and Barbara Tedlock (New York, 1975). For more on the Sioux cosmic-symbolic universe, see William K. Powers, *Oglala Religion* (Lincoln, Neb.: 1977), and for the symbolism of the tipi (from "inipipi" = "the new life lodge") see *The Indian Tipi* by Reginald and Gladys Laubin (Norman, Okla.: 1977). See also DeMallie and Lavenda, n. 8.

[24]Gene Weltfish, *The Lost Universe* (New York, 1965). Gene Weltfish writes that the Pawnee house "was a microcosm of the universe and as one was at home inside, one was also at home in the outside world. For the dome of the sky was the high-arching roof of the universe and the horizon all round was the circular wall of the cosmic house. Through the roof of the house the star gods poured down their strength from their appropriate directions in a constant stream," (p. 621).

[25]*The Earth. The Temple, and the Gods* (New York, 1969).

[26]Virginia Irving Armstrong, ed., *I Have Spoken* (Chicago, 1971), p. 103.

[27]*I Have Spoken,* p. 146.

[28]*Northwest Sahaptin Texts* (New York, 1934), p. 8.

[29]*A Sand County Almanac* (New York, 1949), p. 215.

[30]*Regeneration Through Violence: The Mythology of the American Frontier, 1600–1860* (Middletown, Conn.: 1973), p. 4. Books which face these myths squarely are Dee Brown's *Bury My Heart at Wounded Knee* (New York, 1971), and *The Westerners* (New York, 1974). The former is well known, the latter is not. Nor is John Upton Terrell's *Land Grab* (New York, 1972).

[31]*Fathers and Children: Andrew Jackson and the Subjugation of the American Indian* (New York, 1975), p. 7.

[32]"Mexico and the United States," *The New Yorker* (September 17, 1979), p. 40. It is interesting to note that Paz has moved toward an Indian explanation for the difference between the U.S. and Mexico. In 1969, he wrote that Latin Americans are children of the Counter Reformation, whereas citizens of the U.S. are "children of the Industrial Revolution." This accounts for Americans being out of "close touch with reality," pragmatic, future-oriented. Reality for them "ceases to be a substance and is transformed into a series of acts." See "A Literature of Foundations," *TriQuarterly* 13/4 (1968/9): 9.

[33]For Thoreau's relationship to Indians, see Robert F. Sayer's *Thoreau and the American Indian,* (Princeton, 1978). And for a critique of the book, see Arnold Krupat's article, "Ethnohistory and Literature," in *The Centennial Review* 23, no. 2 (Spring 1979), pp. 141–52.

[34]*The Content and Style of an Oral Literature,* p. 1.

Part One: CONTEXT AND OVERVIEW

Kenneth Lincoln: NATIVE AMERICAN LITERATURES

"—old like hills, like stars"

"LISTEN"

*N*ative Americans: the stress falls on a hemispheric complex of original peoples, histories, languages, cultures, ecologies, radically diverse and no less than forty thousand years "native" to America. Perhaps Native Americans trace even farther back, "older than men can ever be—old like hills, like stars," Black Elk, the Lakota holy man, dreams his tribal ancestors; the peoples' own origin myths speak of emerging out of this land.[1] And the literatures of these many cultures are deeply rooted in America. "I do not know how many there are of these songs of mine," the Netsilik Eskimo, Orpingalik, told Knud Rasmussen. "Only I know that they are many, and that all in me is song. I sing as I draw breath."[2]

From at least five hundred original cultures in North America, perhaps four to eight million peoples speaking five hundred distinct languages, by Vine Deloria's count three hundred and fifteen "tribes" remain in the United States alone.[3] They compose roughly seven hundred thousand full-bloods or "bloods," as the reservation idiom goes, mixed-bloods (parents from different tribes), and "breeds" (one non-Indian parent). There are probably another half million blooded Indian people who live as whites.[4] The working definition of "Indian," though criteria vary from region to region, is minimally a quarter blood and tribal membership.

Each tribe, whether an Alaskan Tlingit fishing village of forty extended kin or the Navajo "nation" of one hundred and forty thousand in Arizona, Utah, and New Mexico, can be traditionally defined through a native language, an inherited place, and set of traditions—a daily speech, a teaching folklore, ceremony and religion, a heritage passed on generation to generation in songs, legends, jokes, morality plays, healing rituals, event-histories, social protocol, spiritual rites of passage, and vision journeys to the sacred world. These cultural traditions evolved before the Old World "discovered" the New World, and many have adapted to changing circumstances and remain strong today. The literature here in translation "surprises by its contemplative perception of the visual world, its delicacy, its magic, and its terseness," as Jorge Luis Borges has said in teaching American Literature from George Cronyn's early anthology, *The Path of the Rainbow* (1918).[5]

Given their diversities, Native American peoples commonly acknowledge a long inherited time in the land. They traditionally idealize ancestral ties, spiritual observ-

3

ances, oral cultural traditions, tribal life-styles of shared goods and responsibilities, and an ecological interdependence (the principle of "sacred reciprocation" in the words of the anthropologist Barre Toelken[6]). Personal concerns are communal matters. Black Elk opens his life story, a remembered history that is carried on as tribal literature of the Oglala Sioux: "It is the story of all life that is holy and is good to tell, and of us two-leggeds sharing in it with the four-leggeds and the wings of the air and all green things; for these are children of one mother and their father is one Spirit."[7] Literatures, in this sense, do not separate from the daily contexts of people's lives; the spoken, sung, and danced language binds the people as the living text of tribal life.

Ideally then, Native American Studies is a holistic art—imagining indigenous tribes contiguous with their environments, grounded in their traditions, enacting their histories. Its methods should be interdisciplinary and exploratory; its research questions assumptions in order to learn, rather than assert.[8] In *Tristes Tropique* Lévi-Strauss recalls that as a beginning student he declined philosophy and law as self-referential, skirted geology as too widely defined in non-human terms, and by-passed psychology as too individually oriented; he thought as an anthropologist, open to improvisation, to fuse geological time, psychological humanism, and the epistemological concerns of philosophy with the disciplines of legal reasoning.[9] Lévi-Strauss's structural anthropology offers one international approach in native cultural studies, balanced by the more immediate ethnography of scholars in direct contact with tribal peoples.

The many native peoples with ancient tenure in America remain as varied as the land itself—forest, prairie, river, valley, seacoast, mountain, tundra, desert, and cliff dwelling peoples who were traditionally farmers, fishermen, food gatherers, and hunters inseparable from the land. Their cultures and histories differ as widely as terrain and climate, flora and fauna; but all tribes acknowledge ties distinct from those of other Americans—indigenous time on this "turtle island," as original myths relate, unified in an ancient ancestral heritage. The Hopi village of Old Oraibi, on the third mesa in northern Arizona, has stood for at least eight hundred and fifty years. Canyon de Chelly, on the Navajo reservation near the Four Corners area, has been occupied for two and one half thousand years. In contrast, the landscape east of the Mississippi carries slim living evidence of once powerful tribes who settled the forests—among many others, the Powhatans who saved Jamestown colony with gifts of green corn in the first severe winter of 1607 (the colonists, unprepared for the climate, were starved to the point of eating their own dead), the Five Civilized Tribes in the Southeast, the Ohio River and Great Lakes tribes, and the Iroquois Confederacy, five and then six tribal allies who treated "at the forest's edge" as equal powers with the Confederation of United States in the eighteenth century (Jefferson, an expert in Indian language and culture, along with Franklin, is said to have translated "Iroquois" as "We-the-people"). Some eastern tribes did survive displacement and revitalize over several centuries, as Anthony Wallace records of twenty thousand Iroquois now living on reservations in New York, Quebec, and Ontario (*The Death and Rebirth of the Seneca*).[10]

Beginning in the 1830s many Indian cultures were "removed" to the "Great American Desert" west of the Mississippi—a diaspora under Presidential decree and military escort. Andrew Jackson promised the eastern tribes, through agents:

> *Say to them as friends and brothers to listen to their father, and their friend. Where they now are, they and my white children are too near to each other to live in harmony and peace. . . . Beyond the great River Mississippi. . . . their father has provided a country large enough for them all, and he advises them to move to it. There their white brothers will not trouble them, and they will have no claim to the land, and they can live on it, they and all their children, as long as grass grows and waters run.*[11]

Already settled there, the Plains Indians resisted, protesting encroachment from eastern tribes shoved west while fighting the invasion of land-grabbing, gold-searching, buffalo-slaughtering, treaty-violating White immigrants who brought with them the railroad, guns, ploughs, fences, plagues, alcohol, and the Bible. When "the very animals of the forest" began fleeing "the hairy man from the east," Luther Standing Bear notes, "then it was for us that the Wild West began."

The "Indian Wars" lasted from the 1860s to the Wounded Knee Massacre in 1890. From 1881 to 1883 the government employed marksmen to slaughter the remaining two and a half million buffalo, once fifteen million in 1700, that were the tribes' main life-support.[12] The seasonal migrations of the tribes, following the game, were disrupted forever. Soldiers herded the survivors onto "reserves" of waste land, issued "citizen's dress" (coat and trousers), and ordered them to "civilize." The Secretary of the Interior commented in 1872 on killing the buffalo to starve Indians onto reservations: "A few years of cessation from the chase will tend to unfit them from their former mode of life, and they will be the more readily led into new directions, toward industrial pursuits and peaceful habits."[13] The transition did not take place so easily or soon; over a hundred years later many Indian peoples are still caught between cultures, living under the worst conditions of both.

The many treaties and speeches spanning three centuries of contact represent the first recorded Indian literatures, documenting the precision and eloquence of Indian oratory. Constance Rourke sees these documents as the first American "chronicle plays,"[14] and Lawrence Wroth observes that the Indians "spoke as free men to free men, or often indeed as kings speaking to kings."[15] For over two hundred years even military defeat could not dislodge the Indian spirit of rightful place in America. After fleeing seventeen hundred miles into the bitter winter of 1877, Chief Joseph grieved with dignity as he surrendered the Nez Percé:

> *My people, some of them, have run away to the hills and have no blankets, no food. No one knows where they are—perhaps they are freezing to death. I want to have time to look for my children and see how many of them I can find. Maybe I shall find them among the dead. Hear me, my chiefs, I am tired. My heart is sad and sick. From where the sun now stands I will fight no more forever.*[16]

There still is honor in this sense of defeat. And in 1883 Sitting Bull, the Lakota warrior extradited from Canada, told reservation bureaucrats from Washington:

> *I am here by the will of the Great Spirit, and by His will I am a chief. My heart is red and sweet, and I know it is sweet, because whatever passes near me puts out its tongue to me; and yet you men have come here to talk with us, and you say you do not know who I am. I want to tell you that if the Great Spirit has chosen anyone to be the chief of this country, it is myself.* [Senate Report #283][17]

The "Indian" Bureau was first established in 1824 under the War Department. Indigenous to cultural and geographical diversities, Native Americans are aligned on one point: they compose the only ethnic group within its boundaries that the United States has warred against and made treaties with—389 broken treaties. Vine Deloria discusses these claims in *Of Utmost Good Faith*, the opening words of a Continental Congress treaty signed by George Washington, the Northwest Ordinance of 1787:

> *The utmost good faith shall always be observed toward the Indians, their lands and property shall never be taken from them without their consent; and in their property rights, and liberty, they shall never be invaded or disturbed, unless in just and lawful wars authorized by Congress; but laws founded in justice and humanity shall from time to time be made, for preventing wrongs being done to them, and for preserving peace and friendship with them.*[18]

". . . they were chasing us now," Black Elk remembers of the 1870s, "because we remembered and they forgot."[19]

While fighting to preserve their own cultural integrity and life-styles, Indians have survived national policies of removal, starvation, warfare, and genocide. F. Scott Fitzgerald eulogized the national myth of a virgin land, "the green breast of the new world" in *The Great Gatsby*, revised by the historian Francis Jennings in *The Invasion of America*: "The American land was more like a widow than a virgin. Europeans did not find a wilderness here; rather, however involuntarily, they made one. . . . The so-called settlement of America was a *resettlement*, a reoccupation of a land made waste by the diseases and demoralization introduced by the newcomers."[20] It is an old and shameful story—a history largely fabled in the popular mind, seldom taught honestly in American schools, of murder and cultural suppression and displacement from native lands. It is most commonly dramatized in the 1830s Long March "removal" of the Five Civilized Tribes, when over a third of the people died on forced relocation to Oklahoma. Asked his age by a census taker in 1910, the old Creek, Itshas Harjo, answered with a memory purely elegiac:

> *I have passed through many days and traveled a long way,*
> *the shadows have fallen all about me and I*
> *can see but dimly.*
> *But my mind is clear and my memory has not failed me.*
> *I cannot count the years I have lived.*

All that I know about my age is that I was old enough to draw the bow
and kill squirrels at the time of the second emigration of the
Creeks and Cherokees from the old country under
the leadership of Chief Cooweescoowee.
I was born near Eufaula, Alabama, and left there
when about fifteen years of age and the trip
took about a year,
for the peaches were green when we left Alabama
and the wild onions plentiful here when we arrived.[21]

Despite such natural poetry, Indian traditions were dismissed as barbaric, heathen, pagan. The Commissioner of Indian Affairs stated in 1889:

The Indians must conform to "the white man's ways," peaceably if they will, forcibly
if they must. They must adjust themselves to their environment, and conform their
mode of living substantially to our civilization. This civilization may not be the best
possible, but it is the best the Indians can get. They cannot escape it, and must either
conform to it or be crushed by it.[22]

Even the skilled ethnologist, James Mooney, could write paternalistically in 1898, "The savage is intellectually a child, and from the point of view of the civilized man his history is shaped by trivial things . . ."[23] Children "kidnapped" into government boarding schools, as Indian people saw it, were ridiculed for their Indian names, stripped of their tribal dress, and punished for speaking native tongues; eventually their elders were shamed out of beliefs in the ancestral spirit world, animal totems and vision quests, a speaking landscape sacredly reciprocal with the people.

Culture after culture, beginning with Cortez's destruction of Tenochtitlan in 1521, witnessed deicide as conquered tribes were forced to abandon their own religions and buckle on Christianity. The Indian encounters with missionaries are recorded in penetrant irony. Red Jacket, the Seneca sachem, asked missionaries near Buffalo in 1805:

. . . you say that you are right, and we are lost; how do we know this is to be true? . . .

Brother, you say there is but one way to worship and serve the Great Spirit; if there is
but one religion, why do you white people differ so much about it?

. . . we will wait a little while and see what effect your preaching has upon them
[other whites]. If we find it does them good, makes them honest, and less disposed to
cheat Indians, we will then consider again what you have said.[24]

The missionaries denied any "fellowship between the religion of God and the works of the devil," and they turned away refusing to shake hands. A century later and graced with the humor of native courtesy, the bi-cultural Hopi, Don Talayesva, could recant modern civilization and return to the old ways on the desert:

I had learned a great lesson and now knew that the ceremonies handed down by our fathers mean life and security, both now and hereafter. I regretted that I had ever joined the Y.M.C.A. and decided to set myself against Christianity once and for all. I could see that the old people were right when they insisted that Jesus Christ might do for modern whites in a good climate, but that the Hopi gods had brought success to us in the desert ever since the world began.[25]

Pressures on Indians to assimilate date farther back than Southwest mission ruins. In preparing for the 1876 Centennial in Philadelphia, the Smithsonian Institution set about gathering Indian curiosities to be displayed in the "Great Wigwam." One hundred Indians from eighteen tribes were invited to encamp at the exhibition, but each had to satisfy a thirteen point checklist: every householder would be pleasant, the "cleanest and finest looking," influential in the tribe, and speak English. He would be attended, the invitation stated, by one wife "well skilled in household arts," a clean child, a dog, and a pony.[26] That year, 1876, the government bartered the Sioux out of the sacred Black Hills for five cents an acre (George Custer two years before had broken the Red Cloud Treaty leading prospectors to gold "from the grass roots down," the richest deposits still in North America). Shortly after Custer charged fifteen thousand Sioux and Cheyenne in villages on a Sun Dance retreat at the Little Big Horn, the Centennial Indian invitations were rescinded.

A more insidious oppression threatens Indians today under melting-pot policies of assimilation: direct and indirect federal coercion of tribes to adapt to mainstream American culture. The disastrous "termination" policies of the 1950s are currently being revived in Congressional bills to abrogate treaties, and "when someone says 'termination'," an anthropologist of the Montana Blackfeet writes, "the Indians hear 'extermination'."[27] This essay then seeks to defend cultural independence, as reflected in the literatures of many hundreds of tribal societies in America.

America's most diverse minorities hold the status, independently, of "domestic dependent nations" (Chief Justice Marshall's opinion of 1831), that is, nations within a nation whose members are legally "wards" of the federal government, and yet remain "sovereign." They occupy separate land bases of some fifty-three million acres, salvaged from the one hundred and forty million acres allotted under the 1887 Dawes Act.[28] The lands contain half the uranium and one third the strip mine coal in the United States (the coal alone worth perhaps a trillion dollars) and yet some reservations suffer the worst hardship in America—incomes at half the poverty level, five years average schooling, the highest national alcoholism and suicide rates, substandard housing and social services, infant mortality, tuberculosis, and diabetes in multiples beyond any other minority in the country, average life-spans of forty-four years.[29]

Historical ironies notwithstanding, traditional Indian literatures, taken mostly from religious and healing ceremonies, idealize the balance of spiritual and worldly concerns in harmonies throughout the world. Within this context of native visions, fueled by pastoral myths of the noble savage and regression to the Garden of Eden, there is a tendency, among Indians and non-Indians alike, to gloss contemporary reservation life and visions of the-way-things-used-to-be. We still fail to see the Native American as an individual with a tribal, human identity. "To be an Indian in modern American society," Vine Deloria writes in *Custer Died For Your Sins,* "is in a very real sense to be unreal and ahistorical."[30] The transparent "Indian," a film and fictional stereotype, lingers more a silhouette—the only minority anonymously enshrined on our currency, the "Indian-head" nickel. And the true history of national Indian affairs shapes an oftentimes bitter resistence to "the American way." D.H.Lawrence wrote in *Studies in Classic American Literature* (1923):

> *The desire to extirpate the Indian. And the contradictory desire to glorify him. Both are rampant still, to-day.*

> *The bulk of the white people who live in contact with the Indian to-day would like to see this Red brother exterminated; not only for the sake of grabbing his land, but because of the silent, invisible, but deadly hostility between the spirit of the two races. The minority of whites intellectualize the Red Man and laud him to the skies. But this minority of whites is mostly a high-brow minority with a big grouch against its own whiteness.*[31]

When America catches the shadow of native peoples on its money and names professionally competitive teams the Warriors, the Indians, the Redskins, or the Aztecs, the stereotype surely reaches down through a sentimental myth of the noble savage into "the bloody loam" of national history—a refracted image that covers several million lives destroyed or violently "removed" from their native earth.[32] And today, there seem "so few of them left," Frederick Turner observes in his *North American Indian Reader,* "so far away from the centers of population."[33] This, too, is open for discussion, since Native Americans represent the fastest growing minorities in America, doubling in population between 1950 and 1970, and more than half now live off-reservation, many in major cities. If the people are few in number, proportionately, they remain many in ancient diversities and stand mythically large in the national consciousness. We would do well to appreciate their literatures as origins of cultural history in America.

"TRANS-"
"To the other side of, over, across"

Crossings: every word *translates* the world we live into the world we think we know. When the process of language works, our known world comes alive *in* words, animate and experiential. Among other forms of human expression (music, dance, costume, drama, sculpture, painting), words embody reality:

> *—through metaphor to reconcile*
> *the people and the stones.*
> *Compose. (No ideas but*
> *in things) Invent!*[34]

When more than one language and culture and space/time lie at either end of this multiple and metaphoric process, the translator must look two ways, at least, at once: to carry over, as much as possible, the experiential integrity of the original, and to *re*generate the spirit of the source in a new verbal performance. Two languages and artists live at the beginning and end, neither simultaneous nor identical, but reciprocal—and recipient to differing audiences.

Native American literature, in brief, is literature in translation. When the tribal ear listens ceremonially at one end of this continuum, and the existential eye scans the printed page at the other, questions of form and function, how and why one uses language, the designs of literature, naturally come into play within cultural cross-studies. "Firmly planted. Not fallen from on high: sprung up from below," Octavio Paz, the Mexican poet, says *In Praise of Hands*. The voiced word, like the hand-made object, the right-told tale, the well-shaped poem, speaks of "a mutually shared physical life," not as icon, commodity, or art for its own precious sake. "A glass jug, a wicker basket, a coarse muslin huipil, a wooden serving dish: beautiful objects, not despite their usefulness but because of it."[35]

If the tribal poet begins in an integrated context of beauty, ethics, and use among his people, how can the translator carry Native American oral traditions—hundreds of indigenous literatures permeated with religion, mythology, ritual, morality and heuristics, national history, social entertainment, economic skills and magic formulas, healing rites, codes of warfare and hunting and planting and food-gathering, visions and dreams, love incantations, death chants, lullabies, and prayers—into printed words in books for modern audiences? One language may be assumed magically powerful, the other only a functional transmission of ideas. "From what you say," Ikinilik told Knud Rasmussen, "it would seem that folk in that far country of yours *eat* talk marks just as we eat caribou meat" (Utkuhikhalingmiut Eskimo). Peter Nabokov reminds us that the first Cherokee shamans to adapt Sequoyah's 1821 syllabary, the earliest known "talking leaves" north of Mexico, in fear of exploitation hid their transcriptions in trees and attics.[36] There are two (or more) sides to words here.

"Good translation of any literature," Jeffrey F. Huntsman posits, "requires a native or near-native sensitivity to both languages, and few translators have the foresight to request a bilingual birth." So the working model might be collaborative translation, truly reciprocal and inter-tribal, in contrast with the isolate poet-maker's little cosmos (see, for examples, such collaborative works as *Sun Chief, Son of Old Man Hat, The Autobiography of a Papago Woman, Crashing Thunder, My People the Sioux, Black Elk Speaks,* and *Lame Deer Seeker of Visions,* among others). An artist's creativity is participatory with things-as-they-are. And further: "The inherent differences between languages, combined with symbolism, figurative or metaphoric manipulation of ordinary language, secret or esoteric language, and fossils of earlier, now archaic language, all contribute to a maddening Arabesque of many varieties of meaning that only the most perceptive and careful translator should confront."[37]

The basic translative paradigm is one person listening to another tell his story. But consider the variables in *Black Elk Speaks, Being the Life Story of a Holy Man of the Oglala Sioux* (1932), perhaps the most ubiquitous text in Native American Studies, "*as told through* John G. Neihardt (*Flaming Rainbow*)."

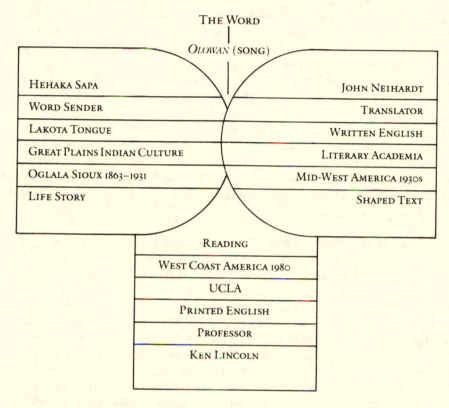

THE WORD

OLOWAN (SONG)

HEHAKA SAPA	JOHN NEIHARDT
WORD SENDER	TRANSLATOR
LAKOTA TONGUE	WRITTEN ENGLISH
GREAT PLAINS INDIAN CULTURE	LITERARY ACADEMIA
OGLALA SIOUX 1863–1931	MID-WEST AMERICA 1930S
LIFE STORY	SHAPED TEXT

READING

WEST COAST AMERICA 1980

UCLA

PRINTED ENGLISH

PROFESSOR

KEN LINCOLN

My nation, behold it in kindness!
The day of the sun has been my strength.
The path of the moon shall be my robe.
A sacred praise I am making.
A sacred praise I am making.
[Heyoka Song][38]

At any one moment (or "word") here, three overlapping sets of at least six variables come into play:

1. the *individual* in his own genetic/psychological complex,
2. his *role* in the event at hand,
3. the *medium* involved,
4. the *space/time* of the event (synchronic),
5. the *cultural matrix* around the event (diachronic),
6. and the *performance* itself.

Hehaka Sapa (Black Elk) sat on the South Dakota prairie for days with John Neihardt, family, and friends in the spring of 1931, recalling half a century of his life as an Oglala Sioux healer. His son, Ben Black Elk, translated the spoken Lakota into English speech, as Neihardt asked questions, translated back into Lakota by Ben Black Elk, recorded in stenographic notes by Neihardt's daughter, Enid. A purblind *wicasa wakan* or "holy man," Black Elk sat at the vortex of a textual performance, distinct from a set story, among his extended family, interspersed with his friends' commentaries (Standing Bear, Iron Hawk, Fire Thunder); Neihardt later translated these "translations" into a written text, exercising poetic license with the notes; the reader, still half a century later, assimilates the published account into his own life. From Black Elk's memories through Neihardt to the reader's present spans a century. The process moves from visionary-healer-singer-teller through poet-translator to literate recipient; from spoken recall through written translation to reading a book; from field anthropology, the where and when of each person involved to the next; from the cultural transitions and histories of each to another; from informant through creative writer to reader. To note these passages stimulates care for the translative details; it raises questions about how one moves toward, or slides away from, genuine translations.

Translation is a projection (Charles Olson says of all poetry) from one place "over to" another, if an original oral performance is to survive in a written poem (tradition, from Latin *trans* + *dare* or "to give over," bears a cognate etymology). But language unfolds not just as a cognitive system, intense as its logical intricacies may be. The translated event, in its new form, must re-emerge as a poem, a musical pattern with origins in dance and song, an insight into this world, an arrangement of sound and sense like no other, an ancient revelation of the workings of human nature, perhaps ceremonial or traditional in the tribe. And all the while, without distorting the original, ". . . a free translation bases the test on its own language. It is the task of the translator to release in his own language that pure language which is under the spell of another, to liberate the language imprisoned in a work in his re-creation of that work" (Walter Benjamin).[39] Poems must work, word by word, line by line, *as poetry* when translated. Transliterated ethnography in itself is not necessarily poetry, no more than folkloric motifs or anthropological paradigms, and may betray the original by failing to carry over its music, tribal value, or clarity and depth of perception.

"A real translation is transparent," Benjamin argues; "it does not cover the original, does not block its light, but allows the pure language, as though reinforced by its own medium, to shine upon the original all the more fully."[40] Within its cultural integrity, *all* poetry, in original text or rendered into another language/culture, is an act of translation *into* the medium of language. The original "poem" or song, described by Black Elk as the "sacred language" of "a great Voice . . . silent" in a vision, springs from a pre-verbal illumination in the seer's imagination, perhaps from the gods. In *Selected Translations 1968–1978* the American poet, W.S. Merwin, adds: "When I tried to formulate practically what I wanted of a translation, whether by someone else or by me, it was something like this: without deliberately altering the overt meaning of the original poem, I wanted the translation to represent, with as much life as possible, some aspect, some quality of the poem which made the translator think it was worth translating in the first place."[41] And many removes later we ask of the translation: Does the poem *honor* the source of the original (its inherent cultural values)? Does the poem *sing* with an echo of the original music (rhythm, tone, syntax, structure)? Does the poem freshly *penetrate* things (insight and meaning in the world)? Does the poem give *expression* to a genuine and arresting truth (accurate form and style)? To question authenticity in translation, to look back to a poem's origins, is to look forward to issues concerning the very nature and uses of poetry itself.

Since the early ethnology and folklore of almost a century ago, gestating the new "sciences" of archeology, anthropology, and linguistics, a new literary interest in Native America has developed, accelerated by alternative cultural explorations in the 1960s. Anthologies of traditional Indian song-poems, dream visions, narrative cycles, speeches, and life-stories illustrate the remarkable variety and depth of literature in hundreds of tribal cultures. Beginning with George Cronyn's *The Path of the Rainbow* (1918), other anthologies followed in time: Margot Astrov's *The Winged Serpent* (1946), A. Grove Day's *The Sky Clears* (1951), John Bierhorst's *In the Trail of the Wind* (1971), *Four Masterworks of American Indian Literature* (1974), and *The Red Swan* (1976), Thomas Sanders and Walter Peek's *Literature of the American Indian* (1973), Gloria Levitas's *American Indian Prose and Poetry* (1974), Frederick Turner's *North American Indian Reader* (1974), Alan Velie's *American Indian Literature* (1979), and the more experimental (and controversial) *Shaking the Pumpkin* (1972) by Jerome Rothenberg and *The Magic World* (1971) by William Brandon. Indeed, a number of America's writers, from Thoreau with the word "Indians" on his dying breath, to novelists such as Cooper and Melville, Faulkner and Hemingway, Berger and Kesey, to contemporary poets Snyder, Merwin, Rexroth, Olson, Levertov, Bly, Rothenberg, Creeley, Kelly, Berg, Simpson, Wagoner, Norman, and Tedlock, have found a need to "go native," however genuinely, seeking their more integral place in this land, their uses among people, their tribal language and audience, their raw material in the myth and history and imagination of America. These poets seek to reinvent, on their own terms, an original relationship to the spoken word, a sensitivity to spirit of place and natural environment, a responsive bond with a tribal audience. The artist's interest in America's first poetries signals his involvement in the life and immediacy of his own "language of the tribe," as Williams wrote. "Not for himself surely to be an Indian, though they eagerly sought to adopt him into their tribes, but the reverse: to be himself in a new world, Indianlike" (*In the American Grain*).[42]

Non-Indians cannot be Indians; but they can translate, discover or re-discover, their own tribal place in this earth. "We won't get Indian culture as cheaply as we got Manhattan," William Bevis quips.[43] Granted the sometimes good intentions of faulty translations, how can we correct "the 'wilderness' poet approach which finds a tranquilly recollecting rhymer in every tree," noted by Jeffrey Huntsman?[44] How see Native America for the many and diverse peoples and pasts and regions they comprise, rather than after-images of the feathered, naked, promiscuous, lawless, cannibal stereotype of the misrepresented Brazilian Tupinamba in the first New World woodcuts surfacing in Germany in 1505: "They also fight with each other. They also eat each other even those who are slain, and hang the flesh of them in smoke. They live one hundred and fifty years. And have no government" (*The New Golden Land*)[45]? How avert the commercial travesty and cultural exploitation of *Hanta Yo,* a will-to-power rendition of the Teton Sioux under a Lakota title— meaning, not as Ruth Beebe Hill supposes, "Clear the path," but more "Get out of the way?"[46] How ward off ethnic slumming among Indians?

A translation can miss the truth of place and cultural history, looking sideways in space, or mar the delicacies of re-creative poetry, mirroring itself. A well versed Indian anthropologist wrote me that he queries the artifice of Brandon's *The Magic World* and Rothenberg's *Shaking the Pumpkin* because they "decontextualize so much that, very often, one can no longer recognize from where— from what people's singular genius—a given piece came after they have worked it over" (correspondence, 16 September 1979). At the same time, in a recent issue of *Western American Literature,* H.S. McAllister defends the "revolutionary" thrust of Rothenberg's experiments in "total translation," even if all the reworkings do not work all the time. With Trickster's room "for messing around," Rothenberg attempts a poem-for-poem translation "not only of the words but of all sounds connected with the poem, including finally the music itself."[47] His former co-editor of *Alcheringa,* Dennis Tedlock, succeeds more consistently in *Finding the Center: Narrative Poetry of the Zuni Indians.* Surely these are matters of cultural understanding and poetic taste, of who does the translating and re-working, of how skillfully they re-create the song-poem. Levertov's Aztec adaptations in *Pumpkin* ring true, Olson's Mayan myths touch us with ancient narrative arts, and Merwin's "Crow Versions" graze the spirit-echo of the original songs notated by Lowie:

> *I am climbing*
> *everywhere is*
>
> *coming up*

McAllister defends the intent, apart from the total success: "These new translations, like the originals, are vital poetry, and the essential alienness of the originals has been translated as well as the words."[48]

McAllister goes on to discuss participatory immersion within the environmental "field" of a poem, taking leads from Edward Hall, Marshall McLuhan, Walter Ong, and Barre Toelken, among others:

> *For us, the word is a third-hand, highly abstracted symbol, finite in the sense that its quantity is determined by its letters, discrete in the sense that it occupies visual space on the page. Its "thingness" is the visual structure we call the alphabet. Because of our deeply grounded literacy, which impinges on our total sense of language, the*

word is for us primarily (though not exclusively) a visual entity. For a non-literate poet or culture, the word is unambiguously oral/aural.

The aural word, though not infinite, is finite in a continuum rather than being clearly bounded like the visual word; the aural word is a portion of the flow which makes up our sound environment. The non-literate is more comfortable than the literate with the sense of language as a flow of sound, because that is how his ear perceives language, and he has not had the perception contradicted by knowledge of the discrete segments of meaning that appear on the page. However, he also perceives words as discrete "things," but this individuation is different from ours, again because of the lack of an abstracted visual mode like our alphabet. With the image of written language to cue us, we have no difficulty imagining what the aural poet means if he says that words are pebbles of meaning, but that very image of written language makes us see as a metaphor what he may mean as a literal statement.[49]

Yes, and perhaps this is why Rothenberg and others seem strained at times or gimmicked, self-indulgently Westernized in attempts at free translation from oral cultures. Disregarding the integrity of the original transcriptions too often, Brandon has been charged with abusing the texts in *The Magic World*, even though his spatial arrangements and verse compositions go far in revitalizing the song-poems *as poems*.[50] Form is never free, poets say, any more than insight, regardless of new or old discoveries. Still, more critically, what is the proper re-creation to carry perform-ance into print, dance onto the page, ceremony into the classroom, one language and sense of reality over into new ones? In brief, begin with caution against defacing the original; listen truly; proceed with attention to the way *translated* language takes shape, on the page, relayed in the mind and body, *as a poem*.

"The poem's form is the sound it makes when spoken," McAllister offers.[51] Translations must risk the forms of reality in song/poems, then, since the world does not lie flat on a page or always justify its margins or behave only according to conventional rhyme and meter. The page serves as visual canvas, with dimensions, perspectives, and energies around words-as-objects-in-space, moving according to acoustic design among other objects in space. At the same time, this translative risk cannot violate a second audience's expectations, *vis-á-vis* the boundaries of reality, or the behaviors of poetry—to push too hard on the re-creative metaphor is to lose song and shape through over-stylization. A poem may hang mobile in space like the leaves on a tree. It may serpentine through a Hopi rain dance in stately choral strophes, arrange itself in a Navajo origin myth as patiently as strata in a canyon wall, or burst freely around Plains drumming and chanting. A poem may lap quietly as lake ripples beaching on a Chippewa shore, or stalk powerfully through darkness over a broken Iroquois terrain. It may soar with the Trickster Raven over the Pacific northwest, or descend into itself, as Kachina gods disappearing into a kiva. The original song, in its human reality, the transplanted poem, in its spatial equivalent, are measured, shaped, imaged, pitched movements in space.

Good Christ what is
a poet—if any
   exists?

a man
whose words will
 bite
  their way
home—being actual

having the form
   of motion

At each twigtip

new

upon the tortured
body of thought

 gripping
the ground

a way
 to the last leaftip
[Williams, "The Wind Increases"] [52]

One should listen to the song-poets on these issues, from all cultures, for their life *is* poetry, not theory, and they certainly master poetic form and function beyond the ethnologists, linguists, structural anthropologists, or literary critics, who by and large do not write, perhaps even seriously read, poetry in any language.

All the warm nights
sleep in the moonlight

keep letting it
go into you

do this
all your life

do this
you will shine outward
in old age

the moon will think
you are
the moon
[Swampy Cree][53]

Who knows more about the makings and performings of the word than the "word senders" themselves?

I do not know how many there are of these songs of mine. Only I know that they are many, and that all in me is song. I sing as I draw breath. [Orpingalik, Netsilik Eskimo][54]

It was the pictures I remembered and the words that went with them; for nothing I have ever seen with my eyes was so clear and bright as what my vision showed me; and no words that I have ever heard with my ears were like the words I heard. I did not have to remember these things; they have remembered themselves all these years. [Black Elk, Oglala Sioux][55]

A description in the Iliad *or the* Odyssey, *unlike one in the* Aeneid *or in most modern writers, is the swift and natural observation of a man as he is shaped by life.* [W.B. Yeats, Irish][56]

No tool 'gainst tiger,
no boat for river.
That much, no more,
and they know it;
but above all to be precise
at the gulf's edge
or on thin ice.
[Confucius, Chinese, *Shih-Ching*][57]

To me it seems more and more as though our customary consciousness lives on the tip of a pyramid whose base within us (and in a certain way beneath us) widens out so fully that the farther we find ourselves able to descend into it, the more generally we appear to be merged into those things that, independent of time and space, are given in our earthly, in the widest sense worldly, existence. [Rainer Maria Rilke, Austrian][58]

. . . if he is contained within his nature as he is participant in the larger force, he will be able to listen, and his hearing through himself will give him secrets objects share. And by an inverse law his shapes will make their own way. [Charles Olson][59]

The author's conviction on this day of New Year is that music begins to atrophy when it departs too far from the dance; that poetry begins to atrophy when it gets too far from music. . . . [Ezra Pound][60]

In regard to the songs, Dreamer-of-the-Sun told me that I may pray with my mouth and the prayer will be heard, but if I sing the prayer it will be heard sooner by Wakan' Tanka. [Red Weasel, Standing Rock Sioux][61]

I am ashamed before the earth;
I am ashamed before the heavens;
I am ashamed before the dawn;
I am ashamed before the evening twilight;
I am ashamed before the blue sky;
I am ashamed before the sun.
I am ashamed before that standing within me which speaks with me.
Some of these things are always looking at me.
I am never out of sight.
Therefore I must tell the truth.
I hold my word tight to my breast.
[Old Torlino, Navajo][62]

First and finally, the words must *sing,* as Albert Lord says of oral formulaic tradition, not *"for* but *in* performance," applicable no less to Native American oral literatures, now finding voice in written languages, than to Homeric epics. "Text" is only a stop-time facet of the embracing mode and texture of a cultural performance, as Toelken and Dundes and others remind us. "But the Indian, you take away everything from him, he still has his mouth to pray, to sing the ancient songs" (Pete Catches, Pine Ridge Sioux medicine man).[63]

A translator must take care not to package chants and ceremonial texts (music, religion, medicine, history) into technological and commercial artifacts, as print can temporarily ossify the spirit of dance, song, narration, healing ritual, prayer, or private witness in a world alive to interior needs: "Because there is a difference, and there will always be a difference," Lame Deer, the Rosebud Sioux healer believed, "as long as one Indian is left alive. Our beliefs are rooted deep in our earth, no matter what you have done to it and how much of it you have paved over. And if you leave all that concrete unwatched for a year or two, our plants, the native Indian plants, will pierce that concrete and push up through it."[64] Not everyone wants his or her shadow caught, notwithstanding Edward Curtis's genius, and some cultures don't care to "share" tribal ways and values with the non-Indian world (witness the Northern Cheyenne controversy over *Seven Arrows).* The traditionalists resent sacred implements on display in museums (the Smithsonian or Southwest Museum, for example, as antiquarian dumping grounds for native North America) and resist the recording of songs, ceremonies, and customs as data in Bureau of Ethnology and American Anthropological reports. Vine Deloria, the Sioux political trickster of *Custer Died For Your Sins,* dubs most anthropology the work of "ideological vultures" scavenging for tenure.[65] In this regard, anthropology bears the bite of a restless Westering society that imperializes, knowingly or unknowingly, with an indiscreet appetite for *other* cultures, for travel and exploration and conquest, for the new and exotic and untouched, out of a dearth of self-definition within inchoate cultural traditions. Though Susan Sontag (*Against Interpretation*) eulogizes the anthropologist Claude Lévi-Strauss as the modern cultural hero in his international cross-overs, a Navajo who never met the man might wonder how a few younger years of field work in South America equips a French academic, for all his Western brilliance, to deep-structure "the savage mind" (read "neolithic" or pretechnological) through a windstorm of library research.[66] "The Indian has been for a long time generalized in the imagination of the white man," N. Scott Momaday (Kiowa) observes. "Denied the acknowledgement of individuality and change, he has been made to become in theory what he could not become in fact, a synthesis of himself."[67] Deloria finds this living in the "shadows of a mythical super-Indian."[68] Of what *use,* the Native American might question today, is a taxonomic system of anthropological equivalences among diverse tribes, discontinuous in space and time, scattered all over North and South America, and faced with immediate survival? This won't hold many sheep, Henry Yellowman would observe to Barre Toelken.[69] To rephrase Deloria, "Anthro, Know Thyself."

> *[In Washington] I have heard talk and talk, but nothing is done. Good words do not last long unless they amount to something. Words do not pay for my dead people. They do not pay for my country, now overrun by whitemen. . . . Good words will not give my people good health and stop them from dying. Good words will not get my people a home where they can live in peace and take care of themselves. I am tired of talk that comes to nothing. It makes my heart sick when I remember all the good words and the broken promises. There has been too much talking by men who had no right to talk. Too many misrepresentations have been made, too many misunderstandings have come up between the white men about the Indians.* [Chief Joseph, Nez Percé, 1879 speech to Congress][70]

"The people" themselves want to be heard, not spoken for or paraphrased. There must always be an attention that ceremonial texts are not reduced to market products or cultural oddities, but instead that translations preserve their traditional contexts, respond to their participant audiences, maintain their sacred and/or medicinal powers (even if this means protection *from* translation), and keep alive their improvisational and traditional tellers and singers. "The best story teller is one who lets you live if the weather is bad and you are hungry," William Smith Smith told Howard Norman, Swampy Cree translator. "Maybe it won't be easy to hear, inside the story, but it's there. Too easy to find you might think it was too easy to do."[71]

"I go backward, look forward, as the porcupine does," Jacob Nibènegenesábe said of Swampy Cree traditions.[72] The past is always "back there." A people's inherited burrow may "look forward" to their present lives, rounded on the quills of time: personal and collective history manifesting itself in who we are, where we make our home, how we live with one another, why we place ourselves in nature as-we-are. And the stories and songs: the origins of things are always with us. Rightly translated, sung, and told, the old ways rise up through the new ways. The true spirits in the world renew us continually, constantly, without fear of change, trusting seasonal continuities. Controversies over breed and blood, urban and "res," conservation and progress, "going back" and coming forward, your tribe and mine, set up the dynamics of being who we are in the world, native to ourselves, tribal to our people, relative to all life forms, ritual to powers that spirit us.

ANCESTRAL VOICES
Tribal Poetics

Except for the Mayan and the Aztec, North American tribal peoples evolved without written languages. They lived as oral cultures, traditions generating mouth to mouth, age to age, alive only as the people passed on a daily culture. Their literatures came down as remembered bodies of myth and ritual, song-poetry and narrative tales, legends and parables. Once these oral literatures carried through the double translation into English, onto the printed page, America began to recognize, belatedly, the long presence of Native American literatures.[73]

How do Indian cultures look upon language and literature? A. Grove Day writes in *The Sky Clears*:

> *The Indians made poems for many reasons: to praise their gods and ask their help in life; to speak to the gods through dramatic performances at seasonal celebrations or initiations or other rites; to work magical cures or enlist supernatural aid in hunting, plant-growing, or horsebreeding; to hymn the praises of the gods or pray to them; to chronicle tribal history; to explain the origins of the world; to teach right conduct; to mourn the dead; to arouse warlike feelings; to compel love; to arouse laughter; to ridicule a rival or bewitch an enemy; to praise famous men; to communicate the poet's private experience; to mark the beauties of nature; to boast of one's personal greatness; to record a vision scene; to characterize the actors in a folk tale; to quiet children; to lighten the burdens of work; to brighten up tribal games; and, sometimes, to express simply joy and a spirit of fun.*[74]

Ideally generative in the world, words make things happen in Native America; language is the source of a world in itself. "In the beginning, the word gave origin to the Father," a Uitoto creation myth begins.[75] The primacy of language interfuses people with their surroundings and natural environment—an experience or object or animal or person lives inseparable from its name. And names allow the people to see, as words image the spirits within things. Black Elk says of his Great Vision, a life-long image of his place in the world: "It was the pictures I remembered and the words that went with them; for nothing I have ever seen with my eyes was so clear and bright as what my vision showed me; and no words that I have ever heard with my ears were like the words I heard. I did not have to remember these things; they have remembered themselves all these years."[76]

A common tribal language is essential. Oral traditions gather the people tribally, as they poeticize the common speech. For the most part, tribal cultures still live through spoken literatures, and the peoples' "literary history" is a function of memory, imagination, and ritual in daily recurrence and seasonal patterns. The arts of language remain communally open; the word is tribal bond. The original names of twenty-seven different tribes meant in various forms "the people," Vine Deloria catalogues in *God Is Red*: "the people" (Arikara), "real people" (Cherokee), "the flesh" (Zuni), "men of men" (Pawnee), "the allies" (Lakota), "first people" (Biloxi), "people of the real speech" (Winnebago).[77] Scott Momaday tells of the Kiowa arrow-maker who sat working in his tepee with his wife. He fashioned and straightened arrows in his mouth, and the best arrows carried teeth marks. Once at night he saw a stranger looking in from the darkness. The arrow-maker said, in Kiowa, that if the outsider understood the language spoken in the tribe, he would give his name and be welcome. The stranger remained silent. Casually the arrow-maker bent his bow in one direction, then another, and then killed the outsider with a single arrow.[78] Words are penetrant arrows—the craft, ceremony, power, and defense of the tribal family. A well-made word pierces the heart.

Oral tribal poetry remains for the most part anonymous, as the tribal poet feels himself essentially a keeper of the sacred word bundle. He inherits rhythm, vision, craft, nature and the word as truths larger than himself that precede and continue beyond his temporal life. The song-poet discovers nature's poems, never pretending to invent the "poetic" world apart from nature, permitted to husband songs as one tends growing things. A poet sings his place in the tribe and nature, taking no credit, giving thanks that the song has chosen him. The anonymity leaves him both unassuming and dignified, twice honored. He gives the song back to those powers granting him voice, humbling himself before nature's tribal circle, his visions feeding into public rituals vital to tribal health—communal, open, of use to the people. His aesthetics prove utilitarian; he believes that tribal life necessitates beauty. Among the Pueblos "good" and "beautiful" are represented in one word.[79]

Tribal life centers in a common blood, a shared and inherited body of tradition, a communal place, a mutual past and present. The tribe is imaged in a circle. Black Elk questions why the grass is kept penned up with the people in cities, since the spirits have shown him the "sacred hoop" of the world: "You have noticed that everything an Indian does is in a circle, and that is because the Power of the World always works in circles, and everything tries to be round."[80] Daily relationships preserve this continuity, at once personal and ceremonial; all tribal members are specially kin, as a parent to a child or a brother to a sister. Tribal values include sharing material and spiritual wealth, loyalty to the kinship system, care for one's place in the world, an extended familial identity for the individual, and kindness in the older sense of the word, that is, "of the same kind" and "kind" or generous within that bond. So to be giving and gracious is natural among kind people.

Despite their separate histories, Native American tribes and literatures interconnect in a poetics resisting European ideas of the artist's primacy as word and world maker (Latin *poeta*, from the "maker" in Greek), his craft that would order nature, the fixity of the printed word. Native American literatures, given their diversities, intersect in a common, organic aesthetics—a poetic kinship that tribalizes "the people," creatures, the gods, and a natural environment.

Rooted Words

Genetic cultural sources within nature, words are the roots of continuing tribal origins. Indian literatures are grounded in an ecological language that often focuses on a single detail.

> *The bush is sitting under a tree and*
> *singing*[81]

Secure within nature, the bush sings its own poetry "under a tree." The poem is landscaped with a care that conditions singing, rather than a triumph of song. The language remains spare, neither more nor less than the evoked "thing" itself. Words-as-things carry their essential meanings as the minimal world elicits poetic attention. Small detail sharpens a response to the larger world; an insect orders the night's darkness, a portent of death.

> *The water bug is drawing*
> *the shadows of the evening*
> *toward him on the water*[82]

The poems sing the origins of people, creatures, things in *local* revelations, exactly where they exist. The people glimpse truths unexpectedly, out of the corner of the eye, as nature compresses and constantly surprises with a rich mystery. All things are alive, suggestive, sacred.

A Sioux holy man addresses a stone with reverence, *Tunkashila,* a word that also means Grandfather. On the Great Plains, where everything exists through vast emptiness, an isolate rock provides the world's cornerstone, a resting place for restless spirits, as in the Omaha fragment:

> *unmoved*
> *from time without*
> *end*
> *you rest*
> *there in the midst of the paths*
> *in the midst of the winds*
> *you rest*
> *covered with the droppings of birds*
> *grass growing from your feet*
> *your head decked with the down of birds*
> *you rest*
> *in the midst of the winds*
> *you wait*
> *Aged one*[83]

Nature here bases wandering spirits—winds, birds, grasses that come and go—even their droppings on the earth origins. The rock's patience serves as the poem's refrain: "You rest . . . you rest . . . you rest . . . you wait / Aged one." Time is here a permanence of place.

Words do not come after or apart from what naturally is, but are themselves natural genes, tribal history in the bodies of the people. People are born into their heritage of the tribal tongue as they enter the world. They do not make up words any more than they make up nature. Singers chant songs, drawing tonally on the voice as an interpretive human instrument, words living in the mouth and body; pitch modulates and brings out meaning, accent cadences the way meanings draw together. Instead of rhyming words (the poem as unifying technique) the songs rhyme perceptions, moods, natural objects, the world-as-word (the poem as unifying association). A lyric threads the story through poetic time as symbolic chords tie the song together harmonically. The Tewa sing to the Mother Earth and the Father Sky, and a weaver's loom appears:

Then weave for us a garment of brightness;
May the warp be the white light of morning,
May the weft be the red light of evening,
May the fringes be the falling rain,
May the border be the standing rainbow.[84]

Formulaic repetition ritualizes the sky's interwoven lights, and resonances between rhymed events stretch the song taut over the sky loom (fringes—falling rain; border—rainbow). The craft is discovered in a natural "house made of dawn":

May it be beautiful before me
May it be beautiful behind me
May it be beautiful below me
May it be beautiful above me
May it be beautiful all around me
In beauty it is finished.[85]

The Navajo tribalize nature through correspondences:

cotton
     motion
          clouds
frogs
   hail
     potatoes
         dumplings
cloud water
     fog
       moss

> smoke
>   cloud
>   rain
>   acceptance
>   breathing in[86]

"Do you picture it," a Zuni asked Dennis Tedlock in the middle of translating, "or do you just write it down?"[87]

Minimal Presence

The poetries suggest a philosophic awareness of things, their resonances, their places. Space shapes objects just as silence determines sound; objects in turn are defined at their circumferences, where they cease to exist. Shadows and echoes silhouette origins. "Listen!" the poets sing, invoking silence as the initial chord of a song-poem, the essential words depending on the silence from which they originate. The true poets listens as he sings:

> *There is in the Indian towns also a sense of timelessness and peace. No one who has watched the winter solstice ceremonies at Jemez can have failed to perceive the great spiritual harmonies which culminate in those ancient rites. None who has heard the deep droning concert of the singers and the insistent vibration of the drums can have mistaken the old sacred respect for sound and silence which makes for the magic of words and literature.*[88]

The strengths of the very young and old cross in the poet, sensing words in desert silence, pattern in forest shadows, design in the falling stars, the return of the summer sun at the winter solstice.

Poetry and morality fuse in storytelling where listening is occasion for learning tribal values. Morals lie inherent in the tales, the performing context of the story, the participation of audience and teller, the season of telling.[89] The storyteller does not gloss his tales or tell too much, so the listener can imagine his place in the story.

Just as silence speaks primally to the mind, so space is fertile without objects. "Nothing" can be suggestive presence, as echoed in the Southwest deserts or resonant on the Great Plains or shadowed in the Northern woodlands. A tribal people learn to know richness in a sense of loss, knowing through a necessary economy that more is not always better. The tribe is dependent on natural growth cycles for survival, and to go over or under necessity threatens the balance. People in tribal cultures learn to give to live, witness the ceremonial "give-aways" and potlatches and rituals of sacrifice. Thoreau records that the Iroquois practiced a "busk" ritual of burning all possessions every fifty years to begin anew. Nature is ever alive with spirits, powers, mysteries, sacred objects, and sacred spaces.

Sacred Play

A truly sacred world allows for an inverting sense of mockery and play. Tribal kinsmen joke to liven their feelings, play to loosen an encumbering seriousness; their play at once tempers and includes the serious world. Seneca poetry, Jerome Rothenberg observes, "works in sets of short songs, minimal realizations colliding with each other in marvelous ways, a very light, very pointed play-of-the-mind, nearly always just a step away from the comic (even as their masks are), the words set out in clear relief against the ground of the (meaningless) refrain. Clowns stomp & grunt through the longhouse, but in subtler ways too the encouragement to 'play' is always a presence."[90]

A storyteller mythologizes holy foolishness to release light spirits into their own place next to dignity. Sioux *heyokas* sport sacramentally as clowns, just as the trickster gods play with men. To become a *heyoka* one dreams a power vision of lightning, the spiritual connection between sky and earth. Southwest *kachina* gods called "Mudheads" use laughter to cleanse with magic license. Those touched by the gods at play—saints, clowns, priests, idiots, children, the elders—become holy and foolish in one gesture (in like manner English "silly" traces a double lineage back to the Old English "saelig," meaning holy and foolish).

Laughter, song, dance, and chant move the tribe through public ritual dynamically into nature. In healing ceremonies and celebrations the people dance to draw life from touch with the earth; they grieve to voice sorrow openly. "You have noticed," Black Elk says,

> that the truth comes into this world with two faces. One is sad with suffering and the other laughs; but it is the same face, laughing or weeping. When people are already in despair, maybe the laughing face is better for them; and when they feel too good and are too sure of being safe, maybe the weeping face is better for them to see.[91]

Tribal stories pivot on contrasts, releasing sorrow, sparking laughter, inspiring invention, purging primal fears. They give humankind a range from the animals and the earth to the gods and the sky. Black Elk laments that the sacred hoop of his tribe is broken and the flowering tree is withered after the Wounded Knee Massacre— "a people's dream that died in bloody snow"; a Nez Percé narrative poem is entitled "Coyote borrows Farting Boy's asshole, tosses up his eyes, retrieves them, rapes old women and tricks a young girl seeking power";[92] in a Cochiti story Coyote talks Beaver into exchanging wives, to Coyote's chagrin and his wife's pleasure;[93] in a Hopi tale Coyote Old Man deflowers the tribal virgin, whom both gods and men court unsuccessfully, he escapes and parades his genitals on a distant hill, then the rain god hunts him down and kills him;[94] the Maricopas tell how the Creator gave teeth of sun's fire to a gentle snake, as protection against a bullying rabbit, and the creatures in vengeance killed their Creator.[95] In all these tales gods and spirits walk the earth at one with plants, animals, and humans. Powers of transformation interrelate animate and inanimate beings in a reverse form of spiritual anthropomorphism: instead of projecting human forms on animals and the gods, men take their personal characteristics, family names, and clans from the animal and natural world—Black Elk, Crow Dog, Lone Wolf, Eagle Heart, Crazy Horse, Two Moons, Sun Chief, Star Boy, Sweet Grass Woman.

The natural world speaks for itself without shame or self-consciousness, dancing its life and language. The Makah sing:

> *Mine is a proud village, such as it is,*
> *We are at our best when dancing.*[96]

A decorous medium of the senses blossoms in the "orchidean" cultures of the Mayan and Aztec cultures, elegized by William Carlos Williams.[97] As the dance plays itself through, Aztec flowers bloom on the poet's lips, singing: a word is a flower is the dawn is a *quetzal* bird is a dewdrop is human life—beautiful, sexual, changing, perishable. "The flower in my heart blossoms in the middle of the night."[98] Passion. And human sacrifice. The terror of beauty.

No single mood corners nature's temperaments. No single curiosity exhausts the possibilities of surprise. Given a respect for nature's range, tribal peoples are freed to experiment with natural rules, discovering inherent truths by trial and error, their own investigation of traditions and moralities. Trusting tribal boundaries and a local sense of origin frees the people to explore their given heritage and environment while taking it on. The Pueblo moves over a space small as a mesa top, down through kivas into the earth, among family and extended kin, back into a communal past working itself out in the present. A plainsman, in contrast, once roamed a thousand miles a season on horseback, at home in motion. The "traditional" freedoms, unconfined by either a maximal or minimal sense of space, empower a tribal member to celebrate his life beyond a sense of restriction, momentary hardship, dislocation, or self-pity. Plenty-Coups, chief of the Crow, told the White "Sign-talker":

> *I am old. I am not graceful. My bones are heavy, and my feet are large. But I know justice and have tried all my life to be just, even to those who have taken away our old life that was so good. My whole thought is of my people. I want them to be healthy, to become again the race they have been. I want them to learn all they can from the white man, because he is here to stay, and they must live with him forever.*[99]

Sense Magic

The Indian world is magic through symbolic detail, and if attentive, one *sees* as a natural visionary. Lame Deer, the Sioux medicine man, says:

> *But I'm an Indian. I think about ordinary, common things like this pot. The bubbling water comes from the rain cloud. It represents the sky. The fire comes from the sun which warms us all—men, animals, trees. The meat stands for the four-legged creatures, our animal brothers, who gave of themselves so that we should*

live. The steam is living breath. . . . We Indians live in a world of symbols and images where the spiritual and the commonplace are one. To you symbols are just words, spoken or written in a book. To us they are part of nature, part of ourselves— the earth, the sun, the wind and the rain, stones, trees, animals, even little insects like ants and grasshoppers. We try to understand them not with the head but with the heart, and we need no more than a hint to give us the meaning.[100]

The world, as tribal seers know it, suggests endlessly. The seer feels the world "real" enough to be guided by and trust what he feels, seeing from "the heart's eye," as Lame Deer says. He heeds intuitions, believes in a perceptual reality cognate with nature's reality. If dreams are unreal, Momaday's grandmother spirit cautions him, then so are the dreamers.[101] A seer walks the Yaqui *brujo's* "path with heart": "'The world is all that is encased here,' [Juan Matus] said, and stomped the ground. 'Life, death, people, the allies, and everything else that surrounds us. The world is incomprehensible. We won't ever understand it; we won't ever unravel its secrets. Thus we must treat it as it is, a sheer mystery!'" Castaneda, the stumbling anthropologist and shaman's apprentice, must be surprised into knowledge. "'We have exhausted nothing, you fool,' [Juan Matus] said imperatively. '*Seeing* is for impeccable men. Temper your spirit now, become a warrior, learn to *see,* and then you'll know that there is no end to the new worlds for our vision.'"[102]

"Go to a mountain-top and cry for a vision," the Sioux holy men counsel.[103]

The spirit world and the natural world interpenetrate through dreams, most intense in the traditional vision quest, whether a Papago on pilgrimage from the desert to gather sea salt, an Eskimo shaman who drops to the bottom of the sea to ask forgiveness from the earth daughter, or a Sioux warrior lamenting in a vision pit on a lonely mountain-top. Seers know the world with care, attune themselves with natural magic. Their healing aligns the people with natural health and energies in the universe. A medicine-man ties the people's needs into things of the world, releasing the spirits in things to move through the tribe. A thought is a spiritual act, a word the magic power to actualize spirits.

Dreams relay visions from the spirit world; sacramental songs ritualize the dream myths, bearing visions into the world (a shaman is midwife to the gods). A Sioux *heyoka* sings:

> *The day of the sun has been my strength.*
> *The path of the moon shall be my robe.*
> *A sacred praise I am making.*
> *A sacred praise I am making.*[104]

Such song-poems are tribal conductors of dream power, and "sometimes dreams are wiser than waking," says Black Elk.[105] The spirits and ancestors speak to the living in dreams, giving their daily lives a sacred strangeness. Incantations, dream visions, totems, and imitative magic set up conduits of well-being and power in forces imag-

ined beyond the limits of people in this world. Dreams heighten the people's awareness, as does fear positively regarded, proving medicinal, therapeutic, because they
cleanse and energize the tribal spirit. The word-medicine of a Navajo chant heals
one asking health from the gods. The formula: chant, learn, be healed, remember—

> *The singer stroked the patient's body*
> *and pressed his body to the patient's body.*
>
> *Have you learned? they asked him*
> *and he answered, Yes.*
>
> *They sang all night, and the patient learned*
> *and was well.*
>
> *Then he was told to be sure and remember all that*
> *he had been taught, for everything forgotten went*
> *back to the gods.*[106]

The healing power of these words is inspired by the gods and yet communal, so that
the sacred world is again common, as in the mythic origins of religious thought.
Black Elk's "great vision" is of no healing power until his people perform it tribally
and ceremonially locate it in their daily life. The Navajo sing from the Night Chant:

> *In beauty*
> > *you shall be my representation*
> *In beauty*
> > *you shall be my song*
> *In beauty*
> > *you shall be my medicine*
> *In beauty*
> > *my holy medicine*[107]

A singer works at dreaming and seeing, but does not dwell on the work. The work
ethic can be transcended by a dream ethic, an intuitive morality inspired by the
spirit world. "Men who work cannot dream, and wisdom comes in dreams," the
Nez Percé, Smohalla of the Dreamer Religion, warned. "You ask me to plow the
ground. Shall I take a knife and tear my mother's breast? Then when I die she will
not take me to her bosom to rest."[108]

Tribal Song

> *I*
> *the song*
> *I walk here*[109]

This Modoc chant is imagined apart from any song-maker. The people come to it
for life, tradition, medicine, play; the tribe lives in the song's daily presence. Such

oral literature arises out of the common ceremonies of people speaking day to day, opening into tribal song. Many tribes speak of hearing the earth's heart in their songs. The chanted rhythms rise with the heartbeat, drums, moving feet, and through them the people dance the earth's pulse. The singing lives in tribal time, in rhythm with nature's cyclic time—the seasons of planting, growing, harvesting, and returning to the living earth.

Oral poetry is kinetic ritual. The body dances and sings alive with the mind. Black Elk says of the grandfather stallion's song in his vision: "It was so beautiful that nothing anywhere could keep from dancing. The virgins danced, and all the circled horses. The leaves on the trees, the grasses on the hills and in the valleys, the waters in the creeks and in the rivers and the lakes, the four-legged and the two-legged and the wings of the air—all danced together to the music of the stallion's song." [110] To know is to be moved by song, to be alert, quick—as the Yaqui *brujo* speaks of wisdom, "light and fluid." [111] A man of knowledge dances his wisdom.

Song cadences balance one another and play in running rhythms; the song-poet groups words in parallel phrases and rhymes thoughts, as though words also gather tribally, corresponding in kinships. A human condition rhymes with a natural phenomenon, man with animal origins.

> *The divine* quechol *bird answers me as I, the singer,*
> *sing, like the* coyol *bird, a noble new song,*
> *polished like a jewel, a turquoise, a shining*
> *emerald, darting green rays, a flower song of*
> *spring, spreading a celestial fragrance, fresh*
> *with the dews of roses, thus have I the poet sung.* [112]

A Tlingit singer laments,

> *It is only crying about myself*
> *that comes to me in song.* [113]

A Nootka complains against the fog,

> *Don't you ever,*
> *You up in the sky,*
> *Don't you ever get tired*
> *Of having the clouds between you and us?* [114]

or sings to bring fair weather,

> *You, whose day it is, make it beautiful.*
> *Get out your rainbow colors,*
> *So it will be beautiful.* [115]

The sensibility here, in Frederick Turner's words, lies "rooted so deeply in things that it goes through them and beneath them" to ancient truths in the world. [116]

Poetry as Survival

The Sioux doctor Ohiyesa says that Native American poetry survives as "a perilous gift."[117] The songs remain alive by necessity and choice, living humanly in the mouth, the torso, the heart, the limbs. As oral poetry, they compel listeners immediately, or lose their audience, their right to be. The language is by definition, Momaday says, one generation from extinction. A Wintu singer chants:

> *Down west, down west we dance,*
> *We spirits dance,*
> *Down west, down west we dance,*
> *We spirits dance,*
> *Down west, down west we dance,*
> *We spirits weeping dance,*
> *We spirits dance.*[118]

While the chant drops "down" to "weeping," simultaneously it moves out toward life, against death's descent. The lament works its way toward healing, countering the downward thrust of dying. The poem ritualizes pain through repetition and accretion, stylizing grief into the life of the dance, the pulse answering death's prone stasis. An ancient Kiowa woman sings as she prepares the earth for the Sun Dance—and the older the old woman grows, the more she frees herself, by necessity, playing to live.

> *We have brought the earth.*
> *Now it is time to play;*
> *As old as I am, I still have the feeling of play.*[119]

And within the Sun Dance play lies a sense of ancient, sacred processional. "But I was not the last," Black Elk envisions,

> *for when I looked behind me there were ghosts of people like a trailing fog as far as I could see—grandfathers of grandfathers and grandmothers of grandmothers without number. And over these a great Voice—the Voice that was the South—lived, and I could feel it silent. And as we went the Voice behind me said: 'Behold a good nation walking in a sacred manner in a good land!'*[120]

A warrior prepares for death with philosophic counsel and bearing. "Let us see, is this real, / This life I am living?" a Pawnee warrior chants, his battle a metaphysical question.[121] Life is a warrior's perishable gift, the world his mystery and challenge. Fear inspires him, brings him to life in humility before his task.

> *Wa-kon'da,*
> *here needy he stands,*
> *and I am he.*[122]

Requesting bravery and power from the spirits, a warrior respects "the power to make-live and to destroy," the interdependent powers that Black Elk, cousin to Crazy Horse, receives from his Grandfather in the western sky. Black Elk is given a bow and a wooden cup filled with rainwater—the terror of a thunderstorm, the gentle life force of its moisture.[123]

The warrior meets death directly, honestly, with no illusions, confronting the defining fact of life, that is, not-life. His bravery grows out of self-accepted smallness in the face of the universe, realizing that the spirits one day will take back the life given him for the moment. "Have pity on me," sings the Assiniboine warrior, crying his vulnerability.[124] White Antelope, a Cheyenne war chief, stood with folded arms and sang this death song as he was ambushed and killed at the Sand Creek Massacre of 1864:

Nothing lives long
Except the earth and the mountains[125]

Tribal Circles

The tribal Native American finds power in natural circles—sun and moon, stars, nest, tepee, flower, rainbow, whirlwind, human contours, nature's seasonal cycles. The singers of a tribally poetic world live in the circular presence of spoken words. The mouth rounds out in speech and song; the printed page remains fixed, rectilinear. Black Elk laments that Indians must live penned up on islands, and Lame Deer questions the power of a society living in squares and plastic bags.[126]

The vision quest is circular, requiring solitude but not corners for hiding; the visionary leaves his tribe periodically in order to return. "Help yourself as you travel along in life," the Winnebago, Crashing Thunder, counsels. "The earth has many narrow passages scattered over it. If you have something with which to strengthen yourself, then when you get to these narrow passages, you will be able to pass through them safely and your fellow-men will respect you."[127] Like the warrior, the song-poet lives individually for the sake of the tribe, and his singing is a matter of life or death for the people. He does not celebrate himself separately, his vision apart from the natural world, but sings his kinship in the tribal circle.

A "49" verse sung at contemporary powwows reminds the people,

When the dance is over, sweetheart,
I will take you home in my one-eyed Ford.[128]

NOTES

[1]John Neihardt, ed., *Black Elk Speaks* (Lincoln: University of Nebraska Press, 1961; 1932), p. 25. Simon and Schuster have reissued the book in a Pocket Book

edition (New York, 1972).

[2]Knud Rasmussen, *Across Arctic America. Narrative of the Fifth Thule Expedition* (New York: G. P. Putnam's Sons, 1927), p. 164.

[3]I use Vine Deloria's figure of 315 culturally functional tribes in the United States (*Custer Died For Your Sins. An Indian Manifesto.* New York: Simon and Schuster, 1969, p. 13). As a Standing Rock Sioux, former president of the National Congress of American Indians, and legal counsel for Indian affairs, Deloria is in a position to arbitrate figures that vary from two hundred to six hundred extant "tribes." *Wássaja* (vol. 7, Jan.–Feb. 1979) published a Federal Register list (February 1979) of 280 "tribal reservation entities" having a government-to-government relationship with the United States and another 40 Indian groups petitioning for federal acknowledgement through the Bureau of Indian Affairs. The statistics for aboriginal population are even less firm. Harold E. Driver cites Kroeber (1934, 1939) with the lowest estimate of 4,200,000 for the North American continent in 1492 and Dobyns (1966) with about 60,000,000. He revises to estimate perhaps 30,000,00 for the continent (*Indians of North America.* Chicago: University of Chicago Press, 1961, 1969, pp. 63–64). Dobyns' most liberal estimates are ten to twelve million people north of the Rio Grande, roughly two thousand cultures speaking a thousand languages (Henry F. Dobyns, "Estimating Aboriginal American Population: An Appraisal of Techniques with a New Hemispheric Estimate," *Current Anthropology* [1966] 7: 414). In response to this controversy, Alfonso Ortiz, the Tewa anthropologist, wrote to me that "no responsible anthropologist known to me believes that there were several thousand aboriginal cultures in Native America north of the Rio Grande, nor were there a thousand languages spoken. Five hundred languages and as many cultures is a commonly agreed estimate. On population eight million is the most liberal upper estimate with any following at all. True, the figures keep getting revised upward slowly as retrieval and sampling techniques improve, but until they do even more, anything beyond what I cite is at best conjectural" (personal correspondence, 25 January 1979).

[4]Harold E. Driver, *Indians of North America* (Chicago: University of Chicago, 1969; 1961), pp. 527–28. Bureau of Indian Affairs and United States Census figures.

[5]Jorge Luis Borges, "The Oral Poetry of the Indians," *Literature of the American Indians: Views and Interpretations,* Abraham Chapman, ed. (New York: New American Library, 1975), p. 277.

[6]Barre Toelken, "Seeing with a Native Eye: How Many Sheep Will It Hold?" in *Seeing with a Native Eye. Essays on Native American Religion,* Walter Holden Capps, ed. (New York: Harper, 1976), p. 17.

[7]Neihardt, ed., *Black Elk Speaks,* p. 1.

[8]See selected papers and discussion from a UCLA symposium on American Indian Studies as a graduate program, UCLA *American Indian Culture and Research Journal,* 2, nos. 3–4 (1978): 1–46. Also see *Contemporary Issues of the American Indian,* college course designs published by the National Indian Education Association, Minneapolis, Minnesota. The Modern Language Association is projecting a book of sample course curricula for teaching Native American Literatures, edited by Paula Gunn Allen. UCLA begins the first Masters Program in American Indian Studies, Fall 1982.

[9]Claude Lévi-Strauss, "The Making of an Anthropologist," *Tristes Tropique*

(New York: Atheneum, 1974; 1955), trans. by John and Doreen Weightman.

[10]Anthony F. C. Wallace, *The Death and Rebirth of the Seneca* (New York: Random House, 1969).

[11]D'Arcy McNickle, *Native American Tribalism. Indian Survivals and Renewals* (New York: Oxford, 1973), p. 72.

[12]See Francis Haines, *The Buffalo* (New York: Crowell, 1970) and Tom McHugh, *The Time of the Buffalo* (New York: Knopf, 1972).

[13]Edward S. Curtis, *The North American Indian. The Indians of the United States and Alaska* (New York: Johnson, 1970; 1908) 3: 11.

[14]Constance Rourke, "The Indian Background of American Theatricals" in Chapman, ed., *Literature of the American Indians*, p. 257.

[15]Lawrence C. Wroth, "The Indian Treaty as Literature" in Chapman, p. 327.

[16]Margot Astrov, ed., *American Indian Prose and Poetry*, originally published in 1946 as *The Winged Serpent* (New York: Capricorn, 1962), p. 87.

[17]Dee Brown, *Bury My Heart at Wounded Knee* (New York: Holt, Rinehart, & Winston, 1970), p. 424.

[18]McNickle, *Native American Tribalism*, p. 51.

[19]Neihardt, ed., *Black Elk Speaks*, p. 138.

[20]Francis Jennings, *The Invasion of America. Indians, Colonialism, and the Cant of Conquest* (Chapel Hill: University of North Carolina, 1975), p. 30.

[21]William Brandon, ed., *The Magic World. American Indian Songs and Poems* (New York: Morrow, 1971), p. 115.

[22]Report of T. J. Morgan, Commissioner of Indian Affairs, to the Secretary of the Interior, 1 October 1889. Chapman, ed., *Literature of the American Indians*, p. 16.

[23]James Mooney, *Calendar History of the Kiowa Indians. Extract from the Seventeenth Annual Report of the Bureau of American Ethnology* (Washington, 1898), p. 154.

[24]Astrov, ed., *Americna Indian Prose and Poetry*, pp. 163–64.

[25]Ibid., p. 248.

[26]Robert A. Trennert, "The Indian Role in the 1876 Centennial Celebration," UCLA *American Indian Culture and Research Journal* 4, no. 1: 7–13.

[27]Malcolm McFee, *Modern Blackfeet. Montanans on a Reservation* (New York: Holt, Rinehart, & Winston, 1972), p. 64.

[28]See Vine Deloria's argument for a pan-Indian political coalition based on a separate land base and tribal sovereignty in *Custer Died For Your Sins*.

[29]Howell Raines, "American Indians Struggling for Power and Identity," *New York Times Magazine*, 11 February 1979; Edgar S. Cahn, *Our Brother's Keeper: The Indian in White America* (Washington: World Publishing, 1969).

[30]Deloria, *Custer Died For Your Sins*, p. 2.

[31]D. H. Lawrence, "Fenimore Cooper's White Novels" in *Studies in Classic American Literature* (New York: Viking, 1966; 1923), p. 36.

[32]Williams first wrote on American violence as a mythic act of regeneration soaked into "the bloody loam" of the country's history (*In the American Grain*, New York: New Directions, 1956; 1925), and Richard Slotkin has developed a "mytho-poeic" reading of American cultural archetypes through a study of colonial and frontier literary history (*Regeneration Through Violence: The Mythology of the American Frontier, 1600–1860*, Middletown, Wesleyan University, 1973). New studies

on Indian stereotyping and image-making are revising old myths about civilization and savagery: among many recent statements see Hugh Honour, *The New Golden Land* (New York: Random House, 1975), Wilcomb E. Washburn, *The Indian in America* (New York: Harper, 1975), Frederick W. Turner III, *The Portable North American Indian Reader,* Introduction (Kingsport: Viking, 1973), and Fredi Chiappelli, *et. al,* eds., *First Images of America: The Impact of the New World on the Old,* 2 vols. (Berkeley: University of California, 1976).

[33]Turner, *Portable Reader,* p. 9.

[34]William Carlos Williams, "A Sort of a Song" in *Selected Poems* (New York: New Directions, 1969; 1949).

[35]Octavio Paz, *In Praise of Hands: Contemporary Crafts of the World,* published in conjunction with the first World Crafts Exhibition held at the Ontario Science Center in Toronto (Greenwich, Conn.: New York Graphic Society, 1974).

[36]Knud Rasmussen, *Across Arctic America: Narrative of the Fifth Thule Expedition,* (New York: G. P. Putnam's Sons, 1927), p. 195. Peter Nabokov, "American Indian Literature: A Tradition of Renewal," ASAIL Newsletter 2 (Autumn 1978): 31–40.

[37]Jeffrey F. Huntsman, "Traditional Native American Literature: The Translation Dilemma," Native American Issue of *Shantih* 4 (Summer–Fall 1979): 6.

[38]*Black Elk Speaks; Being the Life Story of a Holy Man of the Oglala Sioux,* John G. Neihardt, trans. (Lincoln: University of Nebraska, 1961; 1932), p. 193. For issues surrounding Neihardt's translation see Robert F. Sayre, "Vision and Experience in *Black Elk Speaks,*" *College English* 32 (February 1971): 509–35 and Sally McCluskey, "*Black Elk Speaks:* and So Does John Neihardt," *Western American Literature* 6 (Winter 1972): 231–42.

[39]Walter Benjamin, "The Task of the Translator" in *Illuminations,* Harry Zohn, trans. (London: Collins, 1973; 1955), p. 80.

[40]Ibid., p. 79.

[41]W. S. Merwin, *Selected Translations 1968–1978* (New York: Atheneum, 1979), p. xi.

[42]William Carlos Williams, *In the American Grain* (New York: New Directions, 1969; 1949), p. 137.

[43]William Bevis, "American Indian Verse Translations" in Chapman, *Literature of the American Indians,* p. 321. First published in *College English,* (March, 1974).

[44]Huntsman, *Shantih,* p. 6.

[45]Hugh Honour, *The New Golden Land: European Images of America from the Discoveries to the Present Time* (New York: Random House, 1975), p. 12.

[46]See William K. Powers, "The Arachic Illusion," Review of *Hanta Yo: An American Saga* by Ruth Beebe Hill, *American Indian Art Magazine* 5 (November 1979): 68–71 and Alan Taylor, "The Literary Offenses of Ruth Beebe Hill," Review Essay in UCLA's *American Indian Culture and Research Journal* 4 (1980): 75–85.

[47]H. S. McAllister, "'The Language of Shamans': Jerome Rothenberg's Contribution to American Indian Literature," *Western American Literature* 10 (February 1976): 293–309. Jerome Rothenberg, "Total Translation: An Experiment in the Presentation of American Indian Poetry" in Chapman, *Literature of the American Indians,* p. 298 and p. 294.

[48]McAllister, "The Language of Shamans," p. 296.

[49]Ibid., pp. 297–98.

[50]Brandon offended ethnologists and linguists by wanting to see Native American literature as literature apart from anthropological contexts. He also took liberty to rearrange and in some cases reinvent texts. See William Bevis, "American Indian Verse Translations" in *College English* 35 (March 1974): 699. Reprinted in Chapman, *Literature of the American Indians*, p. 308–323. Also see Gretchen Bataille, "American Indian Literature; Traditions and Translations," *Melus* 6 (Winter 1979): 17–26.

[51]McAllister, "The Language of Shamans," p. 299.

[52]Williams, *Selected Poems*.

[53]*The Wishing Bone Cycle: Narrative Poems from the Swampy Cree Indians*, Howard A. Norman, trans. (New York: Stonehill, 1976).

[54]Rasmussen, *Across Arctic America*, p. 164.

[55]Neihardt, ed., *Black Elk Speaks*, p. 49.

[56]William Butler Yeats, "Why the Blind Man in Ancient Times Was Made a Poet" (1906) in *W. B. Yeats: Selected Criticism*, A. Norman Jeffares, ed. (London: Macmillan, 1964), p. 153.

[57]Ezra Pound, trans., *Shih-Ching: The Classic Anthology Defined by Confucius* (Cambridge: Harvard University, 1954), p. 111.

[58]Rainer Maria Rilke, letter of 11 August 1924, quoted in Martin Heidegger's "What Are Poets For?" in *Poetry, Language, Thought*, Albert Hofstadter, trans. (New York: Harper and Row, 1975; 1971), pp. 128–29.

[59]Charles Olson, "Projective Verse" in *The Poetics of the New American Poetry*, Donald Allen and Warren Tallman, eds. (New York: Grove Press, 1973), p. 156. First published in *Human Universe* (1951).

[60]Ezra Pound, "Warning" in *ABC of Reading* (New York: New Directions, 1960), p. 14.

[61]Frances Densmore, *Teton Sioux Music*, Smithsonian Institution Bureau of American Ethnology, Bulletin 61 (Washington, 1918; Da Capo Press Reprint, New York, 1972), p. 88.

[62]Astrov, *American Indian Prose and Poetry*, p. 3.

[63]Albert B. Lord, *The Singer of Tales* (Cambridge: Harvard University Press, 1960), p. 13. John (Fire) Lame Deer and Richard Erdoes, *Lame Deer Seeker of Visions: The Life of a Sioux Medicine Man* (New York: Simon and Schuster, 1972), p. 127. Also see: Alan Dundes, "Texture, Text, and Context," *Southern Folklore Quarterly*, 28 (December 1964): 251–65; Dell Hymes, "Louis Simpson's 'The deserted boy,'" *Poetics* 5 (1976): 119–55; Dell Hymes, "Discovering Oral Performance and Measured Verse in American Indian Narrative," *New Literary History* 8 (1976–1977): 431–57; Dennis Tedlock, *Finding the Center: Narrative Poetry of the Zuni Indians* (Lincoln: University of Nebraska, 1978; 1972); J. Barre Toelken, "The 'Pretty Language' of Yellowman: Genre, Mode, and Texture in Navajo Coyote Narratives," *Genre* 2 (September 1969); J. Barre Toelken, *The Dynamics of Folklore* (Boston: Houghton Mifflin, 1979).

[64]John (Fire) Lame Deer and Richard Erdoes, *Lame Deer*, p. 163.

[65]Vine Deloria, Jr., *Custer Died For Your Sins*, p. 95.

[66]Claude Lévi-Strauss, *The Savage Mind* (Chicago: University of Chicago, 1966; 1972).

[67]N. Scott Momaday, "The Morality of Indian Hating," *Ramparts* (Summer

1964), p. 30.

[68]Deloria, *Custer,* p. 82.

[69]J. Barre Toelken, "Seeing with a Native Eye: How Many Sheep Will It Hold?" in *Seeing with a Native Eye: Essays on Native American Religion,* Walter Holden Capps, ed. (New York: Harper and Row, 1976).

[70]Jarold Ramsey, ed. *Coyote Was Going There: Indian Literature of the Oregon Country* (Seattle: University of Washington, 1977), pp. 38–39.

[71]*Wishing Bone,* Norman, trans., p. 172.

[72]Ibid., p. 4.

[73]A literary scholar is accountable to certain works of folklore, ethnology, anthropology, and biographical history—Paul Radin's *The Trickster* (1956) and *The Autobiography of a Winnebago Indian* (1920; 1963), Theodora Kroeber's *Ishi* (1961), Ruth Underhill's *The Autobiography of a Papago Woman* (1936), Luther Standing Bear's *My People the Sioux* (1928), Frank Waters' *Pumpkin Seed Point* (1969) and *The Book of the Hopi* (1963), Charles Eastman's reflections on Lakota childhood, especially *The Soul of the Indian* (1911), and Hyemeyohsts Storm's *Seven Arrows* (1972), to name only a few not cited elsewhere in this essay. An entire field of American literature, written by non-Indians, focuses on American Indians, from captivity narratives and explorers' accounts and artist's impressions to Fenimore Cooper's Leatherstocking tales, frontier and western sagas, Mari Sandoz's *Crazy Horse* (1942) and Stanley Vestal's *Sitting Bull* (1932), Thomas Berger's serio-comic *Little Big Man* (1964), Claire Huffaker's *Nobody Loves a Drunken Indian* (1967), Dan Cushman's *Stay Away Joe* (1952), a favorite on reservations, and Arthur Kopit's play, *Indians* (1969), a surreal drama of the history and show business in Buffalo Bill's "Wild West." Leslie Fiedler's critical study, *The Return of the Vanishing American* (1969), offers the most lively discussion of these materials, while Richard Slotkin lays the mythic-historical groundwork in *Regeneration Through Violence* (1973).

The most complete annotated bibliography on American Indian literature will appear in an anthology of traditional song-poetry edited by Alfonso and Margaret Ortiz, *To Carry Forth the Vine* (forthcoming, Columbia University). See also Arlene B. Hirschfelder, *American Indian Authors: A Representative Bibliography* (New York: Association of American Indian Affairs, 1970).

[74]A. Grove Day, *The Sky Clears: Poetry of the American Indians* (Lincoln: University of Nebraska, 1964), pp. 4–5.

[75]Astrov, *American Indian Pose and Poetry,* p. 20.

[76]Neihardt, ed., *Black Elk Speaks,* p. 49.

[77]Vine Deloria, Jr., *God Is Red* (New York: Grosset & Dunlap, 1973), pp. 365–66.

[78]N. Scott Momaday, *The Way to Rainy Mountain* (Albuquerque: University of New Mexico, 1969), p. 46.

[79]Octavio Paz, the Mexican poet, argues that the beauty in art still is "good" and useful in pre-technological cultures where the arts are functional crafts; pottery, weaving, wood and metal work, song-poetry and story-telling carry the touch of human hands (*In Praise of Hands*). W. H. Auden felt that cooking was the only functional art, both necessary and aesthetic, left to western technological cultures.

[80]Neihardt, ed., *Black Elk Speaks,* p. 198.

[81]Ojibwa, Brandon, ed., *The Magic World,* p. 96.

[82]Quechuan, Brandon, ed., *The Magic World,* p. 96.

[83]Omaha, "The Rock (Fragment of a Ritual)," Brandon, ed., *The Magic World,* p. 83.

[84]Astrov, ed., *American Indian Prose and Poetry,* p. 221.

[85]From the Navajo Night Chant, Astrov, ed., *American Indian Prose and Poetry,* p. 186.

[86]Jerome Rothenberg, ed., *Shaking the Pumpkin: Traditional Poetry of the Indian North Americas* (Garden City, N.Y.: Doubleday, 1972), pp. 310–11. I have adjusted the line spacing.

[87]Dennis Tedlock, *Finding the Center. Narrative Poetry of the Zuni Indians* (Lincoln: University of Nebraska, 1978; 1972), p. xxxi.

[88]N. Scott Momaday, lecture at UCLA, May 1970.

[89]See Barre Toelken, "The 'Pretty Language' of Yellowman. Genre, Mode, Texture in Navaho Coyote Narratives," in *Folklore Genres,* ed. Dan Ben-Amos (Austin: University of Texas, 1976), pp. 145–70.

[90]Jerome Rothenberg, "Total Translation. An Experiment in the Presentation of American Indian Poetry," in *Literature of the American Indians: Views and Interpretations,* ed. Abraham Chapman (New York: New American Library, 1975), p. 295.

[91]Neihardt, ed., *Black Elk Speaks,* p. 192–93.

[92]Rothenberg, ed., *Pumpkin,* p. 105.

[93]Brandon, ed., *The Magic World,* p. 54.

[94]Ibid., p. 44.

[95]Astrov, ed., *American Indian Prose and Poetry,* p. 267.

[96]John Bierhorst, *In the Trail of the Wind: American Indian Poems and Ritual Orations* (New York: Farrar, Straus and Giroux, 1971), p. 45. Originally published in Frances Densmore, "Nootka and Quileute Music," *Bureau of American Ethnology, Bulletin 124,* (1939), p. 81.

[97]William Carlos Williams, "The Destruction of Tenochtitlan," *In the American Grain* (New York: New Directions, 1956; 1925), p. 27.

[98]Nahuatl, Brandon, ed., *The Magic World,* p. 32.

[99]Shirley Hill Witt and Stan Steiner, *The Way: An Anthology of American Indian Literature* (New York: Knopf, 1972), p. 16. The quote is from Frank B. Linderman's *Plenty-Coups, Chief of the Crows* (Omaha: University of Nebraska, 1962).

[100]John (Fire) Lame Deer and Richard Erdoes, *Lame Deer,* p. 108.

[101]N. Scott Momaday, "An American Land Ethic," *Sierra Club Bulletin,* 55 (February 1970): 9.

[102]Carlos Castaneda, *A Separate Reality: Further Conversations with Don Juan* (New York: Simon & Schuster, 1971), pp. 105, 264, 187.

[103]Rothenberg, ed., *Pumpkin,* p. 197.

[104]Neihardt, ed., *Black Elk Speaks,* p. 193.

[105]Ibid., p. 10.

[106]Brandon, ed., *The Magic World,* pp. 64–65.

[107]Ibid., p. 62.

[108]Astrov, ed., *American Indian Prose an Poetry,* p. 85.

[109]Thomas E. Sanders and Walter W. Peek, *Literature of the American Indian* (Beverly Hills: Glencoe, 1976), p. 47.

[110] Neihardt, ed., *Black Elk Speaks,* pp. 41–42.

[111] Castaneda, *A Separate Reality,* p. 16.

[112] Aztec, Day, *The Sky Clears,* p. 176.

[113] Sanders and Peek, *Literature of the American Indian,* p. 47.

[114] Ibid., p. 48.

[115] Ibid.

[116] Turner, *Portable Reader,* p. 15.

[117] Astrov, ed. *American Indian Prose and Poetry,* p. 128. The quotation is from Charles Alexander Eastman, *The Soul of the Indian* (Boston and New York: Houghton, Mifflin, 1911).

[118] D. Demetracapoulou, "Wintu Songs," *Anthropos* 30 (1935): 483–494.

[119] Momaday, *Way to Rainy Mountain,* p. 88.

[120] Neihardt, ed., *Black Elk Speaks,* p. 36.

[121] Astrov, ed., *American Indian Prose and Poetry,* p. 109.

[122] Omaha Tribal Prayer, Astrov, ed., *American Indian Prose and Poetry,* p. 135.

[123] Neihardt, ed., *Black Elk Speaks,* p. 26.

[124] Astrov, ed., *American Indian Prose and Poetry,* p. 95

[125] George Bird Grinnell, *The Fighting Cheyenne* (Norman: University of Oklahoma, 1956; 1915), p. 178.

[126] Black Elk speaks of travelling with Buffalo Bill's "Wild West" Show to New York and "across the Big Water": "Afterwhile I got used to being there, but I was like a man who had never had a vision. I felt dead and my people seemed lost and I thought I might never find them again. I did not see anything to help my people. I could see that the Wasichus did not care for each other the way our people did before the nation's hoop was broken. They would take everything from each other if they could, and so there were some who had more of everything than they could use, while crowds of people had nothing at all and maybe were starving. They had forgotten that the earth was their mother" (p. 221). Black Elk had gone with Buffalo Bill "because I might learn some secret of the Wasichu that would help my people" (pp. 218–19), but the pilgrimage failed. "Well, it is as it is. We are prisoners of war while we are waiting here. But there is another world" (p. 200).

[127] Paul Radin, *The Autobiography of a Winnebago Indian* (New York: Dover, 1963; 1920), p. 80.

[128] Alan R. Velie, ed. *American Indian Literature: An Anthology* (Norman: University of Oklahoma, 1979), p. 176. Songs collected by Raymond Tahbone from Anadarko, Oklahoma.

Kenneth M. Roemer: NATIVE AMERICAN ORAL NARRATIVES: CONTEXT AND CONTINUITY

Most non-Indians "know" about "Indian tales." But as Vine Deloria, Jr. argues in *Custer Died for Your Sins,* what non-Indians "know" about Indians can often be, to say the least, inaccurate.[1] Because of the ways most non-Indians learn about Native American oral narratives, they tend to associate them with "quaint" or "primitive" fairy tales, folklore, or superstitions. Part of the explanation for these misconceptions is that the popular written and mass media forms of transmitting information about Native American oral narratives often strip away the cultural and literary contexts of the stories. Furthermore, the narratives are usually associated with the dead past of the Vanished American.

The following survey is an attempt to correct these popular misconceptions by stressing the contexts and continuities of Native American oral narratives. I realize that much of the material presented in this essay will be familiar to scholars who specialize in Indian oral traditions. But some of the examples and approaches may be new to the specialists, and I hope that the non-specialists will find my overview useful, particularly if they plan to introduce this type of literature to colleagues, students, and friends.[2]

ONE

In general collections of mythology, legend, and folklore, and even in anthologies of Native American literature, Indian stories are frequently presented in a vacuum. The narratives are reprinted—often from fifty-year old Bureau of Ethnography translations—and either left standing alone or framed by a brief headnote and a briefer footnote. Ideally these frames should be expanded to indicate the *type* of narrative reprinted and the many *contexts* of the story.[3]

Anthropologists, ethnologists, folklorists, linguists, and literary critics, guided by storytellers and interpreters, have established the general characteristics of important types of traditional oral narratives. For example, the introductions to several well-known collections of stories—Stith Thompson's *Tales of the North American Indians,* Tristram Coffin's *Indian Tales of North America,* Susan Feldmann's *The Storytelling Stone,* and John Bierhorst's *The Red Swan*—provide definitions of various types of oral narratives that serve as useful frameworks for understanding traditional Indian stories.

One of the oldest and most significant types of narratives is the origin story: a tale of an "earlier world" that often explains present conditions.[4] These stories may be creation narratives, such as the Cheyenne account of Maheo, the All Spirit, who created the great oceans but needed the help of the lowly coot who could dive below the water to retrieve the ball of mud that Maheo transformed into the land with the help of Grandmother turtle. Or origin stories can be emergence narratives, such as accounts of the trials of the ancestors of the Navajo, who journed upward through several underworlds, or the Zuni Moss People, who followed the two Ahayuuta, the Bow Priests, up through the four "rooms" of the Earth. Origin narratives can also take the form of migration tales, such as the second part of the Zuni story of "The Beginning" that tells of the discovery of the Middle Place, the site of the present Zuni village in New Mexico. In all of the origin stories, whether they be creation, emergence, or migration tales, the characters are divinities or prototypes of people or animals—the Navajo call them "mist people."

"Mist people" also populate the worlds of a second important category of oral narratives, the Trickster stories. The Trickster has been called the "most familiar figure" in Native American stories and the "great personage of North American mythology."[5] In the far North on the Pacific Coast he might be the greedy Raven; further south the erotic Mink; still further south along the coast the ambitious Bluejay. In the Southwest he often appears as Coyote, though the Kiowa's Saynday can transform himself into a man. On the Plains he could be Old Man; near the Great Lakes he could be the human-like Wakdjunkaga of the Winnebago or the human-like Manabozho, the benefactor of mankind who was drastically transformed into Hiawatha by Longfellow. On the North Atlantic coast he may appear as the culture hero, Wisaka.[6] Trickster's behavior can run the gamut from animal lusts, to incredible stupidity, to conscious and more often unconscious acts that are heroic and even godlike. Thus, Paul Radin, probably the best-known student of Trickster, argues that the Trickster is the most inclusive image of the range of human nature found in Indian literature: the Trickster "became and remained everything to everyman—god, animal, human being, hero, buffoon, he was before good and evil, denier, affirmer, destroyer and creator. If we laugh at him, he grins at us. What happens to him happens to us."[7]

Other well-known types of traditional narratives include hero tales, journeys to other worlds, and accounts of animal wives, husbands, and parents. The heroes, who are frequently twins, are more human than the characters in the origin and Trickster tales, but they usually have divine parents. For instance, the Sun and Changing Woman (a holy being associated with Earth and the change of seasons) are the parents of the Navajo's Monster Slayer and Child of Water. Like Hercules and Ulysses, these heroes are continually tested, and the plots of the tales hinge upon victories over monsters and escapes from clashing rocks, knife-like reeds, and boiling sands.[8] The tales about journeys to other worlds can include variations of the popular "Star Husband" motif in which one or two women journey to the stars, or to the Sun in the Kiowa version. Or the journey may take the form of a visit to the land of the dead, whether it be the arcadian "Over the Hill" land of the Arapaho or the two afterworlds described by the Hopi: the place of the Kachinas in the San Francisco peaks and the desert country of the Two Hearts. The animal wives, husbands, and parents stories can begin with a sexual encounter. In one translation of a tale from the Blackfeet, for instance, the opening sentences are: "Once a young man went out and came to a buffalo-cow fast in the mire. He took advantage of her situation. After a time she gave birth to a boy."[9] But an animal-human relationship can also be established when a parent deserts an unwanted child, as in the Zuni "Boy and the Deer" tale, or when a wanderer is adopted by an animal family, as in the "Wolf Woman" story of the Lakota.

The origin, Trickster, hero, journey to other worlds, and animal wife, husband or parents stories encompass tens of thousands of tales collected by thousands of Europeans, Anglo-Americans, and Native Americans—a heritage of collecting that spans almost five centuries including the efforts of Columbus' priest Ramon Pane, Spanish missionaries, French Jesuits, early nineteenth-century Indian agents, such as Henry Rowe Schoolcraft, late nineteenth-century ethnologists who published in the Bureau of American Ethnology bulletins and reports, and twentieth-century collectors such as Franz Boas, Stith Thompson, and Dennis Tedlock.[10] But even a thumbnail sketch of several important types of Indian oral narratives is not complete without two very important qualifications. First, all Native American stories do not fit neatly into one of the major categories. There are many short tales that don't "fit." Moreover, most introductions to collections include a warning similar to Susan Feldmann's advice in *The Storytelling Stone*: the "classes of tales flow freely into one another, and the difference between folktales and myths characteristic of Western cultures breaks down almost completely for the North American Indian."[11] Some of the examples already offered demonstrate how difficult it can be to categorize a particular story. The Zuni accounts of "The Beginning" share elements of origin and hero tales and many of the episodes in the Great Lakes and Eastern Woodland Trickster cycles are similar to hero tales. The other qualification is that even though the traditional categories represent thousands of tales recounted in hundreds of tribes over many centuries, they do not tell the whole story of Native American oral narratives. The narratives of more recent origin (discussed in the second part of this essay) also deserve attention—narratives such as adaptations of European tales, historical accounts, contemporary reservation and urban stories and jokes, and versions of oral narratives transformed into fiction and poetry by Native American authors.

Most editors do include brief statements about the type of narrative included in their anthologies, but only rarely do the editors of general classroom texts provide the philosophical, cultural, historical, environmental, linguistic, stylistic, or performing contexts. Establishing the philosphical context, for example, helps to explain why storytelling was and is so important to Native Americans—why the Laguna poet and novelist, Leslie Marmon Silko, should choose to say in an introductory poem to her novel *Ceremony* that "You don't have anything / if you don't have the stories."[12]

To explain the importance of storytelling, anthropologists frequently emphasize specific functions performed by the narratives. The stories contain information that the listeners needed or still need to understand themselves, their culture, and their environment. To cite just a few examples: the Zuni emergence stories contain religious detail about dieties and heroes, descriptions of the social roles of priests who follow the two heroic Bow Priests, formal greeting customs when the Bow Priests speak to the priests in the fourth room, and important information about geographical formations and abandoned, as well as inhabited, villages in Arizona and New Mexico. Similarly one of the Cheyenne "River Monster" tales explains why traditional Cheyenne who cross the Mississippi are supposed to drop a meat offering; the Navajo "River of Separation" account delineates traditional sex roles; the Lenni Lenape "Walam Olum" serves as a history text; the Tewa migration stories offer symbolic and factual data about constellations and obedience; and countless other tales provide guidelines related to planting corn, hunting skills, animal and human traits, and related practical matters. Furthermore, several anthropologists have argued that the sharing of familiar tribal stories helps Indians to withstand many of the rapid changes of the twentieth century.[13]

N. Scott Momaday and Paula Gunn Allen would probably agree that the specific storytelling functions delineated by anthropologists do help to explain the endurance of many oral traditions. But these two Native American authors go beyond specific functions to emphasize several general appeals. In his essay "The Man Made of Words" Momaday stresses the storyteller's ability to express humanity's "capacity for wonder, meaning and delight." He also calls attention to the influence of a fundamental paradox. A story is "tenuous" because any tale handed down by "word of mouth" is "always but one generation removed from extinction." Yet it is "held dear, too, on that same account."[14] In her essay, "The Sacred Hoop," Allen presents narratives as a means of bringing the "isolated private self into harmony and balance with . . . reality."[15] In part, this sense of harmony and balance is achieved because of the encyclopedic scope of traditional narratives. To quote the nineteenth-century Anishinabe chief, George Copway, "nearly every beast and bird is the subject of the storyteller. . . . Every moving leaf would seem to be a voice of a spirit."[16] But the stories can help the "isolated private self" to establish harmony and balance with realities far beyond day-to-day experiences. The constellation tales give listeners relatives in the sky. Thus, Momaday's observations about what can be lost when techological societies abandon oral traditions and the sense of harmony they offer testifies to the importance of Indian narratives: "We may be perfectly sure of where we are in relation to the supermarket and the next coffee break, but I doubt that any of us knows where he is in relation to the stars and to the summer solstices."[17]

A reader also should have some relevant knowledge of the particular tribe's culture, history, and environment, as illustrated by a Winnebago and a Lakota story. Paul Radin's *The Trickster* is probably the best-known study of the traditional Trickster tale. One of the most fascinating episodes of this Winnebago text is number fifteen in the cycle:

> *On Trickster proceeded. As he walked along, he came to a lovely piece of land. There he sat down and soon fell asleep. After a while he woke up and found himself lying on*

his back without a blanket. He looked up above him and saw to his astonishment something floating there. 'Aha, aha! The chiefs have unfurled their banner! The people must be having a great feast for this is always the case when the chief's banner is unfurled.' With this he sat up and then first realized that his blanket was gone. It was his blanket he saw floating above. His penis had become stiff and the blanket had been forced up. 'That's always happening to me,' he said. 'My younger brother, you will lose the blanket, so bring it back.' Thus he spoke to his penis. Then he took hold of it and, as he handled it, it got softer and the blanket finally fell down. Then he coiled up his penis and put it in a box. And only when he came to the end of his penis did he find his blanket. The box with the penis he carried on his back.[18]

Taken out of context, this episode could be read as pure ethno-pornography on a rather grand scale. But without a knowledge of the Winnebago, readers would miss entirely the central social satire of the episode. Wakdjunkaga, commenting on the chief's banner, exclaims, " 'Aha, aha!' " Radin explains that "the satire here is directed at one of the most important Winnebago feasts, that given by the chief of the tribe once a year, at which he raises his emblem of authority, a long feathered crook. It is his obligation at the feast to deliver long harangues admonishing his people to live up to the ideals of the Winnebago society."[19] In other words, this episode ridicules in a socially acceptable way the chief's admonishments. The Trickster's words and behavior comically and imaginatively vent social tension.

Another story demonstrates the need to know a tribe's environment and history. "A Man Called Redleaf" is a Lakota narrative recorded in 1976 by Vine Deloria, Sr., on Canyon Records. The tale is not one of the five traditional types described earlier. It is an example of a more recent story about a nineteenth-century historial figure who was a member of the White Swan community of the Yankton Sioux. The story opens with Redleaf as a strong, old man of ninety-nine who has outlived his wife, his daughter, and his granddaughter. He is cared for by his great granddaughter. Deloria casually sets the time period as "way back in 1868, or something like that." One day, for no apparent reason, Redleaf announces to his great granddaughter, "tonight at midnight I am going to leave for the other world." The great grand-daughter offers to send her boys down to the river to pick out a tall tree with a very large limb, so that they can place Redleaf's body where he can always see his "beloved Missouri." Redleaf surprises her by saying that he wants to be buried underground much further away from the river. He explains that he has a feeling that if he were laid to rest on the limb, he would not "rest in peace." Almost eighty years later the Ft. Randall Dam was built near that part of the Missouri, and the flood waters would have covered the tree and disturbed any "speck" of Redleaf's bones that remained. But the unusual burial site he selected is still over 200 yards from the highest flood waters. "How do you like that?" Deloria concludes.

As in the case of the Winnebago Trickster episode, a non-Indian can certainly enjoy this tale without knowing anything about Lakota history. He could also appreciate the importance of the specific environment, since the story revolves around a particular burial ground near the Missouri River. But the narrative takes on new dimensions when the listener realizes that the year 1868, which is mentioned by Deloria in an aside, is the year when the Sioux nations signed a crucial treaty that was not kept by the government. 1868 figured crucially in several Indian demonstrations during the late 1960s and early 1970s, especially at Wounded Knee, South Dakota. It is also significant that during the last few decades, one of the most controversial actions relating to several Sioux reservations has been the flooding of timberland from large dam projects on the Missouri. (As a boy I recall a quiet and genial Sioux woman, Ruth Fire, telling me about the fine cottonwood firewood she gathered as a child in Ft. Thompson, South Dakota. As we rounded a brown grassy knoll, she pointed down at a flood area. Only stagnant water and rotting stumps remained.)

Most non-Indians and many Indians, unfamiliar with linguistic and literary contexts, are at the mercy of interpreters, translators, and editors of oral narratives. Therefore, in order to gain some sense of the accuracy of a translation and the reasons for certain features of the characterization, plot development, descriptions of settings, and the structure of the tale, the reader needs to know relevant information about the language, genre, and style of the story.

How this can be accomplished in a concise and meaningful way is demonstrated in Dennis Tedlock's *Finding the Center; Narrative Poetry of the Zuni Indians*. Tedlock was working with a difficult language that "has no clear relationship with any other American Indian language."[20] With the help of Joseph Peynetsa, a young relative of one of Tedlock's storytellers, Tedlock learned Zuni and carefully transcribed his recordings of Zuni stories. Gradually he became aware of certain word connotations and constructions that influenced his translations. For example, in one trickster tale, he noticed that the esoteric word "sani" instead of the ordinary term "suski" was used sometimes for the word "coyote." To suggest this nuance, he translated the esoteric term as "prairie wolf," "the less common of the two English terms" for coyote.[21] In other stories he noticed word order inversions that were common in Zuni. "For example, a strictly literal treatment would produce some lines like, 'Her clothes / she bundled' or 'His kinswoman / he beat.'" Tedlock decided that since "'Her clothes / she bundled' sounds like ordinary Zuni, it ought to be transformed into 'She bundled / her clothes' which sounds like ordinary English."[22] Tedlock's two storytellers, Andrew Paynetsa and Walter Sanchez, also made it clear to him that there were two distinct genres of Zuni oral narratives. The telapnaawe, or tales, are considered fiction and have to begin with the untranslatable word "Son'ahchi" and end with "Lee——/semkonikya." They can be told at night from October through March, and if a listener falls asleep during the tale or does not stand and stretch at the end, he may become a hunchback. The other type of narratives are the stories of the chimiky'ana'kowa, or "The Beginning." They are considered to be "true" and can be told any time during the day or year; but if they are told in a ceremonial context, they must be chanted. These stories begin with "Well then / this / was the BEGINNING" or "Well then / at the beginning . . ." and conclude simply with "that's all."[23]

Of course, such literary conventions are not limited to the Zuni. In most tribes storytellers associate certain types of tales with particular styles, or they correlate particular stages in long story cycles with different types of characterization. Radin has demonstrated this with the gradual acquisition of human traits by Wakdjunkaga in the forty-nine episodes of the Winnebago trickster cycle. Once we begin comparing stories from different tribes, it also becomes obvious that in spite of the many differences, there are important structural similarities that characterize most of the oral narratives. The most obvious similarity is the use of various types of repetition, which can be used to emphasize important information, to build suspense, to give the listeners the feeling that they know more than the characters (foreshadowing is quite common), to create a trance effect, to add multiple meanings to a story, and to achieve a structural sense of harmony and balance. For instance, in the Arapaho story "Raw Gums and the White Owl Woman," included in John Bierhorst's collection *The Red Swan,* there are at least four types of repetition. The first part of the story describes the deeds of a voracious monster baby equipped with a full set of teeth. In a series of parallel episodes the child escapes from his cradle at night, "wanders off," and devours old chiefs. Second and third types of repetition occur with the parents' discovery of the baby's teeth and how he uses them. First the sinister evidence is repeated: "The mother saw him open his mouth, and she saw in his teeth fresh morsels of human flesh. 'Say, [husband], turn and look at those teeth with morsels of human flesh.'" Later the entire drama of the discovery is repeated when the husband describes the occurrence and the acts of the baby to a group of men assembled in his tepee. The fourth type of repetition, which Bierhorst calls "self-reiteration," involves a subtle "kind of duplication in which . . . an entire story is transposed to a new level of meaning." In this case, the voracious monster baby is miraculously transformed into a handsome young man just as he is about to be devoured by dogs. Now instead of encounters with old, male chiefs, the young man encounters an old woman—Old White Owl Woman. The man is tested in a series of parallel incidents. First, he and Old White Owl Woman succeed twice in their attempts to provide food for each other. Then the man answers six riddles and is permitted to murder the old woman, not by devouring her, but by splitting her skull with a stone sledge. He bursts her head and "scatter[s] the brains, which [are] the snow [flakes], melting away gradually." Thus the second part of the tale reveals the origin of spring.[24]

All the contexts discussed so far are important, but they overlook one crucial fact: Native American stories were not created to be read in anthologies. They were and still are performed by respected storytellers. Before discussing the continuity and vitality of traditional and less traditional narratives, it is necessary to comment briefly on the significance of the performance and the performer.

A good storyteller uses his body and his voice. Often physical gestures are self-explanatory because they are linked directly to the content of the tale. At the conclusion of one of the Zuni coyote tales, one of Tedlock's storytellers, Andrew Peynetsa, pointed to his molars to indicate where the coyote had no teeth.[25] But in some cases the gestures can take on an importance of their own. In *Cheyenne Memories* John Stands-in-Timber recalls that the old Cheyenne storytellers began their sacred narratives by smoothing the ground and going through a brief ritual of marking the dirt and touching their bodies. This indicated that the "Creator" made humans and the earth and that "the Creator was witness to what was to be told."[26]

Until 1972, few efforts were made to capture the voice of the storyteller on the printed page. Instead, stories were transcribed into acceptable English sentences and paragraphs and presented as "prose" (in 1962 one of the best-known collections of traditional Indian literature, *The Winged Serpent* by Margot Astrov, was even retitled *American Indian Prose and Poetry,* the poetry being the ceremonial texts and song lyrics, the prose being the stories). During the late 1960s, as Dennis Tedlock was preparing his tape recordings of Zuni stories for publication, he became increasingly dissatisfied with the prose approach to oral narration. After several experiments, he finally decided that one way to capture at least some of the voice of a performer was to present careful translations in the form of narrative poetry. He broke up the Zuni narratives into lines. The line breaks and the amount of space between the lines were dictated by the pauses in the storytellers' voices. To indicate changes in voice dynamics, Tedlock used three sizes of type. Occasional changes in the duration of syllables, pitch, stage directions, and audience response were represented respectively by lines or repeated letters, raising or lowering the line of type, and parenthetical comments in italics. This simple typographical system encourages the reader to hear the tale without the distraction of elaborate typographical gimmickry. Tedlock's *Finding the Center* (1972) is truly remarkable.

A sense of Tedlock's achievement can be gained by reading two versions of a very brief extract from one of the Zuni telapnaawe trickster tales entitled "Coyote and Junco." In the first version I have transformed Tedlock's translation into a typical prose rendition that replaces untranslatable or esoteric words with familiar English phrases, adds words or rearranges the order of words to approximate ordinary sounding English syntax, eliminates repetition, and molds the words into acceptable sentences. The second verson comes from *Finding the Center.* The superiority of Tedlock's translation should be self-evident.

> *Once upon a time long ago Old Lady Junco had her home at Standing Arrows. Coyote was at Sitting Rock with his children. Old Lady Junco was separating the chaff from pigweed and tumbleweed by tossing them in the air above her basket. Coyote was hunting for his children when he came upon her.*

Now Tedlock's version:

SON'AHCHI.
        LO——NG A
   SONTI   *GO*
               •

AT STANDING ARROWS
OLD LADY JUNCO HAD HER HOME
and COYOTE

Coyote was there at Sitting Rock with his children.
He was with his children
and Old Lady Junco
was winnowing.
Pigweed
and tumbleweed, she was winnowing these.
With her basket
she winnowed these by tossing them in the air.
She was tossing them in the air
    while Coyote
Coyote
was going around hunting, going around hunting for his
    children there
when he came to where Junco was winnowing.[27]

Unfortunately, even Tedlock's typography or recent studies such as Richard Bauman's *Verbal Art as Performance* cannot capture the personality of the performer. The best way to experience this most personal context of Indian oral narratives is to know and listen to a good storyteller. This was how Paul Radin learned to interpret many of the differences between the versions of Winnebago stories told to him by the deeply religious, quiet, and conventional Jasper Blowsnake and his non-religious, sociable, and articulate brother, Sam. If this type of contact with a storyteller is impossible, an acceptable substitute is the use of a video-tape series such as "Words and Place; Native Literature of the American Southwest." This series was developed at the University of Arizona and includes tapes of storytellers speaking in their native languages. Introductory comments and English subtitles provide the context and content of the stories, and the tapes offer visual impressions of storytellers' uses of gesture, tone, and inflection and hints about the tellers' personalities. A controversial but still valuable introduction to the significance of performance and personality in Indian storytelling is provided by Hyemeyohsts Storm in his fictionalized history of the Cheyenne, *Seven Arrows*. As the readers learn about the lives of the principal storytellers in the book, they can see how the personalities of these men guide their selections of narratives and shape the tales they tell. Reading Storm's text also reveals the importance of audience response to particular types of storytellers. Laughs, expected and unexpected questions, and even an uninvited bee buzzing around the head of Green Fire Mouse affect both tellers and listeners in *Seven Arrows*.

Two

If non-Indians were aware of the various contexts of Native American oral narratives, they would be less likely to perceive Indian stories as childish fairy tales and superstitions. Furthermore, if they had the opportunity to hear Vine Deloria, Sr.'s Canyon Records tales, or to listen to Andrew Peynetsa, Sam Blowsnake, or the Laguna, Hopi, and Apache storytellers in the "Words and Place" video-tape series, they would understand how a personality could shape a story. They also would know that Native American oral narration is not an artifact of a bygone era. It is a lively art expressed in many old and new forms.

The endurance of the traditional stories is impressive. In the "Introduction" to *Tales of North American Indians* Stith Thompson notes that several tales, including an Iroquois creation story, have the same form in the twentieth century as they did when the Jesuit Fathers recorded them in the early 1600s.[28] But the major categories of traditional oral narratives aren't simply preserved. They often improve, incorporating new types of material. John Bierhorst believes that the version of "The Boy and the Deer" recorded by Tedlock in 1965 is "clearly superior" to versions of this Zuni animal-parent tale collected earlier.[29] Another sign of the vitality of oral narration is the creative ability of storytellers to incorporate non-Indian stories. During the late nineteenth century, for example, Frank Hamilton Cushing collected an imaginative blending of a traditional Zuni story about a girl responsible for tending a flock of turkeys and the Cinderella story. In this Zuni story the fairy godmother is replaced by turkeys whose ritual dances transform the rags of a beloved poor girl into a "beautiful white embroidered mantle" and other gorgeous clothing so she can attend a festival. In one way the Zuni maiden is more fortunate than Cinderella. She is not limited to one Prince Charming; the elders invite her to dance with all the young men. But unlike Cinderella, she doesn't get a second chance. She fails to return to her turkeys at the appointed hour. As a result, the turkeys, who have been her only joy in life, desert her. Her fine clothing is again changed to rags, as they are torn and soiled in her futile efforts to recapture the turkeys.[30]

The narratives told by reservation and urban Indians today are not restricted to traditional tales or creative blends of Indian and non-Indian stories. There are also other types of tribal narratives. Vine Deloria, Sr.'s "A Man Called Redleaf" is a good example of a Lakota story based upon nineteenth- and twentieth-century tribal history. Leslie Marmon Silko, a Laguna poet, novelist, and teacher, stresses the vitality of another popular type of tribal story. In an interview for *Sun Tracks: An American Indian Literary Magazine,* she points out how contemporary stories can give "identity to a place."[31] A Navajo trash fight at a Laguna feast, a young woman who disappeared for a few days after a dance, an old man who lost a team of horses in the quicksand, or the many stories of secret meetings by the river below Laguna village—all these can be the germs of stories to be fashioned and shared at the post office or far beyond the village when two Laguna meet.

Stories shared far beyond reservation boundaries are not always limited to local history or contemporary tribal tales. Half of the over one million Native Americans in the United States live in urban areas and most of the reservation Indians have day-to-day contacts with non-Indians and Indians from tribes other than their own. Therefore, it should come as no surprise that one particularly lively area of oral narration today is the story that transcends tribal boundaries.

Some of the best short examples of these narratives are jokes. In *Custer Died for Your Sins* Vine Deloria, Jr. offers a delightful sampler of jokes shared by Indians around the country. Two of the most common kinds of historical jokes concern Columbus and Custer: "Columbus didn't know where he was going, didn't know where he had been, and did it all on someone else's money. And the white man has been following Columbus ever since." One of Custer's soldiers at the Little Big Horn realizes that his side is losing, so he strips, paints his face with mud, and crosses over to the Cheyenne lines. When a Cheyenne warrior looks "puzzled" and asks the "soldier why he wanted to change sides," the soldier replies, "Better red than dead!" Government agencies, government policies, task forces, B.I.A. and Interior Department officials, presidents, Indian demonstrations and their leaders, and current events are all fair game for stories and jokes. For instance, the Chippewas, or Anishinabe (their native name), like to "tease the Sioux about the old days when they ran the Sioux out of Minnesota. It was, they claim, the first successful relocation program." During the 1960s another popular target for jokes was the Vietnam war. Supposedly, "a survey was taken and only 15 percent of the Indians thought that the United States should get out of Vietnam. Eighty-five percent thought they should get out of America!" Anthropologists are frequently ridiculed: One day Popovi Da, a Pueblo artist, was approached by an inquisitive anthropologist. He asked the artist, "What did the Indians call America before the white man came?" Popovi Da responded, "Ours!" The hundreds of jokes shared by urban and reservation Indians today should make suspect, or at least help to compensate for, the conventional observation by folklorists about the lack of traditional puns, riddles, and sayings. The joking should, moreover, undercut the stereotype of the grim, stonefaced Indian. As with the traditional Trickster tales, the jokes also offer Indians opportunities to vent criticism and hostility while, as Deloria, Jr. puts it, maintaining the ability to "laugh at themselves."[32]

In a survey of American folklore studies published in *American Studies International* Richard M. Dorson makes the following observation: "For all the flood of publications on North American Indian tribal cultures, no folklorist has sought to analyze in any depth Native American folklore and mythology in relation to American mainstream culture."[33] Fortunately, there are several talented Native American poets and novelists who are attempting to do what, according to Dorson, the folklorists have failed to do.

Sometimes the relationships between mainstream experiences and Indian stories come in brief provocative episodes, such as the concluding leap into the twentieth century in Storm's *Seven Arrows*. Simon Ortiz, an Acoma poet and short storywriter, explores in greater depth the reactions of a traditional Acoma to modern technology in the story "Men on the Moon." One of the old man's responses demonstrates simultaneously his ability and inability to assimilate, understand, and control modern technology. The night after he watches the Apollo moon landing on a new television set, he dreams that Flintwing Boy and Coyote are watching an unstoppable monster with metal legs that crushes trees, grass, and flowers. Flintwing Boy and Coyote face East, pray, breathe on some sacred pollen, take in the breath of all directions and give the cornfood to the earth. Flintwing Boy prepares his arrows and sends Coyote to the village to warn the people and to tell them to "talk among themselves" about what is happening.[34]

Gerald Vizenor, Leslie Marmon Silko, and N. Scott Momaday have written episodes, stories, and entire books that demonstrate the relevance of traditional narratives to contemporary "mainstream culture." At first glance it seems as if Vizenor, a poet and teacher of Anishinabe and French descent, has written a book that has little to do with traditional Indian storytelling. The setting of *Darkness in Saint Louis Bearheart* (1978) is the future—the waning years of the twentieth century when all the oil resources are gone and the United States government has collapsed. The plot follows the strange adventures of a bizarre group of characters, who would delight Federico Felini, as they make a pilgrimage from Northern Minnesota, to New Mexico. But Vizenor's book should not be read as a novel, a picaresque travel narrative, or even as a satirical allegory. It should be approached as an ambitious attempt to blend these European written forms with Native American oral traditions. Proude Cedarfair's journey and his final passage into a different world—the world of human-bear visions—is a restatement of the emergence theme found in many origin narratives. The pornographic scenes, the episodic structure, the sudden appearances and disappearances of characters, the lack of motivational explanations, and the surprising combinations of good and evil, wisdom and stupidity characteristic of several of the pilgrims echo the structure and characterization of Trickster tales. Proude's narrow escapes and his desire to lead the way to a new world recall hero narratives. The journeys to strange places populated by strange creatures evoke memories of the "star-husband" and other journey legends. The many visionary, mental, and sexual encounters with animals recall traditional animal-parent, spouse, and lover tales. Furthermore, the emphasis on balance and harmony, found in many different types of traditional stories, is stressed by Vizenor. Almost all the pilgrims who perish die as a direct or indirect result of selfish passions or inflexible, one-dimensional beliefs that upset fragile balances.

In his Pulitzer Prize winning novel, *House Made of Dawn,* Momaday emphasizes the potential healing effects of parts of Navajo and Jemez Pueblo ceremonial and narrative traditions on a World War II veteran shattered by his childhood experiences as an outsider in a pueblo and by a series of horrible experiences during the war, and afterward in Los Angeles. He is not cured, but by the end of the novel he is beginning to find his "voice"—a metaphor that suggests the continuing significance of oral traditions. Silko's *Ceremony* also dramatizes the struggles of a World War II veteran, a mixed-blood Laguna named Tayo. But in this novel the significance of storytelling is even more important then in Momaday's. One way to read *Ceremony* is as a struggle between the powers of evil and good stories. The evil stories are represented by tribal gossip about Tayo's mother and other reservation figures, by tales of poverty, prostitution, and alcoholism in Gallup, New Mexico and other cities, and by World War II narratives about seducing blonds and redheads in Oakland, San Diego, and Los Angeles, or gory tales about killing Japanese soldiers and stealing their teeth.[35] The good stories are often represented by the traditional tales about the animals and land of the Southwest told by Tayo's uncle, Josiah; traditional Keres stories, presented separately as narrative poetry, that parallel Tayo's story of emergence from chaos and imbalance to new life and harmony; and the stories told by a Navajo medicine man, Betonie—stories that mix traditional Navajo narratives, other tribal stories, and experiences that range from the Sherman Indian Institute in California to railroad stories to the St. Louis World's Fair to a powerful story dramatizing the origin of witchery. Betonie believes that the only stories powerful enough to combat the evils of the modern world encompass traditional Indian narratives and the engulfing, everchanging torrents of the mainstream culture. Fortunately for Tayo, Betonie's stories and his own ability to act them out are powerful enough to ward off the influence of the evil stories—at least for a while.

Momaday's prose poem, *The Way to Rainy Mountain,* rivals Silko's *Ceremony* as an extended, imaginative exploration of the relationships between traditional and modern streams of narrative. Initially the book was a "remarkable body of history and learning, fact and fiction—all of it in the oral tradition" collected by Momaday from Kiowa elders.[36] To this material he added his own personal and family memories and his creative imagination. The results, as Momaday describes them, are "three distinct narrative voices . . . the mythological, the historical, and the immediate."[37] The three voices are presented as a series of twenty-four short trios framed by poems, a prologue, an introduction, and an epilogue. The first voice is printed on the left-hand page and is answered by the other two voices on the right-hand page. The relationships between the voices are complex and change throughout the book, but one trio should at least hint at what Momaday has done.

In section sixteen we first listen to a traditional hero tale that pits mythological beast against a Kiowa warrior. This story is juxtaposed against a contemporary narrative that tells of a spirited but pathetic echo of the heroic encounter between man and buffalo set in the almost too "real" world of Carnegie, Oklahoma. Finally we hear a childhood memory of new birth, danger, and exhilaration. Taken together the voices reveal the double paradox of an oral tradition that was grand but seems powerless as a literal description of modern reality. Still, when perceived through the creative powers of personal memory and the imagination, the narrative tradition is as vital as the morning, a father's companionship, new life, and a mother's love:

> *There was a strange thing, a buffalo with horns of steel. One day a man came upon it in the plain, just there where once upon a time four trees stood close together. The man and the buffalo began to fight. The man's hunting horse was killed right away, and the man climbed one of the trees. The great bull lowered its head and began to strike the tree with its black metal horns, and soon the tree fell. But the man was quick, and he leaped to the safety of the second tree. Again the bull struck with its unnatural horns, and the tree soon splintered and fell. The man leaped to the third tree and all the while he shot arrows at the beast; but the arrows glanced away like sparks from its dark hide. At last there remained only one tree and the man had only one arrow. He believed then that he would surely die. But something spoke to him and said: "Each time the buffalo prepares to charge, it spreads its cloven hooves and strikes the ground. Only there in the cleft of the hoof is it vulnerable; it is there you must aim." The buffalo went away and turned, spreading its hooves, and the man drew the arrow to his bow. His aim was true and the arrow struck deep into the soft flesh of the hoof. The great bull shuddered and fell, and its steel horns flashed once in the sun.*

Forty years ago the townspeople of Carnegie, Oklahoma, gathered about two old Kiowa men who were mounted on work horses and armed with bows and arrows. Someone had got a buffalo, a poor broken beast in which there was no trace left of the wild strain. The old men waited silently amid the laughter and talk; then, at a signal, the buffalo was let go. It balked at first, more confused, perhaps, than afraid, and the horses had to be urged and then brought up short. The people shouted, and at last the buffalo wheeled and ran. The old men gave chase, and in the distance they were lost to view in a great, red cloud of dust. But they ran that animal down and killed it with arrows.

One morning my father and I walked in Medicine Park, on the edge of a small herd of buffalo. It was late in the spring, and many of the cows had newborn calves. Nearby a calf lay in the tall grass; it was red-orange in color, delicately beautiful with new life. We approached, but suddenly the cow was there in our way, her great dark head low and fearful-looking. Then she came at us, and we turned and ran as hard as we could. She gave up after a short run, and I think we had not been in any real danger. But the spring morning was deep and beautiful and our hearts were beating fast and we knew just then what it was to be alive. [38]

These three voices are a part of a large and diversified chorus of American Indian storytelling that has room for origin and coyote Trickster tales that Pre-Columbian Indians and early seventeenth-century Jesuits would recognize, fables that non-Indians raised on Walt Disney could follow, and stories and jokes that range from L.A.'s redheads to the greyhairs of Carnegie, Oklahoma, to the B.I.A. headquarters and Apollo moon landings. The diversity and vitality of these narratives are striking testimonies to the perseverence of North America's oldest art form, which continues to adapt creatively to the present.

Today Native American storytellers, poets, and novelists may not recite the old stories exactly the way their ancestors did, and they may have new tales to tell, but they know that the ancient art of oral narration is a precious gift that must be rediscovered, recollected, and refashioned so that each generation can breathe new life into the gift. A few lines from Leslie Marmon Silko's poem "Skeleton Fixer's Story" express this commitment with warmth and respect. The poem appeared in *Sun Tracks* and is based on a story told at Laguna and Acoma Pueblos. The narrative tells how the Skeleton Fixer discovers and collects Old Coyote Woman's bones. With love and exquisite care he reassembles the bones using both words and actions to give Coyote new life. In these lines Skeleton Fixer, the Old Badger Man, speaks to the bones as he works with them:

'Oh poor dear one who left your bones here
I wonder who you are?'
Old Skeleton Fixer spoke to the bones
Because things don't die

they fall to pieces maybe,
get scattered or separate,
but Old Badger Man can tell
how they once fit together.

Though he didn't recognize the bones
he could not stop;
he loved them anyway.[39]

NOTES

[1]Vine Deloria, Jr., *Custer Died for Your Sins: An Indian Manifesto* (New York: Macmillan, 1969), p. 1.

[2]Parts of this essay were originally prepared for a cassette lecture, *American Indian Folklore* (#1627 in the Cassette Curriculum® *American Folklore Series* edited by Hennig Cohen, ®1979.) Permission to use revised versions of these sections has been granted by Everett/Edwards, Inc., Deland, Florida. I would also like to acknowledge the advice and information I received at the Summer Seminar on Native American Literature sponsored by the Modern Language Association and the National Endowment for the Humanities and held at Flagstaff, Arizona, in 1977. Larry Evers' comments about the contexts of oral narratives were especially valuable.

[3]Several significant books and articles by scholars such as Larry Evers and writers such as Leslie Silko (*Storyteller*, 1981) appeared while this essay was in press. One anthology includes important contextual material: Karl Kroeber, ed., *Traditional American Indian Literatures* (Lincoln: University of Nebraska Press, 1981).

[4]Stith Thompson, "Introduction" to *Tales of the North American Indians,* ed., Stith Thompson (Bloomington: Indiana University Press), p. xviii.

[5]John Bierhorst, "Introduction" to *The Red Swan: Myths and Tales of the American Indians,* ed. John Bierhorst (New York: Farrar, Straus and Giroux, 1976), p. 6; Susan Feldmann, "Introduction" to *The Storytelling Stone,* ed. Susan Feldmann (New York: Dell, 1965), p. 23.

[6]See Erminie W. Voegelin, "North American Native Literature" in *Encyclopedia of Literature,* ed. Joseph T. Shipley (New York: Philosophical Society, 1946), pp. 714–19.

[7]Paul Radin, *The Trickster: A Study in American Indian Mythology* (New York: Schocken Books, 1972), p. 169.

[8]Feldmann, *The Storytelling Stone,* p. 12.

[9]"The Piqued Buffalo-Wife" in Thompson, *Tales of the North American Indian,* p. 150.

[10]Alan Dundes, "North American Indian Folklore Studies," *Journal de la Société des Americanistes,* 56 (1967): 62.

[11]Feldmann, *The Storytelling Stone,* p. 36.

[12]Leslie Marmon Silko, *Ceremony* (New York: Viking, 1977), p. 2.

[13]For example, see Clyde Kluckhohn's "Myths and Rituals: A General Theory," *The Harvard Theological Review* 35 (1942): 45–79.

[14]N. Scott Momaday, "The Man Made of Words," in Abraham Chapman, ed., *Literature of the American Indians: Views and Interpretations* New York: New

American Library), pp. 104, 103, 108.

[15]Paula Gunn Allen, "The Sacred Hoop," in Chapman, ed., *Literature of the American Indians*, p. 113.

[16]George Copway, "Legendary Stories and Historical Tales of the Ojibway Nation," in Chapman, ed., *Literature of the American Indians*, p. 31.

[17]Momaday in Chapman, ed., *Literature of the American Indians*, p. 101.

[18]Radin, *The Trickster*, pp. 18–19.

[19]Ibid., p. 152.

[20]Dennis Tedlock, "Introduction" to *Finding the Center: Narrative Poetry of the Zuni Indians* (New York: Dial Press, 1972), p. xv.

[21]Tedlock, *Finding the Center*, p. xxviii.

[22]Ibid., pp. xx–xxi.

[23]Ibid., pp. xxvii–xxviii, xvi–xvii, 225, 275, 269, 297. For a recent survey of responses to the problem of linguistic contexts see Jeffery F. Huntsman, "Traditional Native American Literature: The Translation Dilemma," *Shantih* 4 (Summer-Fall 1979): 5–9. Revised and reprinted in the present volume.

[24]"Raw Gums and White Owl Woman" in Bierhorst, *The Red Swan*, pp. 141–48, 9–10.

[25]Tedlock, *Finding the Center*, p. 83.

[26]John Stands-in-Timber, "Cheyenne Memories" in Chapman, ed., *Literature of the American Indians*, p. 63.

[27]Tedlock, *Finding the Center*, p. 77.

[28]Thompson, *Tales of the North American Indian*, p. xv.

[29]Bierhorst, *The Red Swan*, p. 31.

[30]See "The Girl Who Took Care of the Turkeys," in Tedlock, *Finding the Center*, pp. 65–73; "Cinderella" in Thompson, *Tales of the North American Indian*, pp. 225–31.

[31]"A Conversation with Leslie Marmon Silko," *Sun Tracks* 3 (Fall 1976): 28–33.

[32]Deloria, *Custer*, pp. 148, 149, 155, 158, 166, 167.

[33]Richard M. Dorson, "American Folklore Bibliography," *American Studies International* 16 (Autumn 1977): 37.

[34]Simon J. Ortiz, "Men on the Moon," in *Howbah Indians* (Tucson, Ariz.: Blue Moon Press, 1978), pp. 11–19.

[35]Silko heard many of these stories as she grew up in Laguna. See "A Conversation," *Sun Tracks* 3: 28–33.

[36]Momaday in Chapman, ed., *Literature of the American Indians*, p. 106.

[37]Ibid., p. 107.

[38]N. Scott Momaday, *The Way to Rainy Mountain* (Albuquerque: University of New Mexico Press, 1969), pp. 54–55. I have quoted this section with the permission of the University of New Mexico Press.

[39]Leslie Marmon Silko, "Skeleton Fixer's Story," *Sun Tracks* 4 (1978): 2.

Part Two: THE QUESTION
OF TRANSLATION
AND LITERARY CRITICISM

Dennis Tedlock: ON THE TRANSLATION OF STYLE IN ORAL NARRATIVE

A discriminating reader, hoping to find collections of American Indian narratives which are at one and the same time thoroughly authentic and respectable as literature, is likely to be disappointed. When he explores the narratives published before the field methods of Franz Boas were widely employed, he may decide that their style seems more Victorian than Indian. If he then turns to modern collections but still avoids publications intended only for the use of scholars, he may find his prospective reading described, as in the case of Jaime de Angulo's *Indian Tales,* as suitable fare for both children and adults.[1] Such a volume will seem about as promising to him as a movie rated G for general audiences.

If our reader dares to venture beyond dust jackets and back covers to read a preface, he may find a comment about an author similar to the following one from Oliver La Farge's preface to Theodora Kroeber's *The Inland Whale:* "She . . . turned writer and retold the stories, a dangerous process here successfully applied. The retelling, one might say, is ethnologically honorable. The stories have not been prettified, elaborated, or laden with pseudo-literary trimmings." This sounds reassuring, but there is more: the stories "have simply been put into a familiar idiom, with restraint and good taste, and in some cases purged of the insistent repetitions and cluttering details that primitive people often stuff into their stories for ulterior purposes."[2]

Wishing for greater authenticity, our reader may turn at last to the vast scholarly collections produced by Boasian anthropologists. But he will soon wonder whether the original style of these narratives was as choppy and clumsy as that of most English translations. If he takes these translations to represent, as Boas claimed, "faithful rendering of the native tales,"[3] and if he remains disappointed with popularizations, he may end by agreeing with La Farge, who said, "The literary value of a great deal of primitive literature, whether myths or tales, is nil. That of much of the rest is apparent, in the raw form, only to connoisseurs, while those who undertake to retell some of it often achieve only emasculation."[4]

Unless it is true that many of the oral narratives of non-Western peoples have little or no literary value, and that what value they do have is untranslatable, then something has gone wrong along the way from the oral performance to the printed page. Through the close examination of a single widely-published narrative tradition, that of the Zuñi Indians,[5] I hope to show that something has indeed gone wrong, and to suggest what might be done differently in the future.

ONE

The Zuñi narratives collected by Frank Hamilton Cushing in the 1880s have always attracted more attention than any others: "The Beginning of Newness" has been anthologized by Astrov and Thompson, "The Poor Turkey Girl" by Thompson and Greenway, and "The Cock and the Mouse" by Greenway and Dundes.[6] But the apparent attractiveness of Cushing's work is anything but a measure of its reliability as a representation of Zuñi literature. "The Beginning of Newness," together with the rest of Cushing's "Outlines of Zuñi Creation Myths," has long been a problem for students of Zuñi culture. Cushing himself says that these "outlines" are just that and not direct translations,[7] but it is his additions to the narratives rather than any deletions which have caused the trouble, for, as Bunzel has written, the work "contains endless poetic and metaphysical glossing of the basic elements, most of which explanatory matter probably originated in Cushing's own mind."[8] The "metaphysical glossing" referred to includes strong overtones of monotheism (also found in Stevensons's work) which reflect the theoretical preoccupations of nineteenth-century anthropology rather than Zuñi belief.

"The Poor Turkey Girl" and "The Cock and the Mouse" are cited by the anthologists as classic examples of the American Indian adaptation of European tales. Cushing relates the history of "The Cock and the Mouse" as follows: he had told an Italian version of it to some Zuñis he had brought to New England; about a year later, back at Zuñi, he heard one of these same men tell (in Zuñi) a considerably adapted and expanded version which was later published.[9] Exciting though the Zuñi version may be, it is not clear what the original Italian version used by Cushing was like, for, as Dundes has pointed out, the Zuñi version contains some distinctly European motifs which are lacking in the Italian version printed beside it in Cushing's book.[10] There are further problems: Cushing necessarily told the story to his Zuñi audience in the Zuñi language (the three men were monolinguals), and some of the "Zuñi" alterations could well have originated with Cushing in the process of the telling. Moreover, as will be seen in detail shortly, Cushing was given to elaborations when rendering Zuñi tales in English, and there is no reason to believe he restrained himself in the present case.

Whatever the special problems with "The Beginning of Newness" and "The Cock and the Mouse," the opinion has been widely held that the quality of Cushing's translations is quite good. The novelist Mary Austin is extravagant with her praise, writing that Cushing "is the only American who notably brought to bear on [primitive lore] adequate literary understanding," and that Cushing's is "the best-sustained translation of aboriginal American literature," and, still further, that Cushing made no effort to "popularize" his stories.[11] Margot Astrov, in the introduction to her anthology, lists Cushing as one of those ethnologists who have best met "the two requirements" of the translator: "linguistic fidelity to the original" (short of strictly literal translation) and the communication of the "cultural matrix" of the original.[12] But Hymes has recently shown how far Astrov has gone wrong in judging the quality of song translations,[13] and in a similar spirit I hope to show here that narrative translations, too, are not always what they seem.

Among the more curious things in Cushing's major collection, *Zuñi Folk Tales,* are the oaths used by the characters. Austin cites these as one of the things she admires most and gives "By the delight of death!" as an example;[14] other oaths include "Soul of my ancestors!" "Demons and corpses!" "By the bones of the dead!" "Oh, ye gods!" and "Beloved Powers!"[15] But the Zuñis have no such oaths; they never make profane use of words denoting death, souls, ancestors, corpses, "Powers," and gods. They do use a goodly number of interjections in tales, such as *tísshomahhá* (dread), *hiyáhha* (fright, female speaking), and *ya' 'ana* (disgust, male speaking),[16] but there is not a single one of these interjections which has any denotation other than the emotion it is supposed to express. In this case, then, Cushing's translations do not represent "linguistic fidelity to the original," and, further, they misrepresent the "cultural matrix" of the tales.

Perhaps the most serious difficulty with Cushing's *Zuñi Folk Tales* is that he embroiders the tales with devices, lines, and even whole passages which are clearly of his own invention and not mere distortions. Similes are totally lacking in all other translations (and in texts as well), but they abound in Cushing's tales: for example, a young man attacked by a swarm of mosquitoes was "crazed and restless as a spider on hot ashes,"[17] and a person outdoors at night saw a "light that was red and grew brighter like the light of a camp fire's red embers when fanned by the wind of the night-time."[18] These passages may have literary merit in English, but they do not even have literary existence in Zuñi.

Another kind of embroidery, not so serious as some of the others, is Cushing's insertion of explanatory material for the benefit of his readers. For example, he begins one tale with a lengthy explanation of the geographical location and appearance of its setting,[19] whereas a Zuñi narrator would take his audience's knowledge of local geography for granted. In another example, Cushing describes how a suitor ate very little when given a meal at a girl's house (which a Zuñi narrator would do) but then adds, "You know it is not well or polite to eat much when you go to see a strange girl,"[20] again a case in which a Zuñi narrator would take his audience's knowledge for granted. Of course it is possible that some of this explanatory material was inserted by Zuñi narrators for Cushing's own benefit, but whatever its origin it does misrepresent normal Zuñi practice.

The most distressing of all Cushing's inventions are his moralistic passages. As I have shown in detail elsewhere, the didactic content of Zuñi tales is usually either implicit or addressed by one tale character to another, and it is never addressed by the narrator directly to his audience.[21] But Cushing begins one tale this way: "Listen, ye young ones and youths, and from what I say draw inference. For behold! the youth of our nation in these recent generations have become less sturdy than of old; else what I relate had not happened."[22] In some other cases he points out the moral in the third person, but his tone is still excessively moralistic, as in this example from the end of an Orpheus tale: "But if one should live as long as possible, one should never, in any manner whatsoever, remembering this youth's experience, become enamored of Death."[23]

It should now be sufficiently clear that Cushing frequently violates the linguistic and cultural requirements which Astrov sets for translators, and that a good deal of what Austin calls "color . . . so delightfully rendered" (including the oaths)[24] looks more like Victorian quaintness on close examination.

The work of Matilda Coxe Stevenson, a contemporary of Cushing, avoids his stylistic embroideries, but her major compendium of narratives in *The Zuñi Indians* is not a translation of actual Zuñi performances but rather a descriptive summary in her own words.[25] Much of the apparent order in these materials is her own: she ignores the possibility of alternate versions and attempts to place each story in a chronological sequence which reflects her own Western preoccupation with history more than actual Zuñi practice. Elsewhere in the same volume, however, she does present one narrative which (though rather abbreviated) appears to be a direct translation.[26]

Beginning in the second decade of the present century a veritable army of Boasian field workers descended upon Zuñi. The first members of this army to publish translations of Zuñi narratives were Franz Boas himself, Elsie Clews Parsons, and Edward L. Handy;[27] hard on their heels came Ruth L. Bunzel and Ruth Benedict.[28] Only Parsons and Bunzel published native-language texts, and only Bunzel published texts in any quantity.[29]

Members of the Boasian School, at Zuñi and elsewhere, typically valued translations that were "direct" or "close" or "literal," published with as few changes as possible from the sort of English used by interpreters or bilingual narrators. Thus Parsons could write, in introducing a collection with which she was particularly pleased, that the tales "interpreted by L—— are as close to the original Zuñi, I think, as it is possible to get in English narrative,"[30] and when she showed these translations to A. L. Kroeber, who had trained her interpreter, he said, "In reading them, I can hear L—— speaking Zuñi."[31] One can indeed "hear L—— speaking Zuñi," especially when awkward choices of English words are preserved or when English words are organized according to Zuñi grammar, as in these passages: "The straps the man carried wood with, in the other room he would hang up," "This way you were going to do to me," and, incredibly, "Then one of his legs he threw up."[32]

The literalism in most other translations of Zuñi narratives, including those of Boas and Benedict, does not reach the absurd extremes of Parsons. Benedict followed the usual practice of her contemporaries in asking her informants to give "literal" translations, but it was her stated intention to smooth out "their inadequate English" in her published versions.[33] She did indeed eliminate obvious grammatical errors, but stylistic inadequacies remain including a choppiness and lack of grammatical complexity common to much of the work of this period. Zuñi narrators, like many others, frequently keep a story in motion by combining strings of clauses into long sentences, and by joining these sentences with parallelism. But one would never know this from reading Benedict's translation:

> Her eyes were almost shut. She was skin and bones. She was too weak to sit up and she scratched herself all the time. He jumped up. He ran to the house of Pekwin's son. His wife was just as old. She had gray hair and was bent double. The two young men were angry. They would not talk to their wives. They drove them away. The two old women went off leaning on their canes. They were too weak to travel. There was no rain. The people were hungry.[34]

Such a disaster probably results not only from informant English, but also from the stops and starts of the dictation process and from a tendency to treat parallelisms as not worth preserving in print. But whatever their sources, Benedict's distortions are not purely the result of dictation: Bunzel's translations, which were based on dictated Zuñi rather than dictated English, have a very different character:

> They laid the deer down side by side. They laid them down side by side and they made the boy sit down beside them. After they had made him sit down they gave the deer smoke. After they had given them smoke they sprinkled prayer meal on them. After they had sprinkled prayer meal on them the people came in.[35]

Probably as a result of dictation, the parallelism here (A, AB, BC, CD, DE) is more mechanical than the parallelism in my own tape-recorded Zuñi narratives, and the sentence length (as elsewhere in Bunzel's work) fails to reach the extremes possible in uninterrupted narration. Despite these flaws the text translations of Bunzel display the qualities of oral performance better than any of the other Zuñi work of this period.

Aside from their frequent lack of parallelism, the narratives of the Boasian school tend to be condensations of what a performer would tell in a normal, spontaneous situation. A. L. Kroeber, Demetracapoulou and DuBois, and Gladys Reichard, all of whom recognized this problem in their own collections of American Indian narratives, place most of the blame on the tediousness of dictation and the consequent absence of a responsive native audience.[36] Substantiating their view is the fact that the narratives in my own Zuñi collection, related in all instances to at least a small native audience and taken down by tape recorder, average nearly twice the length of the narratives in Benedict's collection.[37]

After the 1930s, collection of American Indian narratives went into a rapid decline. Texts and translations (other than Zuñi ones) continued to appear sporadically, but many of these later collections, such as Jacobs' *Clakamas Chinook Texts*,[38] were delayed reports of field work done during the main period of Boasian activity rather than reports of anything new. In the Zuñi case, the thirty years which separated the appearance of Benedict's *Zuñi Mythology* (in 1935) from the beginning of my own field work saw the publication of only one minor collection of fresh narratives.[39]

Generally instead of fresh materials there appeared analytical treatments of old ones that reflected the two main currents in modern narrative theory: Bert Kaplan in "Psychological Themes in Zuñi Mythology and Zuñi TAT's" sees Zuñi myths as possible projections of "the repressed unconscious processes of the id";[40] while Claude Lévi-Strauss in "The Structural Study of Myth" finds Zuñi myths (among others) exhibiting the Hegelian dialectic, which he believes to be a substratum in all human thought.[41]

Two

While advances may have been made in the analysis of oral narrative content since the 1930s, the art of translation has seen no substantial gains since the turn of the century. The tape recorder should improve this situation, but its full possibilities have yet to be exploited. It has been a practical and accurate field instrument for only a short time, and the theoretical interests of many of its users (or potential users) are centered on "content" which they presume enjoys a certain independence from the fine points of "style" and translation. John L. Fischer, for example, says that in sociopsychological analysis the primary concern "is with the semantics of folktale; with the message or 'tale picture' which can be transmitted by the codes of various languages, or by various equivalent constructions in a single language."[42] Lévi-Strauss holds a similar view, though his particular analytical interests differ from those of Fischer: "The mythical value of the myth remains preserved, even through the worst translation. . . . Its substance does not lie in its style, its original music, or its syntax, but in the *story* which it tells."[43]

Even when a scholar does show interest in the stylistic aspects of narrative traditions there is no guarantee that he will give much thought to translation. Melville Jacobs, for example, though he promises that his analysis of style or form in Clackamas Chinook narratives "will greatly enhance enjoyment" of that literature, offers translations which are typically Boasian in being "almost literal."[44] Despite the literal translation, the reader does not experience directly the "terseness" which is supposedly one of the principal characteristics of Clackamas style, for Jacobs has made hundreds of "explanatory" parenthetical insertions to rescue him from that terseness.

In some cases the neglect of translation is doubtless related to a belief that style, or at least the better part of it, is simply untranslatable. Franz Boas and A. L. Kroeber, for example, held that style (or "literary form") was so bound up with the peculiarities of particular languages that it was unlikely to survive translation.[45] If their view of style is combined with the view that content survives even bad translation, then there is no room at all for an art of translation. It may be that no one scholar has ever held both these views simultaneously in their pure form, but many scholars of the past four generations might as well have done so.

Some collectors of American Indian narratives have taken issue with the narrow linguistic view of style. Demetracapoulou and DuBois even go so far as to say that in the Wintu case, given an interpreter or narrator who is fluent in English, a translation involves no distortion at all.[46] Jacobs finds in the Clackamas case that all but a very few features of narrative form are independent of the particularities of Clackamas linguistics,[47] the implication again being that translation problems should not pose any great difficulty. The Zuñi narrative tradition displays more stylistic manipulation in phonology, lexicology, and syntax than Jacobs indicates for the Clackamas, but once more a large part of style lies outside of what is traditionally thought of as linguistics, and I would add that even the linguistic features of Zuñi style do not create insurmountable translation problems.

On the phonological level, Zuñi narrative style involves only two common distortions of normal patterns and both of these also occur in every day speech, although they are more frequent in narrative. One of the distortions involves a combination of stress shift and vowel lengthening: a tale character may start off an ordinary greeting with something like *hom nana,* "My grandfather," with stress on the first syllable of *nana* (as is normal), but if the occasion calls for exceptional formality or seriousness, he will shift the stress and lengthen the final vowel as follows: *hom naná—*. It might be hard to get a similar effect by shifting the stress on "grandfather" in translation, but a syntactic shift to "Grandfather of mine" succeeds, I think, in reproducing the original effect of formality.

The other major phonological distortion in Zuñi narrative involves a combination of intonation change and vowel lenghtening: "Thus they lived on" would ordinarily be intoned as follows, with the lowest pitch at the end:

2   3   1
lesnolh 'aateya'kya

But the length of time involved may be emphasized by shifting the highest pitch to the final syllable and drawing out the final vowel for as much as two or three seconds:

2   1   3
lesnolh 'aateya'kya ———

The same operation may be performed on a verb like *'akya,* "he went," to indicate a long distance (but not necessarily a long time). Such forms might be translated as "Thus they lived on and on and on," and "He went and went and went," but in Zuñi this sort of repetition usually indicates repeated action rather than drawn out action (or state of being), as in lines like, "And all the people who had come killed the deer, killed the deer, killed the deer." To translate drawn out Zuñi verbs as repeated ones would mean collapsing two stylistic devices into one. A more direct translation seems a better solution: "Thus they lived on ———," and "He went on ———" (in which the o's should be held). This rendition may seem strange on the printed page, but comparable lengthening does occur in spoken English, as in, "It's been such a lo——ng time."

There are no grammatical differences between every day speech and formal narrative in Zuñi, except for a greater tendency to construct long sentences in the latter. The following, in strict syntactic terms, is a single sentence (each line break indicates only a slight pause):

Towayalan 'ahayuut 'aach ky'akwap,
he'shoktan 'aatoshle
'aachi
ky'akwap,
'itiwan'an lhuwal'ap,
pinnaawan lhuwal'ap, ky'ak'iima lhuwal'ap,
lesnolh lhuwalaa 'ullapnap, taknan kwayilep, taknan kwayilena kwa' ky'ak
   'aawina' ma.[48]

There is no translation problem here: given as a single English sentence, this runs as follows:

At Corn Mountain the two 'ahayuuta *had their home,*
at He'shokta *the* 'aatoshle
the two of them
had their home,
at the Middle there were villagers,
at Winds' Place there were villagers, at Ky'ak'iima *there were villagers,*
there were villagers all around going out to gather wood, and when they went out to
   gather wood they did not come home.

This is somewhat cumbersome by the normal standards of written English prose, but such length would not be extraordinary for an oral narrator in English (unless he were reading from a written text) or for a large number of English poets.

Most of the remaining "linguistic" manipulation in Zuñi style involves the choice of lexical items or formulaic phrases which would be rare or absent in completely neutral everyday speech. As Newman has shown, Zuñi vocabulary runs along a continuum from items labelled as slang (*penaky'amme*) to items labelled as sacred (*tewusu*), with various shadings and a large unnamed neutral category in between.[49] Anything clearly recognized as slang is systematically excluded from formal narratives, but at least one slightly substandard term is used: *'okyattsik'i,* which Zuñis translate as "old lady." A hideous old ogress named *'aatoshle,* for example, may be referred to irreverently as *'aatoshle 'okyattsik'i;* translating this simply as "Old Lady *'aatoshle*" preserves the original effect quite well.

Except for esoteric origin stories, Zuñi narratives do not include many words or phrases that are clearly sacred, but they do include a fair number of items, mostly archaisms, which fall between the neutral and the truly sacred. Among these items are the formulas used to open and close a fictional narrative, *son'ahchi* and *lee ———— semkonikya,* which Zuñis never use except as story frames and which they declare to be untranslatable. The opening formula, *son'ahchi,* might be rendered as "Once upon a time," which is itself a sort of untranslatable formula, but "Once upon a time" suggests a children's fairy tale and is therefore wholly inappropriate to most Zuñi narratives. It seems best to leave these framing devices untranslated; their positions in an otherwise translated narrative, together with a note to the effect that they indicate fiction, should make their "meaning" clear enough. A number of past translators of Zuñi narratives, including Benedict, have chosen to omit these formulas, but that is like leaving the covers off a book.

Most prominent among the longer archaic formulas used in narratives are greeting exchanges. The usual contemporary greeting in Zuñi is *kesshé,* which has the effect of "Hi," and the reply is the same or *tosh 'iya,* "So you've come." But a tale character, on entering a household other than his own, may say, *Hom 'aatacchu, hom chawe, ko'na'to tewanan 'aateyaye?* and someone will reply, *K'ettsanisshe, ho'naawan cha'le, tosh 'iya, s'iimu.* A straightforward translation of this exchange preserves its stilted quality and even a touch of its archaic connotation: "My fathers, my children, how have you been passing the days?" "Happily, our child, so you've come, sit down."

The archaic interjections used by characters in serious tales are difficult to translate: as was mentioned earlier, these are not oaths, but simply give direct expression to emotions. English interjections having only covert religious reference or lacking such reference, such as "Wow!" "My goodness!" and "Dear me!" sound ludicrous in the mouth of a heavy tale character, and those which are archaic in addition sound even worse, "Gadzooks!" "Zounds!" and "I'll be switched!" for example. Probably most of the Zuñi interjections in serious contexts should be left untranslated; even at that most of them would require little explanatory notation, for contexts usually make their meanings fairly clear. When a young man who has just been turned into an eagle because his wife failed to demonstrate her love begins his lament with *hanáhha!* or when a father who has just been told that his son plans to exchange bodies with a bloody dead man replies with *tísshomahhá!* the reader is not likely to go far astray in judging the feeling tone of these interjections; at least he will not be likely to think them equivalent to "Gosh!" or "Good grief!"

Not all archaisms are serious—some are used to embellish humorous tales. It is difficult to place these on Newman's slang-sacred continuum. The fact that they are old should make the terms highly valued, but, in fact, they are employed to make a character seem foolishly old fashioned rather than serious or sacred. They are probably not of slang origin, but hearing these archaic phrases mouthed by foolish characters is somewhat like hearing someone use out-of-date slang. This makes them easier to translate than serious archaisms. A noodle named Pelt Kid, who has just gotten married but knows nothing about sex, suddenly remembers his grandmother's instructions and says, in his hoarse voice, *'a'ana ha'la! Hom to' kwili yalaa teshunholh hakky'akkya, ha'holh shiwaya kwayip yam shuminnkya kwatoky'anaknanna.*[50] The beginning interjection, *'a'ana ha'la!* is an archaism rarely heard even in tales, and an archaic term is used for "penis" (*shuminne,* sandhied and run together with another word in the quotation). The following translation, which takes these archaisms into account, conveys Pelt Kid's ridiculousness well enough: "Golly whizz! You told me to look for two hills, and if it's steamy there I should put my dingie in."

The onomatopoeic words in Zuñi narratives may be considered a part of linguistic style since they are used more frequently in narratives than in everyday speech, though unlike archaisms they are neutral where the slang-sacred continuum is concerned. Context usually makes the reference of onomatopoeic words obvious enough that it is unnecessary to attempt to translate them, as in this passage (again, each line break represents a slight pause):

> *'an suwe kululunan pololo*
> (low, hoarse voice) *tuu——n teyatip,*
> *'an papa wilo' 'anan pololo, wilo' 'ati*
> (low, hoarse voice) *too——w teyatikya.*
> *Sekwat lo'lii pottikya.*
> *Laky'antolh lhiton 'iya*
> *Lhiton 'ikya, ikyas*
> *'isshakwakwa hish ky'aptom 'el'ikya.*

> His younger brother rolled the thunder
> (low, hoarse voice) *tuu——n* it began,
> his elder brother rolled the lightning, lightning struck
> (low, hoarse voice) *too——w* it began.
> Now the clouds filled up.
> Here comes the rain.
> The rain came, it came
> *'isshakwakwa* the water really did come down.[51]

One might render *'isshakwakwa* as "it splattered" and the thunder sounds as "boom" or "rumble," but no clarity would be gained and the reader would not have his experience of onomatopoeia enriched by the Zuñi words.

Three

While it may be that past translations of Zuñi narratives have suffered somewhat from neglect of the "linguistic" features of style discussed above, they have suffered much more from neglect of "oral" or "paralinguistic" features such as voice quality (tone of voice), loudness, and pausing. Boas wrote long ago that "the form of modern prose is largely determined by the fact that it is read, not spoken, while primitive prose is based on the art of oral delivery and is, therefore, more closely related to modern oratory than to the printed literary style."[52] He might have added, had he not so easily labelled primitive narrative as "prose," that it is also related to that portion of modern poetry in which attention is given to "the art of oral delivery." But Boas and his followers, in translating oral narratives, have treated them as if they were equivalent to written prose short stories, except in cases where the originals were sung or chanted. Jacobs has called for a "dramatistic" approach to oral narratives and has made extensive use of dramatic terminology,[53] but his translations follow the familiar short story pattern, except for occasional notations of voice quality.

The presence of the tape recorder has so far failed to wean post-Boasians from the short story approach. Systematic schemes for the notation of paralinguistic features have been proposed recently,[54] but such notation is not yet in wide use; and no one seems to have given much thought to preserving these features in translations. Yet such features are, at least in the Zuñi case, highly "translatable" and it is possible to represent them without making the result look as formidable as a symphonic score. The necessary literary conventions have been there all along, but they are to be found in drama and poetry rather than in prose. Pausing, as in two of the narrative passages already presented, can be represented by line breaks as in written poetry; unusual loudness can be represented by exclamation points, doubled to represent extreme loudness; and unusual softness, together with unusual voice qualities and various other features, can be noted in parentheses at the left-hand margin, as is commonly done in plays. The straightforwardness of these procedures places minimal barriers in the path of a potential reader.

The control of volume in Zuñi narrative can be illustrated by a pastiche of twenty of the loudest and softest lines from a story of more than five hundred lines; these twenty lines reveal the skeleton of the story, complete with opening and closing formulas and the moments of greatest emotion. For the sake of simplifying their presentation here, I have indicated the soft lines with parentheses rather than with marginal notes:

> Son'ahchi!
> *(The little baby came out.)*
> *("Where is the little baby crying?" they said.)*
> *(He was nursed, the little boy was nursed by the deer.)*
> *("I will go to Kachina Village, for he is without clothing, naked.")*
> *(When she got back to her children they were all sleeping.)*
> "He saw a herd of deer!
> But a little boy was among them!"
> "Perhaps we will catch him!"
> Then his deer mother told him everything!
> "That is what she did to you, she just dropped you!"
> *(The boy became*
> *very unhappy.)*
> And all the people who had come killed the deer, killed the deer, killed the deer!
> *(And his uncle, dismounting,*
> *caught him.)*
> "That is what you did and you are my real mother!"
> *(He put the quiver on and went out.)*
> *(There he died.)*
> This was lived long ago! Lee ——— semkonikya![55]

The extremes of loudness and softness overlap in function in that they both draw special attention to a line. The softness of "He was nursed, the little boy was nursed by the deer" seems more appropriate than a loud rendition, and the line about the killing of the deer seems properly loud, but some other lines could have been rendered either way, "But a little boy was among them," for example.

The manipulation of voice quality in Zuñi narration has a diversity which I have only begun to explore; only a few examples can be given here. One of the narrators represented in my collection delivers the opening lines of his tales, including formulas and the names of the major characters and the places where they live, with a formality which approaches that of a chant: his stresses are heavier, his enunciation more careful, and his pitch control greater (but not as great as in singing) than they would be in his normal narrating voice; as he moves into the first events of the story this formality slowly dissolves, over the space of eight or ten lines, until his voice is normal. The only other fully predictable manipulation of voice quality on the part of this same narrator involves the quotation of story characters: the words of the *'ahayuuta* (twin boys, the war gods), for example, are usually delivered in a high, raspy voice, and most female characters, except where their speeches are long, are given a tense, tight (but not high) voice. Since a native speaker of English might prefer to render female voices in narratives by raising his pitch, one might "translate" the Zuñi "tight" voice into an English "high" one. Neither of these practices is a more objective rendition of the female voice than the other; both represent a selective imitation of the common properties of female speech.[56]

There are many less conventionalized (and less common) uses of voice quality in Zuñi narratives, two examples of which will suffice here. When a character is trying to pull some tough blades loose from a yucca plant, the narrator may render "He pulled" with the strain of someone who is trying to speak while holding his breath during great exertion. When a passage involves intense emotion, the narrator may combine the softness mentioned earlier with a break in his voice, as if he felt like weeping. The use of this voice technique is exemplified in the following passage in which a man is killing three deer who are the foster mother and siblings of his nephew:

> *The third uncle*
> (softly, voice breaking) *dropped his elder sister*
> *his elder brother*
> *his mother.*

Loudness and voice quality are obviously worth noting, but it seems to me that pausing is foremost among the paralinguistic devices that give shape to Zuñi narrative and distinguish it from written prose, and the same could probably be said of many other oral narrative traditions. Stravinsky has said, "I dislike the organ's *legato sostenuto,* . . . the monster never breathes,"[57] and he could have said the same thing of written prose. The spoken word is never delivered in the gray masses of boxed-in words we call prose; indeed, according to Goldman-Eisler, as much as half the time spent in delivering spontaneous discourse is devoted to silence, and "pausing is as much a part of the act of speaking as the vocal utterance of words itself."[58] But of all the past anthropological collectors of so-called prose narratives, only one, Paul Radin, seems to have shown any real sensitivity to pausing. For several passages from Winnebago texts he marks pauses of three different lengths; he also breaks these passages into lines. Here his intention is unclear: each line break coincides with a pause, but there are also pauses within lines.[59] Unfortunately he preserves neither pause marks nor line breaks in his translations.

In dealing with the pauses in Zuñi narratives I have found it best to divide them into two types: "ordinary" pauses, represented by line breaks, and "long" pauses, represented by double spaces between lines. I initially spotted pauses only by ear, running through the tape of a half-hour narrative several times. An oscillograph of the same tape later revealed that my "ordinary" pauses ran from four-tenths of a second to two seconds, with the average at three-fourths of a second. The longer pauses ran from two to three seconds. Some other listener might come up with slightly different boundaries for his ordinary and long pauses than I did, or he might want to make more than two distinctions; but in any case, given a reasonably good year, he could probably make fairly consistent notations without the aid of an oscillograph.

Intonation poses no great problems where Zuñi pausing is concerned. Except for the special intonational device used to lengthen time or space (discussed earlier) and a few other, rarer deviations, Zuñi narrative patterns can be covered by a general rule rather than marked for each line: the boundary between one intonation contour and the next is strongly marked where a change of phrase or sentence corresponds with a pause or where a quote begins, and less strongly marked where a change of phrase or sentence occurs within a line or where a pause occurs within a phrase. This pattern seems close enough to the normal tendencies of an English speaker so as to create no translation problems. As far as the internal details of the contours are concerned, the typical Zuñi contour does not happen to be very different from that of a declarative sentence in English, but it should not matter if the two contours were very different: what is important in translation, except for deviations from typical patterns, is the boundaries between contours.

The following passage, with silences and intonation contours as indicated above, will serve to illustrate most of the properties of pausing in Zuñi narrative ("they" in the first line refers to a herd of deer):

Yam telhasshi k'uushina yalhtookwin' aawanuwa' aayemakkya. 'aayemakna lesnolh
chimkwat 'iskon 'aateya tom sunnhap tutunaa paniye.
'aateya'kya ——— koholh lhana

'ist
'an lhuwal'an   5
'an kyakholh
'imat lhatakky'an 'aakya. Lhatakky'an 'aana
'imat paniinas'ist
'uhsi lak'ist
wi'ky'al'anholh lesna paniina uhsist lak   10

k'uushin yalhtan 'uhsi tewuuli yalhtookwin holh'imat ky'alhkonholh yemakna.

They went back up to their old home on the Prairie Dog Hills. Having gone up they were living there and coming down only to drink in the evening.
They lived on ——— for some time

```
until
from the village                                                      5
his uncle
went out hunting. Going out hunting
he came along
down around
Worm Spring and from there he went on towards                        10
```

the Prairie Dog Hills and came up near the edge of a valley there.

The problems encountered in preserving the original pauses in English are minimal. Occasionally Zuñi word order makes the transposition of lines or parts of lines desirable, but this can usually be done without serious distortion of the effect of the original: in the above passage no transposition seemed advantageous, except that "down" in line 9 of the translation is a partial rendition of *paniinas* in line 8 of the text, but elsewhere in the same story a literal rendition would produce lines like "Her clothes / she bundled," and "His kinswoman / he beat," which call for transposition.

Where the length of lines is concerned, it would be difficult and foolish to slavishly follow the exact Zuñi syllable counts in translation, but it is possible to at least approximate the original contrasts in line length. The importance of such an approximation may be seen from the fact that the length of lines—or, to look at it in another way, the frequency of pauses—is the major source of apparent variations in the rate at which human speech is delivered. Passages with short lines (many pauses) will seem slow, while those with long lines (few pauses) will seem fast.[60] In the above passage, the narrator rapidly tells of the deer-herd's residence on the Prairie Dog Hills (lines 1–2), then slows down, with suspenseful effect, as the man goes out hunting (lines 4–9), and finally speeds up again with the excitement of the man's arrival at the Prairie Dog Hills (line 11). Preserving such patterns in narrative pace obviously precludes the insertion of any but the smallest bits of "explanatory" material by the translator: where the Zuñi word *lapappowanne* means "a headdress of macaw tail-feathers worn upright at the back of the head," for example, he will have to settle for something like "macaw headdress" in his translation and leave the rest to a note or a picture, though Cushing might have done otherwise. And where it is frequently unclear which characters are responsible for quotations, as in Clackamas (but not Zuñi) narratives, the translator may find it best to place the names of the speakers outside the main left-hand margin, as in a play.

One of the most striking things about the lines in Zuñi narrative is that they are not always dependent on the major features of syntax. In the above excerpt some of the pauses do correspond with changes of phrase or sentence, but five of them (the pauses following lines 4, 5, 6, 9, 10) leave the hearer hanging, syntactically speaking, thus adding to the suspense already noted for this passage.[61] The longer pauses in Zuñi stories often correspond to sentence boundaries, but in the present excerpt they occur between two phrases of the same sentence (after line 3) and in the midst of a phrase (after line 10). The first of these pauses is a sort of paragraph marker between the affairs of the herd and the hunting expedition of the man; its location within a sentence keeps the listener on the string in much the same way that the placement of a chapter division within an episode (instead of between episodes) keeps the reader of a novel on the string. With the second of these pauses the narrator keeps the listener dangling for a moment and then suddenly lets him know, in the first words of the next line, that the hunter has arrived at the Prairie Dog Hills, where the herd is.

FOUR

The treatment of oral narrative as dramatic poetry has a number of analytical advantages. Some of the features of oral narrative which have been branded "primitive," on the basis of comparisons with written prose fiction, can now be understood as "poetic" instead. It has been said, for example, that while most of our own prose narrative is highly "realistic," primitive narrative is full of fantasy: a stone moves about like an animal, an animal speaks like a man, a man jumps through a hoop and becomes a coyote. Yet when we encounter gross and unexplained distortions of reality in Yeats, for example, we are apt to call them not "primitive" but "dream-like" or "mystical" and to regard them as highly poetic.

It is also said that "primitive" narrative, again unlike written prose fiction, seldom describes emotional states. This is true enough, but the comparison with prose misses the point: what oral narrative usually does with emotions is to evoke them rather than describe them directly, which is precisely what we have been taught to expect in poetry. In the Zuñi case, such descriptions of emotions as do exist are very simple, "The boy became / very unhappy," for example, but evocations are myriad and sometimes quite subtle, as in this passage:

> *He went out, having been given the quiver, and wandered around.*
> *He was not thinking of killing deer, he just wandered around.*
> *In the evening he came home empty-handed.*

According to both the narrator and a member of his audience, these lines clearly indicate (to a Zuñi, at least) that the person referred to is depressed, and they regarded this person's death three days later as a sort of suicide, though it was described in the story as an accident.

Another distinguishing feature of "primitive" narrative, according to Boas and many others, is repetition, ranging from the level of words or phrases to that of whole episodes.[62] At least one of the kinds of repetition in Zuñi narrative is indeed rare in our own prose (and poetry as well), and that is the linking of two sentences or major clauses by the conversion of the final element of one into the initial element of the next, as in these lines (from the last passage quoted in the previous section): "His uncle / went out hunting. Going out hunting / he came along. . . ." But the same device is common in epic poetry, as in this Yugoslav example: "And may God too make us merry, / Make us merry and give us entertainment!"[63] Unless we want to call epic poetry "primitive," this particular kind of repetition must be properly understood as "oral" and not "primitive," and the same thing goes for the repeated use of stock formulas in both epic poetry (epithets, for example) and Zuñi narrative (greeting exchanges, for example).

When it comes to the repetition of whole passages, "primitive" narrative may be compared to epic poetry and also to refrains in songs (from both literate and nonliterate cultures) and in written poetry. Refrains are often varied from one rendition to the next, and the same is true (although in a less structured way) for the repeated passages in Yugoslav epic, as shown by Lord,[64] and in Zuñi narrative. In the following Zuñi passage, a boy's foster mother is quoting to him what he must say when he addresses his real mother, who abandoned him as a baby:

> *My Sun Father*
> *made you pregnant.*
> *When you were about to deliver*
> *it was to Nearing Waters*
> *that you went down to wash. You washed at the bank.*

But when the boy actually confronts this real mother later in the same story, this is what the narrator has him say:

> *My Sun Father*
> *made you pregnant.*
> *When he made you pregnant you*
> *sat in there and your belly began to grow large.*
> *Your belly grew large*
> *you*
> *you were about to deliver, you had pains in your belly, you were about to give birth to*
> *   me, you had pains in your belly*
> *you gathered your clothes*
> *and you went down to the bank to wash.*

The remaining kinds of repetition in Zuñi narrative are of the sort we approvingly call "parallelism" (or something of the sort) when we find them in our own poetry. A line like, "And all the people who had come killed the deer, killed the deer, killed the deer!" cannot honestly be called primitive unless we call Shakespeare primitive when he has Hamlet say, "You cannot, sir, take from me anything that I will more willingly part withal: except my life, except my life, except my life." And not all of the parallelism in Zuñi narrative involves simple repetition:

> *Tewuuli kolh nahhayaye. Nahhayap*
> *lalholh 'aksik ts'an 'aksh 'allu' 'aye, kwan lheyaa k'ohanna.*
> *Muusilili lheya'kwip 'an lapappowaye.*
> *Lapappow lesnish 'aawanelap, ten 'aktsik'i*
> *'ottsi*
> *ho''i 'akshappa.*

In the valley was the herd of deer. In the herd of deer
there was a little boy going around among them, dressed in white.
He had bells on and was wearing a macaw headdress.
He was wearing a macaw headdress and was handsome, surely it was a boy
a male
a person among them.

What all this means, simply stated, is that (remarkably enough) there was a human being among the deer, but the narrator chooses to explore the fact in half a dozen different ways.

Repetitions and other poetic features of oral narrative have implications even for those who focus on content analysis and choose to ignore "style." The implications for psychological analysis, which is normally based on the content of prose translations, may be illustrated by the following passage, in which a boy has just exposed the woman who secretly abandoned him as a baby (parenthesis indicate softer portions):

At that moment his mother
embraced him (embraced him).
His uncle got angry (his uncle got angry).
He beat
his kinswoman
(he beat his kinswoman).

This passage might have appeared in a conventional prose rendition (by Benedict, for example) as, "At that moment his mother embraced him. His uncle got angry. He beat his kinswoman," thus having lost the nuances and greater intensity given it by the repetition, the changes of loudness, and the frequent pauses.

The complications of poetic style have especially strong implications for those who seek to measure the social and psychological content of narrative by means of word-counts. "Killed the deer," repeated three times in a line quoted above, might well have been reduced to a single occurrence in the translations of the past. Moreover, it seems crude to give the same weight to a word like "killed" when it is shouted and when it is rendered flatly. And the indirect expression of emotion, as in the case of the depression and suicide mentioned earlier, would escape a word counter entirely.

Lévi-Strauss and other structuralists operating on an abstract level assume that almost any translation will do for their purposes, but poetic subtleties have a potential for radically altering surface meanings, irony being an obvious example. The more concrete structural analysis proposed by Hendricks, on the other hand, does take the "linguistic" aspect of poetics into account, since each basic element in his system consists of a single semantic "function" which may be served by several lower-level "linguistic" (phonological, morphological, or syntactic) elements.[65]

But even Hendricks overlooks "paralinguistic" matters, though it is precisely at the level of semantic function that the arbitrary wall between "linguistics" and "paralinguistics" collapses. In Zuñi narrative, for example, the semantic function of marking the start of a quotation may be served by such "linguistic" devices as a sharp intonation change or the words, "The deer spoke to her son," but it may also be served by such "paralinguistic" devices as a pause or a change in voice quality.

The treatment of oral narrative as dramatic poetry, then, clearly promises many analytical rewards. It should also be obvious that there are immediate esthetic rewards. The apparent lack of literary value in many past translations is not a reflection but a distortion of the originals, caused by the dictation process, an emphasis on content, a pervasive deafness to oral qualities, and a fixed notion of the boundary between poetry and prose. Present conditions, which combine new recording techniques with a growing sensitivity to verbal art as performed "event" rather than as fixed "object" on the page, promise the removal of previous difficulties. "Event" orientation, together with an intensified appreciation of fantasy, has already led modern poets to recognize a kinship between their own work and the oral art of "primitives." As Jerome Rothenberg points out in *Technicians of the Sacred,* both modern and primitive poets are concerned with oral performance, both escape the confines of Aristotelian rationalism, both transcend the conventional genre boundaries of written literature, and both sometimes make use of stripped-down forms which require maximal interpolation by audiences.[66] This last point recalls the Clackamas "terseness" discussed by Jacobs, and I am reminded of the Zuñi who asked me, "When I tell these stories do you picture it, or do you just write it down?"

The effort presented here is intended more as an experiment than as the final word on the poetic features of oral narrative and their presentation on the printed page. I hope it will encourage others to make further experiments.

Notes

[1] Such an evaluation is made in one of the blurbs on the back cover of the paperback edition of this book (New York: Hill and Wang, 1953). In the preface de Angulo says, "I wrote these stories . . . for my children" (p. 5).

[2] Theodora Kroeber, *The Inland Whale* (Berkeley, Calif., 1963), pp. 8–9.

[3] Franz Boas, *Race, Language and Culture* (New York, 1940), p. 451.

[4] Kroeber, *The Inland Whale,* p. 7.

[5] In using "Zuñi" rather than "Zuni" I follow the practice of the journal where this essay originally appeared. But the English-speaking residents of the Zuñi area, including bilingual Zuñis, use "Zuni" in both spelling and pronunciation. Academics frequently render "Zuñi" as "zoonyee" (rather than the Spanish "soonyee"), so that the final result after retaining the ñ is still an English corruption of what is already a Spanish corruption of the Keresan corruption of the Zuñis' word for themselves, which is *Shiwi.*

[6] Cushing's translations may be found in Frank Hamilton Cushing, "Zuñi Fetiches," *Annual Report of the Bureau of American Ethnology* 2 (1883): 13–19, 21–24;

in "Outlines of Zuñi Creation Myths," *Annual Report of the Bureau of American Ethnology* 13 (1896): 379–447; in *Zuñi Folk Tales* (New York, 1901; New York, 1931); and in *Zuñi Breadstuff*, Museum of the American Indian, Heye Foundation, Indian Notes and Monographs 8 (1920): 20–54, 58–124, 270–88, 395–515. Two additional Cushing interpretations were recorded by men who visited him in the field: John G. Bourke, *Diary* (unpublished MS in the library of the U.S. Military Academy at West Point, 1881), pp. 2565–85; H.F.C. ten Kate, "A Zuñi Folk Tale," *Journal of American Folklore* 30 (1917): 496–99. "The Beginning of Newness," from "Outlines of Zuni Creation Myths" (pp. 379–81), is reprinted in Margot Astrov, *The Winged Serpent* (New York, 1946), reprinted as *American Indian Prose and Poetry* (New York, 1962), pp. 240–42; and in Stith Thompson, *Tales of the North American Indians* (Bloomington, Ind., 1929, 1966), pp. 17–19. "The Poor Turkey Girl," from Cushing, *Zuñi Folk Tales* (pp. 54–64), is reprinted in Thompson (pp. 225–31) and in John Greenway, *Literature Among the Primitives* (Hatboro, Pa., 1964), pp. 228–34. "The Cock and the Mouse," from Cushing, *Zuñi Folk Tales* (pp. 411–22), is reprinted in Greenway, pp. 151–58, and in Alan Dundes, *The Study of Folklore* (Englewood Cliffs, N.J., 1965), pp. 269–76.

[7]Cushing, "Outlines of Zuñi Creation Myths," *Annual Report* 13: 375.

[8]Ruth L. Bunzel, "Zuñi Origin Myths," *Annual Report of the Bureau of American Ethnology* 47 (1932): 547.

[9]Cushing, *Zuñi Folk Tales*, p. 411.

[10]Dundes, *Study of Folklore*, p. 274.

[11]Cushing, *Zuñi Folk Tales* (1931), pp. xix–xx, xxvi.

[12]Astrov, *American Indian Prose and Poetry*, p. 5.

[13]Dell Hymes, "Some North Pacific Coast Poems: A Problem in Anthropological Philology," *American Anthropologist* 67 (1965): 316–41; reprinted in *Stony Brook* 1–2 (1968): 179–204.

[14]Cushing, *Zuñi Folk Tales*, p. xxviii.

[15]Ibid., pp. 134, 182–83.

[16]The orthography used for these and other Zuñi words herein is as follows: vowels should be given their Continental values; double vowls (*aa*, etc.) are like the long vowels in Greek. Consonants should be pronounced as in English, with the following exceptions: *p* and *t* are not aspirated; *lh* is like English *h* and *l* pronounced simultaneously; double consonants (*kk, ll,* etc. except that *ch* becomes *cch, lh llh,* and *sh ssh)* are like those in Italian; and ' is the glottal stop, which, when it follows *ch, k, kw, ky* or *ts,* is pronounced simultaneously with these sounds. Stress is on the first syllable of a word; exceptional words are marked with ´.

[17]Cushing, *Zuñi Folk Tales*, p. 6.

[18]Ibid., p. 24.

[19]Ibid., p. 203.

[20]Ibid., p. 3.

[21]Dennis Tedlock, *The Ethnography of Tale-Telling at Zuñi* (Ann Arbor, Mich: University Microfilms, 1968), chap. 3.

[22]Cushing, *Zuñi Folk Tales*, p. 185.

[23]Ibid., p. 53.

[24]Ibid., p. xxvii.

[25]Matilda Coxe Stevenson, "The Zuñi Indians," *Annual Report of the Bureau of American Ethnology* 23 (1904): 23–61.

[26]Ibid., pp. 135–37.

[27]Franz Boas, "Tales of Spanish Provenience from Zuñi," *Journal of American Folklore* 35 (1922): 62–98. Elsie Clews Parsons and Franz Boas, "Spanish Tales from Laguna and Zuñi, New Mexico," *Journal of American Folklore* 33 (1920): 47–72. Elsie Clews Parsons, "Notes on Zuñi, Part II," *Memoirs of the American Anthropological Association* 4 (1917): 302–27; "Pueblo-Indian Folktales, Probably of Spanish Provenience," *Journal of American Folklore* 31 (1918): 216–55; "The Origin Myth of Zuñi," *Journal of American Folklore* 36 (1923): 135–62; "The Scalp Ceremonial of Zuñi," *Memoirs of the American Anthropological Association* 31 (1924): 28–34; "Zuñi Tales," *Journal of American Folklore* 43 (1930): 1–58. Edward L. Handy, "Zuñi Tales," *Journal of American Folklore* 31 (1918): 451–71.

[28]Ruth L. Bunzel, "Zuñi Origin Myths"; "Zuñi Katchinas," *Annual Report of the Bureau of American Ethnology* 47 (1932): 837–1086 (narratives are scattered throughout this work). *Zuñi Texts,* Publications of the American Ethnological Society 15 (1933). Ruth Benedict, *Zuñi Mythology,* Columbia University Contributions to Anthropology 21 (1935).

[29]Parsons, "Zuñi Tales" (texts are given for only two of these narratives); Bunzel, "Zuñi Origin Myths," and *Zuñi Texts.*

[30]Parsons, "Zuñi Tales," p. 2.

[31]Ibid., p. 2 (quoted by Parsons).

[32]Ibid., pp. 6, 30.

[33]Benedict, *Zuñi Mythology,* 1: xxxviii.

[34]Ibid., 1: 219.

[35]Bunzel, *Zuñi Texts,* p. 109.

[36]A. L. Kroeber, "A Mohave Historical Epic," University of California *Anthropological Records* 11 (1951): 133; D. Demetracapoulou and Cora DuBois, "A Study of Wintu Mythology," *Journal of American Folklore* 45 (1932): 400; Gladys A. Reichard, "An Analysis of Coeur d'Alene Indian Myths," *Memoirs of the American Folklore Society* 41 (1947): 5.

[37]Tedlock, "The Ethnography of Tale-Telling in Zuñi," pp. 279–330; *Finding the Center: Narrative Poetry of the Zuñi Indians* (New York, 1972; Lincoln, Nebr., 1978).

[38]Melville Jacobs, *Clackamas Chinook Texts,* Publications of the Indiana University Research Center in Anthropology, Folklore, and Linguistics 8 (Bloomington, Ind., 1958) and 11 (1959).

[39]Anna Risser, "Seven Zuñi Folk Tales," *El Palacio* 48 (1941): 215–26.

[40]Bert Kaplan, "Psychological Themes in Zuñi Mythology and Zuñi TAT's," in *The Psychoanalytic Study of Society,* ed. Warner Muensterberger and Sydney Axelrod, vol. 2 (New York, 1962) p. 255–62.

[41]Claude Lévi-Strauss, "The Structural Study of Myth," *Journal of American Folklore* 68 (1955): 428–44; reprinted in Claude Lévi-Strauss, *Structural Anthropology* (Garden City, N.Y., 1967), pp. 202–28.

[42]John L. Fischer, "The Sociopsychological Analysis of Folktales," *Current Anthropology* 4 (1963): 237.

[43]Lévi-Strauss, "The Structural Study of Myth," p. 430.

[44]Melville Jacobs, *The Content and Style of an Oral Literature,* Viking Fund Publications in Anthropology 26 (1959): 3, 6.

[45]Boas, *Race, Language, and Culture,* p. 452; A. L. Kroeber, "A Mohave Historical Epic," p. 133.

[46]Demetracapoulou and Dubois, "A Study of Wintu Mythology," p. 386.

[47]Jacobs, *The Content and Style of an Oral Literature,* pp. 7–8.

[48]Tedlock, Tale H-9, personal collection.

[49]Stanley Newman, "Vocabulary Levels: Zuñi Sacred and Slang Usage," *Southwestern Journal of Anthropology* 11 (1955): 345–54; reprinted in *Language in Culture and Society,* ed. Dell Hymes (New York, 1964): 397–402.

[50]Tedlock, *Finding the Center,* pp. 191–213.

[51]Tedlock, Tale H-9, personal collection.

[52]Boas, *Race, Language, and Culture,* p. 491, from an article originally published in 1925.

[53]Jacobs, *The Content and Style of an Oral Literature,* p. 7.

[54]George L. Trager, "Paralanguage," *Studies in Linguistics* 13 (1958): 1–12; reprinted in *Language and Culture and Society,* ed. Dell Hymes, pp. 274–79. Robert E. Pittenger, Charles F. Hockett, and John J. Danehy, *The First Five Minutes* (Ithaca, N.Y., 1960), pp. 194–206.

[55]This and all further Zuñi narrative quotations are from "The Boy and the Deer," in *Finding the Center.*

[56]Tightness, or "squeeze," is more common among women than among men, according to Pittenger, Hockett, and Danehy, *The First Five Minutes,* pp. 202–3.

[57]Igor Stravinsky, album notes to *Symphony of Psalms,* Columbia Records 6548.

[58]Frieda Goldman-Eisler, "Discussion and Further Comments," in *New Directions in the Study of Language,* ed. Eric H. Lenneberg (Cambridge, Mass., 1964), pp. 118–19.

[59]*The Culture of the Winnebago: As Described by Themselves,* Memoirs of the International Journal of American Linguistics, vol. 2 (1949) pp. 42–44, 61–62, 103, 106–8. I infer from Radin's remarks on p. 42 that these pauses were reconstructed rather than recorded in the field.

[60]Goldman-Eisler, "Discussion and Further Comments," p. 120; she adds that the rate of syllable articulation (between pauses), by contrast with the rate of pausing, is almost constant.

[61]One-third of the lines produced by my principal Zuñi narrator involve this kind of phrase splitting, which is twice the proportion of splitting (or "necessary enjambment") reported for Yugoslav epics, by Albert Lord in *The Singer of Tales* (New York, 1965), p. 54.

[62]Boas, *Race, Language, and Culture,* pp. 491–93.

[63]Lord, *Singer of Tales,* p. 32.

[64]Ibid., p. 82.

[65]William O. Hendricks, "On the Notion 'Beyond the Sentence,'" *Linguistics* 37 (1967): 32–35.

[66]Jerome Rothenberg, *Technicians of the Sacred* (Garden City, N.Y., 1968), pp. xxii-xxiii.

John Bierhorst: AMERICAN INDIAN VERBAL ART AND THE ROLE OF THE LITERARY CRITIC

The Esotericism of Ritual Utterances, the odd allusiveness of certain myths and their sometimes densely ornamented texture, whether drawn from one of the more complex milieus, such as the precontact Mexican, or from a tribe like the Navajo, or even from the very few (now extinct) Anambé of Brazil, suggests a distinction that is no doubt tacitly accepted if not much exploited; namely, that there exists in most New World cultures an identifiable, if broad, threshold between folklore and what we may call literary, or privileged, art. If such a distinction does indeed exist, then there is a function that literary criticism can perform, or, at the very least, an opportunity for folklorists to assume on occasions the mantle of the literary critic,[1] if, as they once did, they still can claim the whole of non-Eurasian verbal art as a part of their province.

It is perhaps not too much to suggest that there are verbal productions still waiting to be elucidated that compare in perfection to the dry paintings of the Navajo Mountain Chant or to the elegant pavilions at Uxmal. In the case of representational or plastic art we do not need to be convinced; the interplay of complex symmetries is largely available even to the untutored eye. But where the composition is verbal, its formalism may be accessible only through symbol or by reference to arcane lore. As it comes down to us in English, Spanish, or German, it may be further obscured by bad paragraphing and inexact translation. The effort to grasp it in all its particulars and even the quest for better translation must begin, inevitably, in that fundamental department of criticism known as explication or content analysis; and this effort, for the most part and despite numerous promising starts, is yet to be seriously made.

Over the past hundred years folklorists and anthropologists have been presented with three highly seductive approaches to the business of unraveling literary content, each of which has been rejected by the majority or is in the process of being rejected. These are nature mythology, psychoanalysis, and structuralism. For the purposes of the present discussion we may define nature mythology as the search for annual, seasonal, diurnal, lunar, or astral rhythms as they occur, or are thought to occur, in ritual texts and in myth; psychoanalysis as the study of that peculiar process wherein the ontogenetic drama, communicated by signals from the non-conscious, is printed out in dreams, actions, and utterances of whatever kind; and structuralism as a hypothesis seeking to uncover the natural arrangement of non-conscious emissions, their points of repulsion and attraction, and their latent far-flung symmetries through what may be described as a crystallography of the soul.

In a way it is not surprising that such open-ended disciplines, inviting the free fall of subjectivity, have been kept at a distance by those who see themselves as scientists. Yet it is interesting to recall that the label "science" has been claimed by all three. Literary criticism, in general, will make no such claim, even if it will borrow, and has borrowed, liberally from both psychoanalysis and structuralism and even from nature mythology—and even if a critic like Northrop Frye or an anthropologist like Munro Edmonson might hint that the study of literature ought properly to imitate science.[2]

To adapt a phrase from the critic and novelist Vladimir Nabokov, criticism will seek to combine the passion of the scientist with the precision of the artist.[3] In other words it will allow itself to be fired by alien taxonomies while coming to terms, finally, with the cold symmetry of the work itself. The essential difference, then, is this: the three disciplines to which I have alluded are superorganic; they approach the single myth or the single ritual as a pool of data from which one extracts a few drops of truth to sustain a general theory; the residue, and there is always a residue, remains unused. But criticism, that is to say explicative criticism, exalts the single work and will not rest until its form has been entirely revealed and its contents analyzed down to the last few puzzling scraps.

This would seem an obvious procedure, yet in practice it has rarely been carried out. If a work of Indian literature is superlative, if it is truly worth knowing, then the labor of getting to know it will be very hard. Lovers of New World literature can point with some satisfaction to the studies of the late Angel Garibay, whose recensions and exegeses have carried Aztec lyric poetry to the point where there may now be a real hope of mastering it, perhaps in another twenty or thirty years.[4] Garibay's efforts, if incomplete, amount to genuine criticism, and while they have drawn on the resources of ethnography they have also added to and enriched those resources.

Among Americanists who have devoted themselves primarily to ethnography, some, like Paul Radin, have been acutely aware of the role of criticism and have themselves practiced it. Radin's analysis of the Winnebago Trickster cycle is a case in point.[5] It is to be regretted, however, that he did not leave us his commentary on a much more promising work, the Winnebago ritual text he chose to entitle *The Road of Life and Death* (New York, 1945).

We must wait and see whether Munro Edmonson or his former student, Dennis Tedlock, whose recent translations from the Quiché and the Zuni, respectively,[6] have displayed such extraordinary sensitivity to the requirements of literary art, will now favor us with specimens of literary analysis. Other names could be cited as well, but it will be granted, I think, that the elements of criticism, though they have not been missing from New World studies, have yet to coalesce into a viable tradition.

We may dispense with the functionalist criticism of latter-day Malinowskians, the sentimental criticism of those literary anthropologists who confuse myth with the modern novel, and the descriptive "criticism" that has always been practiced by certain ethnographers. These approaches, at best, serve to highlight random features, providing whole interpretations of none but the simplest of texts.

The only brilliant critic of native American literature has been and is Claude Lévi-Strauss, whose structuralist readings of selected myths have clearly indicated the richness of the material even if they have not succeeded in making it comprehensible. It is true that Lévi-Strauss, with time, has broadened his approach and that his later commentaries are more satisfying, perhaps, than his earliest ones. Thus the rigidity of his early essay on the Tsimshian myth of Asdiwal is felt less keenly in his later, more expansive discussion of the North American Star Husband tale, where not only structuralism but nature mythology is brought into play.[7] These later studies, however, are piecemeal, treating individual myths as mere segments of an inter-mythic superstructure, which, so the theory goes, must be viewed as a whole or not at all.

Lévi-Strauss, increasingly, does not exalt the single work. But he has given us a magnificent four-volume anthology, calling attention to dozens of myths worthy of special study, singling out in particular two "key" myths: the now famous Bororo myth of Geriguiguiatugo and the Tukuna myth entitled The Hunter Monmaneki and His Wives.[8] It would be a most worthwhile project for literary criticism to unravel these "key" myths, also Asdiwal and The Star Husband, selectively utilizing or rejecting the clues that have been offered; and to ask the interesting question, Why did these myths attract Lévi-Strauss in the first place and what do all four have in common? Of this more later.

I would here like to offer an example of what criticism, proceeding from straightforward observation, can actually accomplish. The excerpt that follows is part of the myth of Quetzalcoatl, recorded in the Aztec language by Fray Bernardino de Sahagún in the mid-sixteenth century, probably in the borough of Tlatelolco, and included in Book III of his *Historia general de las cosas de Neuva España*.[9] The passage appears near the close of the myth as the hero is completing his mysterious flight toward the east. The translation, from the Aztec, is my own:

> *And they say that he left a great number*
> *of traces behind him—his signs—by which*
> *he was signified:*
>
> *At a certain spot on a mountain, they*
> *say, he would frolic [and] tumble [and]*
> *fall to the bottom, and for his recovery*
> *he left in place a towline [of maguey].*
>
> *At another site he laid out a ball court*
> *all of stone. And through the middle, where*

the center line lay, it was entrenched. [And]
the entrenchment ran deep.

And in another place he shot a ceiba,
shooting it so that he himself passed through
the heart of the ceiba.

And in another place he built a house
underground. [And] the site is called
Mictlan.

And in yet another place he erected a stone,
a great stone phallus. They say that
anyone might once have pushed it with his little
finger. It had indeed been set in motion,
rocking back and forth. Yet, they say,
when many pushed it, then it absolutely
would not move. Though many together
might make the effort, desiring to push it,
it could not be moved.[10]

Anthologists presenting the Quetzalcoatl story have almost always omitted this passage, casting it aside as one of those seemingly crude bits of stuffing that mar, or appear to mar, the story line. But I hope to demonstrate that the passage, far from crude, is elegant, and that without it the story makes no real sense.

The myth as a whole may be epitomized as follows: the aging culture hero, Quetzalcoatl, driven off by the sorcerer Tezcatlipoca and sent journeying eastward, passes through five quasi-earthly localities where he is initiated, step by step, into the mysteries of death. Continuing eastward, he embarks upon the curious itinerary of signs, quoted above, then proceeds to his ultimate goal, Tlapallan, the land of the rising sun.

Let us begin by recalling that just prior to the itinerary of signs, the hero, in a manner of speaking, is dead. I will not quote the lengthy passage in question but merely summarize it by noting that Quetzalcoatl (1) had discovered his own senescence, (2) had left behind him a memorial, (3) had crossed a river, (4) had renounced his jewels, and (5) had fallen into a drunken sleep. The number 5, by the way, is obtained without trickery or manipulation. It is in fact what the composer of the myth intended, and each of the five stages, or localities, is given its own mytho-geographical designation: (1) Huehue-Cuauhtitlan, "Place of the Old-Age Tree," (2) Temacpalco, "Where the Handprints Are," (3) Tepanohuayan, "At the Stone Bridge," (4) Cozcahapan, "At the Water of the Jewels" and (5) Cochtocan, "Where He Lay Sleeping." Turning now to the itinerary of signs, quoted above and in full, we note that there are again five stations: (1) the mountain, (2) the ball court, (3) the ceiba (*Ceiba pentandra,* the kapok tree), (4) the house underground, and (5) the stone phallus.

It must also be noted that the hero, near the beginning of the myth, when warned of his fate, was nonetheless promised: *Auh in iquac tioalmocuepaz, occeppa tipiltontli timochioaz* ("And when you return, you shall have again been made a child").[11] If we take the mythmaker at his word, and there is no reason not to, then we may be permitted to look ahead in the story for some kind of resurrection or mystical rejuvenation.

Let us look more closely now at the itinerary of signs. The opening incident recapitulates a widespread North American trickster tale in which the playful or foolish trickster slides down a slope, leaving behind him a scar, a growth of lichens derived from the skin of his buttocks, or, in the present case, a landslide scar plus an invading growth of (xerophytic) magueys, whose fiber, incidentally, was a source of rope.

The second stop involves a ball court, a scene of ritual combat; and indeed, in the folkloristic Quetzalcoatl legend recorded by Gerónimo de Mendieta, the hero was defeated on a ball court by his sorcerer opponent, Tezcatlipoca.[12] This as a prelude to his famous flight.

The encounter with the ceiba tree is explained in another folkloristic source, the so-called "Histoyre du Mechique," where we read that the hero, on his flight to the east, shot an arrow into a tree and opened a hole large enough to accommodate his person; he thereupon literally entered the tree—and died.[13] (Stories in which a chief, a king, or a god is buried within a tree, especially a sacred tree like the ceiba or cottonwood, are of course very common and can be garnered from Peru, Mexico, the Great Plains, and as far north as Iroquoia. There is sometimes an implication of rebirth.)

The fourth stop is Mictlan ("Dead Land"), the Aztec underworld.

Fifthly and lastly, the hero exhibits his erect penis, as he does also in another version of the Quetzalcoatl myth, one of almost equal poetic merit, in which at the moment of victory over death we encounter the double entendre, *acoquiza in iyollo quetzaltototl,* translated (1) "the heart of the quetzal rose upward," or (2) "the inner part of the precious penis rose upward."[14] It is of interest, perhaps, though by no means essential, to note the significance of phallic exhibitionism in South American lore; in a Tukuna myth, for example, it is the visible phallus that distinguishes the living from the dead; in a ritual of the Urubu the exhibition of the glans penis is said to symbolize victory over the underworld.[15] In our text, moreover, the phallus becomes an immovable object, recalling—or indeed, deliberately incorporating—the common folkloristic motif whereby a narrator effectively perpetuates his hero, turning him into stone.

As a tentative step toward interpretation we may now characterize the itinerary of signs as a progression through (1) youth, (2) maturity, (3) demise, (4) limbo, and (5) resurrection. But there is still much more to be noted.

Is it of any significance that the fourth station, Mictlan, or limbo, as I have just characterized it, also can be read as "north?" *Mictlan + pa* (directional postposition) =

mictlampa ("north"). And are there any other potential allusions to the compass in this itinerary of signs? Not at first glance. But we may hold in reserve the impression that it would not be inappropriate to find the third station, the place of demise, associated with the west, or the second station, the place of ritual combat, associated with the south (inasmuch as warfare is often linked with this direction in Aztec lore), or, indeed, the place of youth and resurrection established in the east. I share these assumptions because it is already implicit in the use of the number 5 that we may be dealing, in covert form, with the so-called ritual of the four world quarters.

The ritual is widespread and variable, but it must always be this: the celebrant must recognize each of the four directions in contiguous order; he must, in effect, "go round the world." The order may be clockwise or counterclockwise, and the sequence may begin at any one of the four points. It will be considered finished after four stops or, as in many cases, five stops, that is, after a return to the point of origin. The ritual essentially is a charm against death, though it may be given various corollary interpretations such as charm against disease, pursuit of wholeness, prayer for peace, and so forth. In Quetzalcoatl's itinerary of signs, if there is an allusion to the four world quarters and if there is a prescribed order, it must be as follows: (1) east, (2) south, (3) west, (4) north, and back again to (5) east. This incidentally is the famous "sunwise" circuit practiced in certain phases of Navajo ritual and, needless to say, widespread in Plains lore.

But if the hero himself is being turned through a sunwise circuit of revival, there is also a level at which the topography is involved. Each of the five signs is in fact a landmark: (1) the avalanche scar grown over with magueys; (2) the stone "trench," perhaps a canyon; (3) ?; (4) probably the pre-Aztec archaeological site (with tombs) in the modern state of Oaxaca, known today not as Mictlan but as Mitla; and (5) the balanced rock. We may now look back upon the earlier journey, summarized above, in which the hero progressed toward a drunken sleep, and note that not only does it correspond numerically and therefore artistically (in terms of Aztec mythopoetics) to the five-stage itinerary of signs, but that it, too, has topographic, or geographic, associations. It is beyond the scope of the present discussion to trace the seasonal allusions that appear at various points in the Quetzalcoatl myth, but it will be at least granted as a tentative observation that the world itself—or as Theodor Gaster has styled it, the "topocosm" [16]—accompanies the hero through death and rebirth.

There is a seeming flaw, however, in the itinerary of signs; the third sign, the ceiba, is no sign at all. Yet the composer of the myth was evidently aware of this problem and took the trouble to phrase the passage so that it could be read two ways. I have already given the primary translation in context, above. The secondary translation:

> *And in another place he shot a ceiba*
> *[as though it were an arrow], shooting*
> *it so that it itself passed through the*
> *heart of [a second] ceiba, [thus forming*
> *a cross].*

If this reading seems contrived, it must be pointed out that we have Sahagún himself as the authority for it.[17] It is not untypical, moreover, of the sometimes startling cleverness to be found in Aztec literature. The reading is gratifying from another point of view in that it introduces, by implication, the missing cross which, as we know from the pictographic codices, was an emblem of the four world quarters. Thus the hero who had been dead is revived, as promised, through a circular, or cruciform, itinerary of signs in which his life is rehearsed in its entirety and made new. The point I hope to have established is that what might at first strike the eye as an ill-digested jumble of folkloristic motifs is in fact both organic and flawless in terms of the work as a whole. And though my demonstration has been laborious, it must be kept in mind that the educated Aztec listener, steeped in the lore of the world quarters, his ear attuned to the symbolic language of myth, need have experienced no difficulty whatsoever in grasping the full meaning of this remarkable passage, which might be admired, moreover, not only for the richness of its content but for its very economy and tasteful restraint.

But in emphasizing through the use of this isolated example the explicative function of criticism, perhaps even what T. S. Eliot once dubbed the "lemon-squeezer" tactic,[18] I do not mean to overlook the full range of duties that the critic must contemplate. Textual criticism will of course be included, as well as genre studies, comparative studies, literary theory, and, inevitably, value judgments. Yet the main thing, and it is worth repeating, is that criticism cannot flourish unless it is rooted in a firm understanding of the individual work.

Once we begin to gain this understanding we can widen our prospects. For example, using the material that has just been presented, we may now view with renewed suspicion that portion of the Florentine Codex in which the first of the five stations in the itinerary of signs is construed not as one but as two stations;[19] Seler's recension (which I have borrowed) obviates the discrepancy, and so we give it our endorsement,[20] noting that Sahagún's Spanish version of the same passage serves as a corroboration.

For comparative study we may entertain a myth like the Asdiwal text, mentioned above, which Lévi-Strauss has characterized as a specimen of the "court literature" of the Tsimshian nobility. The Sahaguntine corpus is likewise a court literature and we may look for fruitful comparisons with this observation as a starting point. And the range may be extended to the shamanistic and priestly literatures of such cultures as the Navajo and the Zuni, and in general to those mythic texts, wherever they may be found, that have been characterized by Lévi-Strauss as *versions plus savantes*.[21] In the realm of pure content we may take note of the fact that the hero Asdiwal's career, on the geographical level, is a counterclockwise circuit of the world quarters, beginning in the east and also terminating in the east, whereupon he is changed into a monument of stone; and we may ask, with justification, whether this myth and the myth of Quetzalcoatl are drawing upon a common theme.

The search for pervasive themes, metaphors, and motifs will prove a rewarding one, as indeed it has already for those who have followed the guidelines of nature mythology and psychoanalysis and even for those who have contented themselves with statistical studies. Moreover, and this from a strictly literary point of view, we will find mythopoets in widely separated cultures drawing their materials into the framework of a standard plot. I have discussed in another place this "centripetal" tendency of Indian mythology and will here only touch upon it, noting that guilt, death, and the quest for food are among the principal forces binding a varied panoply of lore.[22] Asdiwal, Quetzalcoatl, Geriguiguiatugo, The Star Husband, and The Hunter Monmaneki and His Wives may all be revealed as reworkings of this basic plot. But though we will admit the use of widespread, even universal patterns, I hope it is clear from the analysis developed in the preceding pages that we need not rely upon Jungian formulations; we may keep simple diffusion before us as a working hypothesis (to be challenged perhaps at a later date), concentrating for the time being upon what can be provided by ethnography, by internal evidence, and by native criticism—that is, those texts referred to by folklorists as "variants," for the variant by its very nature constitutes a gloss and is of course our best, often our only, source of native commentary.

NOTES

[1] As in fact they have in other contexts. See Daniel G. Hoffman, ed., "Folklore in Literature: A Symposium," *Journal of American Folklore* 70 (1957): 1–24.

[2] Frye, *Anatomy of Criticism* (Princeton, 1957), pp. 7–8; Edmonson, *Lore: An Introduction to the Science of Folklore and Literature* (New York, 1971).

[3] See Alfred Appel, Jr., "Nabokov: A Portrait," *The Atlantic* 228, no. 3 (1971): 84. See also Appel, "An Interview with Vladimir Nabokov," in *Nabokov: The Man and His Work,* ed. L. S. Dembo (Madison, Wisc., 1967), p. 33.

[4] See especially *Poesía náhuatl,* 3 vols. (Mexico, 1964–68).

[5] *The Trickster: A Study in American Indian Mythology,* 2nd ed. (New York, 1972).

[6] Edmonson, *The Book of Counsel: The Popol Vuh of the Quiché Maya of Guatemala* (New Orleans, 1971). Tedlock, *Finding the Center* (New York, 1972).

[7] "The Story of Asdiwal," in *The Structural Study of Myth and Totemism;* ed. Edmund Leach (London, 1967), pp. 1–47. *L'Origine des manières de table* (Paris, 1968), pp. 161–266.

[8] *Le Cru et le cuit* (Paris, 1964), pp. 43–45. *L'Origine des manières de table,* pp. 17–20.

[9] For the Spanish text see ed. Angel M. Garibay, vol. 1 (Mexico, 1969), pp. 278–91. For the Aztec text see Eduard Seler, *Einige Kapitel aus dem Geschichtswerk des Fray Bernardino de Sahagun* (Stuttgart, 1927), pp. 268–92; also Arthur J. O. Anderson and Charles Dibble, *Florentine Codex,* pt. 4, (Santa Fe, 1952), pp. 13–36.

[10] Reprinted (with minor revisions) from *Four Masterworks of American Indian Literature* (New York, 1974), pp. 62–63.

[11] Seler, *Einige Kapitel,* p. 273.

[12] *Historia eclesiástica indiana* (Mexico, 1870), p. 82.

[13] Edouard de Jonghe, ed. *Journal de la Société des Américanistes,* nouvelle série. Tome 2 (1905), p. 38.

[14] For the Aztec text see Walter Lehmann, *Das Geschichte der Königreiche von Colhuacan und Mexico* (Stuttgart and Berlin, 1938), p. 91.

[15] Curt Nimuendaju. *The Tukuna,* University of California Publications in American Archaeology and Ethnology, vol. 45 (1952), p. 117. Francis Huxley, *Affable Savages: An Anthropologist Among the Urubu Indians of Brazil* (New York, 1957), p. 262.

[16] *Thespis* (New York, 1950), p. 4.

[17] Garibay, vol. 1, p. 291.

[18] *On Poetry and Poets* (New York, 1957), p. 125.

[19] Anderson and Dibble, *Florentine Codex,* pt. 4, p. 35.

[20] Seler, *Einige Kapitel,* p. 291.

[21] As for example in *L'Origine des manières de table,* p. 120.

[22] *The Red Swan* (New York, 1976).

Jeffrey F. Huntsman: TRADITIONAL NATIVE AMERICAN LITERATURE: THE TRANSLATION DILEMMA

The true and lasting treasure of every human community lies in its words. When the graves of Mycenae yielded up their splendid contents, the golden masks were mute—timeless and magnificent, but as empty, as alien, and ultimately as profoundly frightening as the mouths of the Stonehenge trilithons. But in words is power and strength and wealth, and only those without songs are truly poor and alone. Until recently, Native Americans have been treated as if they were peoples, not just without a treasure in words, but almost without words of any kind. The image of the stoic, silent redskin is most obviously a staple of Anglo linguistic and cinematic literature, but even in historical studies, particularly those which attempt to chart the intricacies of Indian-Anglo relations, the Indian is nearly always a *fantoccio,* a passive object to be transformed, destroyed, pitied, catalogued, and, finally, sadly and safely mourned. The Indian is too often Unperson, dead or assimilated, defamed as ruthless, depraved, nomadic, and now, most cruelly, a shiftless welfare sponge, drunkenly and ungratefully awaiting the princely gratuity that is the monthly check from the BIA.

Although the particular charges have changed over the centuries since the White European invaded the Western hemisphere, the maligning of the Native American through omission and commission, whether deliberate or mistaken, has not. In the earliest contacts, the Indian was seen either as a simple, Rousseauean pure being or as a subhuman but essentially harmless savage: in Anglo literature these types are represented by Chateaubriand's Atala and Shakespeare's Caliban. During the first three-quarters of the eighteenth century, the Indian came to be seen as a more dangerous savage for the simple reason that, as the Anglo population grew and expanded inland, it consumed more and more Indian land, a process that the Indian came quite naturally to resent and then to resist. These savages were savages because they were not civilized, and being uncivilized could obviously have no true culture. However good, even idyllic, their life might immediately seem, it was still a savage life, although natural and therefore virtuous. The dilemma for the Christian American, then—and all Americans who wielded power were by definition Christian Americans—was how to reconcile with savagism the God-given moral and intellectual virtues that the pre-Christianized Indian, like the prelapsarian Adam, had in fruitful and natural abundance. The solution that Anglo-Americans found characterizes the entire American experience: Progress. In the words of historian Roy Harvey Pearce, "the Indian was the remnant of a savage past away from which civilized men had struggled to grow. To study him was to triumph over the past."[1] Certainly, almost quintessentially, such a being must lack a literature; what few words the aboriginal North American inhabitant might have, must lack not only Christian values but even the pagan but civilized values of the Ancient World.

Once Indian cultures were thought to be destroyed, it became possible to study the pieces, to pity, and to comprehend. Anthropologists and apologists of various persuasions could safely talk about Native Americans without fearing that they might reappear at the door. These later discussions usually take one of several common forms, but each says more about Anglo perspectives on Indians than Indian on Indians. Most common, especially in even today's public school texts, is the contributions approach where the "gifts" of Indian life are listed: moccasins, crops, medicine, inventions, politics, tribalism, the names of natural features, cities, and states, and now ecology ("ecological man" has recently replaced "marginal man" and "noble savage" as an Indian sobriquet). Another angle is the "great person" or "hero" perspective which considers the so-called political and moral leaders who worked in what Anglo histories consider to be the Indian cause. Yet another approach (more common recently) involves Anglo self-flagellation, the "fraudulent treaty" or "unjust deposition" approach, which, while calling attention to past wrongs, usually conveniently ignores the fact that treaties *still* are being broken today in spirit or in letter. Finally, and of most interest here, there is the "wilderness poet" approach which finds a tranquilly recollecting rhymer behind every tree.

What is wrong with all of these views on the Native American is that they presuppose Anglo values. The "contributions" are meant to upgrade Indians in Anglo eyes. The "heroes" require a belief in an essential cultural identity and an assumption about a congruent function of certain types of leaders in both cultures. The "fraudulent treaty" assumes identical legal values for both groups and a predisposition toward useless Anglo guilt. And the "wilderness poet" finds an unctuous moper, plucking the same *chordae cordis* as Longfellow and Southey, and whose literary event appears to have an appalling soporific sameness. Even when the attributes of Indian culture and personality are presented as worthy of respect and emulation, they are so frequently taken out of context, viewed as "Indian," not Ute or Dakota or Malecite, that they are nearly meaningless except as artifacts of *Anglo* literature.

But culture does not consist centrally of artifacts or history. It is a congeries of mental constructs which describes how people think or evaluate, and only secondarily how they act. Indeed, the term *culture* is more restrictive than that: it is only those aspects of thinking that are shared by a community, that are publicly acknowledged, overtly or covertly, as meaningful. Between Anglo and Indian cultures are rather striking differences in the organization and importance of things. For Anglos, life is characterized by encounters with relative strangers, lasting a few moments or months. We invest ourselves with our independent histories and are so acutely aware of our personal uniqueness that a sense of community is usually impossible, unless it centers on a largely unsatisfying totemic label like *linguist, Texan, Jew*. But for Indian people, as for other small, stable societies, the culture frames a coherent network of reciprocal relationships. In the order of organisms, individuals are born, live some brief term, and die, leaving the enduring system of organization fundamentally unaltered (although the details of the culture may change, often radically, over time). Anglos generally value the innovative above the traditional, both personally and societally, and therefore reveal themselves nakedly but proudly, regardless or whether that literature is purportedly personal (lyric) or societal (epic). The poet is inventor, creating a purposefully unique artifact. For the Native American, however, the self is traditionally unobtrusive and its art in words paradoxically private and public at the same time. Although traditional Indian poetry is "owned" by its maker, and this ownership recognized even long generations after its maker and sometimes his or her name has died, it is the immediate and intimate possession of all who know it. Its owner is both creator and audience, the audience likewise creator and owner. Since it is shared, traditional Indian literature does not instruct except obliquely, but, like the more familiar sacred literature of Western Europe, celebrates and invokes. Even the most individualistic experiences, the vision quests of the peoples of the High Plains, are truly meaningful and powerful only when they have been remade in song. The truth of the vision quest, in other words, is not realized, for either questors or their community, until it has been "published."

Here in these fundamentally different cultural realities lies the prime and most vexing problem in translating Indian literature. In searching for the essence of a piece, the translator must choose between satisfying the requirement that the translation preserve the literal content of the work—neither adding concepts or images perhaps implicit in the original and unconsciously inferred by the native speaker/hearer, nor deleting "useless" repetitions or "blatant" commonplaces that surprise and tire the English reader—and satisfying the requirement that the translation convey the spirit of the original. Good translation of any literature requires a native or near-native sensitivity to both languages and few translators have the foresight to request a bilingual birth. Too often, even large-scale cultural differences are overlooked by translators concentrating on the details of word and phrase. For all the interactive closeness of their societies (especially when viewed with an Anglo perspective), the peoples of the High Plains were oriented in their individual experiences toward their unitary Godhead and their personal conduct as discrete members of a profoundly symbiotic world. Their poetry tends to be highly personal, epigrammatic, and—to use the least misleading European term—lyrical. Therefore, relatively literal translations of Dakota or Cheyenne poems are meaningful and moving works of art for most American readers, and the success of W. S. Merwin's translations from Crow is due in considerable part both to Merwin's own terse style and to the individualistic tendencies of the Anglo-American way of life. But the more close-knit, more systematized societies of the Pueblo peoples turn inward, the reciprocal symmetries of their life and literature are consequently more alien and more elusive to Anglo translators and readers, and their literature is more properly termed epic than lyric.

Even on the apparently simplest level of language, the issues are far from clear. The Whorf-Sapir hypothesis—that the normal categories, relations, and collocations of a person's language influence to a large degree what may be perceived—is useful in some measure. But outsiders can make too much of a given phrasing because they fail to understand fully the force—or lack of force—the phrase may have for its ordinary users. To cite a set of trivial but effective examples: If we compare French *J'ai faim* (lit. 'I have hunger') with Irish *Tá ocras orm* (lit. 'It is hunger on me') with English *I am hungry,* should we dwell on the imagistic effectiveness of the Irish phrase, the intimate identification of person and plight of the English, or the subtle and philosophical detachment of the French? And what then are we to make of the Navajo, which translates literally 'Hunger is trying to kill me'? Such pretty judgments would be utterly foolish, of course, because each phrase is the most commonplace formulation available and invokes not the tiniest *frisson* of poetic delight in a native speaker. Translation is possible with the aid of a native informant, to be sure, but the translator must at least know which questions to ask. Indian poetry is typically spare and even the lengthy and complex Navajo chantways abound with rarefied and elusive symbolism which seems to defy elegant translation. The inherent differences between languages, combined with symbolism, figurative or metaphoric bendings of ordinary language, secret or esoteric linguistic formulations, and fossils of earlier, now archaic diction, all contribute to a maddening Arabesque of many varieties of meaning that only the most perceptive and careful translator should confront.

Compounding these semantic tangles is the fact that most Indian literature has an intimate place in a larger context of ceremony that cannot be reproduced in print at all. The inflections of song, the rhythms of drum and dance, the delicate and insubstantial gestures of the teller, are impossible to replicate in the most careful of explanatory notes, and it is this inability to provide the echoes of longhouse, lodge, or hogan that has led translators like Jerome Rothenberg to alter radically the form and even content of the Indian originals. Much has been written about the deficiencies of such an approach (for example, William Bevis' fine article "American Indian Verse Translations"[2]) and those who have searched for texts to reach or simply to read will need few examples.

Bevis considers in detail the four-stage "development" of a Pawnee Hako ceremony song. The original was collected by Alice G. Fletcher and published in the Twenty-second Annual Report of the Bureau of American Ethnography, accompanied by a careful, word-for-word explanation of the text. (Fletcher's rather free translation, however, introduces a number of what Natalie Curtis Burlin called "hidden meanings.") The original, as translated by Bevis using Fletcher's notes, is as follows:

   I. *Ho-o-o*
     Mother earth you arise now;
     Mother earth you arise now;
     Dawn is born now;
     Mother earth you arise now.
   II. *Ho-o-o*
     Mother earth she has arisen now;
     Mother earth she has arisen now;

Dawn is born now;
Mother earth she has arisen now.

III. *Ho-o-o*
Brown Eagle you arise now;
Brown Eagle you arise now;
Dawn is born now;
Brown Eagle you arise now.

IV. *Ho-o-o*
Brown Eagle she has arisen now;
Brown Eagle she has arisen now;
Dawn is born now;
Brown Eagle she has arisen now.

V. *Ho-o-o*
Brown Eagle speaks in the lodge standing now;
Brown Eagle speaks in the lodge standing now;
Dawn is born now;
Brown Eagle speaks in the lodge standing now.

VI. *Ho-o-o*
We understand your words in the lodge now;
We understand your words in the lodge now;
Dawn is born now;
We understand your words in the lodge now.

VII. *Ho-o-o*
My son you arise now;
My son you arise now;
Dawn is born now;
My son you arise now.

VIII. *My son he has arisen now;*
My son he has arisen now;
Dawn is born now;
My son has arisen now.

Enter William Brandon, whose volume *The Magic World*[3] presents a dawn-drawn falcon of dubious parentage:

Earth our mother, breathe forth life
all night sleeping
now awaking
in the east
now see the dawn

Earth our mother, breathe and waken
leaves are stirring
all things moving
new day coming
life renewing

Eagle soaring, see the morning
see the new mysterious morning
something marvelous and sacred
though it happens every day
Dawn the child of God and Darkness

Brandon has wrenched the poem out of context and radically rearranged its content; Bevis notes that "even if the idea of light born of God and Darkness is apt, the form of its expression was destroyed. Instead of coming as a culminating shock . . . the idea should appear in the third line of each stanza ('Dawn is born now') and thus provide the assumed, secure context for the rebirth of all life and the parallel awakening of the ceremonial son (who disappeared when Brandon dropped the last two stanzas)."[4] This carnage Brandon excuses in his introduction with the dashingly negligent remark, "All that we want from any of it is the feeling of its poetry. Let the ethnologists keep the rest."

Jerome Rothenberg also comes up wanting in Bevis' evaluation, although parts of his work are both reasonably reliable translations and effective English poetry. Whatever the failings of Rothenberg's reworking from a critical standpoint, as a practical matter his "total translations" can be very useful in the classroom. Most of us who teach Native American literature find our classes filled with the scions of the white middle class, who typically have little acromatic experience. Having the class divide into groups and chant Rothenberg's versions of the Seneca *Ídos* songs, say, will hardly wing them away to the council fire, but it may give them some idea of what it means to be part of a small, coherent, esoteric group, participating in a meaningful community event.[5]

T h e		H E	H E	H H	H E	H
		H E	H E	H H	H E	H
The animals are coming by	H E	H **U H**	H E	H
n i		H E	H E	H H	H E	H
m a l s		H E	H E	H H	H E	H

Rothenberg admits to remaking the poems:

translation makes a poem in this place that's analogous in whole or in part to a poem in that place. The more the translator can perceive of the original—not only the language but, more basically perhaps, the living situation from which it comes &, very much so, the living voice of the singer—the more of it he should be able to deliver. In the same process he will be presenting something—i.e., making something present, or making something as a present—for his own time and place.[6]

Until recently, of course, Indian literature was exclusively oral—formulated, communicated, and preserved in the spoken, changed, and sung word, and that compelling quality still can be evoked by translations that fail on scholarly or critical grounds. Rothenberg intends his versions to be replications "not only of the words but of all sounds connected with the poem, including finally the music itself."[7] The language of Frank Mitchell's "Tenth Horse Song" differs from ordinary spoken Navajo by the presence of vocal ornamentation, distortion, and the prolongation of sounds, tones, and rhythms. The following sample of the Navajo song presents the text respectively as sung, as it would ordinarily be spoken, and as literally translated.[8]

Yikai hye' ne yane	*'eshikiye*	*shi*	*nishliyigo 'ohye-la*
Yikai yii'naayá	*'eshkii*	*shi*	*nishłįįgo*
'Dawn within-reared	*boy*	*I*	*I-am-then*

'Esdza shiye' ehye-la	*'esdza shiye' ehye-la ŋaŋa yeye 'e*
'Esdzą́ą́ shiye'	*'esdzą́ą́ shiye'*
'The Woman, my-son	*The Woman, my-son'*

Rothenberg selects the features of nasality and repetition for emphasis in his version:

Because I was thnboyngnng raised ing the dawn NwnnN go to
  her my son N wnn N wnn N nnnn N gahn

However little they sound like the Navajo originals, Rothenberg's poems are engrossing and there is much to be gained from the excitement they generate when they are performed.

One final matter: the distinction usually carefully made in studies of Western literature between poetry and prose, no less than that between poetry and song, blurs into virtual insignificance. As Frederic Webb Hodge noted,

> *Prose rituals are always intoned, and the delivery brings out the rhythmic character of the composition. Rituals that are sung differ from those that are intoned in that the words, in order to conform to the music, are drawn out by vowel prolongations. If the music is in the form of a chant, but little adjustment is required beyond the doubling or prolongation of the vowels; but if the music is in the form of the song, the treatment of the words is more complex; the musical phrase will determine the length of a line, and the number of musical phrases in the song the number of stanzas. . . . In many of these [other, secular] songs the words are few, but they have been carefully chosen with reference to their capability of conveying the thought of the composer in a manner that, to the native's mind, will be poetic, not prosaic.[9]*

This high, oral art has dimensions that involve factors like the methods and limitations of memorization, intonation, precision, brevity, inflection, rhythm, pace, and dramatic effect. And even those pieces that most closely correspond to our Western folktales tend to be repeated with few variations from telling to telling or even teller to teller.

By way of example and conclusion, I would like to quote some rarities: recent and excellent translations of living Indian literature. The three poems quoted here are from a series called the "Wishing Bone Cycle." They were related on several occasions in virtually identical forms by Jacob Nibènegenesábe ('Slowstream') in Swampy Cree, mixed with some Anishinabe (Ojibwa). Although they are, strictly speaking, in prose (that is, they are not sung or chanted), the terseness, vivid imagery, and lack of variation from telling to telling make them more nearly equivalent to European poetry; hence the translator's choice of form. The translator, Howard Norman, learned Cree as a second language. For the first poem, I give the translator's transcription and literal translation.

koo ché ho	*I try*
púko sey eémo	*making wishes*
kwo és kun	*right way right*
se púko eme místik	*then I wished a-tree*
otitupú stáo	*upside down*
wuikwun kwasakána	*branches [turned-into]*
okapíse	*roots*
ochapikése	*roots*
akóspe unikwúchos	*then the-squirrels*
koónechemutinéswe	*[went-needing-to] ask*
nuspatiniskwe	*moles*
tannése muhukiáno	*how do we dig-travel*
pátchenetuchéwato	*down*
ewéque washkúhikun	*to [get] home*
payakwúhe nikótoo	*one-time happened*
ipoestéyek ooenetispéte	*that-way*
uyaohutáhto nikóhtoo	*[also] then there was*
kiséw	*a time*
kiskískew puyúta mosis	*I remember it [clearly]*
toník	
se púko eme tiníte	*I wished a-man'upside*
utitopu stáo	*down*
wey otúan elísheek	*his feet [turned-into] his hands*
wayoisteew otúan	
pawtawseó	
ewapun kakésa páyaw	*[and] in the-morning*
otúan muskísm	*his shoes had to ask*
koonechemutinéswe	
aka payásew	*the-birds*
tannese yasépu yehoo	*how do we fly up to [get]*
washkúhikun	*home*
payakwúhe nikótoo	*one-time happened*
ipoestéyek ooenetispéte	*that-way*

I try to make wishes right
but sometimes it doesn't work.
Once, I wished a tree upside down
and its branches
were where the roots should have been!
The squirrels had to ask the moles
"How do we get down there
to get home?"
One time it happened that way.
Then there was the time, I remember now,
I wished a man upside down
and his feet were where his hands
should have been!
In the morning his shoes
had to ask the birds
"How do we fly up there
to get home?"
One time it happened that way.

In the telling of the poem, only the intimacy varied: once Nibènegenesábe changed "a man" to "my brother." Here are two other examples of these striking translations.

Over there is a cave I wished up.
Some darkness goes in and lives there.
Some water goes in.
Some blind animals go in.
And the darkness and the water
and the blind animals
never steal from each other.
Where would they put what they stole?
The darkness couldn't find it.
The water would drown it.
The blind animals might put it
in the wrong place
and it would get lost or drown.

*   *   *   *

A snake lost his eyes once.
Don't blame this one on me!
It was the snowy owl.
He was playing the moon.
That owl closed his eyes
and sat in the fog tree
with his white face.
The snake looked up through the fog

and saw that round face
and said "Moon, show me a meal!"
Then that moon came down and took his eyes.

The final narrative of the cycle gathers the wishing bone together with the other bird bones and the feathers, and they all fly south for the winter. Norman comments: "The *ice trees* refers to the story of what happens, according to the Cree, to the trees in winter. It is believed that the trees turn to ice in the winter. Then in spring they all turn back into trees, except for one. This one tree melts into the water that will provide nourishment for all the new-born of the earth."

"I see you bird bones!
You better get up and back together!
Where are the feathers?
It's cold and my teeth are rattling
the rest of me.
The ice trees are coming
and the weasel has his snow
all over him already!"
I said this at the beginning of winter.
I found those other bones lying there
and leaped in with them.
Then we went looking for the feathers.
I had my sack of old wishes with me.
Then, we found the feathers.
They were on a little tree
that had no leaves, and trying
to make it fly!
Ha! They thought those twigs were bones!
Then all the feathers leaped on us
and we flew south. This is what happened.
This is how I went to make wishes somewhere else.
I brought my sack of old wishes with me.[10]

The problems confronting the translator (and reader) of Native American literature are immense. The history of European-Indian relations has obscured many original Indian values and attitudes and has substituted a set of simplistic and unreal Anglo attitudes that translators must transcend, both for themselves and for their audiences. But the peoples of Native America have not vanished, and in general their societies still maintain their unique character, whatever superficial changes might have occurred. Culture, those elements of belief and action shared by a community, dies hard and is seldom destroyed by mere material alterations (Navajo culture has no more been destroyed by the pickup truck than it was by the horse three centuries earlier). Even when Native Americans like James Welsh, Leslie Silko, and Simon Ortiz create word-art on European models, in English, their creations can illuminate a distinctively Indian world; it must be no less true with translations. But the linguistic differences posed by widely divergent languages and the particular psycho-logical character of Indian cultures, the elliptical austerity of a closely-shared world-view and the natural refinement, complexity, and reserve of highly-developed art forms—all make access to the traditional world of the Native American difficult. Nonetheless, good translation, faithful to the original and moving in the result, is possible, as demonstrated by Howard Norman's *Wishing Bone Cycle* and Dennis Tedlock's *Finding the Center: Narrative Poetry of the Zuni Indians.*[11] The effort required is great but clearly worth it. For the state of human *being* is an idea, an idea we have of ourselves. Only when we are embodied in an idea and the idea is realized, as in language, can we take possession of ourselves. We then comprehend our humanity most fully in such art, and traditional art becomes the moral summation of its people.

NOTES

This essay is reprinted, with modifications, from *Shantih: A Journal of International Writing and Art: Native American Issue,* eds. Brian Swann and Roberta Hill, vol. 4, no. 2 (1979), pp. 5–9. Earlier versions of this article appeared as "Traditional Native American Literature: The Problems of Translation," *ASAIL Newsletter,* March 1975, pp. 2–5, and as "Problems of Translation," ERIC Document ED 102 585 (abstract published in *Resources in Education* 10, no. 7 [July 1975]: 47).

[1]Roy Harvey Pearce, *Savagism and Civilization* (Baltimore: Johns Hopkins Univ. Press, 1965), p. 49.

[2]William Bevis, "American Indian Verse Translations," *College English* 35 (March 1974): 693–703.

[3]William Brandon, ed., *The Magic World: American Indian Songs and Poems* (New York: William Morrow, 1971), p. 68. Bevis's third line alters Brandon's "awaking" to "awakening," and his thirteenth, "marvelous" to "marvellous."

[4]Bevis, "American Indian Verse Translations," p. 697.

[5]Jerome Rothenberg, ed. and trans., *Shaking the Pumpkin: Traditional Poetry of the Indian North Americas* (Garden City, N.Y.: Doubleday, 1972), p. 16.

[6]Jerome Rothenberg, "Total Translation," *Stony Brook* 3/4 (1969): 301.

[7]Ibid., p. 293.

[8]David P. McAllester, "The Tenth Horse Song [of Frank Mitchell]," *Stony Brook* 3/4 (1969): 311.

[9]Frederic Webb Hodge, *Handbook of the American Indians North of Mexico,* Bureau of American Ethnography, Bulletin no. 30, (Washington, D.C.: Bureau of American Ethnography, 1907).

[10]Sixteen poems of the cycle appeared in *Alcheringa* 5 (1973): 112–19; most were reprinted, slightly altered, with many others in Norman's *Wishing Bone Cycle: Narrative Poems from the Swampy Cree Indians* (New York: Stonehill [Farrar, Straus & Giroux], 1976).

[11]*Finding the Center* (New York: Dial, 1972; rpr., Lincoln: University of Nebraska Press, 1979).

Karl Kroeber: THE WOLF COMES: INDIAN POETRY AND LINGUISTIC CRITICISM

There never has been such a thing as "Indian" poetry in North America: there were, and are, different kinds of poetry created by different Indian peoples. I use the term "Indian poetry" to stand for a diversity of traditional North American Indian poems, because all Native American poetry is radically different from Western European poetry. The contrast presents an opportunity to examine the foundations of our critical procedures. Most contemporary theorists claim, explicitly or implicitly, universal validity for their hypotheses about the nature of poetics. An obvious test of such universality is provided by poetry at least superficially antithetical to ours. Thus:

> *Waila yawixne*
> *Waila yawixne*
> *Waila yawixne*
> *Wine nisu*
> *Wax metu weineke*
> *Awitsnatsaka*
> *Hila yawixne*
> *Waila yawixne*
> *Eha yawixne*
> *Waila yawixne*[1]

I try in this essay to explain how this Nez Percé song is in part amenable to, and in part resistive to, linguistic principles we perceive as essential to poetic art. I leave to another occasion the problems of whether or not the evidence of Indian literatures supports our faith in the universality of certain psychological and aesthetic archetypes.

Even without knowledge of the Nez Percé language, one is bound to wonder if the few words above can possess irony, ambiguity, metaphoric originality, or any of the characteristics our commentators regard as necessary to a poetic use of language. For the moment, however, let us attend only to the most obvious feature of the song, its frequent repetitions, apparent even without translation. Repetition, characteristic of virtually all Indian poetry, is a feature little noticed by our criticism because it is a minor element in our poetry. But repetition has been scrutinized by those searching for linguistic principles underlying literary poetics—above all by Roman Jakobson, the most celebrated linguist of the past generation. One of his essays in particular, "Linguistics and Poetics," has been repeatedly cited as defining central linguistic presuppositions upon which modern criticism must be based.[2] His schematization there of "factors inalienably involved in verbal communication" (p. 353) has been widely reproduced and has served as a model for aestheticians as diverse as Ricoeur, Jameson, Hernadi, and Lodge.[3]

In communication according to Jakobson (p. 353)

> *The* addresser *sends a* message *to the* addressee. . . . *the message requires a* context *referred to. . . . seizable by the addressee, . . . either verbal or capable of being verbalized;* a code . . . *common to the addresser and addressee; and, finally,* a contact, *a physical channel and psychological connection between the addresser and addressee enabling . . . them to enter and stay in communication. All . . . factors involved in verbal communication may be schematized as follows:*

$$\text{context}$$

$$addresser–-–-–\frac{message}{contact}–-–-–addressee$$

$$code$$

The nature of any communication is determined by which of these six fundamental elements is emphasized. Emphasis on addressee makes for "imperative" communication, whereas focus on the addresser makes for "expressive" or "emotive" communication, and "focus on the message for its own sake" establishes "the *poetic* function of language" (p. 356). From this scheme Jakobson develops a more precise definition of "poetic function, the essential characteristic of *all* poetry, *poeticité.*[4]

> *What is the empirical linguistic criterion of the poetic function? In particular, what is the indispensable feature in any piece of poetry? To answer this question we must reall the two basic modes of arrangement used in verbal behaviour,* selection and combination. . . . *chosen words combine in the speech chain. The selection is produced on the base of equivalence, similarity, and dissimilarity, synonymity and antonymity, while the combination, the build up of the sequence, is based on contiguity.* The poetic function projects the principle of equivalence from the axis of selection into the axis of combination. *Equivalence is promoted to the constitutive device of the sequence.* [p. 358]

The hazard in such bold reductionism is illustrated later in the essay, where we read:

> *In poetry not only the phonological sequence but in the same way any sequence of semantic units strives to build an equation.* [p. 370]

None of the many scholars who have based their work on Jakobson's article appear to have noticed that this statement contradicts his heavily emphasized earlier distinction:

> *Poetry and metalanguage, however, are in diametrical opposition to each other: in metalanguage the sequence is used to build an equation, where in poetry the equation is used to build a sequence.* [p. 358]

One reason for the contradiction (and for later critics overlooking it) is readily discernible. Jakobson wants to distinguish poetry from metalanguage, language about language, but the probability of confusing them is high because he so rigidly separates *message* from *context* and has little concern for the function of *contact*. Insisting that the "poetic function" is "focus on the message for its own sake," and condemning any linking of it to its referent, that is, condemning concern with the "object language" of the message, Jakobson is inevitably drawn toward describing poetry as a form of metalanguage, even though that is not his intention.

Because he does not believe that a poet is deeply involved with matters of contact and context (though poets in oral cultures must be so involved), Jakobson goes on to distinguish poetry from prose by identifying the former with metaphor, which is "original" and relatively detached from ordinary uses of language, and the latter with metonymy, which is closer to "practical" language references. Jakobson's purpose is to deny the importance of referentiality in poetry. To prose, however, he must allow considerable referentiality, and therefore "the prosaic variety of verbal art" must present "more entangled problems for poetics, as does any transitional linguistic area." Prosaic art makes "the translation . . . between strictly poetic and strictly referential language" (p. 374). But, to the detriment of logical consistency,

> *the same linguistic methodology, which poetics use when analyzing the metaphorical style of romantic poetry, is entirely applicable to the metonymical texture of realistic prose.* [p. 375]

This fuzziness in Jakobson's discussion of prosaic art is inevitable, because he locates it on an uncalibrated spectrum only limited by polar opposition between "poetic" and "referential" language. This conceptual antithesis is deeply rooted in modern critical thinking. Whether or not they follow I. A. Richards in dividing "emotive" from "scientific" language, modern critics define *poeticité* in contrast to "ordinary" or "practical," that is, referential uses. And this critical practice reflects a central distinguishing feature of modern Western poetry, its aesthetic self-sufficiency. Jakobson's scheme, then, is not eccentric: its difficulties, especially those arising from making metaphor the key to poetry and defining metaphor in opposition to metonymy carries us into the heart of modernist poetry and poetics.

Yet Jakobson's principles are useful for understanding Indian poetry/song. No other theoretical enunciation so precisely explains why the Nez Percé song I quoted above is a poetical work. If poetry is "projecting the principle of equivalence from the axis of selection into the axis of combination," the Nez Percé song is pure poetry, because its different phrases all mean the same thing: "the wolf comes." So far as the Indian song is exactly repetitious, the "principle of equivalence" from the axis of selection subsumes the axis of combination. Repetition, a primary characteristic of Indian song, is in fact an important if little noticed feature in the process which Jakobson sees as distinguishing poetic utterance. And herein would lie an explanation for the powerful effect of very slight variations in Indian poetry unsupported by effects of metaphor or ambiguity. So as not to stress too much the Nez Percé song, which is of interest so far as it is representative, I'll illustrate with other examples, first the translation of a Wintu song.

> *Down west, down west we dance,*
> *We spirits dance,*
> *Down west, down west we dance,*
> *We spirits dance,*
> *Down west, down west we dance,*
> *We spirits weeping dance,*
> *We spirits dance.*[5]

If we assume the English lexical items accurately reflect Wintu originals, the poem can be seen to consist of just four elements "down west" (land of the dead), "spirits," "we dance," and "weeping," the final item appearing only once as a combined formal/emotional linchpin of the song. But the structure that "weeping" holds together is constituted of what I call superimposed repetitions. Not only are the words reiterated, but the singing dancers perform, literally enact, the words, being "spirits" who dance.

Jakobson's perception that variation *per se* is not the essential feature of poetic art (but, instead, indicates the primacy of the superinduction of the axis of selection upon the axis of combination) can be illustrated not only by particular Indian songs but also by the function of songs in large, complex ceremonies. A song from the lovely Pawnee *Hako* ceremony makes the point clear.

> *Hoòòò!*
> *H'Opirit rira risha* [repeated four times]
> *Hoòòò!*
> *H'Opirit ta ahrisha* [repeated four times]
> *Hoòòò!*
> *Reshuru rira risha* [repeated four times]
> *Hoòòò!*
> *Reshuru ta ahrisha* [repeated four times]

The first line after the invocative Hoòòò means "Morning Star breathing life approaches from far, vanishing and reappearing," the second, "Morning Star breathing life approaches nearer but his brilliance fades," the last two lines being identical except for substituting "Dawn" for "Morning star."[6] The repetition within this song which is sung while the celestial morning star actually fades into the light of dawn, and then dawn, in turn, fades into daylight, microcosmically repeats the function of the song as a whole in the total macrocosm of the ceremony, in which it is repeated four times. Phrases, words, even sounds, furthermore, are systematically repeated in other songs, so that the entire ceremony, which involves scores of people travelling many miles and singing more than a hundred songs, is structured by diversely reiterated superimpositions of selection upon combination. The range is from phonemic patterns to choreographic movements of large groups of participants. The climactic song of the ceremony, in which a child is blessed some days after the first singing of the Morning Star-Dawn song, reproduces some of its sounds (as well as those from other songs) in an eight-times repeated, highly condensed lyric.

> *Hoòòò!*
> *H'I re ra!*
> *H'I re ra!*
> *Pira uta hao!*
> *Ira uta, uta hao!*

The basic meaning is that the principal divinity ("Tirawa" here represented by "I") "breathing life comes from far—let this child be fully his."[7] The internal reiterations and their relation to the song quoted above are apparent even without translation or description of the ceremony.

The ceremonial context of the *Hako* songs does raise a question to which Jakobson (like other linguistic critics) directs little attention: *why* does poetry operate by projecting the principle of equivalence from the axis of selection to the axis of combination? If we can avoid the temptation to leap to specific anthropological explanations, the Indian poems may help us to an answer more readily than our own lyrics. The singer of the Wintu poem (which follows a patterning of "lines" common to many Wintu songs) explained it by telling how shortly after her best friend had died, that friend returned in a dream in company with other female spirits, weeping, dancing, and singing this song, which was then sung and danced publically. One notices a conjunction of the intensely personal and private with formal, social, public performance. The song is not merely "about" the singer's dream, it is part of the dream itself, a dream of the loss of the singer's dearest personal relation. Yet formally everything adheres to Wintu cultural patterning, the dancing, the form of the song, the special meaning of certain words, "down west" = "land of the dead." Even the singer's making her dream of private grief public fulfills Wintu custom.[8] The poem is an integration of personal psychology and cultural ordering.

Hence the essential tension in the poem is formal rather than substantive: the Wintu singer in no sense questions her culture, or sets up an opposition between herself and her society, as a modern, self-conscious Western poet usually does. The tension in the Indian poem is at a deeper level—in the poetic process itself as defined by Jakobson. Selection, as he indicates, is choice of the individual, and, speaking broadly, combination derives from the rule-system of the language. One can treat the axis of selection as a personal dimension, equivalent to Saussure's *parole,* projected upon the axis of combination, the cultural or social dimension, equivalent to Saussure's *langue.* The Indian song allows us to perceive the inherent tension of this "speaking situation," because in the song both parts of the dialectic are necessary. The potency of utterance of loss is dependent upon prescribed cultural forms. These, in turn, are effectively, that is, affectively, realized in the individual act of superinduction.

But even as Indian poems reveal the utility of Jakobson's analysis, they illuminate some of its limitations, indeed, call into doubt many verbal and rhetorical features today assumed to be essential to *poeticité.* The repetition of Indian song supports the idea of a promotion of the axis of selection but would seem to preclude, for example, the kind of ambiguity and irony we conceive of as indispensable in poetry. More complicated and more fundamental is the question of metaphor, which for Jakobson, as for many modern theorists, principally discriminates poetic language from prosaic. Extensive repetition would seem to run counter to any high valuation of vivid, original metaphor. The first fact to notice in facing this question is that, unlike Jakobson, Indians *never* define poetry against prose. Traditional Indian poetry was sung, was language conjoined to music. And "prose" in our sense, Dennis Tedlock has argued, is unknown in oral cultures, is a "modern," post-writing invention.[9] Even if we don't go so far as Tedlock, we must recognize that oral cultures do not operate by polarizing "prose" and "poetry." We may, then, hypothesize that the vivid, original metaphors characteristic of Western poetry are not essential to all poetry, just as our prosaic art is more nearly unique than universal.

To reverse Tedlock's argument, let us observe how rare in any form of Indian literature are metaphoric figures, similes, for instance, being so unusual as at times to be touchstones for an inaccurate translation, e.g., Cushing's Zuni tales. This absence would be less important did we still accept the traditional idea of metaphor, originating with Aristotle, which classifies metaphor as a verbal trope of condensed comparison, as Ricoeur puts it, "the application to one thing of a name belonging to something else."[10] But modern aestheticians, beginning with I. A. Richards, have rejected this "ornamental" concept, metaphor as merely the pleasing substitution of a figurative term for a more literal one. Since Richards, the prevailing view has been that metaphor is a tension between apparent incompatibilities. Kenneth Burke, for example, although beginning with language close to Aristotle's (metaphor is "a device for seeing something in terms of something else"), transforms the old idea by observing that "to consider A from the point of view of B is, of course, to use B as a *perspective* upon A."[11] Burke's position has been supported and refined by subsequent thinkers to the point where his perspective has become *model.* Thus Gilbert Ryle in *The Concept of Mind* says that metaphor "represents the facts . . . as if they belonged to one logical type or category (or range of types or categories) when they actually belong to another." And Colin Turbayne, in his famous analysis emphasizing the consciousness involved in the metaphoric process, stresses that "the use of metaphor involves the pretense that something is the case when it is not," and that in making metaphor "we are aware, first, that we are sort-crossing, that is, re-presenting the fact of one sort in the idiom appropriate to another . . . secondly, that we are treating the world and man as if they belonged to new sorts." Such approaches lead naturally to Ricoeur's recent formulation that "metaphor presupposes a literal interpretation which self-destructs in a significant contradiction."[12]

The centrality of metaphor in our literature is neatly summarized by Monroe Beardsley's definition of metaphor as "a poem in miniature."[13] The implications of "miniature poem" are realized fully in Max Black's treatment of metaphor as a theoretical *model,* a heuristic fiction which can "reveal new relationships." And Black has illustrated how such models function by means of what has become a traditional exemplification, happily appropriate to the Nez Percé song: "man is a wolf."

> *The effect, then, of (metaphorically) calling a man a 'wolf' is to evoke the wolf-system of related commonplaces. If the man is a wolf, he preys upon other animals, is fierce, hungry, engaged in constant struggle, a scavenger, and so on . . . Any human traits that can without undue strain be talked about in 'wolf-language' will be rendered prominent and any that cannot will be pushed into the background.*[14]

Black's carefully logical prose reveals his lack of interest in real wolves, his indifference to any actual experience of a wolf. And his intellectual detachment illustrates the irony that modern analysts, though discarding the old "ornamental" concept of metaphor, more decisively than the ornamentalists separate metaphor from referential functions. Like most contemporary theoreticians, Black is more comfortable with an example that is a verbal and philosophic cliché than with an original metaphor. For if poems are self-sufficient, if poetry is language ordered artistically by being deployed non-referentially, the efficacy of poetic metaphor will indeed be difficult to analyze. The self-sufficient poem, by definition, attempts to stand clear of context-contact, and metaphor is "a poem in miniature." But need all poetry be self-sufficient? As I've pointed out, a discrimination of prose from poetry, the literary base for Jakobson's metaphor-metonymy distinction, becomes questionable when tested against American Indian art.[15] And does not the very concept of metaphor as model, as heuristic fiction in our jargon, imply a function for poems quite different from that we observe in Pawnee, Wintu, and Nez Percé dramatic songs? Let us at least consider the possibility that the paucity of vivid, original metaphors in American Indian poetry may indicate that such metaphors, so characteristic of Western poetic art, *substitute* for efficacies of another kind in other cultures.

Pursuit of this hypothesis at least forces one to rethink our usual terminology of linguistics and rhetoric. Most Indian poetry appears to be built more upon a form of metonymy, synecdoche, than upon metaphor. A popular song of seventy years ago derived from an Ojibwa song illustrates how an Indian poet could work by synecdochic omission instead of by inventing metaphors. First, the words that delighted some of our grandparents:

> *In the still night, the long hours through,*
> *I guide my bark canoe,*

My bark canoe, my love, to you.
While stars shine and falls the dew,
I seek my love in bark canoe,
In bark canoe, I seek for you.
It is I, love, your lover true,
Who glides the stream in bark canoe;
It glides to you, my love, to you.[16]

The sins of whites against the red man are many, but in this case the translator, Frederick Burton, felt cheated when he had a literal version of the song given him, for he'd been told it meant "I am out all night on the river seeking for my sweetheart." The literal transcription ran:

Chekabey	*Throughout*
tebik	*night*
ondandeyan	*I keep awake*
chekabey	*throughout*
tebik	*night*
ondandeyan	*I keep awake*
ahgahmah-sibi	*upon a river*
ondandeyan	*I keep awake*

Burton wanted to know what had happened to the sweetheart. She is not there, his informant replied, explaining the significance of *ondandeyan* occurring three times.

That mean, he said, I keep awake. I get tired, yes, and sleepy, but I no sleep. I keep awake. That word (tebik) is night. Now you see. Why does a man keep awake all night when he want to sleep? . . . Only one reason. I go to find my sweetheart. The words is not there but we understand it. We know what is meant . . . we know that the man who made this song was looking for his sweetheart, and we do not need the word there.

Burton concluded that Ojibwa songs were never "complete in themselves," each depending "upon something external, a story or ceremony." Comparing his own compositions to those of the Ojibwa, he decided the Indian song had to be defined as a "mnemonic summary," in other words, as a synecdoche.[17] A Papago phrased it better: "the song is very short because we understand so much."[18]

Scholars have come to equivalent recognitions. Paul Radin, speaking of the active engagement of "primitive" audiences in performances, observes that "there are no 'illiterate' nor ignorant individuals." Every member of "an audience . . . comes prepared."[19] Of what that preparation for participation consists is illustrated by the ease with which Burton's informant moves in his interpretation from third person to first person singular, back to third person, and finally to first person plural. The informant's perception that the song is inseparable from the facts of Ojibwa courtship is no sign of aesthetic impoverishment. Rather, the song's synecdochic character shows why there is no *need* for striking metaphors, which would in fact impede the participative communication between audience and anonymous composer. The synecdochic character of Indian song affirms the total group, tribe or nation as the appropriate "audience" for each individual as poet-singer. Poetic utterance articulates what the individual *shares* with his social group—which may well be, among Plains Indians, for example, a determined insistence upon the integrity of each member's individuality. But such articulation precludes the pretend, sort-crossing, metaphor-as-model art described by aestheticians, who, significantly, refer to poems as *texts*. Because an Indian poem exists as a socio-cultural synecdoche, performance is essential to its form. All Indian poems, as I've said, are songs, and most are integral to a "ceremonial situation," sometimes religious, sometimes secular, sometimes highly formalized, sometimes quite "open." But always the Indian poem exists as utterance. It never exists as text, only as act. To make clear the importance of this apparently trivial distinction, I'll try to return the Nez Percé song to something like the context from which I have so far isolated it.

The song was performed in the Guardian Spirit Dance, *Weékwetset,* literally "Dance of the Dream Faith," a winter ceremonial, among the most religious of the Nez Percé, in which individuals performed in honor of their special guardian spirits. The variations upon the core meaning "the wolf comes" are in part concealments, because a song such as this was private, its full meaning known perhaps only to the singer, for the songs were either inherited or obtained through sacred vision. One mode of concealment, guaranteed to drive a translator mad, was through the use of special rather than everyday names for animals, in this case a disguising probably of *himim,* "wolf."[20] The singer would begin his song with an accompanying dance by himself, then others would take up his words and join in the singing. Those who had not had success in obtaining their own vision could not sing as individuals, but they could join in such a chorus. The singer/dancer was usually costumed, with his body painted to indicate in stylized fashion the sacred animal of his song. His dance would mimic the animal through bodily movements and appropriate sounds. Sometimes this dramatizing extended to concealed bladders filled with blood, broken to show wounds. Sometimes the violence of the performance would bring the singer/dancer to a state of physical collapse. Often, too, several dancers would cooperate to make the representation more realistic—in "The Wolf Comes" the lead dancer might be joined by others, since wolves hunt in packs.

The ceremonial dramatization I have just sketched is, in fact, an artistic macro-structure corresponding to the verbal microstructure described by Jakobson. The dramatic performance of "The Wolf Comes" is a supervention of the "axis of selection," the individual dream, heritage, identity, upon the "axis of combination," the Guardian Spirit dance-ceremony which re-affirms the ritualized forms expressive of Nez Percé culture. As in the Pawnee *Hako,* wherein the ceremony depends on, indeed, *is,* a linking of minute units of language, even phonemes, to the total shape of an extended and complicated tribal ritual journey, so the "Dance of the Dream Faith" unifies the many diverse identities of the dancers without obliterating, to the contrary, affirming dramatically, the integrity of each as an individual unique by heritage, private vision, and personal exploit.

Exactly the same pattern can be observed in the Wintu dramatic performance of "Down West." But our terms such as "dramatic" and "performance" may obscure what they are intended to clarify because for us they imply contrast to the "real."[21] For Indians, there was immediate, practical, continuous back-and-forth flow and interpenetration of actuality and representation of actuality. The interpenetration appears in the "ceremonious" fashion in which Indians perform many acts we perform casually or in a routinized manner. And their formalized ceremonials tend to be folded into the processes of "real" phenomena. Song and dance, as in our Nez Percé example, frequently contain strong elements of mimicry, or literally utilize actuality, as in the *Hako* song performed at the fading of the morning star into the light of dawn, or as in the Wintu dance/song the women and her companions *become* the singing/dancing spirits. Ceremonies are physically continuous with both personal and tribal existence, "realizing" rather than "standing for" the actualities they celebrate. Indian "drama" cannot be separated from Indian "non-dramatized" life. "Performance" of the Nez Percé song is a focal point in the individual's life, even as the whole ceremony is focal for tribal life. In our terms, the individual is synecdochic of tribe and his performance is synecdochic of its culture.

A tribal ceremony's meaning, for both individual and tribe, consists in its practical contribution to the on-going continuity of personal/tribal existence. As one must understand "The Wolf Comes" in the context of its performance in the "Dance of the Dream Faith," so one must understand this ceremony in the context of the continuity of Nez Percé's society's "performance." Perhaps I can sketch enough of the socio-religious aspects of this larger performance to convey a sense for the cultural values of which the ceremony is synecdochic.

Like many American Indians, the Nez Percé, a hunting and gathering rather than a farming people, lived democratically, with little hierarchical organization. Each household was the responsibility of the father; each village had a chief, who had little power, however, to settle intra-family matters. In disputes between villages, an *ad hoc* council of chiefs and elders would adjudicate. Murder of someone not a member of the tribe was not classed as a crime, but murder within the tribe required blood revenge by kin of the dead, though blood-money payment was sometimes possible, especially if the victim had been notoriously quarrelsome. A similar pattern held for adultery, the injured party being entitled to kill both man and woman, but the matter often being adjusted by adequate payment. Public contempt was the punishment for lying, the worst sin: an ultimate Nez Percé epithet of insult was "liar."

Each individual owned his own work implements and weapons and horses, and might own slaves, men and women captured in war, and usually treated with consideration. The kill of each hunter belonged to his family, except during a large communal hunt, but there was no private ownership of land. Inheritance, through the male line, included songs and names, and personal property was distributed according to the wishes of the deceased at a funeral feast. There were not a large number of rites, and few were elaborate. Women lived separately during menstrual periods and pregnancy. There were no special birth or puberty ceremonies. The

Nez Percé had no cosmogonic myths but some animistic beliefs in spirits, both good and bad, and liked fetishes and good-luck pieces, stones, bear claws, wolf's teeth, usually worn around the neck.

Major festivals and ceremonies were usually intertribal, with certain localities used as traditional meeting places. One dance ceremony was performed by a special company, to which admission was obtained only by inheritance or special dream. There were war and scalp dances, but the most important was the "Dance of the Dream Faith" in celebration of guardian spirits associated with the sacred vigil, probably the fundamental Nez Percé socio-religious rite. At about age ten a child (boys and girls alike) went into the mountains to fast, usually for five days. If an animal appeared in a dream during this vigil its name was adopted as the child's sacred name, and it became the child's guardian spirit for life.

The child went alone to one of the high peaks and there heaped up a pile of stones next to which he seated himself. He took no food or drink and kept awake as much as possible. After three or four days an animal might appear in a vision, give him a name, and teach him a sacred song. Many failed to have a vision, and they were regarded as unfortunate and seldom became influential adults. The child told no one of the result of his vigil on his return; the first time any had a chance to guess the nature of his guardian spirit was when the child sang a new song at the next Guardian Spirit dance. Although friendship often sprang up between those who shared the same guardian spirit, no special groupings or societies were formed around it: the primary significance of the vision remained individual. Yet sacred names and songs obtained in a fasting vigil were inheritable, so some had a right to perform as many as a dozen songs at a ceremony, whereas others had no right to any of their own.[22]

Despite its superficiality, this sketch may suggest the remoteness from physical realities of Professor Black in his discussion of "man is a wolf." Black's rationalistic style, his concentration on the verbal as verbal, his insistent intellectual analysis are representative of the mode of modern criticism. And this style and focus of interest reflects that commitment to self-referentiality of poetic language which is fundamental to Jakobson's linguistic schematization. Surely Black, Jakobson, and other theoreticians are responding to the thrust of modernist poetry, which has intensified the Western emphasis upon the isolated quality of the literary artifact. The Nez Percé singer/dancer, to the contrary, realizes "wolf" in his performance because he has seen and heard wolves in the wild and he has been visited by one in a vision. His language and experiences (physical and spiritual) totally interact. His vision, moreover, occurred spontaneously within a situation culturally structured, thus confirming a religious sanction of the firm yet fluid and unhierarchic yet discriminating social mores of the Nez Percé, which I so roughly outlined above. Given this contrast between poem as isolated artifact and poem as means by which energizing power flows between man and world, divine and natural, individual and cultural community, it does not seem unreasonable to suggest that the vivid, original metaphor crucial to our poetry, and central to our critical theorizing, may not be essential to *poeticité*, but may be a phenomenon of our culture. Our poetic metaphor, specifically, may be a verbal substitute for a vanished socio-cultural efficacy directly operative in traditional American Indian songs.

NOTES

[1]Herbert Joseph Spinden, "The Nez Percé Indians," *Memoirs of the American Anthropological Association,* vol. 2, Pt. 3 (1907–15), pp. 165–274, 263. My subsequent descriptions of the Nez Percé are drawn from this standard monograph, though I have used other sources, such as G. L. Coale, "Notes on the Guardian Spirit Concept Among the Nez Percé," *Internationales Archiv für Ethnographie* 48 (1958): 135–48, D. R. Skeels, "The Function of Humor in Three Nez Percé Indian Myths," *American Imago* 11 (1954): 248–61, as well as material cited below. For purposes of this essay I accept Spinden's translation, although I hope elsewhere to discuss some issues it poses. Various kinds of translating problems are discussed in the volume *Traditional Literatures of the American Indian* which I edited for the University of Nebraska Press (Lincoln:, Nebr., 1981). Before we try to deal with the translation difficulties of American Indian literatures we must deal with the problems in poetics they bring forward. Because usually we've had the translation cart before the poetic horse, we've not used Indian literatures as we might to challenge our critical/linguistic assumptions, which in effect relegate such literature to second-class aesthetic status. I'd prefer to present the Nez Percé wolf song without any translation; those interested in its complexities might begin with Haruo Aoki's *Nez Percé Grammar* (Berkeley: Univ. of California Press, 1970), though Aoki's mode of presentation is difficult for the non-specialist, and (far more fascinating) the interlinear translations of Archie Phinney (himself a Nez Perce) in "Nez Percé Texts," *Columbia University Contributions to Anthropology* 25 (New York: Columbia University Press, 1934). Two recent essays of mine deal with psychological and aesthetic structurings, here slighted for emphasis on metaphor: "Poem, Dream, and the Consuming of Culture," *The Georgia Review* 32, no. 2 (1971): 266–80 (reprinted in this volume), and "Deconstructionist Criticism and American Indian Literatures," *Boundary 2,* 7, no. 3 (1979): 73–89.

[2]The essay is one of the "closing statements" from a conference at Indiana University in 1958 in *Style in Language,* ed. Thomas A. Sebeok (Cambridge, Mass: M.I.T. Press, 1960), pp. 350–77. Quotations from it in this essay are hereafter cited by page number in the text.

[3]Paul Hernadi, "Literary Theory: A Compass for Critics," *Critical Inquiry* 3 (1976): 369–86; Frederick Jameson, *The Prison House of Language* (Princeton: Princeton University Press, 1972), pp. 202–03 and pp. 122–23 on Jakobson's "influential theory of the opposition of metaphor to metonymy." The latter is the focus for David Lodge's essay, "Metaphor and Metonymy in Modern Fiction," *Critical Quarterly* 17 (1975): 75–93, subsequently expanded in *The Modes of Modern Writing* (London: Arnold, 1977). Paul Ricoeur, of course, frequently has utilized Jakobson's work: in the recent *Interpretation Theory: Discourse and the Surplus of Meaning* (Fort Worth: Texas Christian University Press, 1976), Ricoeur bases his analysis on the "schema of communication described by Roman Jakobson in his famous article" (p. 26). A careful evaluation of the presuppositions underlying structuralist/formalist criticism

will be found in Mary Louise Pratt, *Toward a Speech Act Theory of Literary Discourse* (Bloomington: Indiana University Press, 1977), with an analysis of Jakobson's essay on pp. 29–37.

[4]The term is emphasized in Jakobson's "Qu'est-ce que la poésie?" *Poétique* 7 (1971): 299–309, esp. 307. This essay derives from Jakobson's "Poetry of Grammar and Grammar of Poetry," *Lingua* 21 (1968): 597–609, the English version of an earlier article.

[5]D. Demetracopoulou, "Wintu Songs," *Anthropos* 30 (1935): 483–94. Ms. Demetracopoulou does not provide original texts, but her knowledge of Wintu linguistic and artistic forms seems extensive.

[6]Alice C. Fletcher, "The Hako: A Pawnee Ceremony", *Annual Report of the Bureau of American Ethnology* 22, pt. 2 (Washington, D.C., 1904): 128, where the music is also transcribed; analysis of the song runs through p. 130.

[7]Ibid., pp. 257–59.

[8]Demetracopoulou, "Wintu Songs," pp. 484, 489.

[9]Dennis Tedlock, "On the Translation of Style in Oral Narrative," *Journal of American Folklore* 64 (1971): 114–33 (reprinted in this volume).

[10]Ricoeur, *Interpretation Theory,* p. 47.

[11]Kenneth Burke, *A Grammar of Motives,* (New York: Prentice-Hall, 1945), pp. 503–04.

[12]Gilbert Ryle, *The Concept of Mind,* (New York: Barnes and Noble, 1949), p. 16; Colin Turbayne, *The Myth of Metaphor* (Columbia: University of South Carolina Press, 1970), pp. 13, 17; Ricoeur, *Interpretation*, p. 50.

[13]Monroe Beardsley, *Aesthetics* (New York: Harcourt, Brace, 1958), p. 134. See the same writer's excellent "Metaphor" in the *Encyclopedia of Philosophy,* ed. Paul Edwards (New York: Macmillan, 1967), vol. 5, pp. 284–89. For recent considerations one may consult with profit the collection of essays in *Critical Inquiry* 5:1 (Autumn, 1978), *Metaphor: The Conceptual Leap.* Among these perhaps the most relevant to my discussion is Donald Davison's challenging "What Metaphors Mean," pp. 31–48.

[14]Max Black, *Models and Metaphors* (Ithaca: Cornell University Press, 1962), p. 46.

[15]The foundation for the distinction is described in the chapter "Two Aspects of Language and Two Types of Aphasic Disturbances," Roman Jakobson and Morris Halle, *Fundamentals of Language* (Mouton: the Hague, 1956), pp. 55–82.

[16]The song was composed by Frederick R. Burton, from whose amusing but perceptive account of its origin I quote original song, translations, and the informant's commentary: *American Primitive Music* (New York: Moffat, 1909), pp. 149–63.

[17]Burton, *American Primitive Music,* p. 162. He goes on to distinguish the Indians' literary art by observing: "our poetry is or aims to be self-dependent; our songs are or should be complete in themselves; the Ojibwas' are consciously incomplete statements of the situation, feeling, or events which find expression through them." The self-dependence or self-sufficiency of our poetry is related to the intense subjectivity of our art. Paula Allen, herself a Native American poet and critic, has commented on a Kiowa song that its "statements are not metaphorical . . . for no Indian would take his perception to be the basic unit of consciousness in the Universe," "Symbol and Structure in Native American Literature: Some Basic Considerations," *College Communication and Composition* 24 (1973): 267–70. Ralph

Linton observed that the aim of a "primitive" artist is "to present his subject as he and his society think of it, not as he sees it." "Primitive Art" in *Every Man His Way,* ed. Alan Dundes (Englewood Cliffs: Prentice Hall, 1968), pp. 353–63, 358.

[18]Ruth Underhill, ed., *The Autobiography of a Papago Woman*, The American Anthropological Association Memoirs, vol. 46 (Menasha, 1936), p. ii.

[19]Paul Radin, "The Literature of Primitive People," *Diogenes* 12 (1955): 1–29.

[20]Spinden, "The Nez Percé Indians," p. 247. Besides changes in languages over the course of time, inaccuracy of reporters, and other peripheral difficulties in the study of Indian literatures, there is the problem of dialects, exacerbated in the present case by the possibilities for personal distortion by the performer. And what dialect is being distorted? Phinney and Aoki give the same common name for "wolf" that Spinden does, but Aoki's *teqelixnikét,* "wolf" in the special Nez Percé "mythic" vocabulary does not correspond with Spinden's. This is perhaps enough to suggest why one needs a separate essay on the translation problems of Indian songs. Larger issues involved in these problems, however, have been treated by at least two distinguished scholars. Dell Hymes during the past twenty years has contributed several major studies. Among these of special relevance to my argument I'd cite "Some North Pacific Coast Poems: A Problem in Anthropological Philology," *American Anthropologist* 67 (1965): 316–41, and "An Ethnographic Perspective," *New Literary History* 5 (1973): 187–201, and in the same journal more recently "Discovering Oral Performance and Measured Verse in American Indian Narrative," 8 (1977): 431–58. In the same issue Dennis Tedlock, whose *Finding the Center: Narrative Poetry of the Zuni Indians* (New York: Dial Press, 1972) is a landmark among studies into oral literature, provides a stimulating essay "Toward an Oral Poetics," pp. 507–19.

[21]This point is developed impressively by Wolfgang Iser, "The Reality of Fiction: A Functionalist Approach to Literature," *New Literary History* 7 (1975): 7–38, beginning with the observation that in Western criticism " 'fiction' and 'reality' have always been classified as pure opposites: (p. 7), and going on to explore the inadequacies of this polarity. Iser's ideas are given full expression in *The Act of Reading* (Baltimore and London: The Johns Hopkins University Press, 1978).

[22]Analogous vigils occurred in many tribes. The non-specialist will find authentic autobiographical accounts in Frank B. Linderman, *Plenty-Coups: Chief of the Crows* (New York: John Day, 1972 [1930]), and John G. Neihardt, *Black Elk Speaks* (New York: Pocket Books, 1972 [1932]), the latter a classic of Native American religious literature. The procedures and cultural significancies of visions and vision quests differ markedly from tribe to tribe.

Willard Gingerich: CRITICAL MODELS FOR THE STUDY OF INDIGENOUS LITERATURE: THE CASE OF NAHUATL

The study of native American texts as literature has begun to take on features of critical seriousness in North America but is still struggling to discover a critical language which can do justice to the modes of these oral indigenous texts and their derivatives. Nahuatl, the tradition with which redaction of oral indigenous literature begins in the Americas (1520s), is the primary case in point. It is surely the more ironic of the many paradoxes which abound in the history of Mexico, that the Nahuatl language texts of the 16th and 17th centuries, whose overt literary qualities have been so emphatically and continuously remarked, should continue so little analyzed and understood as literature in 1982, four full centuries after many of these texts were first redacted. Even after four centuries of critical scrutiny, some of the most basic characteristics of genre, mode, and function in 16th century Nahuatl texts have yet to be described.

My intention here is to survey, in the briefest possible fashion, the record of serious Nahuatl literary analysis (particularly the contributions of Garibay), note some current contributions, and finally to suggest some promising sources and models for the unique and culture-specific critical language which will be needed to describe adequately the Nahuatl literary legacy. I should add, for the sake of clarity, that when I say "literary texts" I refer to the entire body of 16th and 17th century written codices characterized by the figurative, repetitious, polysynthetic and often occult *tecpillatolli* style—which is itself still one of the primary mysteries of Nahuatl literature. This includes almost everything, but most particularly I have in mind all the scattered *huehuetlatolli* texts (primarily the Sahagún and Olmos collections), the narrative texts of Sahagún in their various manuscripts as well as Books I and II, the Cronica Mexicayotl, most of the Anales de Cuauhtitlan, the Leyenda de los soles, the Anales de Quauhtinchan, the Anales Historicos de la Nación Mexicana, the narrative parts of Chimalpahin, the "Conjuros" of Ruiz de Alarcón, and of course the Cantares mexicanos and the Romances de los Señores collections.

Scarcely a single clerical historian failed to make some passing comment on the metaphorical or convoluted nature of these Nahuatl texts, and the need for some "special attention" to those qualities on the part of the listener, or reader. Durán is most explicit:

All the native lays are interwoven with such obscure metaphors that there is hardly a man who can understand them unless they are studied in a very special way and explained so as to penetrate their meaning. For this reason I have intentionally set myself to listen with much attention to what is sung; and while the words and terms of the metaphors seem nonsense to me, afterward, having discussed and conferred [with the natives, I can see that] they seem to be admirable sentences, both in the divine things composed today and in the worldly songs. [Durán, p. 300]

Boturini pointed out the difficulty of explicating texts which "mystify historical facts with constant allegorizing" (in Brinton, 1887, p. 27). Carochi makes reference to the "extravagant . . . poetic dialect [of] the ancients" (Ibid., p. 29); Clavigero points out the confusing use of interjections, vocables, and meaningless syllables in these texts and called their language "pure, pleasant, brilliant, [and] figurative" (Ibid., p. 28). Brinton was of the opinion that "the Nahuatl language . . . lends itself with peculiar facility to ambiguities of expression and obscure figures of speech" (Ibid.), and Garibay who returned to these problems time and again speaks of Nahuatl literature's "impenetrable obscurity" (Garibay, 1953, p. 73), of the "exorbitant profusion" of its metaphors (Ibid., p. 76), concluding that "it is undeniable that many poems have various meanings. The supremely difficult and tentative thing is trying to determine exactly the meanings they have" (Ibid., p. 74). "A detailed study of the technique of metaphor in these poems," he notes, "would be useful to their understanding" (Ibid., p. 76)—a study, I must point out, that has still to be published, more than a quarter-century after Garibay's indication. As late as 1977, in that *tour de force* of historical analysis, *The Toltecs,* Nigel Davies laments the many episodes in the old texts "to which it is hard to attach a historical significance," episodes which are the impositions of "ancient legend . . . upon the historical record" (Davies, 1977, p. 74). But it is still Sahagún, with his sure eye for the demonic, who most emphatically strikes his own metaphor of the Nahuatl texts, and identifies the origin of their notorious obscurity:

Our Enemy [the Devil] planted in this land a forest or wilderness filled with thick underbrush from which to do his business and in which to hide himself safely, as do the wild beasts and the most dangerous serpents; . . . this forest or over-grown hill are the chants. . . . They sing to him, and without ability to understand, except for those who are natives well-versed in this language. [Garibay, 1953, p. 73]

Were it not in archaic Spanish, we might guess this was some contemporary culture-commentator lamenting the supposedly inaccessible and invidious nature of modern poetry.

In order to assist the achievement of that "special attention" Durán considered necessary for comprehension of Nahuatl literature, a number of early grammarians added commentaries on the figurative modes of the language to their works. In 1547 Father Olmos dedicated the entire 8th Chapter of the Third Part of his *Arte,* or "Grammar," to explication of what he called "The Manner of Speech of the Elders in their Ancient Discourses." Father Juan Mijangos added a translation of 195

"Phrases and Modes of Elegant Speech among the Ancient Mexicans" to his book of sermons in 1621, and Sahagún listed 83 proverbs (*tlatlatolli*), 46 conundrums (*zazanilli*), and 92 metaphors (*machiotlatolli*), with translations in Chapters 41–43 of his book of rhetorical orations.

Until the emergence of Father Garibay as a commentator on Nahuatl manuscripts around mid-century, all discussions of literary aesthetics, mode, genre, or interpretation in these texts were made by scholars for whom the problems of anthropology or history were vastly more significant than the preoccupations of literary historians or critics, and whose critical vocabulary was minimal.

Seler and his German descendents set rigorous standards for interpretive scrutiny of indigenous texts, contributed immensely to the arts of paleography and translation, and to sorting out the baroque inter-dependencies of the various 16th and 17th century clerical writings; the problems of iconography interpretation and historical veracity of the chronicles, however, greatly overshadowed their concerns for literary structure. Daniel Brinton, a personal friend of Walt Whitman, included three volumes of Nahuatl texts in his 8-volume "Library of American Aboriginal Literature," but his paleographies were distorted and his commentary on poetic structure limited to outlining some of the Nahuatl terminology referent to chant practice and its accompanying instruments (Brinton, 1887, p. 13–30). It is not altogether coincidental that Brinton, a somewhat literary anthropologist, was also emphatic in his attack on the strictly historical method; in an 1882 essay on the Quetzalcoatl-Tezcatlipoca narrative he wrote,

> *Let it be understood, hereafter that whoever uses these names in an historical sense betrays an ignorance of the subject he handles, which were it in the better known field of Aryan or Egyptian lore, would at once convict him of not meriting the name of scholar.* [Brinton, 1882, p. 35]

The effort to develop a critical vocabulary of Nahuatl literature has gone on always in the shadow of historical, anthropological, and more recently, linguistic commentary. Not that this is necessarily detrimental: anthropological linguistics especially offers new tools for developing a critical language for Nahuatl literature, and literary texts themselves, while generated by antihistorical forces, always reflect their historical contexts. But Brinton's comment, his vehemence, reflects the very secondary status of literary commentary in Nahuatl studies at the close of the 19th century, particularly in reference to narrative texts. Even as late as 1974, in his commentary on the Sahagún and Cuauhtitlan narratives of Quetzalcoatl, John Bierhorst finds it necessary to protest the "strong admixture of euhemerism" (the attribution of the origin of myth to historical men and events) which he feels characterize mid-twentieth century Mexican studies (Bierhorst, 1974, p. 77). The trouble with euhemerism for the literary scholar, of course, is that it reduces all problems of myth to questions of historical identity, and worse, directs all attention away from the texts themselves and their imaginative qualities to some vaguely conceived "real events."

Not until the work of Father Garibay do we find a serious scholar who attempts a sustained analysis of Nahuatl texts for literary quality, an attempt embodied primarily in his edition of the Los Romances Manuscript, his partial edition of the Cantares Manuscript, his edition of the 20 Hymns from the Sahagún Manuscripts, and his 2-volume *Historia de la literatura náhuatl,* the first and still only comprehensive attempt to survey all primary Nahuatl texts for their literary structure and identity. His survey of lyrical, religious, and dramatic genres of poetry focused attention on regional style names such as *otoncuicatl* (Otomi Song) and *huexotzincayotl* (in the Huexotzinco style), on functional or performance designations such as *teponazcuicatl* (hand drum song), *ahuilcuicatl* (pleasure song), and *cuecuechcuicatl* (ticklish dance song), and on the three major lyric genres: *cuauhcuicatl* (eagle songs), *xopancuicatl* (green-time songs), and *icnocuicatl* (songs of anguish). He sketched the panorama of lyric imagery and thematics, and identified four basic stylistic procedures: parallelism (in 3 patterns), the diphrase (which he claimed was unique to Nahuatl), refrain (in 3 variants), and "clasp" words. He emphasized the oral-musical character of the original text, and their associations with dance and performance, and suggested five types of metrical phrasing. He outlined fragments of "epics" and "sagas" in various manuscripts, pointing out the generic terms *xiuhtlapoalli* (the year-count), *itoloca* (things said about people), *icacoca* (spoken things); he identified the *huehuetlatolli* (discourse of the elders) as a literary genre and found fragments of a dramatic literature. His edition and commentary of the 20 Hymns from the Sahagún manuscripts added another major chapter to the on-going scrutiny of those 329 lines of hieratic, iconographic literature.

There, however, with certain brilliant exceptions, the case still rests for our generally accessible knowledge of Nahuatl literary structure, even though as Garibay himself was the first to point out, he never intended his survey of literary forms and genres to be anything more than "rudimentary" (Garibay, 1953, p. 21).

In matters of stylistics, Munro Edmonson has indicated the present need to expand Garibay's rudimentary terminology:

> *A peculiar problem is posed by the stylistic features of the more traditional texts, and particularly by what Garibay baptized* difrasimo: *the coupling of two images to suggest a third meaning. It is becoming clear that the poetic features of Nahuatl style are even more complex than Garibay believed, including not only couplet parallelism as a general feature and Garibay's binominal* difrasimo *as an embellishment, but also polynominal repetition with both semantic and poetic force.* [Edmonson, 1974, p. 12]

Father Garibay's literary survey is marred in several points by the models and critical language he draws from Classical and Romance Studies. In the attempt to define the genres of "epic" and "drama," in particular, Garibay suggests some parallels which can only throw the Nahuatl texts into a shadow. Beginning with a Sahagún comparison between Tula and Troy, he touches on the Aristotelian definition of epic, and goes on to mention Homer, the Ramayana and the Mahaparatha. He tentatively proposes trochaic tetrameter as the Nahuatl "epic meter," but then is impelled to offer four reasons why no meter at all can be found in many texts of "epic" material, finally concluding: "the Nahuatl metric had not arrived at a clear regularity such as we see in Sanscrit or Greek" (Garibay, 1953, p. 283). This cannot bode well for the Nahuatl, of course, and Garibay finds himself led time and again to refer to "fragments" and "vestiges" of epic cycles, eventually determining that

> *A rudimentary epic form has arrived to us, but of sufficient force to merit consideration. It will not sustain comparisons with Homer nor even with the Icelandic Eddas, but neither can its value, within the limits of its relativity, be denied.* [Garibay, 1953, p. 328]

For what might seem apparent reasons, therefore, Father Garibay closes with the disclaimer that this survey of the "epic" seems to him the least satisfactory chapter of his entire *Historia*. Even then he had a sense of the Nahuatl texts betrayed by inappropriate models and false formal analogies.

A similar conclusion, which I need not document here, is developed in the *Historia* for dramatic poetry. In both cases, and in various other segments of his work, Garibay falls prey to formal literary models taken from Greek, Hindu, Hebrew, Germanic, or Spanish traditions, models which pose expectations the Nahuatl texts have no chance of fulfilling and which obscure the real accomplishments of the Nahuatl artists. To discuss Ce Acatl Quetzalcoatl and Aeneas as cultural heros or ancestor figures may make clear sense, but to compare Book III of the Florentine Codex or the Annals of Cuauhtitlan to the *Aeneid* is literary folly. Which does *not* mean the Nahuatl texts cannot stand on their own merits. They are clearly evolved from a refined literary tradition whose vocabulary, mythical resources, and textual subtleties are perhaps as extensive as those of Virgil, but whose modes, intentions, functions, and formal ideals are generated from a wholly distinct aesthetic and cultural ethos. Until the unique genius of that Nahuatl tradition has been generally exposed through a sufficiently extensive, resilient, and independent critical vocabulary, the kind of conclusions which Garibay reluctantly arrives at, abounding in the terms "rudimentary," "fragmented," and "embryonic," will be inevitable.

So where are the post-Garibayan studies in modes, intentions, functions, and formal ideals of the Nahuatl literary artists and their texts coming from? As I've suggested above, with noteable exceptions, they're not. But before looking at those exceptions and then at some suggested resources that might be useful in development of a Nahuatl critical vocabulary, perhaps it would be helpful to step back for a moment and identify what exactly we mean by "literary concerns," what the basic objectives of literary scholarship are in themselves, so we can see more clearly what we still don't know about Nahuatl literature as literature.

Literary study is the analysis of any given text according to one of two foci, depending on the immediate purpose of the study. The first is to examine and describe as accurately as possible the ontology of the text itself. Since a literary text is a mental or linguistic object and does not conform in any physical sense to the shape of the oral or print medium in which it is embodied, this means apprehending fully and then describing the complete mental structure or form of a particular occasion of an extended use of language. Translated, that means literary study is an extended linguistics, the analysis and description of a large linguistic object called, for example, *Moby-Dick* rather than single words, or phrases, or sentences. When there have accumulated among us several linguistic objects of the general mental form of *Moby-Dick,* say *Lord Jim, Farewell to Arms,* and *Los de abajo,* we may advance to description of some abstract, general thing called the novel, whose formal characteristics and cultural ideals as an aesthetic mental experience we might then codify and use in turn as a basis for judgment of such new linguistic objects of that general shape as might appear among us, for example, *Cien años de soledad.* The focus of this analysis stays strictly on the text or texts in question, describing its "behavioral" features as it were, its "gestures" to use an anthropological analogy. The investigator looks carefully at all the linguistic devices by which meaning is encoded into an aesthetic artifact, into a particular, individual, and unique mental object which gives pleasure to its reader or listener and performs some social or personal function necessary to him; how its particular uses of image, metaphor, accent, tone, semantic reference and all their extended forms interact and work together to produce the style or the actuality of that particular text. The other focus of literary study—and it goes without saying that these are complementary, almost inseparable activities—is the description of meaning. What is the unique, particular, and individual knowledge or vision of things that this particular conglomeration of linguistic signs has embodied? Having carefully and precisely observed the tracks, what can we say about the animal that made them? The immediate object of this focus of study is the author's mind, whether considered as an individual system or emblematic of a socio-historical process. Both conscious and unconscious intentions and assumptions fall within the scholar's sustained attempt to determine as accurately as possible what the given text in question, as representative of the mind of its creator, actually says about reality. Questions of agreement or disagreement are extraneous, of course, to the study itself. And in the search for meaning, each reader brings his own pattern of reference to the text; in this regard literary scholars are no different from anthropologists, historians, philosophers, in their uses of Freudian, Marxist, Jungian, structuralist, millennialist, or other frames of reference.

There is a third activity that literary scholars often engage in which looks like literary analysis: the discovery of sources, the discussion of the author's biography, the exploration of social conditions in which the work was composed, all may contribute to the discovery of further subtleties of form in a work, but are in themselves more properly historical than literary investigations.

While these two foci of literary study *per se,* the description of form and the translation of that form into meaning, are always complementary, they are not reversible. The interpretation of meaning in literature is always subservient to and dependent on the identification of the text's formal elements. We cannot talk about the meaning of animalism in *King Lear* until we have discovered the chains of images that suggest it. It is precisely for this reason that the analysis of formal qualities in the Nahuatl texts must proceed if we are to deliniate further those subtleties and refinements whose presence in the Nahuatl mind we can now only infer.

There are three sources from which a critical terminology of sufficient resiliency and precision to describe Nahuatl literature justly and fairly might be generated: first and most importantly is the embedded terminology of the texts themselves; next is the growing body of performance-oriented and "ethnography of speaking" studies by U.S. anthropological linguists and ethnomusicologists; and finally the testimony of contemporary indigenous poets still in touch with whatever survives of their traditional oral modes.

In the search to uncover an indigenous Nahuatl terminology of literary form, major advances since Garibay have been made by Dr. Miguel León-Portilla, most notably in the description of a native aesthetic. Often following up suggestions Garibay left dangling, León-Portilla also has advanced our knowledge of the biographies of actual individual poets, of the roles literary artists fulfilled in Nahua society, and has refined Garibay's outlines of the philosophical dialogues suggested by the lyrical texts. His key studies for these concerns are *La filosofía náhuatl estudiada en sus fuentes, Trece poetas del mundo azteca*, and *Los antiguos mexicanos através de sus cronicas y cantares*. In spite of its promising title, *Las literatures precolombinas de México,* is only a compendium of introductory remarks and adds nothing to the critical terminology of the other works. Taking off from an appendix to Garibay's *Historia, Trece poetas* is an anthology of the historical sleuthing León-Portilla does so well: he identifies thirteen documented poets (and poetesses) of the preCortesian period, summarizes the attested biographical facts and supplies a sample of their attributed work. In 1972, quatre-centenary of the poet-King's death, León-Portilla expanded his section on Nezahualcoyotl in a separate publication, including all the poems he felt could be reliably attributed to the King. Recently he has demonstrated, from the manuscripts of Chimalpahin, that the erotic *Chalca Cihuacuicatl* (Song of the Chalcan Women) was composed by Aquiauhtzin of Amecameca, probably about 1479. But the key León-Portilla discussions for literary students are those on aesthetics, found in *Los antiguos mexicanos* and the ever-expanding *Filosofía náhuatl*. In these books Dr. León-Portilla analyzes the indigenous terms of what he believes is the old, high Toltec tradition of artistic ideal and practice. At the center of that tradition he identifies the concept of the self as *in ixtli, in yóllotl* (the face, the heart), a concept of dynamic interchange and balance between the inner forces and the exterior appearances of the individual. Closely implicated in this concept is an educational ideal identified as *yolmelahualiztli* ("the rectification of the heart") and *ixtlamachiliztli* ("the action of teaching wisdom to the face"). The supreme goal of the artist he identifies as the *yolteotl* ("the deified heart") and the artist's task as *tlayolteohuiani* ("continually putting a divine heart within things"). The true artist is he who becomes *moyolnonotzani* ("one who continually converses with his own heart"), (León-Portilla, 1961, pp. 149–50, 169–70). In fact, so essential does León-Portilla feel these concepts are for Nahuatl ethnohistory that he speaks finally of "an aesthetic conception of the universe and life," according to which beauty and truth are literally one and the same (León-Portilla, 1974, p. 322). Here León-Portilla makes his most radical and exciting contribution to the tradition of Nahuatl critical literature, a contribution which pulls literary considerations off the periphery of Nahuatl studies and plunks them down in the middle of an entire theory of Nahuatl ethnology and metaphysics. What he proposes is nothing less than that the entire Nahuatl epistemology, its basic truth-concept, rests on this aesthetic vision of reality, in which poetry is the fundamental index of man's ability to speak the truth of his existence: "There is only one way to stutter from day to day 'the truth' on this earth," says León-Portilla in his paraphrase of the Nahuatl epistemology: "It is the road of poetic inspiration: 'flower and song'. On a foundation of metaphors conceived in the deepest element of the self, or perhaps 'sent from within the heavens,' with flowers and songs [with poetry], the truth can perhaps in some form be indicated" (León-Portilla, 1974, p. 319). Confronted with such a theory it becomes absolutely imperative to have the study of Nahuatl metaphor Garibay called for thirty years ago. If León-Portilla is right, or even close to right, then the literary modes, structures, and aesthetics of the Nahuatl texts become not curious ornaments and interesting devices of relaxation and diversion, but primary indices to the most basic assumptions and patterns of Nahuatl culture itself. Art, and literary art in particular, must become central subjects of investigation in Nahuatl studies.

Another post-Garibayan investigator who has directly assisted the development of an indigenous terminology and formal description is Thelma Sullivan, English translator of numerous texts, including portions of the Cronica mexicayotl and a fine version of that Mesoamerican masterpiece, "The Prayer to Tlaloc," from the Sahagún manuscripts. For our present interests, Sullivan's most direct contribution is in her study of those supreme expressions of the *tecpillatolli* style, the so-called *huehuetlatolli* discourses, an on-going study most accessibly summarized in her article "The Rhetorical Orations, or *Huehuetlatolli*, Collected by Sahagún," included in the Edmonson anthology on the Sahagún manuscripts titled *16th Century Mexico*. After surveying all the available descriptions of *huehuetlatolli* and the ethnohistorical data on their collection and redaction by Sahagún, she classifies them according to five functional categories: prayers, court orations, orations of parents, orations of the merchants, orations relative to the life cycle—this latter with five thematic sub-categories. An extensive list of six tables classifies the eighty-nine orations that Sullivan identifies as *huehuetlatolli* in the Sahagún manuscripts. While reserving full commentary on the rhetorical style for another study, she indicates it is "characterized by the extensive use of metaphor, complementary phrasing, synonyms, and redundancy" (Sullivan, 1974, p. 98). "While these orations appear to be set in an established framework," she notes, "within that framework they move and flow with a high degree of freedom and imagination." Based on her functional analysis, Sullivan defines the genre of *huehuetlatolli* as "enculturistic . . . orations handed down from generation to generation and delivered on key occasions, both religious and secular, for the purpose of perpetuating and preserving the religious, social, moral and even historical traditions" (Ibid., p. 99).

Another scholar who has contributed to the debate over rhetorical terminology is Joséfina García Quintana, who in the introduction to her translation of the primary Olmos discourse, suggests the more widely attested native term for these orations is *tenonotzaliztlatolli* or "Discourses of Admonition" rather than *huehuetlatolli*. Obviously, only an analysis of the use of both terms in the original documents will clarify the issue.

A final project which must be mentioned in this category, though it has not yet emerged in publication, is the complete English edition of the Cantares manuscript now being prepared by John Bierhorst. When completed it will offer paleograph, translation, and possibly a concordance of the entire 85 folios. Presumably there will be extensive commentary on the text's formal qualities as well.

Midway between the contributions of those who have examined directly the generic and aesthetic terminology of the Nahuatl texts and the studies of anthropological linguists which offer scattered models only, stands one book which must be mentioned as the most coherent example available of the thorough taxonomy of native, oral literary practice that Nahuatl studies still needs. Taking "a holistic, contextual approach to traditional verbal behavior" of the Chamulas, Gary Gossen, in his *Chamulas in the World of the Sun,* sets forth the formal and genre classifications of their oral traditions based on terms obtained from the Chamulas themselves. "Folk taxonomies . . . consistently demonstrate," he points out, "that Western genre labels do not correspond precisely to folk genre labels" (Gossen, 1974, p. ix). Out of this native classification Gossen identifies, describes, and relates to specific acts of performance four levels of oral genres incorporating seven major forms— such as "true recent narrative," "true ancient narrative," "language for rendering holy," "prayer," and "song"—with twenty-seven sub-genres, and five other "marginal genres." "Oral traditions," Gossens asserts, "are as diverse as cultures. Herein lies the need for a model that allows a specific oral tradition to speak for itself, in its own categories of meaning" (Ibid., p. x). No single study better exemplifies the systematic formal survey, swept clean of Western, latinate vocabulary, of which Nahuatl literary analysis presently stands in need.

Gossen's study is partially a product of a movement which has oscilated for some years between North American anthropologists and linguists, particularly among students of native American cultures and languages, under the rubric "ethnology of speaking" taken from the Dell Hymes essay of 1962, which identified the field of inquiry. In 1974, with the publication of a bulky six-part anthology titled *Explorations in the Ethnology of Speaking,* the discussions achieved that dubious intellectual status of a "school." Judging by the sample studies of this group that I have seen, probably no other body of scholars currently working outside the Nahuatl texts themselves offers more in the way of analytic models and terminology. In contrast to Freudian, Marxist, and Lévi-Straussian analysis, all of which seek to decipher from the verbal text an unconscious, "true" significance which is lost to the native mind or to history, ethnography of speaking looks at "communicative competence" on the part of the speaker or artist and puts primary value on his conscious intent and control of the speech or "performance" event. The notion of oral literature as individual, discrete performances in specific social contexts is intrinsic to this mode of analysis, not necessarily to cast light on the social order, but to understand the particular behavior and textual choices of the oral artist in performance. Section V in *Explorations in the Ethnography of Speaking* is addressed to "The Shaping of Artistic Structures in Performance" and includes another Gossen analysis of Chamula aesthetic canons, developed from a metaphor of heat, used in native judgment of a given oral performance. There is also a taxonomy of Tzotzil oral genres.

The attention of these speech ethnographers to literary artistry as a central subject is nowhere better illustrated than in the fine analysis by Keith Basso of the use of metaphor in a speech genre of the Western Apache known as "Wise Words," a genre which has remarkable similarities to the Nahuatl *machiotlatolli* (metaphors) recorded in Sahagún's Book VI. Nor is Basso satisfied only to develop a scheme of lexical hierarchies demonstrating the semantic categories of Apache metaphoric thinking; he goes on to develop a theory of metaphor itself, a theory which assumes the linguistic competency model of Chomsky, but insists that Chomsky's model cannot account for figurative speech; it must be broadened, Basso suggests, to include "appropriately ill-formed," ungrammatical utterances such as the Apache "Wise Words," if generative grammatical theory is also to encompass the obviously creative ability of metaphor to generate "novel semantic categories" in a language, if it is to account for the total "command" of a linguistic system that oral artisans display in the creation of metaphoric artifacts such as the "Wise Words."

There would appear to be one great obstacle, however, to the appropriation of these ethnography of speech models for use in the study of Nahuatl texts. Every one of these linguists works with a living language and culture, usually spending time in the field with his informants, observing and tape-recording their oral performances, checking and re-checking his taxonomic lexicon, and questioning, often with the aid of prepared questionaires, every relevant detail of the social context of the performance. How are we to observe a performance of poetic or narrative texts redacted into print medium four centuries ago? How are we to question the singer on his canons of style when his voice is long gone to dust? How, in other words, are we to extract the components of performance which these ethnographers are demonstrating provide essential formal concerns in every oral literary tradition? Dennis Tedlock in his work with Zuni story-tellers has developed a basic orthographic system, employed in his collection *Finding the Center,* of heavy and light print, raised letters, line endings, spacing, italics and parentheses in order to fix in print the "paralinguistic" style features of loudness, pausing, tonal quality, and rate of delivery present in the aural experience of a literary performance. How can Nahuatl scholars ever hope to find a transcription system that elaborate in any 16th century text? The latinate orthography of the time was not even capable of transcribing the very essential Nahuatl phonemic contrasts of vowel length or the glottal stop.

The first answer to this problem is that we, in fact, do know a great deal from the ethnohistorical record about oral performance in Mesoamerica and especially among the Nahuas. From accounts of Durán, Pomar, Mendieta, Chimalpahin, Tezozómoc, and Ixtlilxochitl we can reliably reconstruct the social milieu of performance for *huehuetlatolli,* lyric songs, and some sacred ritual texts in considerable detail. We know the instruments which often accompanied performance and in some cases how they were played. We have scattered, in great profusion and with surprising consistency, through the lyric texts the transcription of vocables, the non-lexical elements of pure sound. We have the still undeciphered drum notations in the Cantares manuscript. And finally we know the educational system of the schools in which the pictographic texts were performance-read. All this adds up to a potentially vast store of information about Nahuatl oral performance, were it once assembled, surveyed, and analyzed. Secondly, and perhaps even more significantly, some of the very linguists who cultivate performance analysis most intensely have indicated the tape recorder is not indispensible to it. Donald M. Bahr, in a study based entirely on printed texts with practically no performance notations, is able to identify two distinct genres, "prose myth narrative" and "chant," in four cognate narratives of the emergence myth from the Zuni and the Pima. But more explicitly, Dell Hymes himself, in a re-study of some Chinook narratives that is fundamental for understanding how all this discourse and performance analysis can apply to the Nahuatl texts, concludes that

> . . . *to lack tape recordings would be to miss something, the realization in performance to which Tedlock so rightly and creatively calls attention;* but it would not be to lose everything. *Poetic structure could still be found. The indispensible tool would not be a tape recorder, but a hypothesis.* [Hymes, 1977, p. 454]

Hymes describes in this study how he discovered, in the print text of some narratives he had previously examined, a complex "poetic and rhetorical form" of lines, verses, stanzas, and scenes delineated by a set of discourse features in the printed text itself. He found the markers of these lines and verses not in phonological patterns of stress, syllable counts, or pauses, but in recurrent initial particles like "Now" and "Now then" and in the distribution of verbs between the particles. This discovery led him to believe Tedlock had exaggerated the need for recorded performance in order to adequately analyze the oral poetic:

> *In short, one can accept a minimal definition of poetry as discourse organized in lines. . . . One does not fully face the issue posed by the claim that a body of oral narrative is poetic, in the sense of organization into lines, until one goes beyond the existence of lines to principles governing lines and relates such principles to the organization of texts in other respects as well. Older texts make us face the issue directly. If they are manifestations of a tradition of organization into lines, that organization can be discovered only in the lines themselves, and in their relations to one another, for that is the evidence available.* [Ibid.]

In other words, the basic structural and formal features of an oral performance text are likely to be found in the linguistic record itself, even if the stylistic refinements of the performance have been lost.

No one has better demonstrated this possibility for the Nahuatl texts than the linguist-historian team of F. Karttunen and J. Lockhart, whose study "Structure of

Nahuatl Poetry as seen in its Variants" provides without question the most serious advance in our knowledge of Nahuatl lyrical form since the surveys of Garibay. Through a lengthy comparison of the structural features of three song-texts which are repeated in the Cantares and Romances manuscripts, Karttunen and Lockhart isolate what they call "the basic unit of Nahuatl poetry . . . the verse," a unit they define as a relatively self-contained statement of varying length which practically always ends with a coda of non-lexical or exclamatory material (MS, p. 2). These verses, they find, link together in what they identify as "verse pairs" which can be "strong" or "weak" according to the amount of shared material which manifests the pairing. Further, they find most poems "tend to consist of 8 or 10 verses with a strong predilection for 8." So strong, in fact, do they find that predilection, that they claim: "The 8-verse sequence must be granted a place in Nahuatl poetry at least as prominent as that of the sonnet in European tradition" (MS, p. 5). The structure of verse pairs into whole poems is done, they find, according to no hierarchical or narrative order. "Rather, it is as though the verses were arranged about a center—a theme, mood, character—to which they relate directly in a comparable way. . . . The order of the verses is far less important than their relevance to the common theme and their pleasing symmetrical arrangement" (MS, p. 2). This verse, verse-pair, 8-verse pattern of structure extends through the entire corpus of the lyric, they claim, with no distinction between *icnocuicatl, xopancuicatl, yaocuicatl, melahuaccuicatl* or any other generic denominations—terms which these investigators assert are semantic rather than phonological categories.

At the verse-internal level, the level corresponding to the line in Hymes's discussion, Karttunen and Lockhart admit to some foundering in their search for a more basic unit of structure. "No suprafoot unit within the verse, comparable to the line in European poetry has yet emerged," they report. So, they add, "not finding a line, one looks for a foot." Employing the traditional latinate metrical vocabulary, they locate several occasions "in which it appears that the intention is to achieve a [dactylic] foot," but are forced to conclude that "as with other apparent metrical regularities, this one applies only to a small portion of the corpus in any straightforward way." Recently, Dr. Karttunen informed us that they have still to survey possible phonetic patterns of vowel length and glottal stops in the continuing search for an intra-verse meter. I might suggest, based on the revelations of the ethnographers of speech, first that no latinate metrical taxonomy can ever be made to stick on native American texts (it has been largely abandoned, at least since Pound, by contemporary poets), and second that some more basic unit, corresponding to the line Hymes located in the Chinook texts, might yet be found within the Nahuatl verse, if we can only come to see the particular principles of relationship which Hymes points out must govern their manifestation. The use of non-lexical vocables, the *ahuiya, ohuaya's*—which Karttunen and Lockhart discover, incidentally, are copied with remarkable accuracy from variant to variant—may play some part in that manifestation.

Let me close off this survey of models and achievements in Nahuatl literary study with one final suggested resource. There are presently among us writers who straddle the void between Western, Euro-American history and indigenous tradition in the reality of their own being. Writers like N. Scott Momaday, Simon Ortiz, and Leslie Silko whose education in and experience of the Euro-American modes of self-hood, behavior, and aesthetics have not destroyed the vestiges of native knowledge to which they find themselves heir, but has brought that knowledge to sharp relief in their individual minds. As these writers become increasingly conscious of themselves as artists, they make critical or autobiographical statements of various sorts about the nature and origins of their art and their aesthetic ideal. Through these voices, sensitized to both our academic literary jargon and their own oral traditions, we have a unique occasion to see into those oral traditions from an intuitive, visceral perspective that no anthropologist, including Carlos Casteñada, can ever afford us.

I'm thinking of passages like the sermon by the half-Christian Sun Priest Tosamah in Momaday's *House Made of Dawn,* and of Simon Ortiz's meditation on art in language titled *Song, Poetry, and Language—Expression and Perception.* In the latter Ortiz examines what a song is for his Acoma people, specifically for his father. He finds a complete indifference to breaking the song into parts: "It doesn't break down into anything," he is told; "It is complete." He speaks also of the "context" of the song-performance, but he means something more than the physical details of context the anthropologists speak of: "The emotional, cultural, spiritual context in which we thrive," he says, "in that, the song is meaningful. The context has to do not only with your being physically present, but it has to do with the context of the mind. . . . The context of a song can be anything or can focus through a specific event or act but it includes all things." I would suggest that observations such as these have direct implication for what we can or cannot say about structure, meaning, and function of indigenous texts.

While these personal self-explorations will seldom provide terminology to directly explicate oral texts, and while they are far removed from 16th century Mexico, certainly Acoma is closer to Anahuac than Rome is, and Kiowa thinking about language should be no less relevant to Nahuatl thinking than are the theories of Noam Chomsky.

BIBLIOGRAPHY
Bahr, Donald. "On the Complexity of Southwest Indian Emergence Myths." *Journal of Anthropological Research* 33 (1977): 317–49.
Bauman, Richard and Joel Sherzer. *Explorations in the Ethnography of Speaking.* Cambridge: Cambridge University Press, 1974.
Basso, Keith. "'Wise Words' of the Western Apache: Metaphor and Semantic Theory." *Meaning in Anthropology,* ed. Basso and Selby. Albuquerque: University of New Mexico Press, 1976, pp. 93–121.
Brinton, Daniel. *Ancient Nahuatl Poetry.* Philadelphia, 1887.
Durán, Fray Diego. *Book of the Gods and Rites and the Ancient Calendar.* Trans. F. Horcasitas and D. Heyden. Norman: University of Oklahoma Press, 1971.

Edmonson, Monro, ed. *16th Century Mexico*. Albuquerque: University of New Mexico Press, 1974.

Garibay, Angel M. *Historia de la literature náhuatl*, 2 vols. México: Porrúa, 1953–54.

———. *Poesía Náhuatl*, 3 vols. México: UNAM, 1964–68.

———. *Llave del Náhuatl*. México: UNAM, 1961.

———. *Viente himnos sacros de los Nahuas*. México: UNAM, 1958.

Gossen, Gary H. *Chamulas in the World of the Sun*. Cambridge: Harvard University Press, 1974.

Hymes, Dell. "Discovering Oral Performance and Measured Verse in American Indian Narrative." *New Literary History* 8 (1977): 431–57.

Karttunen, Frances and James Lockhart. "The Structure of Nahuatl Poetry as Seen in its Variants." Manuscript.

León-Portilla, Miguel. *Trece Poetas del Mundo Azteca*. México: SEP/SETENTAS, 1972.

———. *PreColumbian Literatures of Mexico*. Norman: University of Oklahoma Press, 1969.

———. *Los antiguos mexicanos através de sus crónicas y cantares*. México: Fondo de cultura económica, 1961.

———. *La filosofía náhuatl estudiada en sus fuentes*. 4th ed. México: UNAM, 1974.

Mijangos, Fr. Juan. *Primera parte de sermonio dominical*. Cd. México, 1623.

———. "Frases y Modos de Hablar Elegantes . . ." Ed. A.M. Garibay. *Estudios de cultura náhuatl VI*, 1966, pp. 11–27.

Miliani, Domingo. "Notas para una poetica entre los nahuas." *Estudios de cultura náhuatl IV*, 1963.

Murphy, William. "Oral Literature," *Annual Review of Anthropology* 7 (1978): 113–36.

Olmos, Andrés de. *Arte para aprender la lengua mexicana*. Ed. Rémi Siméon. Paris, 1885.

Ortiz, Simon. *Song, Poetry and Language—Expression and Perception*. Tsaile: Navajo Community College Press, 1977.

Osuña Ruiz, Rafael. *Introducción a la lirica prehispánica*. Maracaibo: Editorial Universitaria de la Universidad de Zulia, 1968.

Rothenberg, Jerome. *Technicians of the Sacred*. Anchor Books. Garden City: Double-day & Co., 1968.

———. *Shaking the Pumpkin*. Garden City: Doubleday & Co., 1972.

Sahagún, Bernardino de. *Florentine Codex*, 12 Books. Eds.: Arthur J.O. Anderson and Charles Dibble. Salt Lake City: University of Utah Press, 1950–69.

Sullivan, Thelma. "Náhuatl Proverbs, Conundrums and Metaphors, collected by Sahagún." *Estudios de cultura náhuatl IV* (1963): 93–178.

———. "The Rhetorical Orations, or *Huehuetlatolli,* collected by Sahagún," in Edmonson, 1974, pp. 79–109.

Tedlock, Dennis. "On the Translation of Style in Oral Narrative." *Journal of American Folklore* 84 (1971): 114–33. (Reprinted in this volume.)

———. *Finding the Center*. New York: Dial Press, 1972.

———. "Pueblo Literature: Style and Versimilitude" in *New Perspectives on the Pueblos*, ed. A. Ortiz. Albuquerque: University of New Mexico Press, 1972, pp. 221–40.

Part Three: FOCUS ON STORIES

Dell Hymes: VICTORIA HOWARD'S 'GITSKUX AND HIS OLDER BROTHER': A CLACKAMAS CHINOOK MYTH

This myth represents an aesthetic principle and an ancient conception. I shall try to indicate briefly both. But first, a few words as to the source.

In 1929 the late Melville Jacobs, recently trained in linguistic anthropology at Columbia University by Franz Boas, discovered that the Clackamas Chinook language was still spoken by one or two people. One of them, Mrs. Victoria Howard, living near the ancestral home of the Clackamas at what is now Oregon City on the Willamette River in Oregon, proved a veritable storehouse of narrative. Born in 1870 on the Grande Ronde Reservation, she had absorbed much of what was still known of Clackamas tradition from her grandmother and mother-in-law. That knowledge poured into the notebooks of Jacobs just a year or so, as it happened, before her death. A generation later Jacobs typed, and Indiana University was able to publish, the resulting two volumes of texts (1958a, 1959). These volumes, and two volumes of analysis (Jacobs 1958b, 1960) constitute the richest heritage of Native American literature from the region.

The present myth was published in the second volume of texts (1959: pp. 315–31) and discussed by Jacobs in his second book of analysis (1960: pp. 208–29). There Jacobs says rightly (p. 228): "Perhaps no other Clackamas myth draws so convincing an outline of a personality, or rather a number of personalities, as the product both of goodness in people and the decisive circumstances of their immediate kin-in-the-household relationships. . . . stress is never on abstracted large segments of personality. It is on specific pressures from relations who are closest. Each man usually does what he has to because of his nearest kin. In fact in this myth the spirit-powers at no point tie in with delineations of male actors and their behavior. *That is why this is really a woman's drama.* (My emphasis). It is a woman's spirit-powers that ultimately resolve a chronically perilous situation which has been created by another woman."

CONCEPTION

A trail of names and texts can be found that leads to a great deepening of this perception.[1] A book is required to report the journey and findings. A summary can start from the name of the Grizzly Woman who is at the center of the present myth. In Clackamas she is invariably named with the stem -*kitsimani*. (The hyphen shows that a prefix may precede the stem; alternation in prefixation proves to have expressive significance, for which see my "Reading Clackamas texts"). A name of that length ought to be analyzable into parts in Chinookan, but this one is not. Comparative analysis shows that it is connected to a name for "grizzly bear" in the Miwokan languages of central California. Now, Chinookan and Miwokan belong to a family of languages, Penutian, that extends from central California through parts of Oregon to Tsimshian in Canada. Comparison of the names for "bear" in all the Penutian languages sheds valuable light on the Penutian relationship itself,[2] and on the conception that lies behind the present myth. It appears that the Clackamas and Miwok names (related to names in another Penutian language, Molale, as well) are as old as Penutian itself, that is, some thousands of years. The two languages are too far from each other for one to have borrowed the name from the other under aboriginal conditions. Miwok words and grammar show the name to be an old formation, equivalent to *ki-tse-ma-ni,* and involving an element, reconstructed as **ski-* (Clackamas *tsi-,* Miwok *ši-*), that recurs in names of predators, perhaps especially clawed predators. What one can tell of the name is consistent with the consistent role of Grizzly Woman in Clackamas as a dangerous being.

This name stands for a dangerous female creature, apart from other names for bears (male grizzly, black bear, cinnamon bear) in Chinookan. And it stands apart from a Chinookan name that *Kitsimani* somehow replaces. In the Shoalwater Chinook texts recorded by Franz Boas in 1891 from Charles Cultee, near the Pacific Ocean, Cultee tells how his great-grandfather was sent to obtain the guardian spirit power most important in his family, U-t'ónaqan; how far up in the mountains he heard her shriek and fled in fear for his life; how in the event she revealed herself to him as a person, and conferred on him the power of invulnerability to wounds. An analogous encounter and escape, but lacking the element of guardian spirit power, was told by Mrs. Howard as having happened to her father-in-law's father; and a version of the very same story was heard among the Clackamas, and retold among the more easterly Wasco Chinook. I recorded it from Hiram Smith (cf. my "Verse analysis of a Wasco text"). Now, in the Clackamas story the pursuing creature is called *Kitsimani;* in the Wasco retelling, it is called *A-t'únaqa.*

The three stories are clearly based on a common tradition. Shoalwater *U-t'ónaqan,* Clackamas *Kitsimani,* Wasco *A-t'únaqa* are all described as having very long breasts, such that a person fleeing from her downhill could escape, because she would step on her own breasts. (Going uphill, she could keep them thrown over her shoulders). Yet the common tradition has two names and, indeed, two aspects of the creature at its heart. In the Clackamas story and the Wasco story based on it, the creature is simply dangerous. In the Shoalwater story, she is first dangerous in outer aspect, then revealed as a protector in inner aspect (in vision). Etymology indicates that *T'unaqa* is especially associated with the protective, nurturant aspect. Forms cognate with Chinookan *t'u-* have to do with "good, beautiful, paradigmatic" in Chinookan, Takelma, and with shamans and shamanistic power in both these and other Penutian languages. Comparison shows that a related name occurs among the Miwok. All Miwok were born into one of two moieties, and one of the moities was named *Tunak-:a-* (in the Southern Sierra Miwok form), after its bear ancestor. A related name, Dzo:noq'wa, occurs among the Kwakiutl of British Columbia, probably by borrowing, for a creature both dangerous in the woods and powerful in Potlatch declamation as an ancestral privilege. The Tsimshian of British Columbia have concepts of mythical bear power names that appear to contain the *-naqa* element. A cognate word among the Klamath of southern Oregon refers to a transvestite shaman; and there is reason to think that an association with transvestitism may be linked with the modern Wasco assertion that *-t'unaqa* were never found where they themselves live (plateau country), but only west in the vicinity of the Cascade mountains. To be sure, the Cascades are where the nearest grizzly bears would have been, and that fact reinforces the connection between *T'unaqa* and female grizzly.

What links all these bits of evidence, I believe, is an ancient mode of thought. Animals in myth were a way of thinking about traits of character, motives of personality. The female bear was a way of thinking about the integration of feminine personality. The great age of the two Chinookan names; the dual aspect of the creature in the Shoalwater Chinook story of guardian power; the presence of both names among the Miwok in California; the dual aspect of the Kwakiutl conception associated with the borrowed name; the link with transvestite shamanism among the Klamath and perhaps elsewhere; such things point to a concern with the relation of what to the Indian cultures were "masculine" and "feminine" character traits: the "masculine" dangerously aggressive, the "feminine" protectively nurturant.

Such a context makes significant an otherwise isolated fact in the Clackamas myth of "Thunder and his mother." The hero, Thunder, encounters a *Kitsimani* who is the only figure in Clackamas to have *two* faces. She is the last of five that he encounters and kills, and the only one whom he decides to skin, so as to have her skin as spirit-power regalia. Later the regalia proves too powerful for his companion, Coyote, to control, and Thunder has to rescue it and him. Now, Thunder is the very model of a good son, and cannot be imagined to take for power any regalia lacking in virtue. Coyote is near the apex of mythical beings, and anything too powerful for him must be powerful indeed. I cannot but infer that the two-faced Grizzly Woman embodied both faces of feminine power, protective as well as dangerous; that the unity of the two was what proved too much for Coyote; that the integration of the two is something appropriate for a great power like Thunder and would always be associated with great power.

This mode of thought has not been noticed before, to the best of my knowledge. The ceremonial relation of Indian men to bears, through hunting, is well known. Women figure there only as mediators of the hunting relationship. Here we have a concern of which women themselves are the focus.

There is a complementary tradition also involving ambiguity of sex. Men may disguise as women to gain revenge. The fear of "male" danger in female garb is dramatized vividly in another Clackamas story (Hymes 1977), where it is joined with a concern about untrustworthy caretakers, a concern that emerges in other stories about Grizzly women and about revenge by temporarily transvestite men, both from Mrs. Howard and from another Grande Ronde reservation narrator, Mrs. Frances Johnson, source of the Takelma texts recorded by Edward Sapir. I take these narratives to reflect the breakdown of traditional cultural security, of "home as haven" in the nineteenth century among groups shattered by disease and forced removal to reservations.

In the myth of Gitskux we have a paradigmatic expression of the focus on women themselves. If *Tunaqa* can stand for the archaic type of a Bear-like woman who can protect and save, *Kitsimani* stands for the archaic type of a Bear-like woman who can endanger and destroy. She is far more here than a stock ogress. She is portrayed as a creature who *tries* to be a proper human wife, to take the place of one, and fails. Even her destructive rage is nuanced. Childlike, she cannot help competing with children for a pet; open to human loyalty, she does not at first want to believe she ate the younger sister; but, somewhat as the Hulk of current television and comic strip, rage triggers transformation into the dangerous being she cannot escape. The fundamental theme of the myth is the contrast between such a Grizzly woman and women who do embody the ideal. The older brother's first wife is so strong that she can bring in a deer with one hand. The second wife is first perceived *as* a man, separate from the long-haired woman seen next. She has all the necessary strength, and supernatural foresight as well; takes initiative in their sexual relationship; but then defers to her acquired husband in the traditional male role of hunter. It is she who has "knowledge at a distance" as to the fate of the younger brother, and who conducts his ritual cleansing, and the restoration of his hair, as she had previously seen to the proper burial of the younger sister's head. Perhaps only a woman would have performed a story in which a woman so perfectly unites feminine decorum and sexuality, male strength, and spiritual authority.

Neither Mrs. Howard nor Jacobs identified the myth-time creatures of the story, except, of course, for Grizzly Woman. The two brothers are almost certainly Fisher and Panther. Gitskux has dark hair, takes part in hunting deer, and becomes at the end an animal in the mountains. Of the animals of the mountains near the Clackamas, only the 'fisher' fits these requirements. It is dark or blackish-brown in general color; its strength is such that it can even run down and kill a marten, and commonly kills porcupines. Moreover, it has grayish shoulders and grizzled fur on top of its head, such as might suggest the consequence of the captivity with Grizzly Woman. An animal of the set weasel, ermine, marten, mink, wild cat, is to be expected, since the pattern for older brother-younger brother adventures in the region generally has the cougar (panther, mountain lion) as older brother. Elsewhere in Clackamas Panther and Mink travel together, in Kathlamet Chinook Panther and Mink, in Sahaptin Panther and Wildcat. In Modoc the pattern is stepped down a notch, the sober older brother being Mink, the impetuous younger brother Weasel; and in Kalapuya, Sahaptin and elsewhere, Panther (cougar, mountain lion) can have other junior partners. In a Sahaptin myth there are four: wolf, fisher, weasel, and wild cat (Jacobs, "Northwest Sahaptin Texts," *University of Washington Publications in Anthropology* 2 [Seattle, 1929]). This Clackamas myth fits the pattern particularly because of the habitual hunting of deer. It is particularly the mountain lion (cougar, panther) that hunts deer even today, and there is a Takelma myth in which he has to be prevented from extinguishing the deer. Of the probably junior partners in hunting deer, the fisher is the one large enough to be credible; nor are the smaller animals credible in the noble role enacted by the younger brother in this myth. Weasel and Mink are fierce and mean in Chinookan; marten is not known (and too small); Wildcat is sometimes sympathetic, but again, too small, and of course not dark. The myth, then, preserves an otherwise unremembered name for the 'fisher'; it does not, in fact, really fish; but that is its English name.

This myth is notable for the attention to the detail of relations between brothers, and uncle and nephews, and foregrounding of these. And while the two brothers, the two men, are the actors of the title, around whom the action centers, the ultimate power is held by women. Probably that fact is connected with the story having been told by a woman, who had heard it from her mother's mother; it has been shaped by interests of women. And it has been remembered at great length.

The older brother is a chief, but we learn that only incidentally when the people say that the chief's two wives are fighting. They even live at the end of the village, where usually poor people, rather than a chief, would live. The older brother is almost a background figure, unable to act in regard to the dangerous being that comes to him as a second wife, and his sons from both his earlier and later first wife are closest to their uncle, ultimately going with him when the actors take on their identities for the world after the myth-time. Gitskux plays the standard role of 'youngest smartest,' to be sure, in sensing that Grizzly Woman is dangerous; but that it is Gitskux who brings back a pet raccoon for the two children; who sees and retrieves the younger sister's head, who is described as restored with loving care and black hair hanging to the ground; and who is the one to kill the false wife and restore the true in the last encounter, all this would seem a loving choice on the part of the narrator. Common propriety would have put the older brother first in the title, because older; unless the sequence is simply that just the one name was remembered, putting Gitskux first is a special foregrounding. And if it is just that only his name was remembered, that too suggests special concern.

Women have the ultimate power of action and foresight. It is the concern of the first wife for her children that precipitates the reciprocal killing of pets, and the fight that leads to the first killing of a wife and pretense on the part of Grizzly Woman. This first older brother's wife, and the second, both have the power to have foreseen their fate and prescribe its remedy. Women cannot normally act in their own behalf, but through men; and perhaps each woman makes of herself a decoy to bring about the killing of the dangerous Grizzly Woman wife (as Jacobs suggests). Both, however, have the valued power of foresight. And both are strong. The first brings in deer with one arm, the second appears to the older brother to indeed be a man when bringing in deer. Both combine the strength and knowledge that a fine man

133

might have with proper feminine characteristics as well: preparing food, caring for children and relatives, seeing to ritual necessities, bearing children, even braiding their hair. Older brother becomes the husband of the exemplary woman of the latter part of the myth because she brings it about, through the trickery of flea bites and the power of holding time still. And it is she who initiates their taking on of their identities for the present world. Fundamentally, the story of loyalty among siblings, and care for children, is founded on a paradigmatic contrast between the not-quite human Grizzly Woman who would be a true wife, and two women who *are* true wives, the second more thoroughly shown as a woman of knowledge and power than the first.

To repeat Jacobs (1960: p. 228): "Perhaps no other Clackamas myth draws so convincing an outline of a personality, or rather a number of personalities, as the product both of goodness in people and the decisive circumstances of their immediate kin-in-the-household relationships . . . (and) . . . this is really a woman's drama."

ANALYSIS

The presentation of the myth in terms of its lines of verse makes more perceptible some of these qualities. The mode of analysis is discussed at length elsewhere (cf. Hymes 1976, 1977, "Verse analysis of a Wasco text"). Here let me note that the more than 900 lines of this myth constitute the longest text I have so far analyzed into verse from a published prose version. Like many Chinookan myths, it is discovered to have five main parts, and to have greatest elaboration at the apex or center. A profile of the text in terms of its units gives a sense of its proportions.

PROFILE

PARTS	ACTS	SCENES	STANZAS (VERSES)	LINES
One	I	i	ABC(abc)	19 lines
		ii	A(abc)B(abc)C(abc)	30 lines
		iii	(abc)	7 lines
	II	i	A(abc)B(abc)	15 lines
		ii	AB(abc)	12 lines
		iii	ABC(abc)	18 lines
		iv	(abc)	14 lines
		v	(abcde)	14 lines
	III	i	AB(abcde)C(abcde)	26 lines
		ii	A(ab)B(ab)C(ab)D(abc)E(abc)	37 lines
		iii	A(abc)B(abc)C(abc)	45 lines
Two	I	i	(abcde)	21 lines
		ii	(abcde)	16 lines
		iii	AB(abc)C(abc)	19 lines
		iv	(abcde)	14 lines
		v	(abcde)	15 lines
Three	I	i	AB(abcde)C(abcde)	41 lines
		ii	A(abc)B(abc)C(abcde)D(abcde)E(abcde)	58 lines
		iii	[10 lines in own pattern]	10 lines

PARTS	ACTS	SCENES	STANZAS (VERSES)	LINES
Three I (cont.)		iv	A(ab)B(ab)C(ab)	27 lines
		v	A(abc)B(abc)C(abc)	19 lines
	II	i	A(abcde)B(abc)C(abcde)	44 lines
		ii	A(ab)B(ab)C(a-1,2, b-1,2, c-1,2,3)D(abc)E(ab)	43 lines
		iii	A(abc)B(def)C(ghi)D(abcde)E(abcde)	50 lines
		iv	A(abcde)B(abcde)C(abc)	45 lines
		v	AB(abc)C	20 lines
	III	i	A(ab)B(ab)C(ab)	22 lines
		ii	AB(abc)C(abc)	16 lines
		iii	(abcdefghij)	29 lines
Four	I	i	(abc)	11 lines
		ii	(abcde)	18 lines
		iii	(abcde)	20 lines
	II	i	(abc)	14 lines
		ii	(abc)	10 lines
		iii	AB(abc)C(abc)	27 lines
	III	i	(abc)	10 lines
		ii	(abcde)	19 lines
		iii	(abcde)	20 lines
Five			A(abc)B(abc)C	15 lines

Part of the configuration of the text is shown by a rank ordering of scenes in terms of numbers of lines.

RANK ORDER IN TERMS OF NUMBER OF LINES

58	Three I ii	She becomes his wife.
50	Three II iii	The brothers plan.
45	Three II iv	Grizzly Woman is killed by Gitskux.
44	Three II i	The wife advises about Gitskux.
43	Three II ii	The brothers are reunited.
41	Three I i	He finds a house, woman, food.
45	One III iii	Grizzly Woman is killed.
37	One III ii	Testing the would-be wife.
30	One I ii	Grizzly Woman comes to be the older brother's second wife.
29	Three III iii	The wife combs his (Gitskux's) hair.
27	Three I iv	They bury the sister's head.
27	Four II iii	Testing the would-be wife.
26	One III i	The first wife's foresight.
22	Three III i	The brothers return home.
21	Two I i	Grizzly Woman returns, kills, eats the people.
20	Three II v	Older brother helps.
20	Four I iii	Today!
20	Four III iii	Grizzly Woman is destroyed.
19	One I i	They live there.

RANK ORDER IN TERMS OF NUMBER OF LINES (cont.)

19	Two iii	The brothers retrieve their sister's head.
19	Three I v	She has two boys.
19	Four III ii	Grizzly Woman is killed.

The 22 scenes with 19 or more lines include *all* but one (III ii) scene of the central part III. The elaboration within Two is also its central scene (iii), as well as first (i). In One the elaboration is at beginning and end (I i, iii; all of III (i, ii, iii), and in Four it is at the end of each act (I iii, II iii, III ii, iii). Five is a logical part of intrinsic importance as epilogue, but brief.

The number of lines is an indication of emphasis, but not the only one. The fact that certain short scenes are apparently distinguished at that level of organization is another indication of emphasis; such seems to be the case with Four II i, ii, regarding the children and their uncles. The qualitative rank reflects the attention to personal ties among kin.

A separate indication of emphasis is structural elaboration in terms of numbers, not of lines, but of stanzas.

RANK ORDER IN TERMS OF NUMBER OF STANZAS

5:	ABCDE	One III ii	Testing the would-be wife.
		Three I ii	She becomes his wife.
		Three II ii	The brothers are reunited.
		Three II iii	The brothers plan.
3:	ABC	One I i	They live there.
		One I ii	Grizzly Woman comes . . .
		One II iii	Gitskux brings a raccoon for his nephews.
		One III i	The first wife's foresight.
		One III iii	Grizzly Woman is killed.
		Two iii	The brothers retrieve their sister's head.
		Three I i	He finds a house, woman, food.
		Three I iv	They bury the sister's head.
		Three I v	She has two boys.
		Three II i	The wife advises about Gitskux.
		Three II iv	Grizzly Woman is killed by Gitskux.
		Three II v	Older brother helps.
		Three III i	The brothers return home.
		Three III ii	The wife cleanses Gitskux.
		Four II iii	Testing the would-be wife.
		Five	Epilogue.

The 20 scenes with 3 or 5 stanzas include *all* but two (I iii, III iii) of the central part III. The stanzaic elaboration in Two is only its central scene (iii), and almost so in Four (II iii). In One the elaboration is almost all at beginning and end (I i, ii; III, i, ii, ii-) but also center (II iii). The brief part Five still has 3 coordinate stanzas, the first two of 3 verses each, marked by particles (A) and turns of speech (B).

136

Again, the number of stanzas is not the only indication of emphasis through structural elaboration. The most notable instance is the unfolding of the restoration of Gitskux's hair (Three III iii). The first five verses would suffice; the hair is restored to its previous length. Yet the action continues without break into further combing and five more verses; the hair is made even longer than before. The implication is that the woman has power not only to restore but to strengthen; that the younger brother is not only cleansed and restored as a man, but enhanced in attractiveness and status. The total of ten verses is doubling of the Chinookan pattern number, five. Such elaboration without break is unusual and significant; it shows the narrator's skill and special concern. We have in effect the third of three rituals (the burial of the sister's head, the cleansing of Gitskux, the restoration of his hair), conducted by the woman, and this the most elaborated of the three.

Let me add that I did not experience the ritual effect until analysis had disclosed the sequence of verses. The pacing of verse (instead of prose) is somehow essential to the ritual effect.

All this interpretation, from ancient conception to segmentation of prose into verse, depends upon control of linguistic form, yet the interpretation of linguistic form can sometimes depend upon the interpretation of myth. The scene in which the older brother and his new wife bury the sister's head (Three I iv) is grammatically odd. The three verbs of A(b) (lines 442, 444, 445), the narrative verb of B(a) (line 446), the five narrative verbs of B(b) (lines 449–53), and the first three verbs of C(a) (lines 454–56), all end with a suffix -x (a voiceless velar fricative similar to that in German *ach*). Now, this suffix is identified in Chinookan grammar as "usitative," and it often occurs in ways that can be understood as having to do with something usually done, something done many times. Not so here. It is impossible to imagine that the older brother and his new wife "usually" bury the younger sister's head. The ritual character intrinsic to burial, together with the part of the burial in a sequence of ritual actions initiated by the woman, suggests that the suffix has an additional, or perhaps better, deeper sense. The ritual context suggests a sense of what is "usual" or "habitual" in the sense of what one would expect from a person, given their nature. What is "usual" or "habitual" here, then, is not action, but character. That fits the fact that Chinookan name for "myth," -*k'ani*, does also mean "nature, character."

The effect in any case seems one of ritual, and I have tried to catch something of the effect in translation by differentiating these verbs with "had." Perhaps there is also a suggestion of the sense such ritual itself recurs. The interpretation of the suffix as expressing character is reinforced by use of the same suffix in a short Clackamas version of the Star-Husband story (analyzed in a ms. by Charles Bigelow and Kris Holmes). Mrs. Howard's account (Jacobs 1959: p. 468) has as its point the character of two young girls who sleep out and wish jokingly that two stars come to them as men. The occurrences of the suffix seem to combine the senses of usual action and usual character, the latter with respect to both the girls and the stars they wish for.

Interpretation of form depends upon sensitivity to literary interpretation in another scene (Three I iii), in which the new wife defers to the older brother as hunter. The scene has ten lines, in keeping with pattern numbers, but there is no evident internal division into pattern numbers. Any attempt to divide the scene in terms of groups of 3 or 5 lines appears to violate its integrity. Rather, there appears to be a logic to the sequence of the whole, moving through turns of speech and types of pronoun in an arc. The woman's speech is of course 5 lines. Notice that it moves from "you" (*m*-) through "someone" (*ł*) to "I" (*n*-). It does this within an opening that goes from "the two" (*šd*-) to "she" (*g*-), and a closing that returns from "he" (*č*-) to "the two." Abstracted from the rest of the text, one has: the two, she-him, you, you, someone, I, I, he-her, the two.

Such craft bespeaks concern. This scene is indeed the one in which the paragon wife tells her husband that he is now to be the man of the place. The shaping in terms of pronouns is a shaping in terms of personal relationship. The man, so recently bereft of all kin and the village of which he had been chief, has found a woman who is self-sufficient, capable of herself appearing at first to be a man as she returns from the hunt, but capable also of taking up a woman's proper appearance in the home. She is, moreover, vested with spirit-power greater than any man in the story, giving her knowledge of the man, his history, and his brother's fate, which she confirms through questions. She chooses the man as mate, brings him to her through the indirection of bites of a flea, and crowns their union with suspension of time (recall Athena doing this for Odysseus and Penelope). Given all this, the power to be both man and woman in role, she restores him to the role of hunter, not because it is necessary for him, but because it is proper, and, one can perhaps infer, necessary to him.

In number of lines this scene is short. In its delicate pronominal arc, it expresses a theme of the myth, something as does a sphere that tops a steeple, or better, perhaps, as does the finest-grained bit of wood or cloth or stone in the center of a large construction. These ten lines are indeed the central scene among the five that concern the relationship between the man and woman. And the center is often the apex in Chinookan literary art. That the ten lines stand apart in the way that they are fitted together seems not an accident or slip, but a consummate effect. And the scene teaches the lesson that what is fundamental to such narrative art is not the recurrence of groupings of lines and verses in certain numbers, pervasive though such numerical regulation is, but the patterning of lines as such. Overall, bar-like form (in musical terms) is maintained in the number of lines, but within the scene a different, exactly fitting device, the personal pronoun, becomes the instrument of orchestration.

We see, indeed, that elaboration in terms of lines, of stanzas, and of special craft (as in Three I iii and Three III iii) converge on the central part, Three, where the relations among the two brothers and the new wife are at the fore. Part Three, in effect, presents the paradigmatic true wife at the center of a narrative which before and after deals with the inadequacy of violence of a would-be wife.

Before providing the text itself, let me call attention to one additional nicety of structure. When the brothers are reunited (Three II ii), there are ten turns of speech, five for each brother. Within the ten turns, the roles are reversed. The older brother calls, and the younger brother thinks it is Bluejay deceiving him again. The older brother says it is he, and the younger brother thinks it is Blue Jay deceiving him (expressed with even greater reproach). The older brother responds "no," and tells the younger brother to touch him; the younger brother does and affirms the identity; the seventh turn is again the older brother, but now, not a new initiative, but a confirmation. As fits the alternation, the eighth turn of speech belongs to the younger brother, but now it is an initiative, a question; the older brother's last turn is an answer; and the younger brother's last turn is a confirmation and additional information. Within the strict alternation of turns, then, Older Brother-Younger Brother throughout, speech roles shift, and there are actually four groups of turns: AB, AB, ABA, BAB. I have tried to catch it by grouping together the first three, as center of the recognition scene, leading to the appropriate change in role manifest when the younger brother initiates for the first time. The grouped turns are identified by the *ad hoc* device of adding numbers to the letters that denote verses (a-1, a-2; b-1, b-2; c-1, c-2, c-3) within the central stanza. Devices aside, the interplay of verses and turns is a neat, and in a way moving, effect.

A NOTE ON TYPOGRAPHY

The purpose of the analysis into lines is only partly to reveal patterns and relationships that obtain in the original language. It is also to show the text as something to be read as poetry, rather than prose. The presentation in lines at the very least slows down the eye, and the mind, allowing the original text to unfold at something like its own pace. Whatever questions may remain about the exact organization of lines in the text, there can be no question that its organization is indeed one of lines.

If these instances of the first literature of North America are to be understood as literature, rather than relegated to the status of documents merely, there is no choice but to give them the garb of literature visually as well as analytically. A definition of poetry as organization of lines can be defended as universally applicable, but an analytical and definitional victory is not enough. It is necessary to see the recurrences, repetitions, contrasts and alternations in the original wording, and, if at all possible, to see the original working in an attractive, efficient and effective format.

Such typography has been difficult to obtain. Many journals and university presses will not even consider materials in an Indian language, because of the forbidding appearance of the special symbols and the forbidding cost of typesetting them. Recently Charles Bigelow has developed a font, based on that called "Syntax," designed by Hans E. Meier of the Zurich School of Arts and Crafts. "Syntax" is a contemporary sans-serif based on humanistic letterforms of the Renaissance for superior clarity and legibility in text composition. Bigelow and Kris Holmes have designed needed phonetic characters and symbols with the cooperation of Mr. Meier, and the result is called "Syntax phonetic." It is being made available by Mergenthaler Linotype, in cooperation with D.D. Stempel AG, and with the support of the National Endowment for the Arts and the Oregon Arts Foundation. Its general availability will mean that Native American text can be set reasonably inexpensively in a typeface designed especially for it in keeping with modern principles of design.

(It is an interesting fact that the task of providing a comprehensive typeface in which Native American texts could be set as literature revealed the need to design, for the very first time, capitals for some of the phonetic symbols).

The following pages exemplify Syntax phonetic with four of the most interesting scenes of "Gitskux and his Older Brother." We are indebted to Irish Setter, 1135 S.E. Salmon, Portland, Oregon, for preparing them.

3. I.ii.
[She becomes his wife]

A (a)   Šdá::wixt;
       gagyúlxam,
         «Gigíwam ačmúx̣a,   370
         «Yáxuba amgúkšit!»

(b)   Nix̣łúxwayt,
       «Tə́l: nkíx̣ax̣,
       «Anx̣úkšida.»

(c)   Gayúya,   375
       nix̣úkšit,
         gayugúptit.

B (a)   Dángi číxča,
       nix̣ə́gwitq:
         Ú:::! gałə́xłx níx̣ux̣.   380

(b)   Wínpu gačíxča,
       nix̣łúxwayt,
         «Łúxwan wátułba q̇wáp anx̣úkšidam.»

(c)   Nix̣ə́lačk,
       gayúya q̇wáp wátuł,   385
       nix̣úkšit.

C (a)   Kwálá q̇wáp gayugúptit,
       aga wiťax̣ wínpu nikłxíyukwačk,
        gačíxča.

(b)   Łə́xłx níx̣ux̣,   390
       nix̣ə́lačk,
        nayx̣ə́lkiłx̣.

(c)   Yú::x̣t;
       nix̣łúxwayt,
         «Qánčix̣ łuxwan ayučúdiyayax̣dixa?»   395

(d)   Gayúpa,
           gasixəmknákwačk:
              ákwa gíbix.

(e)   Gayáškupq,
           gíwam číwx̣t,   400
           aga wíťax̣ gayux̣ugákwšitam.

D (a)   Núx̌ix,
           aga wíťax̣ niktxíwkačk wínpu;

(b)   Nix̣túxwayt,
           «Túxwan néšqi anugúptit.»   405

(c)   Yáx̣a áx̣ wagagílak ú:::qiw,
           tá::x̣əlqwalala.

(d)   Nix̣túxwayt,
           «Túxwan kwábá anúya;

(e)   «Kí::mlipsix,   410
              «anx̣agmúkwšit.»

E (a)   Iyax̣əngná:::gwax̣ áx̣ka,
           kwatqí gagíyux̣;
              gaktx̣émitq itbúlmax̣.

(b)   Aga gayúya,   415
           gayax̣agmúkwšit kí::mlipsix.

(c)   Kwálá aga gagyúlxam,
           «Dánba kémlipsix imx̣úkšit?»

(d)   Gagigkítkiq,
           gašx̣úkšit,   420
              gayugúptit.

(e)   Túxwan qánčix̣,
           nix̣égwitq;
              šdúkwtk;
                 aga ayágikal gašx̣élačk.   425

3. I.iii
[He becomes the hunter]

Aga gašdútayt;
   gagyúlxam,
      «Ága máyka amx̣q̇wálalma.
«Amx̣túxwan,

‹Łúxwan iłə́kala łúx̣t.´ 430
  «Daba náyma ganułáytx̣,
«Náyka anx̣q̓wálalma.»
  «Áw,»
    gačúlxam;
Aga kwaλqí gašdə́x̣ux̣. 435

3. II.ii
[The brothers are reunited]

A (a)   Aga káwux gayúya,
     gagix̣ə́nimayx,
      gáx̣ba idə́kaqwłba.
(b)   Aga gayúya,
     yú::::yt; 530
      kwálá::: yúyt,
   aga gačúgikl itxwdə́li;
     nixłúxwayt,
  «Û:: agá łga indímam.»
B (a)   Gayú::giya itgwə́li, 535
     gayuxátxwit;
      nix̣mílaq,
   nix̣əlčə́maq:
     yú:::qəlqt íyamxix;
      qátgí:: iyágwamnił níx̣ux̣. 540
(b)   Gayáškupq,
     gačíglkl íyamxix:
      aga dá:::yma idə́q̓wču.
C (a.1) Gačyúlxam,
     «Á:::wi! Ičə́mxix!» 545
(a.2) «ʔá:::! Ísʔis!»
     gačúlxam.
(b.1) «K̓úya!
     «Náyka.»
(b.2) «ʔá:::í:sʔi:s!» 550
(c.1) «K̓úya!
    ‹Nə́gitga!
     «ngaλákwačk!»›

(c.2)   Gačikλákwačk:
         «A:w áganwi! Ápxu;»   555
(c.3)   «ʔə̂n:::!»
         gačyúlxam.
D (a)   «Qáx̣ba wagałáx̣ aga akíx̣ax̣?»
 (b)   Gačyúlxam,
         «Dábá.»   560
 (c)   «Áw. Mánk áłqičwa,
         aladímama.»
E (a)   Gačíglga,
         gačíyučkč,
         gačílk̓ilxma íyagwamnił.   565
 (b)   Aga gačílqwim,
         nix̣łx̣ələmčk,
         p̓ala níx̣ux̣.

3. III.iii
[She combs his hair]

(a)   Káwux,
        aga wiťax̣ gagíyukwł λáx̣nix,
         aga gakłilgə́čam;
         gagiútxmit iqčáma;   725
              gałə́l:::: gałiq̓ə́lba iłíyaqšu.
(b)   Wíťax̣ gagigútxmit iqčáma,
         náwi idyámčkš nugwagílakwit.
(c)   Iłáłunix gagigútxmit iqčáma,
         gagə́łx̣ga,   730
         náwi ší:ťixbt iyágikaw.
(d)   Wíťax̣ gagigútxmit iqčáma,
         gagə́łx̣ga iłíyaqšu,
         ná:::wi idyáq̓ux̣łax̣bt.
(e)   Wíťax̣ gagigútxmit iqčáma,   735
         náwi wílx gałigútxwit.
(f)   Gagə́łx̣ga núx̣̓,
         gagyúlxam wíyalxt,
         «Qánčix̣bt gánga iłíyaqšu?»
(g)   Gačúlxam,   740

«Aýš gałigútxwitx̣ wílx.»
(h)   Gagyúlxam,
      «Níxwa míya!»
        Gašgíglkl.
(i)   «ʔə́n::,»   745
      gačúlxam,
        «Mánk íłaλqt aga.»
(j)   «Âw,»
      gagyúlxam;
        aga gałáškupq.   750

GITSKUX AND HIS OLDER BROTHER

PART ONE
Grizzly Woman Comes To Be A Wife, Slays, and Is Slain
I. Grizzly Woman Comes
i. [They live there]

A   *The people lived there in a village.*
       Their house was at the end,
          Gitskux, his older brother, his (brother's) wife;
            they had two children,
               one younger sister.   5

B   *Aaaalways the two (men) would go,*
       they would hunt;
          sometimes they would bring back a deer,
           sometimes they would bring raccoons;
             that is what they did.   10

C (a)   *Aaaalways they would bring back some deer,*
       the woman would go out,
          she would bring the deer inside with only one arm;
           she would let it drop,
             now she would butcher it.   15

(b)   *Now she would distribute to people small pieces of meat,*
       (except) the house of the two Greyback Lice.

(c)   *She would become quiet,*
       in the morning again the two would go.

     I.ii. [Grizzly Woman comes to be the older brother's second wife]

A (a)   *Soooon—*   20
       I do not know just when,
          now Grizzly Woman reached them.

(b)   *The two have not gotten back,*
       soon they are travelling along,
          now Gitskux broke his bow;   25

(c)   *He told his older brother,*
       "Hurry!
          Something is wrong!"

B (a)   *They went to their canoe,*
       they went,   30
          they went back home.

(b)   *They got back;*
          she would take the deer with only one arm,
            she would bring it in the house.

(c)   As for those two,   35
            Gitskux got his two nephews,
                they went,
                    they entered the house:
                        there is Grizzly Woman.
C (a)   It became night,   40
            he (the older brother) went and lay down,
                right away Grizzly Woman herself also went and lay beside him.
(b)   They said nothing,
            they were afraid;
                he told them,   45
                    "Let it be!
                        Say nothing!"
(c)Now that is what they did;
            now he had two wives.

I.iii. [They continue to live there, but]

(a)   In the morning,   50
            the two would go;
(b)   Whatever they would bring back,
            now his first wife distributed that to people;
(c)   As for those two children,
            now they did not go to their father,   55
                only to their uncle.

II. Grizzly Woman Kills the First Wife and Puts On Her Skin
i. [Grizzly Woman claims a pet raccoon, the children cry]

A (a)   I do not know just when,
            the two caught a little raccoon,
                they brought it,
                    they brought it back.   60
(b)   Grizzly Woman said,
            "Aaaaana, for me."
(c)   The two children would cry;
            they wanted the raccoon.
B (a)   In the morning,   65
            again they would go.
(b)   Now they would always see the raccoon,
            Grizzly Woman would play with it,
                they would cry.
(c)   Now her (the mother's) heart   70
            it became no longer good.

II.ii. [The mother kills Grizzly Woman's pet]

A   *Some day,*
    now she is cleaning;
        Grizzly Woman is absent;
          she clubbed it,   75
            she killed the raccoon.

B (a)   *Soon now she arrived,*
    she saw her raccoon,
      it is dead.

  (b)   *"Ahhhh!"*   80
    she said,
      "What happened to it?"

  (c)   *She (the mother) paid no attention to her.*

II.iii. [Gitskux brings a racoon for his nephews]

A   *Soon now the two got there,*
    again they brought one back;   85
      Gitskux told his older brother,
        "I will bring it,
          I will bring it to the children."

B   *He brought it,*
    he brought it back,   90
      he brought it to his nephews;
        they were glad,
          they would play with it all day.

C (a)   *As for Grizzly Woman,*
    now she became angry.   95

  (b)   *She told her husband*
    "Why didn't you give it to me?"

  (c)   *He told her,*
    "I did not get it,
      "That uncle of theirs got it,   100
        "he gave it to them."

II.iv. [Grizzly Woman kills the children's pet]

  (a)   *Now they lived there;*
    aaaall day the children would play with it;
      one day they went to the water,
        they went to swim;   105
          only she, Grizzly Woman, is there.

  (b)   *Now she was the one cleaning,*
    she clubbed the raccoon,
      she killed it.

(c) *The children arrived;*   110
   right away they ran to
     where their raccoon was,
      they saw it;
       it is dead;
        they cried.   115

II.v. [The wives fight; Grizzly Woman kills the first wife,
    and puts on her skin]

(a) *Now the two women quarreled,*
   soon now they jumped at each other,
    they fought.

(b) *She killed her,*
   she skinned her,   120
    she put herself down into her.

(c) *The children fled from her.*

(d) *She called out to them,*
   she would tell them,
    "Come *here!*   125
     "Commme *here!*
      "Soon your uncle, those two will come."

(e) Noooo,
   they did not go inside.

III. The Brothers Kill Grizzly Woman and Restore the First Wife
i. [The first wife's foresight]

A *As for that woman,*   130
   she had known about herself;
    when it was morning,
     they went;
      now she told her brother-in-law:

B (a) *"Hurry!*   135
   "Come back home earlier!

(b) *"This day she will kill me,*
   "she will skin me;

(c) *"She will put herself down inside me,*
   "she will lay me behind the house. 140

(d) *"Now bring deer,*
   "keep giving food to her;

(e) *"Keep telling her,*
   "'Eat!'"

C (a) *Now that is what the two soon do;* 145
   now he broke his bow.

(b)   *He told his older brother,*
      "Hurry!
        "Let us go back home!"

(c)   *He (the older brother) told him,*   150
      "Pretty soon."

(d)   *"No!"*
      he told him.

(e)   *He told him,*
      "Your wife now has killed your children's mother."   155

III.ii. [Testing the would-be wife]

A (a)   *Now they went;*
      he got rotten wood;
        he transformed them,
          they became deer.

(b)   *They arrived,*   160
      the children are running about;
        they went ashore.

B (a)   *He dropped the deer at the door,*
      he told her,
        "Now take them in the house."   165

(b)   *She stood,*
      she went;
        in vain,
          she could not begin to lift them.

C (a)   *A long time he stood,*   170
      he pushed her,
        he told her,
          "What is the matter with you?
            "Always you would take it inside with just one arm."

(b)   *"Uhhmmm yes,"*   175
      she told him,
        "Today I have diarrhoea."

D (a)   *He took them inside,*
      now he butchered them;

(b)   *She began to help him,*   180
      she took it;

(c)   *She distributed it to people,*
      she even gave food to the two Greyback Lice.

E (a)   *They said,*
      "Oh dear! When has someone given us food?"   185

(b)   *They stood,*
      they danced,
        they said,
          "When has someone given us food?"

"Someone gave us food!"   190

(c)   That is what they did,
           they sang.

III.iii. [Grizzly Woman is killed]

A (a) Now she went back home,
           she herself arrived;
               as for Gitskux,   195
               now he was cooking;
                   all done,
                       now they began to eat.
   (b) The children did not eat,
           they lay down,   200
               they sleep;
                   now all night he (Gitskux) kept giving her food,
                       she ate.
   (c) Sooooon now she will fall asleep,
           he will awaken her,   205
               he will tell her,
                   "What is the matter with you?
                       "You didn't use to be like that."
B (a) Soon then some meat left.
           "Uhmmm yes,"   210
               she would tell him,
                   "I am ill;"
                       now again she will eat.
   (b) Soon now she will fall asleep,
           he will grab her,   215
               he will sit her up,
                   now in vain she will try to eat:
                       worse.
   (c) Now she is asleep,
           in vain he tried to sit her up;   220
               nooo,
                   he let her drop;
                       now slowly, carefully he took off his sister-in-law's skin:
                           Oh dear! It is Grizzly Woman lying there!
C (a) He brought his sister-in-law's skin,   225
           he put it back on her;
               soon now he covered her about;
                   He went inside the house,
                       back she came following him.
   (b) The two took hold of her (Grizzly Woman),   230
           they brought her outside;
               they made a fire,

        there they laid her on top;
           she burned.

(c)   *They did nothing over her,*   235
        there she lies;
           life had come back to her *(the first wife)*.

PART TWO
Grizzly Woman Returns and Captures Gitskux
i. [Grizzly Woman returns, kills, eats the people]

(a)   *Now they lived there;*
        I do not know just when,
           now again she reached them.   240

(b)   *The two (wives) fought,*
        they fought on,
           the children were crying and screaming;
             the people said,
                "Dear oh dearrrr! Our chief's wives are fighting."   245

(c)   *They came to watch the two,*
        they are fighting on;
           *Grizzly Woman was sat on under*neath.

(d)   *Soon she would raise herself up,*
        now again she (the first wife) would throw her down again;   250
           the people kept calling out;
             anger,
                now that acted on Grizzly Woman.

(e)   *She thought,*
        "Now she injured me;"   255
           now she became a dangerous being,
             she swallowed her;
                now she ate up alllll the people.

[My mother's mother used to say,
    "Only she actually would eat people;   260
        "Other Grizzly Woman did not eat people;
        "They just killed them."]

ii. [The Younger Sister's Head.]   [320:16]

(a)   *She remembered her sister-in-law,*
        she thought,
           "I didn't swallow her."   265

(b)   *She vomited:*
        "Oh Nooooo;"
           she did not swallow her (again).

(c)   *She went to the river,*
      she is at the water,   270
         she washes and washes her.

(d)   *She leaped on her,*
      she seized her,
         her head broke off,
            it went off into the water,   275
            it drifted.

(e)   *In vain she kept trying to seize it,*
      it drifted.

iii. [The Brothers Retrieve Their Sister's Head]

A   *Yonder where those two are,*
        he (Gitskux) told him,   280
          "Hurry!
            "Make haste here!
               "Now your wife has eaten our people."

B (a) *The two made haste,*
        they are goooooing on,   285

(b)   *Soon while they are going,*
      now they saw something,
         it is drifting toward them.

(c)   *He told him,*
      "Let's go close to that thing."   290

C (a) *They paddled to it,*
        he got their younger sister's head.

(b)   *He told his older brother,*
      "Look at it!
         "Our younger sister's head."   295

(c)   *Now he put it away,*
      the two went onnnn.

iv. [They Encounter Grizzly Woman]

(a)   *Close to their house,*
      some woman sits and sits,
         she sits on the bank of the river.   300

(b)   *She hailed the two,*
      she said,
         "Indeeeeed bring me across!"

(c)   *He told his younger brother,*
      "Let's bring her across."   305

(d)   *"No.*
      "That is her,
         "she is tricking us."

(e)   *He told him,*
    "Pay no attention to her;   310
      "Let us *go on."*

v. [Grizzly Woman Captures Gitskux]

(a)   *The two are goooooooing on,*
    they arrive:
      noooooo people.

(b)   *Soon* now *they saw her,*   315
    they fled her,
      they leaped into their canoe.

(c)   *She leaped at him (Gitskux),*
    she caught her little finger in his (long, beautiful) hair,
      she seized him.   320

(d)   *He threw their younger sister's head to him,*
    he told his older brother:
      "Our younger sister's head!
        "Now she got me."

(e)   *Now he (the older brother) went on,*   325
    now he is alone.

PART THREE
The Elder Brother Finds A True Wife, Through Whom Gitskux
    Is Rescued And Restored
I. He Becomes A Husband, Hunter, Father Again
i. [He finds a house, woman and food]

A   *As for that Gitskux,*
    now Grizzly Woman took him,
      to where her house is;
        there she kept him,   330
        she did not kill him.

B (a)   *As for his older brother, he went* on *and on,*
    I don't know where he is going,
      now he reached a very *large house.*

(b)   *Soon he is approaching it,*   335
    he thought,
      "Here I will put away my younger sister's head;"
      he cached it carefully and well.

(c)   *Now he went,*
    he entered,   340
      Dear oh dear! smoke-dried meat.

(d)   *He thought,*
    "Perhaps the people went somewhere."

(e)   *He thought,*
      "I shall be here;   345
        "a little while tomorrow,
          "before I shall go somewhere."

C (a)   *He* sits *and sits there;*
      evening,
        now he heard,   350
          a person is coming:
            a man unpacked his pack.

(b)   *He looked at him,*
      he brought deer inside,
        he went out.   355

(c)   *A loooong time,*
      now a woman entered,
      she washed,
        then twisted her hair into braids.

(d)   *Now he thought,*   360
      "Where did the man go?
      "This person must be his wife."

(e)   *Now she butchered,*
      so now she gave him food;
      he ate,   365
        he finished eating,
        he was through.

I.ii. [She becomes his wife]

A (a)   *The two sit and sit there;*
      she told him,
        "If you should be sleepy,   370
        "Sleep over there!"

(b)   *He thought,*
      "I am tired,
      "I will lie down."

(c)   *He went,*   375
      he lay down,
      he went to sleep.

B (a)   *Something is biting him,*
      he woke up:
        Uuuu! *he scratched himself.*   380

(b)   *A flea was biting him,*
      he thought,
        "Perhaps I should lie near the fire."

(c)   *He got up,*
      he went near the fire,   385
      he lay down.

C (a)   *Soon he was nearly asleep,*
      now again a flea began to crawl about on him,
        it bit him.

  (b)   *He scratched himself,*   390
      he got up,
        he fixed the fire.

  (c)   *He sits there;*
      he thought,
        "How long perhaps until it will be dawn?"   395

  (d)   *He went outside,*
      he looked around:
        it is dark.

  (e)   *He went inside,*
      he is sleepy,   400
        now again he laid himself quite down.

D (a)   *A little while,*
      now again a flea began to crawl on him;

  (b)   *He thought,*
      "Perhaps I will not sleep."   405

  (c)   *That woman on the other hand is sleeeeeping,*
      she is snoooooring.

  (d)   *He thought,*
      "Perhaps I will go there,

  (e)   *"at the very edge (of her bed),*   410
      "I will lie down by her."

E (a)   *She herself had known all about him,*
      that is what she did to him;
        she joined (five) nights together.

  (b)   *Now he went,*   415
      he lay down by her at the very edge.

  (c)   *Soon now she told him,*
      "Why do you lie down at the edge?"

  (d)   *She covered him,*
      the two lay there,   420
        he went to sleep.

  (e)   *I do not know how long,*
      he woke up;
        the two stretch out on their sides;
          now his wife and he got up.   425

I.iii. [He becomes the hunter]

Now the two stayed;
      she told him,
        "Now you will be doing the hunting.
        "You will have thought,

'Perhaps there is some man.'   430
"Here I have lived alone,
"I would be the one hunting."
"Indeed,"
   he told her;
  Now that is what the two did.   435

I.iv. [They bury the sister's head]

A (a)   The two stayed on there,
    a long time;
      now she asked him,
      she told him,
        "Did you not carry something,   440
        "when you got to me?"
(b)[3]   He had told her,
      "Uhmm, yes. My younger sister's head.
      "I had cached it over there,
      "before I had entered."   445
B (a)   "Indeed,"
    she had told him,
      "Go bring it."
  (b)   He had gone,
    where he had cached the head;   450
      he has gotten it,
        he had carried it,
          he had brought it to her.
C (a)   She had washed and washed it,
    she had combed and combed it;   455
      Now she had beaded it,
      she threaded them on her every hair;
      Aaaaall done,
        now she wrapped it entirely up.
  (b)   The two went,   460
    they put it quite away,
      they became quiet.

I.v. [She has two boys]

A (a)   At morning,
    now again he would hunt;
      now that is what he would do.   465
  (b)   As for her,
    now she stayed,
      she smoke-dried.
  (c)   Now she became pregnant.

B (a) *A long time,*
  now she gave birth:
   she got a male child.   470
 (b) *Now they lived on there,*
  he became somewhat big.
 (c) *Now again they all stayed.*   475
C (a) *A long long time,*
  Now again she gave birth,
   again a male child.
 (b) *Their two sons became quite big.*
 (c) *Now all day they will run around,*   480
  they will play.

II. Gitskux Is Rescued, Grizzly Woman Is Killed
i. [The wife advises about Gitskux]

A (a) *Now again she asked him,*
  she told him,
   "Did you come alone?"
 (b) *He would tell her,*   485
  "No.
  "We two, my younger brother.
  "Grizzly Woman took him,
  "Perhaps she ate him."
B (a) *"No,"*   490
  she would tell him,
   "He lives.
  "She did not eat him,
  "She just keeps him to use to wipe her anus.
 (b) *"Now she will nearly kill him,*   495
  "now his hair is nothing,
  "now he is blind,
   "only bones:
    "now make haste!
 (c) *"What do you think,*   500
  "will you go?
  "Hurry!"
C (a) *He told her,*
  "Uhh yes! At morning I will go."
 (b) *"Indeed,"*   505
  she told him.
 (c) *Now she tied up things (for him),*
  she gave him flints.
D (a) *She told him,*
  "Put these on his head."   510

(b)   *"Give him something (emetic),*
             "wash out his 'heart,'
                 "scrape and rinse it out."
E (a)   *She would tell him,*
             "Be goooooing!   515
                 "You will get to him,
                     "aaaall the time he weeps.
     (b)   *"Blue Jay will get to him,*
             he will do every which way to him,
                 he will tell him,   520
                     'It is I (your elder brother),
                         'Now I have come.'"
     (c)   *"He will tell him,*
             "Ohhhh Blue Jay! I am a poor thing,
                 'Thus you do me.'"   525

II.ii. [The brothers are reunited]

A (a)   *Now at morning he went,*
             she showed him the way to
                 where her (Grizzly Woman's) house was.
     (b)   *Now he went,*
             he is goooooing on;   530
                 soooon as he is going,
                 now he saw smoke;
                     he thought,
                         "Uuu now I must have arrived."
B (a)   *He wennt to the house,*   535
             he stood by it
                 he listened,
                 he heard:
                     his younger brother is weeping and weeping;
                     howww his heart became.   540
     (b)   *He went inside,*
             he saw his younger brother:
                 now only bones.
C (a-1) *He told him,*
             "Younger brother! My younger brother!"   545
     (a-2)   *"Ahhh! Blue Jay!"*
             he told him.
     (b-1)   *"No!*
                 "It is I."
     (b-2)   *"Ahhh Bluue Jaay!"*   550
     (c-1)   *"No!*
                 "Take hold of me!
                     "Feel me!"

(c-2) *He felt him:*
   "Ooh it is really so! Older brother!"   555
(c-3) *"Uhh yes!"*
   he told him.
D (a) *"Where is the sun now?"*
 (b) *He told him (his younger brother),*
   "Right here."   560
 (c) *"Indeed. It will be some time later,*
   "she will get here."
E (a) *He took him,*
   he washed him,
    he scraped and rinsed out his 'heart.'   565
 (b) *Now he gave him food;*
   he began to eat;
   he became quiet.

   II.iii. [The brothers plan]

A (a) *He told him,*
   "She will get back,   570
   now she will tell me,
 (b) *"'Arrrrre you here?*
    'Esteemed Wigickúx?
    'My anus-wiper?'
 (c) *"I will tell her,*   575
   'Yes, I am here.'
B (d) *"Now she will go,*
   she will defecate,
   she will come inside;
 (e) *"Now she will tell me,*   580
   'Sit up straight!'
 (f) *Now I will wipe and wipe.*
C (g) *Now she will sit on me,*
   now she will tell me,
   'Now turn turn yourself.'   585
 (h) *Now that is what I do,*
   I wipe her.
 (i) *"Indeed,"*
   he told his younger brother.
D (a) *Now he put flints aaaall over his head;*   590
   he told him:
 (b) *"When she sits upon you,*
   she will tell you,
    'Adíiii your head pricks.'
 (c) *"Now you will tell her,*   595
   'Long ago I had much hair,
    now sofffft you would sit on me.'

(d)   *"Now she will sit on you,*
            now you will stand up and push in her,
                she will get cut and cut,   600
                    her very heart will get cut,
                    you will kill her."

(e)   *"Indeed."*

E (a)   *The two sit there.*
         He told him,   605
            "Where is the sun?"

(b)   *He told him,*
         Now it is long past midday."

(c)   *"Uhmmm yes,"*
         he told him,   610
            "Now it is near the time she will return."

(d)   *He told his younger brother,*
         "What you have usually done,
         "do that same way."

(e)   *Now he left him,*   615
         he went and hid;
            he went around the house,
            he covered himself.

II.iv. [Grizzly Woman is killed by Gitskux]

A (a)   *Soon now he heard,*
        she got back,
            she entered.   620

(b)   *She told him,*
         "Arrrrrre you here?
         "Esteemed Anus-wiper?"

(c)   *"Uhh yes,"*   625
         he told her,
         "I am here."

(d)   *"Indeed.*
         Soon now I will defecate;"
         she went out.   630

(e)   *Soon now she began to shriek,*
         she said,
            "Ádáaaaaa! My anussss!
            "Ádáaaaaa!
         she shrieked.   635

B (a)   *She became quiet,*
        she entered,
            she told him,
               "Now sit up straight, Esteemed Gitskux!
              "Wipe me!"   640

(b)   *He sat straight,*
              she sat on him,
                  she stood up.

(c)   *She told him,*
              "Adáaaaa! What pricks?"   645

(d)   *He told her,*
              "Long ago I had much hair, soft.
                  "You will sit on me however now,
                      "what hair have I?
                          "Only bones now."   650

(e)   *"Uhhmm yes,"*
              she told him.

C (a)   *Now again she sat on him;*
              as soon as she sat on him,
                  now he stood up and pushed in her: 655
                      "Aadaaaaa!",
                          she said.

(b)   *He did it rapidly,*
              he cut and cut her:
                  Guuuu! she fell down.   660

(c)   *He hailed his older brother,*
              he said,
                  "Older brother! Now I have killed her!"

II.v. [Older brother helps]

A (a)   *He went around the house,*
              he went inside: 665
                  she lies there,
                  she is dead;
                      now he told him,
                          "Now I shall take you outside."

B (a)   *He held his hand,*   670
              he took him over to there,
                  he seated him;

(b)   *He told him,*
              "Now remain here!
              "I will go burn her house,   675
              "There she will burn."

(c)   *"Indeed,"*
              he told him.

C   *He went,*
              now he burned her house: 680
                  it burned up every bit,
                      she burned up too,
                          only her bones remain.

III. Gitskux Is Restored
i. [The brothers return home]

A (a)   *He told his younger brother,*
        "Eat a little again;   685
          "You will be tired,
            "We shall go a long way."
  (b)   *Now he took him with him,*
        they went:
        they have arrived close by.   690

B (a)   *He told him,*
        "I will leave you here;
          "I will go inform them."
  (b)   *"Ahh yes,"*
        he told him,   695
        "I will remain here."

C (a)   *He went,*
        he told his wife,
        "Now I have brought my younger brother."
  (b)   *"Indeed,"*   700
        she told him;
        "There,
        "soon I shall bathe him
         "A little while tomorrow
         "I shall fix him properly."   705

III.ii. [She cleanses Gitskux]

A   *Now they went out,*
        they went,
         where he is,
          they reached him.

B (a)   *Now she bathed all his body,*   710
        she made him quite clean;
  (b)   *she got water,*
        she threw it at him;
  (c)   *the fifth time,*
        now his eyes opened.   715

C (a)   *She told him,*
        "Now let us go inside."
  (b)   *They went,*
        he saw his two nephews.
  (c)   *He took them,*
        he put them on his lap.   720

III.iii. [She combs his hair]

(a)   *Morning,*
      now again she took him outside,
        now she combed him;
          she placed the comb on him: 725
           blaaaaack his hair grew out.

(b)   *Again she put the comb on him,*
      right away it covered him to his ears.

(c)   *The third time she put the comb on him,*
      she pulled and combed,
        right away half way down his back.   730

(d)   *Again she put the comb on him,*
      she pulled and combed his hair,
        right away at his knees.

(e)   *Again she put the comb on him,*
      right away it stood to the ground.   735

(f)   *She pulled and combed a little,*
      she told his older brother,
        "To what was his hair before?"

(g)   *He told her,*   740
      "It would just stand to the ground."

(h)   *She told him,*
      "Suppose you go along!"
      The two saw him.

(i)   *"Uhhmm,"*   745
      he told her,
        "It is a little longer now."

(j)   *"Indeed,"*
      she told him;
        now they went inside.   750

PART FOUR
Grizzly Woman, The Would-Be Wife, Returns
I. Return Of The Would-Be Wife
i. [Oversight]

(a)   *I do not know how long after,*
      now those two children became big;
      now she told the two (men):

(b)   *"I forgot.*
      "I did not tell you,   755
        "If you should burn her,
          "You should mash her bones,
            "Blow them away."

(c)   *"Uhh,"*
    he would tell her,   760
      "I merely burned her."

I.ii. [Foresight]

(a)   *"Uhh,"*
    she would say,
      "I do not know where,
        "some day,   765
          "now she will reach us.
(b)   *"She will kill me,*
    "she will skin me,
      "she will lay me down.
(c)   *"Be quick!*   770
    "Do (the necessary) things to her.
      "My body will get bad."
(d)   *"If she reaches us,*
    "Do not be long,
      "Come back home."   775
(e)   *"Indeed,"*
    they told her;
      Gitskux thought,
        "Nowwww again she will do some sorts of thing to us."

I.iii. [Today]

(a)   *I do not know when,*   780
    now she told them,
      "Today now she will reach here.
(b)   *"Be careful!*
    "Make haste!
      "The children will be terrified."   785
(c)   *"Yes,"*
    they told her;
    they went,
      they went hunting;
      as for her,   790
      she is doing chores.
(d)   *Soon now she (Grizzly Woman) arrived,*
    right away she killed her;
      she did not eat her;
      she skinned her,   795
        she put her on herself.
(e)   *She dragged her to the rear of the house,*
    she laid her down,
      she covered her.

II. Detecting The Would-Be Wife
i. [Children and uncles seek each other]

(a)   *The two children are playing I don't know where;*   800
     soon now they went inside,
       they saw their mother;
         they thought,
           "Not like our mother."

(b)   *They did not remain at the house,*   805
     they ran,
       they went to wait for their father and their uncle.

(c)   *As for those two yonder,*
     he broke his bow;
       he told him,
         "Now Grizzly Woman has come to her;"   810
           they went back home,
           they hurried.

II.ii. [Children and uncles meet]

(a)   *Soon they are going,*
     now they met the two children,   815
       at once he said to his nephews,
         "What happened?"

(b)   *"No.*
     "The only thing is
       "that we saw   820
         "our mother is not right."

(c)   *"Indeed.*
     "Let us go indeed."

II.iii. [Testing the would-be wife]

A   *They went,*
     they got back: 825
       she is going about,
         she is doing chores;
           they went inside.

B (a)   *He told her,*
     "Give me the knife!"   830
       She looked for it,
         in vain,
          nooo.

(b)   *He told her,*
     "What is the matter with you?   835
       "Always I tell you,

            "'Give me the knife';
               "In a snap you get it,
               "You give it to me."

(c)   *"Ah*mmm *yes. I forgot."*   840

C (a)   *Now again he told her,*
            "Where is the roasting spit?"
            She looked for it.

(b)   *Now again he stood up,*
            he pushed her,   845
               he told her:
                   "This is it right here standing by us!
                       "It's you that usually put it away."

(c)   *"Aánáaa! I forgot."*
            All of that.   850

III. Destroying The Would-Be Wife
i. [Grizzly Woman Sleeps]

(a)   *Now they ate;*
            She did not feel quite right.[4]

(b)   *They ate,*
            he will tell her,
               "What is the matter with you?"   855
               "Aánáaaa! I am sick."

(c)   *They ate,*
            soooon *now she fell asleep;*
               "What is the trouble with you?"
               "Uhhh *yes! I am sick."*   860

III.ii. [Grizzly Woman Killed]

(a)   *Soon now she was asleep,*
            right where she sits,
               she lay.

(b)   *As for those two children,*
            their father put them to bed,   865
               he lay beside them.

(c)   *Now* slowly, *carefully he (Gitskux) untied her arms,*
            her legs close to her feet,
               slowly, *carefully he took off her skin.*

(d)   *Grizzly Woman* sleeeeeeps;   870
            he took his sister-in-law's skin,
               he put it onto her,
                   he laid her down nicely,
                   he covered her.

(e)   *He went inside,*   875
           his older brother got up,
              they killed her;
                 they dragged her outside,
                    they laid her down.

III.iii. [Grizzly Woman destroyed]

(a)   *Soon now that woman entered;*   880
           she told them,
              "Bring some firewood!
              "We shall build a fire."
                 That is what the two did.

(b)   *They brought wood,*   885
           they built a fire,
              they placed her on it.

(c)   *She burned up,*
           she was completely incinerated:
              only her bones.   890

(d)   *She took them,*
           she gathered them in a heap;
              she mashed them,
              all done;
                 now she took them,   895
                 she blew, *blew them away every bit.*

(e)   *Now she told them,*
             "Now we have killed her,
             "She will not reach us again."

PART FIVE
Epilogue: They Part to Become What They are Now

A (a)   *Now they lived on and on there,*   900
            that is the way they were;
 (b)   *Now the two youths became big;*
 (c)   *Now they separated.*
B (a)   *She said,*
           "I for my part will become a water-being.   905
              "You on the other hand will be in the mountains."
 (b)   *Igitskúx said,*
              "I for my part will go with my two nephews."
 (c)   *The other, her husband, said,*
              "I for my part will go alone."   910
C   *I do not know what they became;*
           they did not use to say,
              what those people became.

      Now myth myth . . .

As an aid in checking this analysis and translation against the original publication, the following table is provided.

LINEATION:
Correlation between published text and verse analysis

JACOBS 1959:315–331.	VERSE ANALYSIS			
315:10	One	I.i.	1–19	19 lines
316:5		ii.	20–49	30 lines
316:15		iii.	50–56	7 lines
317:1		II.i.	57–71	15 lines
317:6		ii.	72–83	12 lines
317:8		iii.	84–101	18 lines
317:16		iv.	102–115	14 lines
318:1		v.	116–129	14 lines
318:5		III.i.	130–155	26 lines
318:13		ii.	156–192	37 lines
319:17		iii.	193–237	45 lines
320:4	Two	I.i.	238–258	21 lines
320:13		[insert]	259–262	4 lines
320:16		ii.	263–278	16 lines
321:3		iii.	279–297	19 lines
321:19		iv.	298–311	14 lines
321:12		v.	312–326	15 lines
321:18	Three	I.i.	327–367	41 lines
322:13		ii.	368–425	58 lines
323:11		iii.	426–435	10 lines
323:13		iv.	436–462	27 lines
324:2		v.	463–481	19 lines
324:9		II.i.	482–525	44 lines
325:2		ii.	526–568	43 lines
325:14		iii.	569–618	50 lines
326:10		iv.	619–663	45 lines
327:3		v.	664–683	20 lines
327:10		III.i.	684–705	22 lines
327:16		ii.	706–721	16 lines
328:1		iii.	722–755	29 lines
328:13	Four	I.i.	756–761	11 lines
328:17		ii.	762–779	18 lines
329:4		iii.	780–799	20 lines

JACOBS 1959:315–331.	VERSE ANALYSIS			
329:10	Four (cont.)	II.i.	800–813	14 lines
329:15		ii.	814–823	10 lines
329:18		iii.	824–850	27 lines
330:7		III.i.	851–860	10 lines
330:10		ii.	861–879	19 lines
330:17		iii.	880–899	20 lines
331:4	Five		900–914	15 lines

NOTES

[1]This paper is indeed part of a study of all the Clackamas narratives having to do with the Grizzly Ogress, which is in turn part of a book-length manuscript, *Bears that Save and Destroy,* completed in 1978–9, but in need of some revision. Portions of the book-length study are adapted as articles in my "Reading Clackamas texts" and "Verse analysis of a Wasco text." Only the English text, revised from the translation published by Jacobs, is given here, for reasons of economy of space and typography. Charles Bigelow and I have in preparation a book that will present a series of Chinookan texts in the original language, according to the kind of verse-analysis shown here, and employing a typography devised by Bigelow for the purpose. A sample precedes the English text.

[2]Most Penutian work so far has concentrated on the California languages, and on limited comparison of semantically unrelated words. When words are compared within a semantic group, new understanding of derivational patterns and meanings may emerge, as has been the case with words for "bears." Evidence accumulates that the ancestral Penutian language had not only inflectional elaboration by suffixes, but also derivational elaboration by pre-posed elements. That discovery, summarized in the slogan "Inflection to the right, agglutination to the left," radically recasts the assumptions of previous comparison of words, and adds many bits of evidence.

[3]The remote past tense on verbs in (b) et seq. makes use of the 'usitative' suffix -x, as has not been the case with preceding verbs. I try to catch something of the effect by using 'had.' The effect seems one of ritual. In the action clearly each verb indicates a single occurrence; the 'usitative' may imply the character of these two people, who would do this proper thing as an expression of habitual character. It may suggest a sense in which the single 'historical' action of myth is repeated each winter; if so, this ritual-like action of respectful treatment for the head of the sister-in-law brings the 'eternal recurrence' of the myth-time event into overt grammatical expression.

[4]Nervous, and sleepy; the skin felt as if smothering her, indicating that its power was greater than she could control.

BIBLIOGRAPHY

Hymes, Dell. "Louis Simpson's 'The deserted boy'." *Poetics* 5, no. 2 (1976), pp. 119–55.

———. "Discovering oral performance and measured verse in American Indian narrative." *New Literary History* 8, no. 3 (1977), pp. 431–57. (Ch. 9 in 1981[b].)

————. *Bears that save and destroy.* MS., 1979(a). (To be revised.)

————. *Myth as verse.* MS., 1979(b).

————. "Verse analysis of a Wasco text." *International Journal of American Linguistics.* (1980). 65–77. (Ch. 5 in 1981[b].)

————. "Reading Clackamas texts." In Karl Kroeber (ed.), *Traditional Literature of the American Indians,* 117–59. Lincoln: University of Nebraska Press, 1981(a). (Ch. 10 in 1981[b].)

————. "In Vain I Tried to Tell You." Philadelphia: University of Pennsylvania Press, 1981(b).

Jacobs, Melville. *Clackamas Chinook Texts, Part 1.* Indiana University Research Center in Anthropology, Folklore, and Linguistics, Publication 8. Bloomington, Ind., 1958(a).

————. *Content and Style of an Oral Literature.* Chicago University Press, 1958(b).

————. *Clackamas Chinook Texts, Part 2.* Indiana University Publications in Anthropology, Folklore and Linguistics, Publication 11. Bloomington, Ind., 1959.

————. *The People are Coming Soon: Analysis of Clackamas Chinook Myths and Tales.* Seattle: University of Washington Press, 1960.

Elaine Jahner: STONE BOY: PERSISTENT HERO

Heroes, by their very definition, require somewhat more than usual human force of character and they display it in wonderfully extravagant gestures. But if they are to have any real staying power through generations of human thought, their exploits must strike some sparks from the flints of home, hearth and dear mundane routine. Among the Lakota Sioux people, Stone Boy (along with the ever vital Trickster figure *Iktomi*) maintains his space-age identity with all the rakish good humor and protective force that he had in ancient mythic times.

In the story of Stone Boy, the links between its images and basic cultural resources have uniquely Lakota features, but the energies generated by these bonds are universal and have intense imaginative power. Showing how the particular opens out into the general is the scholar's task. It involves marshaling every available bit of ethnographic, linguistic and aesthetic information that might help explain the reality of a text.

As we sense the range of possibilities in any given tale and realize that actual narrators shared our intuitions about the power of some of the images, we are developing a finely tuned appreciation for an art almost totally neglected among American people until recently.[1] In the process, of course, we gain a different sense of the people who developed such works. Surely both our gains are argument enough for pursuing even a partial understanding of an elusive art form. As more and more people join the effort, we may be able to bring together the elements of a poetics of tribal folktales. This paper is one step in the direction of such a poetics and a plea for communal efforts to go beyond the point lone scholars can hope to reach.

The Lakota story of Stone Boy has immense possibilities as a starting point for studying the poetics of the folktale. It is still told today so we have a good sense of what elements have survived through time and radical culture change. Furthermore, we have reliable Lakota texts collected between 1897 and 1975 so we can trace some of the ties the story once had to a culture now past.[2] We also have a unique version of the story that seems to be the mythic relative of the more commonly told and collected *ohunkaka* or fictionalized accounts. The collection of available Stone Boy texts could easily be the basis for a monograph that would show that heroes with wit and good faith can survive even the most deplorable human machinations.

One theme is particularly accessible to modern audiences. In fact, its major manifestation is so inescapably obvious that in choosing it, one can at least start with certainty on a journey of interpretation. The meaning of boundaries—the dynamic interplay between inside and outside, security and danger, risk and continuity—is the theme that shapes the one episode surviving in most contemporary narrations.

According to many tellers, Stone Boy went sledding one day in winter with some young buffalo. He coasts behind the children and arranges to slide right over the top of their sleds. Naturally, since he is made of stone, he kills the buffalo children. Some time later, he hears an old buffalo sharpening his horns. Not admitting his identity, he asks the old buffalo what he is planning and learns that the entire buffalo nation is mobilizing to attack him. His response is to build an impenetrable boundary around his home. He tells his family to prepare at least one, sometimes four walls around the home. Then he sits on one of them and watches with glee while the buffalo try but fail to break them down.

Older, Lakota-language versions are longer and more complex than any modern versions I know. Pre-reservation tales clearly relate to the peoples' many feelings about the buffalo. Today, with the buffalo culture a beloved memory, the beast seems an anomalous enemy. Indeed his role is remarkably diminished in Kate Blue Thunder's 1975 version.[3] Kate does not even include the well-known sledding incident. She stresses Stone Boy's canny intelligence as the motive for the attack on his home. "Well, he was smart. So they wanted to kill him cause he was smart and he could do everything. This boy he turned into stone. They say he could talk, you know. So he knew what was coming. So he had them build him a high wall, stone, rock, where he sits, where he lives, a stone wall around him where he lives."

Kate goes on to point out that the buffalo leader is mean. The buffalo seem thinly disguised American troops or bureaucrats. What is important in this version is that Stone Boy creates a haven of safety "where he lives."

One other stylistic feature of her version is important because it occurs in every extant version of the story no matter how old or new. The buffalo attack when a certain kind of cloud appears in the sky. References to the clouds vary. Sometimes they are dark yellow, sometimes brown; but always they presage the beginning of a ferocious plains winter blizzard. In a culture where people counted their ages by the number of winters survived, this detail is important. Time and seasons are boundaries too, and movement through time is comparable to movement through space. The buffalo attack when Stone Boy's people are most vulnerable, beset by danger from the elements as well as from outside forces. The time when a storm is about to begin is a kind of transitional zone, a time of preparation for the challenge of surviving the blizzard. Even with technology, few people in the northern plains feel secure in a raging storm. The story of Stone Boy is always and truly a winter's tale bringing into play powerful and resonant images of security and its opposite. One reason for the power of these images is that stone or *inyan* has meanings that echo throughout all of Lakota life. It is not conceived as inert substance, but as moving yet unyieldingly persistent power. When explaining the meaning of stone to Frances Densmore, Chased-by-Bears chose an image that directly links stones and the sense of protection that comes from a well-guarded dwelling:

> *The outline of the stone is round, having no end and no beginning; like the power of the stone, it is endless. The stone is perfect of its kind and is the work of nature, no artificial means being used in shaping it. Outwardly it is not beautiful, but its structure is solid, like a solid house in which one may safely dwell. It is not composed of many substances, but is of one substance, which is genuine and not an imitation of anything else.*[4]

Stone Boy is living stone; and, as Densmore and almost all other reliable commentators on Lakota culture note, there is a close bond between stone and *Takuskanskan*, or the primal energy. *Takuskanskan* is often translated as "Something-In-Movement." Brave Buffalo, also speaking to Densmore, said "In all my life, I have been faithful to the sacred stones. I have lived according to their requirements and they have helped me in all my troubles."[5]

This background of meaning for stone is part of what gives the story its force and endurance. In pre-reservation times, the story had many more elements than we usually find now and they were intertwined in elaborate ways that we perceive best by studying the Lakota language versions. Fortunately we have a reliable text written by George Sword, somewhere around 1900. Sword was bilingual and claimed that the younger Lakota no longer understood his form of the language. Some of the linguistic matters that he insisted on preserving in the tale give us important clues as to how the story's segments of meaning functioned and related to each other.

This version, and almost all other older versions, begins by mentioning that four brothers live alone. We have the nucleus of a band, the basic unit of Lakota society. Theirs is an organized life where rules and obligations of kinship are keenly observed and the brothers feel their lack of a sister.

Then a woman comes; she arrives and she stands. For the non-Indian reading the story or just skimming the plot, this may not seem a particularly emphatic point or one generating any kind of suspense. But Sword clearly saw this as an important event. When he saw the written version of the story, he objected to combining the notions of arriving and standing into one word, *hinazin*.[6] He complained that only young people, influenced by white teachers, thought it one word and he insisted that its separation into two was very important, since the two ideas of arriving and standing had to be separate. I do not believe that Sword was just quibbling about a linguistic issue. I believe that he was responding to an important artistic point in the story. The concept of arriving outside the brothers' home, and that of just standing until invited in, each carried separate connotative meaning for him.

The woman arrived. Lakota verbs of movement exhibit many identifiable differences from the English patterns in that they mark the nature of point to point movement very precisely. The Lakota verb used for the woman's arrival is *hi*, a verb difficult to explain to English speakers. Ella Deloria translates it as "to arrive coming,"[7] It implies an end to a pre-determined journey, hence the "coming." Eugene Buechel is a bit clearer in his explanation. He says that it means arrival at a place not one's own with the fact mentioned at that place.[8] Generally the idea of purpose and intention to arrive at a particular point is part of the verb's meaning. The Lakota version, then, does not have the sense of some straggler coming haphazardly upon the tipi. Rather it conveys the idea of someone deliberately deciding to join the group. She comes to the boundary of their lives and that is as far as her own powers permit her to go without some response from the brothers. The next move is theirs.

The old folktale world was in many ways comparable to a chessboard. There were only so many moves possible for any given character. The brothers really have only two choices: to risk inviting a woman of unknown character into their tipi or to risk the continuing vulnerability inherent in being a group without a woman. They know that the presence of a woman in their midst is crucial to continuing the game of life. So they invite her in. She crosses the threshold, the crucial boundary. The tipi is now hers since, according to Lakota ways, the tipi belongs to the women of a family. Before bringing her in, the brothers have decided to give her the role of a sister.

It so happens that the intruder is an evil woman and the first narrative clue the Lakota audience has as to her nature is the fact that she does not share the brothers' meal. Because she cannot or will not eat, the brothers know that there is trouble of some kind. First they choose the kindest explanation, excessive shyness, and they leave her with the youngest brother in the tipi. She refuses to share the space with him, asks him to go, but he slyly watches her from the woods. He sees her come out, stand and survey the territory to make sure that she is alone, then go within the tipi. Soon the youngest brother smells cooking meat. Suspicious, he changes form, flies to the top of the tipi, and sees her planning the completion of a macabre robe decorated with the hair of the men she has eaten. Naturally, he warns his brothers that their "sister" will not complete the household but will devour it and complete her own robe.

The four brothers have risked bringing a woman into their space and it proved to be a wrong move. Letting her cross the boundary into their tipi forces them to flee it in order to regain their own territory. One risk requires still another; they can only regain what is lost by going into unknown territory knowing that in time the woman will follow. She does.

Once again the Lakota language version contains clues to what is happening that are not present in the English. In George Sword's version, the words describing the flight are *ku napepi*. *Ku* means "to be on one's way *home*." *Napepi* means "they flee." In another Lakota version,[9] we find a comparable construction *nakipapi*. The *ki* inserted into the verb *napepi* means "to flee to one's own home."

Now since the brothers are running *away* from home, the English version "to flee home" is jarring to the non-Indian's sense of what is happening. Are they fleeing to another place that they consider as home? Subsequent passages in the story indicate that the tipi, temporarily controlled by the cannibalistic intruder, is indeed their only home. What then is happening in this section of the story? What are the particular poetic nuances which give a specially Lakota quality to the idea of home?

I believe that it is safe to suggest that narrators and audiences in pre-reservation times were accustomed to the idea of fleeing various kinds of situations in order to find (or regain) a particular state of mind or well-being that, to them, meant *home*. We find the same kind of flight motif in other stories. We also find whole stories based on flight toward a better life. One observer, recorded in the North Dakota historical archives, gave us a characterization of the Lakota sense of home that links it with a state of mind. "Home . . . consisted of living conditions and environments, visible or invisible primarily and of location secondarily. And yet with this concept of man and people as primary with the location secondary, there was an idealistic attitude toward all environs including this and that definite *location* which was *vital, tenderly joyful, painfully delicate* and *indescribably precious,* different *in specie* from what one meets among white people [emphasis is as in the original text]." [10]

Clearly the brothers' flight signals an effort to return to the fellowship of their previous state with some hope of eventually returning to the definite location of their original home. But first they find themselves crossing many boundaries into the unknown, including that which separates life from death. The evil woman follows them, cutting off the heads of the elder ones and missing the youngest only because a bird (a messenger from a realm above the human) tells him how to kill her.

Then we find a reversal of action. This time, the brothers are outside all boundaries including those of life itself. The youngest must bring them back from realm to realm. First they must cross into life itself, so he builds a sweat bath. In Lakota the word is *inikaga* which means "to make life." It is literally a house of life. He puts his brothers within and soon hears a very formal request to step out. They are alive and he invites them to cross out of one realm into another.

All of them can then return to their home. Soon another woman arrives and stands outside. They face the same risks as before and the text notes that this time they are frightened but they invite her in. This woman acts as a true sister and enhances their home. Yet one change necessitates another. There is now a woman present but she must have a partner; so one by one, the brothers leave to find her one. None ever returns. Even the youngest brother, who until this point in the story has been the primary agent causing movement back and forth across crucial boundaries, disappears. After the brothers leave, his narrative function is assumed by the woman whose anguish forces her to leave the tipi. She stands on a hill and pleads with the higher powers for help. Noticing a small, perfectly round white stone, she swallows it and gets pregnant.

With miraculous quickness, she gives birth to Stone Boy and with equally amazing speed she brings him to maturity merely by wishing him through various stages of development. The conventional narrative technique for the immediate maturation of a hero is throwing the youngster out of the tipi four times until he returns as a man. Sword, however, adds his own poetic touch. He mentions the mother's wishes and notes how she takes the child by the hand and walks with him. With maturity comes a personal destiny and quest. Stone Boy is ready to move out into the unknown and find his uncles.

We know that stone, in the Lakota world, is all-powerful, and Stone Boy clearly represents the mythic *Inyan* alive and acting among the people. So we can be permitted a bit of surprise in discovering that Stone Boy needs and receives from four old women additional magical power. Each is represented by a token that he later uses in a game against the Buffalo People. These powers, though, are not quite like the magical gifts we find in European fairy tale worlds and sometimes even in Lakota tales. The word for Stone Boy's gifts in Sword's tale is *ohan* which can also be translated as *ways* or *customs*. It was a commonly used word and suggests a theme found throughout Lakota hero tales. Once a hero has become part of a *tiyošpaye* or extended family, he is bound by all the cultural ways that everyone else must learn. There is noteworthy realism about Lakota hero tales.

It so happens that Stone Boy's uncles have wandered into the territory of the Buffalo people. Each brother has temporarily ended his life journey once more, for the Buffalo have sent each into the land of the dead again. Stone Boy can bring them back to life but only by passing the game-like tests that the Buffalo people impose. The odds are all in favor of the buffalo. Nevertheless, with the old women's powers (the gifts of human culture), Stone Boy prevails. Finally he can build a sweat lodge, put his uncles' bones back together, bring them back into life and lead them home. But not alone. He wins buffalo wives for each of them. Now the home unit seems complete. The uncles have wives; the extended family exists and the embryonic society has a future. The story could end at this point but it does not. Next the enduring sledding episode occurs. The element that has lasted throughout time seems almost a footnote to Sword's tale.

In Sword's version, the sledding incident has an almost gratuitous character. After passing all the tests that the Buffalo people have imposed on him in their territory, Stone Boy seems deliberately to provoke them to attack him on his home field. Every other incident in the tale involves risk for the brothers. This last event appears to be a celebration of the fact that the home unit, the *tiyošpaye* is now secure. Buffalo come from all over the world to attack it but StoneBoy and his uncles have built four wooden walls around their home. Our undaunted hero finds a piece of metal and takes it within the enclosures where he stands upon it and gleefully watches the buffalo kill themselves trying to get to him. Finally he and his uncles chase the buffalo in a splendid hunt. An old buffalo remarks that they have tried their best but they could not get the life of Stone Boy. He endures. But not alone. His family and his home are safe too. Lakota heroes seem to avoid solitary splendor. They insist on family members to share their accomplishments.

In the story of Stone Boy, there is much crossing and recrossing of life's crucial boundaries, and there is at work the relentless momentum generated by a lifestyle that required risk for continuity. Every member of any audience should be able to sense some of the reality of this interplay of themes. Lakota people in the prairie environment surely have felt these themes with intensity as they fought first to build the magnificently dramatic buffalo culture that was followed so quickly by their resistance to the arbitrary boundaries of reservation life. When these boundaries were finally imposed, the dialectic between inside and outside acquired new political overtones. But always homes have needed protection, and attacks can still occur when the people are most vulnerable. Stone Boy still has his role. And he still has his sense of humor.

The reading of Sword's "Stone Boy" that I have just sketched is, admittedly, a curious combination of objective and subjective elements. I have used ethnographic and linguistic data to give authenticity to some of my interpretations, but my sheer uninhibited delight in the way that certain episodes work after all of my scrambling through old ethnographic remnants of insight is my own emotion. It may or may not have a relationship to the way George Sword or any other nineteenth century Lakota listener knew the tale.

But emotion it is and genuine at that. In a very real way the story lives for me. It is literature. It is poetry. I can read contemporary versions and celebrate the story's survival, delighting in the way the tale adapts to fit the times. And that kind of emotional response is my goal in attempting a poetics of Lakota folktales.

Much of the task of constructing a poetics consists of trying to reconstruct an historical context. At this stage of our effort we brush shoulders with ethnographers, historians, and linguists. Yet, by insisting that we are simple word-lovers working toward a poetic goal, we appropriate our own kind of freedom, with its overtones of terror like all freedoms. We garner every bit of objective data we can find only to transfer it into the realm of the subjective and personal response.

The novelist William H. Gass has written lines about the art of storytelling that probably describe the efforts of every truly convinced teller of tales. "In the act of love, as in all the arts, the soul should be felt by the tongue and the fingers, felt in the skin. So should our sounds come to color up the surface of our stories like a blush."[11] These thoughts are so immediate that it would seem impossible to apply them to the stripped bare bones of tales taken from their vital context and laid to rest in archives. But Stone Boy's uncles kept coming back to life and all our effort is not to try to explain how life was long ago. It is to try to take what we find from way back then and restore some youthful vitality to its sounds and meanings. This distinguishes the poet's efforts from the ethnographers' or the linguists'. The poet feels words. There is nothing exclusively objective about that. So it is that one who seeks the poetics of a folktale not only gathers every available bit of ethnographic and linguistic data but also tries to sense the meaning of that data with the total, simple, complete subjectivity of a lover.

NOTES ON TRANSLATION

Chances are that the very first Native American narrator who shared a story with a curious invader prefaced the tale with cautionary comments about the process of translation. We know that George Sword, the narrator of the tale I am translating, not only voiced his concerns but wrote them. He insisted that the ideas of arriving and of standing outside the tipi were separate. Unfortunately, we know too little about how he considered other elements of the narration.

The difficulties of translation, as Dennis Tedlock has so clearly explained, involve both linguistic features (phonology, lexicology and syntax) and oral or performance features.[12] Tedlock has pioneered methods of transcribing and translating in ways that indicate the peculiarities of both linguistic and performance features in tales he has himself heard from Zuni narrators. But what about texts collected long ago? Is any sort of restoration process possible? If we have the exact words of the narrator and if we know the performance conventions of the culture, I believe that we can achieve enough sense of original conditions to make the effort worthwhile.

The most immediately obvious feature of my translation of Sword's Stone Boy text has to do with performance. The text is structured by the phrases "so they tell" and "they say." These phrases translate the Lakota words "*ske*" and "*keyapi*," features with a two-fold function. They remind an audience that the tale has come through generations of tellers and they mark pauses. The Sioux narrators often stopped at crucial points in a tale waiting for a nod and an "*ohan*," (yes) from listeners. The process also created suspense. Obviously, I cannot assert definitely that the presence of *ske* in the text marks the major pauses and that *keyapi* marks the minor ones, but treating them as such produces a rhythm that approximates very closely the ebb and flow of an actual performance.

Semantic and syntactic issues present more formidable challenges. To be true to the artistry of a story requires the use of English sentences and phrases appropriate to the generic demands and the tone of the Lakota narrative. Sometimes exact transliteration with its absurd English is far more misleading than a freer translation. Yet there always is the matter of semantic elements present in the Lakota which simply do not translate into idiomatic English but which are important to the story's total structure. The primary example in the story of Stone Boy is the phrase that translates as "fleeing home." Most translators simply say "they fled." But the notion of both leaving and returning home as part of the same effort is important to the story. So I have chosen to say that they "were fleeing to get back their home." Sometimes, I have chosen to use somewhat stilted English to mark areas of important diversions between Lakota and English. Naturally, such choice requires decisions about which Lakota elements have connotative meanings crucial enough to require a wrenching of English style in order to preserve them. I hope that my essay explains how I made decisions about which Lakota linguistic peculiarities must be reflected in the English version if the meaning of the story is to have as full an echo in the English as I can possibly give it.

Four young men dwelt in the same tipi and one of them was called Hakela.

So they tell.

And then, from way out there, someone came and stood. They heard something; so they told Hakela *to look. He peeked out and there was a young woman, more beautiful than any he had ever seen. The front part of her hair was bound and she had a great big work bag. Like that, she came and stood.* Hakela *saw her and he said, "Brothers, a young woman is there; she has arrived and she is standing; the front part of her hair is bound and she has a great big work bag. Really." That's what he said.*

So they tell.

And the oldest brother, that one, said this, they say.

So they tell.

"Invite her into the tipi. We have no woman who can be a sister, so she can be our elder sister," he said.

So they tell.

Then Hakela *peeked out and said, "Sister, come in and live with us."*

So they tell.

"Our oldest brother says we have no elder sister so you can be our sister."

The woman said, "fine," and then she moved into their home. They gave her food but she didn't eat. She just kept on sitting there. Those four young men thought that she really wanted to eat but she was too bashful; so they felt sorry for the woman. Then the oldest brother said this.

So they tell.

"My brothers, let's go for a walk. Hakela *and our sister will stay here and she'll get back her appetite," he said. They went for a walk while* Hakela *stayed behind. The woman told him, "My brother, go hunting in the woods."* Hakela *took his arrows and went hunting.*

So they tell.

Near the woods, he sat down. Soon that woman came out of the tipi and stood, looking all around. Then she went back inside. Next the smell of roasting meat came from the tipi, but the smoke odor was unusual. Hakela *made himself into a chickadee and flew to the top of the tipi, alighting on the tipi pole. Then he peeked down into the tipi. Down there was a big metal container and it was full of crushed up scalps. The woman was saying, "I don't want the three young men around on the border so I'll put them over there."*

Hakela, *at the top of the tipi, peeking in, heard it all. Then the woman went on, "Anyway,* Hakela's *hair is awful so it will go here at the bottom."*

Hakela *fainted from fright. That great big bag really was filled with human heads. She roasted and then ate them. That's what he saw.*

About that time, his brothers were all coming back home so he started to fly down to them.

So they tell.

He had made himself into a chickadee; then half-way down, he turned back into a man and ran to them.

So they tell.

The brothers were coming back to their own home so he told them, "Brothers, that very woman who is our sister told me to go hunting so I went hunting in the woods. From there I watched. She came out and stood looking around and then she went back in and smoke came from within with an unusual odor, so I made myself into a chickadee and perched on the tipi poles and all of a sudden she took her great big metal shield with scalps tied all over it and then she said, 'The three young men are not for this particular border. I'll put them there. That's where I'll put their hair.' Then she said, 'Even though Hakela's hair is nasty, I'll put it at the end.' That's what she said."

So those brothers decided, "We'll go home, just like always; but it is true that that food brings us no joy," they said.

So they tell.

The older sister went on acting right at home but she didn't pay any attention to them in the tipi, they say. Together the brothers secretly helped each other, and this is what they did.

So they tell.

They boiled a pack-strap and softened it. They told her to bring a bundle of wood. "As soon as she leaves, we'll go," they said. Only Hakela stayed behind in the woods.

So they tell.

That woman broke the pack strap as she was going along.

So they tell.

That's why she took so long to come home. After some time, Hakela could go back into that tipi of theirs, and he took the container full of men's heads and the metal shield and threw them into the fire.

All the while, the brothers were fleeing to get back their home; then Hakela too got moving. He looked back and saw the woman re-enter the tipi and the very things that Hakela had thrust into the fire, she took back out for herself. Immediately she started the attack on them.

So they tell.

And she caught up with them.

So they tell.

They shot arrows at her but she had that metal shield and they hit only that.

So they tell.

Then she went to the oldest of the young men and cut off his head with a mysterious knife.

So they tell.

And then she caught up to the remaining three and chopped their heads off, one by one.

So they tell.

And she killed all of them.

So they tell.

Hakela was the only one left so she came after him in quick pursuit. Then a chickadee appeared, flying above them and they said it said this, "Hakela, on the forelock," it said.

Then he shot right in the middle of the forelock and only then did he kill the woman, they say.

Next Hakela hurried to find wood and right away he made a sweat lodge.

So they tell.

And all those brothers of his, he dragged them there and then he put them in that sweat lodge and immediately poured water on the stones, they say.

Then all of them groaned and said, "Keep on, you who are so gracious but be good enough to open the door," they said.

So they tell.

Hakela heard them and opened the door.

So they tell.

And they all stood there, alive. They continued the flight to return to their home.

So they tell.

And they kept on coming home to carry on their life in their tipi.

So they tell.

Again a very beautiful young woman, wearing a lot of quill work and carrying a big bag came to their place.

So they tell.

But her forelock was not bound. That is how she arrived there and stood. Of course the brothers were terribly frightened but once again the oldest of the brothers spoke, they say.

"Hakela, *ask her to come inside. We have no elder sister so we will have her as a sister,*" he said.

"*I am very happy to have brothers,*" she said, and came into the tipi and made herself at home.

So they tell.

Quickly they gave her food and, this one, she just as quickly ate.

So they tell.

Then she opened the bag she was carrying and right there in plain view, she finished good mocassins for them, they say.

Then the oldest one of them said, they say, "It is not proper for you to be here alone, so I'll go," he said.

And he started to go somewhere, they say.

Then all of them said the same thing. Now that sister of theirs was all alone and she was heartbroken; all she did was lament, they say.

She stood atop a hill and wept as she walked along looking downward when she saw a transparent stone, so very beautiful. Because she was lamenting, she put it in her mouth.

So they tell.

Because she was completely exhausted, she slept and she swallowed the stone in her mouth.

So they tell.

However, she didn't know this and at once that woman got pregnant, they say, and very quickly the child was born.

So they tell.

His mother said this, they say. "My son, I want you to walk" and she took him by the hand and he walked, they say. She did that four times and now he became a young man, they say. He observed the customs of the tipi and he saw fine visions, they say. And this is what he said.

So they tell.

"*Mother, whose beds are these?*"

This is what his mother told him, they say. "My son, your four relatives are all uncles so these are their beds."

So they tell.

"*They went on a journey and they did not come home,*" she said.

"Mother make me arrows, I'm going to go to look for my uncles," he said. So his mother made him arrows, they say. Now, from there, he started to go seeking his uncles, they say.

He came near the lodge of an old woman.

"Stone Boy, my grandson, where are you going, my grandson?"

"To a ball game."

"I will give you my powers," she said. She made a yellow ball club and said, "Take this and you'll thank yourself for it," she said.

He went on from there and again he came to a lodge. An old woman said, "Grandson, I will give you one of my powers to use in the contest." And she gave him a kingfisher's feather, they say.

He went along and again he came to a lodge and an old woman said, "Stone Boy, grandson, take one of my powers for the contest." He went to her and she gave him a turtle.

So now he went on to look for his uncles, they say. He was going along when he saw a lot of people so he stood on a hill and they said, "Greetings, Stone Boy, come play ball."

These people were the buffalo tribe. They told an old woman to play with Stone Boy, he said.

So they tell.

The ball game was going along and all of a sudden he took that yellow club of his and the yellow eagle plume and he struck. An eagle started to fly.

So they tell.

Again they struck the ball but a large hawk flew by Stone Boy.

That's how Stone Boy won again.

So they tell.

Once again they struck the ball but Stone Boy hit the kingfisher's feather and a kingfisher started to fly.

Ho. That's the way Stone Boy won again.

So they tell.

Now they hit the ball into the water but Stone Boy struck the turtle and won again. Then the old Buffalo woman who had played against him said, "Well now, my son-in-law, shoot me."

He took his arrow and shot her in the neck. She died.

There, he found his uncles' bones, gathered them up and joined them together. He made a sweat lodge and he put them in there and poured water on them until they groaned and came to life.

So they tell.

He had won four very beautiful young buffalo women. His uncles seized them and brought them back home with them.

So they tell.

As they returned, he gave back their powers to the four old women.

When they got back to their own tipi, the mother of Stone Boy hugged and kissed her adopted relatives.

So they tell.

All were of good heart.

So they tell.

One time, though, Stone Boy went traveling again.

So they tell.

He met four really beautiful young women and they had a sled. So he made himself into a little boy with sore eyes and he stood there in front of where the buffalo girls were sitting. One buffalo had black hair, another grey, another had brown hair and the last had yellow hair. That's all there were.

Stone Boy said he wanted to sit where the first one was. But she said, "Oh no!"

So they tell.

He said to the last one in line, "I'll come and sit there," they say.

"All right," she said.

There he was, in the last place. Now they started to slide down together when Stone Boy became a huge boulder and that's how he started to smash the four white buffalo girls, they say.

He took their tongues, they say. And he went home with them, they say.

Another time, he went traveling and he saw a buffalo sharpening the tips of his horns so he asked, "Grandfather, why are you sharpening the tips of your horns?"

That buffalo said, "Grandson, that Stone Boy killed four of my children so I'm going to go attack him," he said.

"Grandfather, when will you go to attack him?" Stone Boy asked.

The buffalo answered, "When the yellow clouds are here above us, then I'll attack."

So Stone Boy answered, "Grandfather, this is who I am," and he shot him.

So they tell.

The buffalo died.

So they tell.

Just like that, Stone Boy killed four buffalo, one by one and took their tongues and went back home with them. Then he told his uncles to make arrows and he told them to make four wooden enclosures.

So they tell.

"Make them strong," he said. They did just that.

So they tell.

Now it was time for the yellow clouds to come and from all over the world the buffalo arrived, just as expected.

So they tell.

Stone Boy brought a great big piece of metal into the wooden enclosure.

So they tell.

And he stood on it. Then an old buffalo ornamented with pure white shells came to the top of the hill and said this.

So they tell.

"Stone Boy, get out of the way. A buffalo with long horns is coming there."

The long-horned buffalo came and gored the wooden structure.

They killed him.

So they tell.

Again he said, "Stone Boy, get out of the way! The Yellow Buffalo is going to try."

He ran up to the wooden enclosure and hit it head-on.

They killed him.

So they tell.

Again, "Stone Boy, get out of the way! The Crazy Buffalo is going to try," he said. Then he ran up to the wooden enclosure and hit it head-on.

He was killed too. Well then, the buffalo came like a flood of water and Stone Boy and his uncles pursued them and sent them into a confused retreat.

Then that old buffalo who wore a pure white shell said, "That's why."

So they tell.

"That was the last time to come to this place of ours. We will not get the life of Stone Boy."

Then the men finished off the buffalo, they say.

Afterwards they went back home and they were very prosperous, they say.

This is the end.

So they tell.

NOTES

[1]The current emphasis on the literary value of Native American folktales is resulting in some important and sensitive critical essays. See Dell H. Hymes, "The 'Wife' Who 'Goes Out' Like a Man: Reinterpretation of a Clackamas Chinook Myth," *Social Science Information* 7: 173–79; Jarold Ramsey, "The Wife Who Goes Out Like a Man Comes Back as a Hero: The Art of Two Oregon Indian Narratives," *PMLA* 92 (1977): 9–18; also "From 'Mythic' to 'Fictive' In Nez Perce Orpheus Myth," *Western American Literature* 13 (1978); Dennis Tedlock, *Finding the Center,* (Lincoln: University of Nebraska Press, 1972); Barre Toelken, "The 'Pretty Languages' of Yellowman: Genre, Mode and Texture in Navaho Coyote Narratives," *Genre* 2, (1969): 211–35.

[2]Two versions of the Stone Boy story are available in the J. R. Walker collection of the Colorado State Historical Society. Both versions will be published in the forthcoming volume edited by Elaine Jahner, *Lakota Myth,* (University of Nebraska Press).

Other Lakota versions are in Eugene Buechel, *Lakota Tales and Texts,* (St. Louis: John S. Swift Co., 1978) and Ella Deloria, *Dakota Texts* (New York: G.E. Stechert & Co. 1932); R.D. Theisz, *Buckskin Tokens,* (Aberdeen, S. Dak.: North Plains Press, 1975).

[3]See Theisz, *Buckskin Tokens,* p. 58.

[4]Frances Densmore, *Teton Sioux Music,* Bureau of American Ethnology Bulletin no. 11, (1918), p. 205.

[5]Ibid, p. 208.

[6]In commenting on Sword's use of the Lakota language, James R. Walker wrote, "Sword contended, and in this was sustained by other old Oglala, that there was no such word as *hinazin* in the Lakota language as it was spoken before contact with white people; that the white people mistook the phrase for the word and wrote it as such . . ." See J. R. Walker manuscript collection, Colorado State Historical Society Archives.

[7]Ella Deloria, "Notes on the Dakota, Teton Dialect," *International Journal of American Linguistics* 8 (1933): p. 97–21.

[8]Eugene Buechel, *Lakota Grammar* (Rosebud, S. Dak.: St. Francis Mission, 1939), p. 165.

[9]See Deloria, *Dakota Texts,* p. 87.

[10]Aaron McGaffey Beede, unpublished manuscript, North Dakota State Historical Society Archives.

[11]William H. Gass. *Fiction and the Figures of Life* (Boston: Nonpareil Books, 1971), p. 29.

[12]Dennis Tedlock, "On the Translation of Style in Oral Narrative," in *New Perspectives in Folklore* (Austin: University of Texas Press, 1972), pp. 114–33.

Pat Carr and Willard Gingerich:

THE VAGINA DENTATA MOTIF IN NAHUATL AND PUEBLO MYTHIC NARRATIVES: A COMPARATIVE STUDY

One of the basic problems of working with Pre-Columbian literary comparisons is the irreparable loss of so much material. Extensive transcribed fragments of Nahuatl pre-conquest literature do exist, but there are, as far as we know, no extant Pueblo manuscripts of corresponding age. There are, however, the narrative myth bowls which illustrated the prevailing Pre-Columbian Pueblo myths.[1] While it is a commonplace that the sixteenth century burning of the ancient Aztec and Mayan books was disastrous, it is becoming increasingly apparent that the breakage of ancient Pueblo pottery by twentieth century treasure hunters (who use bulldozers) is equally disastrous to comparative studies of Pre-Columbian culture. We still do have some comparable literary fragments from both the northern and the southern cultures, and through them we can draw some parallels between the surviving Mesoamerican literature (recorded by Spanish churchmen in the sixteenth century) and the surviving Pueblo literature (recorded by American anthropologists in the late nineteenth and early twentieth centuries).

While the cultural affiliations between Mesoamerica and the American Southwest, what Di Peso calls the Gran Chichimeca, are not fully understood,[2] their literatures contain some very definite correspondences that would appear to derive more from diffusion than from coincidence. Numerous and undeniable narrative parallels appear in the myths of these northern and southern peoples, but from the host of similar characters, plots, and motifs, this pilot study will illuminate the parallels found only in the motifs of the *vagina dentata* and ghost pursuit.

Thompson records some thirty instances of the *vagina dentata* scattered throughout the recorded literature of North American Indians,[3] and the fact that it was a motif of Pueblo literature as early as 1050 A.D. is demonstrated by its explicit depiction on the Mimbres myth bowls. In one of these myth bowls, the central male and female figures are faithfully depicted in the act of copulation while six smaller figures stand decorously around the rim of the bowl with ceremonial bows and arrows and prayer sticks (Figure 1). Many Mimbres bowls contain scenes of copulation, but the significance of this particular bowl is that the club-like male member is inside a vagina carefully surrounded by teeth. There is little doubt that we have in this black-on-white pottery food bowl an eleventh century Pueblo illustration of the toothed vagina.

FIGURE ONE

Mimbres bowl in an anonymous private collection. Drawn by Pat Carr from a photograph in the Western New Mexico State University Museum.

1050 A.D. is the date Di Peso fixes for the appearance of "Quetzalcoatl cultists" at Casas Grandes in Chihuahua, Hachita, Cerrillos, and Chaco Canyon in New Mexico. These cultists of the Plumed Serpent, it seems, came into some form of economic and cultural competition with the earlier "Tezcatlipoca cultists" who had appeared about 150 years earlier and settled further west in the Gila-Colorado-Sonara lowlands. The Mimbres people fall precisely between these two cultural apportionments, and reach their fullest development (ca. 1100) about the time when such cultural competition must have been in its apogee.

No manuscripts have survived from this period, however, and all recorded versions of Pre-Columbian myth in Mexico come to us from sixteenth and seventeenth century manuscript redactions. Unfortunately, as in the case of the Mimbres bowls, it is a fragmented record. All such manuscripts were prepared by Christian priests, by students directly under their supervision, or, late in the sixteenth century, by Indian scholars whose formal education had been thoroughly Hispanic. The Church's first attitude toward indigenous mythic narrative was that it came of demonic origin and should, therefore, be eradicated as thoroughly as possible. Even the later curiosity of churchmen concerning indigenous thought and beliefs was largely motivated by concern to better prepare priests for combating those beliefs. Consequently, students and scholars who took interest in pre-Cortesian oral texts tended to record only that which they felt had some clear "historical" quality, abbreviating or disregarding all other texts. Typical of this attitude is the statement with which Fernando de Alva Ixtlilxochitl, grandson of the Nahuatl Prince Nezahualpilli of Tetzcoco, prefaces his "Summary Relation":

> [I shall not] treat of the fables and fictions which appear in some of their histories, being superfluous things.[4]

We will never know how many myth texts of Ixtlilxochitl's ancestors were lost during the course of the sixteenth century as a result of this attitude. Texts with erotic or sexually explicit details we can assume never found their way into script or print.

Not that Nahua society was sexually "liberated"; it was in fact universally repressive in matters of sex, punishing adultery with death and homo-eroticism with vicious torture. A number of Nahuatl stories do survive, however, in which erotic elements play some part: the seduction of Quetzalpetatl by her drunken brother Ce Acatl Quetzalcoatl (an event more implied than clearly stated) in the Anales de Cuauhtitlan is probably the most significant. The apparition of Tezcatlipoca in Tollan as a naked Huaxtecan chili-vendor whose splendid endowments incite a fury of desire in the daughter of King Huemac (Codice Florentino); the demand of the same Huemac for a Nonoalcan woman measuring at least four hands across the hips[5] (Historia Tolteca-Chichimeca—a demand which led to war in Tollan and the death of Huemac) are other sex related incidents that come immediately to mind. But nowhere in the Nahuatl texts do we find expression of the *vagina dentata* motif with the explicit detail of the Mimbres bowl.

There is, however, one brief narrative in the so-called "Legend of the Suns" manuscript of 1558 (Part III of the Codice Chimalpopoca) which contains a transmuted version of the *vagina dentata* motif, a narrative which turns out to have considerable value in deciphering psychohistorical impulses for a key feature of late Aztec-Chichimec culture: the ritual "War of Flowers" in which sacrificial prisoners were captured. This story, untitled in the manuscript and which we identify as "Xiuhnel, Mimich and the Star Demon," is the only extant Nahuatl narrative text which makes an explicit link between any erotic incident and human sacrifice, and several considerations make clear that it is a version of the charter myth by which at least some of the Chichimec peoples justified the frenetic outburst of militarism and sacrificial warfare which they initiated in the Mexican Altiplano during the tenth to thirteenth centuries. The full text of the story, which has a history of minute but crucial mis-translations,[6] follows:

. . . There came down two deer, each with two heads, and also these two mixcoa *[cloud serpents], the first called Xiuhnel and the second called Mimich, hunting there in Godland [the desert area to the north of the Valley of Mexico, from which the Chichimecs were thought to have migrated].*

Xiuhnel and Mimich pursued the two deer, trying to shoot them.

A night and a day they pursued them and by sunset had tired them.

Then they consulted one another and said, "You make a hut here and I'll make myself one over there."

Ah, soon came the malicious ones!

And then out came they who were deer, who had become women.

They came calling, "Dear Xiuhnel, Dear Mimich; where are you? Come. Come to drink, come to eat."

And when they heard them then they said to one another, "Don't you answer them."

But then Xiuhnel called and said to them, "You come here, my elder sister."

Then she said to him, "Dear Xiuhnel, drink."

And Xiuhnel then drank the blood, then immediately lay down beside her.

And when he laid her down, then she turned herself face down upon him, then she devoured him, tore open his breast.

And then Mimich said, "Iyo! My brother is eaten!"

And the other woman was still standing and calling, "My lover, eat."

But Mimich did not call her.

And then he took the firesticks and lit a fire, and when he had lit it, then Mimich hurriedly threw himself into it.

The woman, pursuing him, also entered the fire.

She followed him there the entire night, until noon the following day.

And then at noon he descended into a thorny barrel cactus, fell into it, and the woman fell down after him.

And when he saw the star-demon had fallen, he shot her repeatedly.

Only then could he turn back.

Then he returned, parting and tying up his hair, painting his face and weeping for his elder brother who had been eaten.

Then the gods heard him, the fire-gods, and they went to bring the woman, Itzpapalotl; Mimich went in the lead.

And they took her and then burned her.

Then she burst open:

First she blossomed into the blue flint;

Thus the second time she blossomed into the white flint, and then they took the white, then they wrapped it in a bundle.

And thus the third time she blossomed into the yellow flint; no one took it, they only looked.

And so the fourth time she blossomed into the red flint; no one took this either.

Thus the fifth time she blossomed into the black flint; no one took this either.

And Mixcoatl then took the white flint for a god, then wrapped it then carried it in a bundle.

Then he went off to make war in a place called Comallan.

He went off carrying the flint, his goddess Itzpapalotl.[7]

Mixcoatl, "Cloud Serpent," is the god-man ur-father regarded by most Chichimec tribes as the priest and chieftain who first led them into the Valley of Mexico from the north. In the narrative which follows this story in the manuscript, he goes on to become the father of One Reed Quetzalcoatl, the great Toltec-Chichimec god-man of Tula, so revered by all Nahua peoples. This little episode of the unfortunate Xiuhnel and his terrified brother clearly indicates that the "star-demon" (*tzitzimitl*), who goes through her transformations from a double-headed deer to two deer, to two women, to one woman, is actually the goddess Itzpapalotl, "Obsidian Butter-fly." Further, it is clear that the story is meant to explain how this goddess, as a chunk of white flint, became Mixcoatl's patron-goddess, and therefore a patroness of all Chichimecs.

The star-demon Itzpapalotl eats Chichimecs and is also their patroness. Mimich escapes by fleeing through fire. Burned herself, she becomes flint, the raw material of weapons and sacrificial knives. Taking her up, Mixcoatl goes immediately off to war. Three other brief textual references confirm these implicit suggestions that this were-deer "star-demon" was a dominating numen of early Chichimec consciousness, and in her "terrible mother" aspect had much to do with the initiation of the *xochiyaoyotl* or "Flower Warfare," ritual battles designed to provide prisoners for sacrifice. Two of these passages occur in Part I of the same Codice Chimalpopoca containing the Legend of the Suns, the Annals of Cuauhtitlan, a treasure-trove of Chichimec history, myth, and legend, and source of the finest Quetzalcoatl narrative surviving in Nahuatl. At two different places in these Annals the goddess Itzpapalotl addresses her people with direct ritual mandates for human sacrifice. The first comes in the very opening lines of the manuscript and is fragmented because of manuscript deterioration:

> ". . . *And when you have gone to shoot in the four directions*
> *place them in the hands of the Lord of Fire [Xiuhtecutli],*
> *the old, old God [Huehueteotl]*
> *whom three will guard: Mixcoatl, Tozpan, Ihuitl."*
> *These are the names of the three hearthstones.*
> *In this way Itzpapalotl instructed the Chichimecs.*[8]

The second passage in the same manuscript makes clear that it is arrows, i.e. war, that are to be shot in the four directions, that "them" are prisoners of war, and placing them "in the hands of the Lord of Fire" means sacrifice by fire:

> *And then you will go to the east*
> *where you will shoot arrows*
> *likewise to the Godland in the north*
> *you will shoot arrows,*
> *likewise in the Region of Thorns*
> *you will shoot arrows,*
> *likewise in the irrigated Flowerland*
> *you will shoot arrows*

And when you have gone to shoot,
have caught up to the gods—
the green, the yellow, the white, the red;
eagle, jaguar, serpent, rabbit, etc.—
then you will place those who will be
guardians of Xiuhtecutli:
Tozpan and Ihuitl and Xiuhnel.
There you will burn your captives.[9]

The third text demonstrates that this "Obsidian Butterfly" figure, syncretized with the ancient Toltec mother-numen, Teteo Innan, "Mother of the Gods," produced the late "terrible mother" figure of the Aztecs, Coatlicue. This text, Hymn 4 in the appendix of Book II, Codice Florentino, is too long for quotation and commentary here, but the following lines from the close of that Hymn make clear how thoroughly Itzpapalotl had become identified with the figure of the Mother of Gods herself in late Nahua-Chichimec religious consciousness. The Hymn is specifically addressed to Teteo Innan and entitled "her Song."

Ahuiya! O Goddess upon the barrel cactus,
Our Mother, Aya, Itzpapalotl.
Xoh! Aya, let us look on her;
on the Nine Plains
she fed on the hearts of deer,
Our Mother, Aya, Lady of the Earth.
Xoh! With new chalk, new plumes,
are you anointed;
in the four directions arrows are broken.
Xoh! To the deer transformed;
Across the Godland to behold you
come Xiuhnel and Mimich.[10]

In others words, the little narrative of "Xiuhnel, Mimich and the Star Demon" describes how a figure central to mythic justification of sacrificial warfare, an institution of great importance in late Nahua society, came into being, came to Chichimec consciousness. It is our observation that this consciousness springs from an explicitly erotic fantasy which is, in fact, a transmuted fantasy of the *vagina dentata*.

The metaphoric figure of vagina as mouth is, in the wonderful algebra of the unconscious, a reversible equation. As Freud pointed out many times, in the unconscious opposites are equal. Vagina as mouth, mouth as vagina—there is no difference in that dream-like state of pre-consciousness from which mythic narrative emerges. Eliade points out that this *vagina dentata* reversal motif is especially prevalent throughout world mythology in Earth Mother figures:

. . . A number of South American iconographic motifs represent the mouth of
Mother Earth as vagina dentata. . . . It is important to note that the ambivalence

FIGURE TWO
Cihuacoatl (from Durán's *Historia de las indias*).

*of the chthonian Great Mother is sometimes expressed, mythically and iconographi-
cally, by identifying her mouth with the* vagina dentata.[11]

The figure of Teteo Innan, as the line "Our Mother, Aya, Lady of the Earth"
demonstrates, is an Earth Mother figure par excellence, as are the syncretic figures
which derive from her.

In "Xiuhnel and Mimich" we find a specific instance of this *vagina dentata* reversal. Xiuhnel responds to a coy sexual invitation in the darkness, but in the moment of possession the deer-woman-demon reverses the situation and eats him, then seeks to consume Mimich with the same trick. In all the later Nahua goddesses derived from the syncretism of the Mother of the Gods and this voracious Obsidian Butterfly, the mouth continues to be an obsessive feature. Cihuacoatl ("Snake Woman"), an avatar of the Aztec Coatlicue ("Skirts of Snakes"), is described by Father Durán as ". . . the main goddess . . . revered and greatly exalted in Mexico, Tezcoco, and all the land."[12] Sahagún's informants list her first among the Nahua female deities, and suggest that she is foremost in potentiality.[13] The informant of Durán particularly remembered the open mouth and ferocious teeth of the idol, and the drawings which accompany the text emphasize that feature (Figure 2). She was a voracious idol, and many prisoners fell victim to her appetite. Fire sacrifice was a feature of her ritual, and numerous details identify her also with the earth.

> *. . . The priests went once a week to visit the sovereigns and warn them that the goddess was famished. Then the rulers provided the repasts; a captive taken in war, to be eaten by the goddess. He was led to the temple and delivered to the priests, who took the prisoner and thrust him into the chamber of Cihuacoatl. He was slain in the usual way: his heart was extracted and offered up. They also ripped off a part of his thigh, casting the body outside crying out loudly, "Take this for it has been gnawed on!" feigning that the goddess had spoken. The priests outside lifted the dead body, considering it to be the "leftovers" of the goddess. It was given back to the owner for having fed the goddess . . . This ceremony was performed every eight days. I* explained that *in pictures the goddess was always shown with a large open mouth.* She was always famished, and thus in this temple and in honor of this goddess more men were slain than in any other.[14]

This description of a central temple ritual at the height of the Aztec period (early sixteenth century) solidly confirms a link in Aztec-Chichimec consciousness between oral fixation and human sacrifice, a link whose genesis we find described in the little narrative of Xiuhnel and Mimich. Mimich escapes, but since this tale became a tribal myth, it must have been understood that in some sense the goddess, transformed to the multicolored flints into which her body blossomed, continued to pursue all Chichimecs, a pursuit which required ritual defense.

Among the Zuni Pueblo Ruth Benedict recorded, in the 1930s, extensive versions of similar myths in which female figures pursue men. These tales likewise involve two brothers, known in Zuni as the Ahaiyute or Little War Twins, who were also among the favorite protagonists in the eleventh century Mimbres myth bowls. In one tale, the twins have been warned by their grandmother to stay away from an old evil woman near Twin Buttes, but they go despite the warning and meet the old woman who combs their hair and then sends them out for firewood.

> *A little later the boys came back, each with an armload of wood, and the old woman made a fire and put lots of stones in the fire to make them hot. She put a big cooking*

pot on the fire and filled it with water. The two boys piled wood on the fire to make it burn hard, and the stones got red hot and the water boiled. Then she said to Elder Brother, "Sit here on my left side." She combed their hair again, and after a while she bit the neck of the elder brother, and he died, and then she bit the neck of the younger one and killed him too.[15]

As with the Nahuatl myth, this act of the female biting the male becomes associated with implicit sexual fears. But the Pueblo myth continues; the Ahaiyute are immortal, and their souls go out of their bodies as the old woman boils one and bakes the other between two hot stones. As she comes back to eat the cooked meat, the souls of the twins plague her by shouting from water jugs or cooking pots that the meat has been defiled by excrement or urine. In her anger, the old woman breaks bowl after bowl until the two brothers at last go into her nostrils, scratch the inside of her nose until she begins to sneeze. Then she coughs, and finally dies.

After she was dead the two Ahaiyute came out of her nose. The old woman lay there dead. Then they took an arrow point and skinned her from her feet up, and left the body in the house. They went out and got grass and weeds and brought them back to the house and stuffed them into the old woman's skin. They stuffed it full and sewed up the feet. They put her dress on it, and it was just like the old woman. They put a stick in each leg and tied a belt around the waist.[16]

They leave the body standing in a corner while they go through the old woman's house, into four rooms, and finally pass from the fourth room into another world. In this other world, they wander into a village, steal ceremonial lightning and thunder-making equipment from the people, who wake up and chase them back to the old woman's house. "The people could not catch them, but they said, 'Never mind, we will get you some day.'"

The Ahaiyute then take the stuffed body of the old woman and tie it to the elder brother who runs as if the old woman were chasing him. The younger brother runs ahead, shouting to his grandmother that the evil woman is about to catch his brother. The grandmother runs out, smashes the old woman's head with a stone as the twins laugh; they point out that the body is already dead, and add, "That old woman was mean, so we killed her. We kill everyone who kills people and now the people need not be afraid any more because we have killed all the monsters in this country." But despite this assurance, as in the Nahuatl myth, the continued pursuit of the Zuni immortals, and hence of the Zuni peoples, by the old woman's avatars has been established.

In a variant of this tale, the old woman is identified as Atocle Woman who delouses the twins before she bites their necks and roasts them. Again, their voices call out that she has eaten dung, and she ejects the boys by sneezing, upon which she falls dead.

Upon being killed, like all kachinas [immortals] she became a deer. They stole all her rainmaking ceremonial objects and stuffed her as a huge deer to fool their grandmother.[17]

In yet another myth, the twins meet the "toothed vagina" more explicitly; in this story, their grandmother warns them specifically to stay away from eight girls living nearby with their grandmother, saying, "Don't go there. They have teeth in their vaginas. They will cut you and you will die." Of course, the twins decide to visit the girls despite the warning, and in preparation make themselves false penises of oak and hickory. Since there are eight girls, the twins invite the six young Lehaci and their grandfather along, and when the girls and their grandmother urge the group to lie with them,

> *All the men took out their false members. They used them cohabiting. They broke the teeth from the women's vaginas. The blood ran. When the oak members were worn out, they put them aside and took the hickory ones. By daylight the teeth of these women were all worn out. They were broken in pieces . . . These women never killed men any more.*[18]

This is the myth depicted on the earlier mentioned Mimbres bowl with the seven figures involved in copulation (Figure 1); the Ahaiyute were often seen as a single character in many of the tales, and hence the seven painted characters would be the six Lehaci and the Ahaiyute. Mimbres potter-Story-Tellers generally depicted the penis as a bar with a circle head, but in this particular bowl, the penis is very definitely clubbed, hockey-stick shaped, and thus the design focuses on the false members fashioned of oak and hickory.

One further myth of the Ahaiyute concerning copulation and then pursuit by the female exists in a number of versions in which the twins have intercourse with a girl (often with a number of girls in succession who then become the same girl) whom they afterwards shoot full of arrows. She, however, pursues them as a ghost, asking in each kiva she passes where her husbands are. As in the Nahuatl narrative, the "tooth vagina" is not specified here, but the ghost pursuit by the female is so terrifying to both the twins and the people with whom they seek protection that it becomes dramatically implicit in the role reversal and female pursuit itself. In the myth, the twins go from kiva to kiva until at last in the Knife Society they are admonished for having killed the girl but are then given a stone knife and a war club with which to dispatch the ghost. They are instructed to scalp the girl, lay her on her back with the injunction to count the stars, a task she can never finish, and then to return to the kiva with the scalp for use in ceremonies; this tale is given as the charter for scalping ritual and ceremonial societies.[19]

In all of these myths and their variants, both Pueblo and Mesoamerican, we have narrative parallels appearing with great clarity and regularity. While not every myth contains all of the elements, when they do appear, these narrative elements almost always appear in the same order,[20] and may be summarized as: The initial curiosity of the male (generally two brothers); the deer to woman (or woman to deer as in the kachina/deer complex); the devouring of the male by the female; the pursuit of the male by the female (or pursuit by the female's followers or possibly even the pretended pursuit); the fear that comes with the pursuing; the use of fire sacrifice in some form; the explosion (or sneeze as a form of explosion); the flint—as arrow point, stone knife, or flakes of stone—and the preservation of the body or some memento of it (or transformation of it) for ceremonial purposes. In every case, the basic thrust of the narrative seems to be the terror generated in the male by the pursuit of the female, and in both Chichimec and Pueblo versions, the tale is used to provide a charter for some type of ritual murder.

While Mimich and the Ahaiyute escape the pursuing female, there is the suggestion in all of the myths that either the transformed evil woman, or her followers from that other world, will continue the pursuit. If this fantasy was adopted as representative of some enduring anxiety (otherwise we would not have the myth), then some answer, some response to or appeasement of the evil was needed. Mimich in the Nahua myth has been provided with fire (for escape as well as a medium of ritual protection) and with a flint goddess to whom he can direct his ceremonial offerings. The Ahaiyute have been presented with rain-making equipments, scalps, the stuffed body of the vanquished woman, flint again in the arrow points and the ritualistic stone knife, and the wooden male members, all of which become ceremonial.

But since a death had to result (the death of Xiuhnel in the Nahua and the symbolic deaths of the twins in the Pueblo stories), there is the suggestion that often an appeasement in the form of a human sacrifice was necessary. If the pursuing female kachina, ghost, or goddess wanted hearts or other parts of the body, then certainly the way to protect one's own body was to offer her someone else's. The war which Mixcoatl goes off to create, carrying the swaddled white flint fragment of Itzpapalotl, is a direct consequence of the encounter between Xiuhnel, Mimich, and the were-deer. It is the first Chichimec *xochiyaoyotl* or "sacrificial flower war" intended to gather "hearts and flowers" in propitiation of the goddess's appetite. Seen this way, the "flower wars" become an elaborate displacement of masculine anxiety from the female sexuality which generates it to the battlefield where it is enacted and then to the temple ritual where it is appeased in fire and blood. It would appear to be a male-dominated development from start to finish and suggests, to say the least, an extensive fear and subjection of women in early Chichimec culture. Certainly not all human sacrifice in the preColumbian world, or even among the Nahua peoples in particular, has its genesis in this single male erotic fantasy of the *vagina dentata*, but it is interesting to note that the stone knife sacrifice, scalping, and the flaying of victims all appear in these particular myths.

Di Peso proposes ritual cannibalism to explain several incomplete burials at Casas Grandes in Chihuahua, but there is no evidence of human sacrifice among the Pueblo peoples in the northern areas of the Gran Chichimeca.[21] At least eight probable instances of cannibalism from the Pueblo period (A.D. 900–1300) have been excavated in the southwest, most recently at Burnt Mesa on the San Juan River. None, however, show evidence of ritual; survival is a likely explanation in several cases.[22] If we see these parallel myths described above as possibly indicative of the human offering to the goddess, there must have been other factors in the south that were not present in the north. In this regard we might point out the homosexual overtones in the myths, and note that although ritual and social homosexuality was widespread throughout the Americas, in the Nahua cities it was brutally and savagely punished.[23]

According to traditional psychoanalytic theory, one of the most common motifs in the psychogenesis of male homosexuality is an irrational castration anxiety generated by the fantasy that the female genital is in some way a castrating instrument.[24] This particular fantasy is found explicitly mentioned or enacted in mythologies from the New Hebrides to the Amazon.[25] The New World myths related above enact such a fantasy in the suggestions of seduction (or the actual seduction in many cases), then the savage attack by the woman, with the neck or the entrails or the heart being substituted for the male genital. This is not to suggest, however, that the preColumbian American male of Mesoamerica and the Gran Chichimeca suffered from homosexual delusions. Psychiatric definitions of homosexuality have considerably deviated from the classical Freudian terms, and the mythic use of an erotic fantasy is often quite different from the individual or personal use of it.

There is, further, specific evidence in the 16th century Nahuatl texts of that masculine anxiety before the energy of female sexuality which we are suggesting lies somehow at the root of the Chichimec obsession with sacrificial warfare. In Chapter 21 of Sahagún's Florentine Codex, Book VI—among the so-called *huehuetlatolli* texts or "discourses of the elders"—we find a lengthy admonition from a noble Nahua father to his son on matters of sexual conduct. The upshot of his advice is "Don't give yourself over to sexual excess," and the threat behind the advice is that he will finally at some point "dry up" and no longer be able to satisfy the desires of his wife, who will then abandon and cuckold him.

> *"And if you ruin yourself impetuously, if too soon you seduce, you discover, women on earth, truly the old men went saying, you will interrupt your development, you will be stunted, your tongue will be white, your mouth will become swollen, puffed; . . . you will be enfeebled, weakened, emaciated. . . . And you are like the bored maguey, you are like the maguey: soon you will no longer give sap. Perhaps it is this way with you, a man, when you have already consumed yourself, when you can no longer say anything, no longer do anything to your spouse. Soon she hates you, soon she detests you, for truly you starve her. Perhaps then her desire arises; she longs for the carnal relations which you owe your spouse. Already you are finished, you have completed everything. Perhaps you are incapable. Then she will ignore you, she will betray you. Truly, you have ruined yourself impetuously, you have consumed yourself."*[26]

And to cap off this warning the father has a "word or two" which he hopes will "inspire" the young man to caution, a final *exemplum* to clarify what awaits old men who do not guard their energies against the insatiable needs of their women.

> *"In the time of lord Nezahualcoyotzin [Priest-King of Tetzcoco from 1430–1472], two old women were seized. They were white-headed; their heads were like snow; it was as if they were wearing shredded maguey fiber. They were imprisoned because*

they had committed adultery, had betrayed their spouses, their old men. It was young priests, youths, who had violated them. "The ruler Nezahualcoyotzin inquired of them; he said to them: 'O grandmothers, listen! How do you feel? Do you perhaps still require the carnal act? Are you not satiated, being as old as you are? And how did you live while still in your girlhood? Just say it, just tell me, since you are here for this reason.' They said to him: 'Master, ruler, our lord, receive it, hear it. You men, you are sluggish, you are depleted, you have ruined yourselves impetuously. It is all gone. There is no more. There is nothing to be desired. But of this, we who are women, we are not the sluggish ones. In us is a cave, a gorge, whose only function is to await that which is given, whose only function is to receive. And of this, if you have become impotent, if you no longer arouse anything, what other purpose will you serve?'"[27]

These *huehuetlatolli* texts are thought to be among the first materials with which Sahagún began his monumental ethnographic labors in the 1540s. Parts of the doctrine, morality, ritual, and rhetoric contained therein certainly must represent the high, old "Toltec" tradition (*Toltecayotl*) of the Altiplano and probably reach back in some form at least to Teotihuacan itself. But just as surely, the received texts are formed in a syncretism of some sort with Chichimec traditions. Numerous prayers to Tezcatlipoca (a diety of Chichimec origin) and evocations of the *xochimiquiztli*, the "flower death" of sacrifice, and the *yaomiquiztli* or "War Death" are found especially in the first chapters of the Sahagún collection. In fact, in the discourse quoted above, several paragraphs earlier, the young man is encouraged to emulate and envy the fate of a certain young Mixcoatl of Huexotzinco "who came to die in war in Mexico." A song in his memory is quoted, in which the dead warrior is exalted for his heart "like fine burnished turquoise" which "comes up to the sun."[28] The juxtaposition of these two texts in a single discourse, one an injunction to sacrificial warfare and the other a warning to beware the early loss of potency and the social consequences of inability to meet the sexual needs of a woman, offer further argument for the psychic interaction of these issues in Nahua-Chichimec consciousness.[29]

We are not prepared on the basis of this initial study to make statements about diffusion of Chichimec and Pueblo myth. Several points are apparent, however. The very close relation between the eleventh century Mimbres bowl and the twentieth century Zuni narrative of the twins and the eight girls (the bowl almost a direct illustration of the tale), demonstrates an incredible cultural continuity of some eight centuries duration in that region. Clearly, there seems to be a more direct line of descent from the eleventh century Mimbres to the twentieth century Zuni than from the Mimbres to the fifteenth century Nahua-Chichimecs. Any link then between Mimbres and Chichimec mythology would seem to refer us back to some pre-Mimbres horizon, perhaps to some original "Chichimec" protomythology. The structural parallels we have indicated would seem to suggest some such early contact or common origin, probably at very remote historical levels. From the evidence of those parallels, we suggest a characteristic of that substrata of belief might have been the deep fear of a female spirit (an aspect of the Earth-Mother perhaps?) whose pursuit of men demanded blood offerings or some type of ritual murder.

NOTES

[1] See the book-length study by Pat Carr, *Mimbres Mythology,* Southwestern Series 56 (El Paso: Texas Western Press, 1979), which establishes the relationship between the myth bowls and the centuries-later redactions of the myths.

[2] Charles C. Di Peso, *Casas Grandes and the Gran Chichimeca* (The Museum of New Mexico, 1972). Reprinted from *El Palacio* 75: 4.

[3] Stith Thompson, *Tales of the North American Indians* (Harvard University Press, 1929), p. 309.

[4] Fernando de Alva Ixtlilxochitl, *Obras Históricas,* ed., Alfredo Chavero, vol. II (Mexico City, 1892), p. 19.

[5] This incident, in its historical aspect, may well be less erotically motivated than it first appears. When King Huemac orders his Nonoalcan subjects (an ethnic minority living within the city of Tollan) to bring him a woman "four hands wide in the hips," the Nonoalcans, predictably, become upset. "Who does he think we are?" they say and arm for rebellion, finally driving Huemac into a cave and shooting him full of arrows—*Historia Tolteca-Chichimeca: Anales de Quauhtinchan,* eds., H. Berlin & S. Rendon (Mexico: Antigua Librería Robredo, de José Porrúa e Hijos, 1947), p. 69. This request was probably not literal, however, but part of a ritualistic examination ceremony to determine legitimacy in the Toltec ruling order, and excluded the Nonoalca because they did not understand the metaphoric intent of the request, thereby demonstrating their illegitimacy in the ruling orders. The evidence for this interpretation is found in Chapter IX of Ralph Roys' edition of the Book of Chilam Balam of Chumayel, a compilation of sacred and historical texts apparently from Xiu Maya tradition. This Chapter, which Roys entitles "The Interrogation of the Chiefs," records a series of ritual questions and answers "in the language of Zuyua" which the neo-Toltec conquerors of Yucatan had used to separate valid candidates for office from the upstarts, the impure, the illegitimate. Apparently only a select few, probably of the pure Toltec line, were taught the correct responses to the questions, and this secret lore became their "shibboleth." On page 97 of Roys' edition this "question" appears:

> "Son, bring me here a farmer's wife, an old woman, a dark-colored person. She is seven palms across the hips. It is my desire to see her." What he wants is the green fruit of the squash-vine. This is the language of Zuyua.

[6] The various translations of this important Chichimec myth offer a classic illustration of how a small ambiguity in the linguistic structure of the original can produce divergent and even contradictory versions in translation, hopelessly confusing any meaningful interpretation. The line rendered "And when he laid her down, then she turned herself face down upon him, then she devoured him, tore open his breast" is ambiguous in the original. In Nahuatl, pronoun objects are indicated by the verbal prefix *qui-* which has no contrasting gender morpheme: "auh in o*qui*tecac niman ipan hualmixtlapachcuep niman ye *qui*cua *qu*elcoyonia." Only the context, therefore, determines whether she devours him or he devours her— obviously a question of some importance for any attempt at interpretation of the narrative. There are, as far as we are aware, no previous English versions of this text and only two Spanish ones: in Primo Velázquez's complete edition of the Legend of the Suns MS (see note 7) and in Angel M. Garibay's anthology of Nahuatl

narrative, *Épica Náhuatl*. Velázquez translates: *Después que se echó con ella, se volvió bocabajo sobre ella, la mordió y la agujeró* (Then he threw himself down with her, turned face-down over her, bit her and opened her). Garibay renders the line rather more explicitly: *Luego con ella se tiende, la oprime, la mordisquea, y al fin la desflora* (Then he lies down with her, presses upon her, bites her, and finally deflowers her).

In short, both Spanish versions read the original Nahuatl as an attack on the female were-deer by Xiuhnel. The object pronoun ambiguity continues through the narrative in such a way that both Velázquez and Garibay are able to follow this rendering through the passage, both interpreting the one who goes weeping as the sister of the devoured or deflowered. But such a translation leaves the flight of Mimich through the fire—very explicit in the original—totally unmotivated and nonsensical, and drops Xiuhnel from the story for no reason whatever. Obviously, the psychohistorical significance of the myth can emerge only when the pronouns are put in their proper order and the flight of Mimich, together with the subsequent sacrifice of the pursuing demon, Itzpapalotl, are understood as consequences of her appetite. Walter Lehmann had already supplied such a version in his 1938 paleograph and German translation of this text (see note 7) previous to both Spanish mistranslations. He renders this important line as: *Und nachdem sie ihn auf den Boden gelegt hat, da wandte sie sich mit dem Gesicht nach unten über ihn, Da frist sie ihn, . . . macht sie ihm ein Loch in die Brust* "And after she has laid him on the ground she turns herself face-down on him. Then she devours him, makes a hole in his breast."

[7] Legend of the Suns MS, Walter Lehmann, ed. and trans., *Die Geschichte der Königreiche von Colhuacan und México*, "Quellenwerke zur alten Geschichte Amerikas," vol. I (Stuttgart, 1938), pp. 358–62. The most accessible version of this text is in Primo F. Velázquez, *Codice Chimalpopoca*, Universidad Nacional Autónoma de México, Instituto de Investigaciones Historicas, 1975), pp. 123–24. Present translation is prepared by W. Gingerich.

[8] Anales de Cuauhtitlan MS, in Lehmann, *Die Geschichte*, pp. 49–52. Also Velázquez, *Codice Chimalpopoca*, p. 3.

[9] Anales de Cuauhtitlan MS, in Lehmann, *Die Geschichte*, pp. 65–66. Also Velázquez, *Codice Chimalpopoca*, p. 6. Notice that the name of the third hearth-stone has changed from "Mixcoatl" to "Xiuhnel."

[10] Codice matritense del Real Palacio and Codice Florentino MSS, in Angel M. Garibay, ed. and trans., *Veinte himnos sacros de los nahuas* (México: UNAM, 1958), p. 66–69.

[11] Mircea Eliade, *Rituals and Symbols of Initiation: The Mysteries of Birth and Rebirth*, trans. W. Trask (New York: Harper & Row, 1965), pp. 62–63.

[12] Diego Durán, *The Book of the Gods and Rites and the Ancient Calendar*, trans. D. Heyden and F. Horcasitas (Norman: University of Oklahoma Press, 1971), p. 210.

[13] Informants of Sahagún, *Florentine Codex*, trans. A. Anderson & C. Dibble, bk. I (Salt Lake City: Univ. of Utah Press, 1950), p. 3.

[14] Durán, *Book of the Gods*, pp. 216–17. (Emphasis ours).

[15] Ruth Benedict, *Zuni Mythology*, (New York: Columbia University, 1935), 1: 59. The Zuni tales have been chosen to represent the body of Pueblo tales in these instances (the versions of the Hopi, Tewa, etc. often vary only in the names given to the characters) because the first anthropologists to reach the Pueblo peoples in the

nineteenth century contended that "the Zuni is almost as strictly archaic as in the days ere his land was discovered." (Frank Hamilton Cushing, "Outlines of Zuni Creation Myths," *Bureau of American Ethnology, Thirteenth Annual Report, 1891–92* [Washington, 1896], p. 341). They believed that the white man had made no impression on the Zuni, and that the Zuni tales did not reflect the customs and beliefs of the contemporary narrators but reflected the customs and traditions of many generations past (Benedict, *Zuni Mythology* 1: xiv). The recordings by Benedict have been chosen because they seem to us to be the most complete and are by far the most readable. Dennis Tedlock, in "On the Translation of Style in Oral Narrative," *Journal of American Folklore* 84 (1971): 114–33, (reprinted in this volume) has expressed a preference for the English style of Bunzel's translations, but the Benedict volumes have the added advantage—for the beginning researcher—of including detailed summaries of and comparisons with the previous tale collections of Cushing, Bunzel, and others.

[16]Benedict, *Zuni Mythology,* 1: 60.

[17]Printed only in abstract, in Benedict, *Zuni Mythology,* 1: 75.

[18]Ibid., p. 54.

[19]Ibid., p. 68.

[20]The significance of this observation is indicated by Vladimir Propp in his *Morphology of the Folktale* (Austin, 1970), pp. 21–23.

[21]Charles Di Peso, *Casas Grandes: A Fallen Trading Center of the Gran Chichimeca,* 3 vols. (Flagstaff, Ariz.: Northland Press, 1974). While there are a few headless skeletons, a few heads without bodies found in Pueblo burials, the examples are so rare that most archeologists seem to conclude at this time that such burials represent a disturbed grave and a reburial rather than the practice of sacrifice and decapitation. (H. S.& C. B. Cosgrove, *The Swarts Ruin* [Harvard, 1932].) And Hamilton A. Tyler concludes that human sacrifice probably did not exist in the Pueblo culture for the simple reason that the culture itself "is so short that any memory of such a practice would still linger among the whole tribe." *(Pueblo Gods and Myths* [University of Oklahoma, 1975], p. 113.)

[22]Lynn Flinn, C. Turner II, and A. Brew, "Additional Evidence for Cannibalism in the Southwest: The Case of LA 4528," *American Antiquity* 41, no. 3 (July, 1976): 308–18.

[23]First on the list of King Nezahualcoyotl's famous Eighty Ordinances (v. 1430–72) is the following provision for punishment of homo-eroticism:

> . . . *The active agent [of the couple] was tied to a pole and all the young men of the city covered him with ashes in such a way that he was buried, and the passive one had his entrails pulled out through the anus before being likewise buried in ashes.* [from Ixtlilxochitl, *Obras Historicas,* 2: 187–88].

[24]Paul Friedman, "Sexual Deviation," *American Handbook of Psychiatry,* vol. 2 (New York, 1959), pp. 594–95.

[25]Mircea Eliade, *Myths, Rites, Symbols,* eds., W. Beane and W. Doty, vol. 2 (New York, 1975), pp. 408–09.

[26]Informants of Sahagún, *Florentine Codex,* bk. 6, p. 117. This version is derived from the Anderson-Dibble translation.

[27]Ibid., p. 118–19.

[28]Ibid., p. 115.

[29]I cannot desist from suggesting that if there is any historical validity to our observations on the nature of the Chichimec psyche as represented in the texts under discussion, then perhaps the fabled Mexican "machismo" of legend and song has its roots even farther back than the conquistador-conquistada complex identified by Octavio Paz in *El Laberinto de la soledad*. Perhaps this ancient anxiety before the feminine has been the Chichimec's most enduring contribution to that marvelous amalgam which is the Mexican culture. (W.G.)

Ekkehart Malotki: THE STORY OF THE 'TSIMONMAMANT' OR JIMSON WEED GIRLS

A HOPI NARRATIVE FEATURING THE MOTIF OF THE VAGINA DENTATA

INTRODUCTION   The tradition of recording Hopi prose narratives is nearly one hundred years old. Most of the Hopi oral artifacts that are available today, we owe to four men. These scholars were endowed with both the necessary foresight and the enthusiasm to collect portions of a people's most precious and revealing heritage, its oral literature. One of the earliest salvage projects of Hopi literature was carried out by the Scottish-born ethnographer Alexander M. Stephen. He started his work in the First Mesa village of Walpi in 1882. His clan legends were compiled for publication by Mindeleff in the mid-1880s. A second collection of his was edited posthumously by Elsie Clews Parsons some forty years later. It included one version of the Hopi origin myth and other tales dealing with events from the times of "prehuman flux."[1] Also presented were stories dealing with feats of culture-heroes, and more recent happenings located in the time span after the Hopi emergence. The two other noteworthy collections from the early Anglo contact days are Fewkes' *Tusayan Migration Traditions* (1897) and *Traditions of the Hopi* (1905) which were assembled by the Mennonite missionary Henry R. Voth. Fewkes collected in the First Mesa area. Voth's material stems almost exclusively from the Third Mesa village of Oraibi. A fourth significant compilation of tales, *Folk Tales from Shumopovi, Second Mesa,* was recorded by Wallis in 1912, but not published until 1936.

The most startling observation made by this author, who has collected intensively in the domain of narratives, songs, and humor in the course of his linguistic research of the Hopi language, is the almost total absence of erotic or obscene elements in the collections mentioned above.[2] The same absence is noted in subsequent publications, most of which were offered in learned periodicals, museum notes, or an occasional master's thesis. Those that surfaced in more popular magazines generally consisted of watered-down tale-plots adjusted to the level of Anglo children. As might be expected, these works are purged of any so-called objectionable references to sex, bodily functions, etc. Often they and other anthologies of Hopi myths and legends actually constitute rewritten versions of the originals, presented in what one recent publication claims to be "poetic prose" and manufactured for the reader's liking, with additional padding based on the collector's empathy for Hopi culture.[3]

With the exception of one genuine bilingual attempt by Kennard and the abortive bilingual series undertaking by the Northern Arizona Supplementary Education Center, the entire body of available Hopi folklore has been collected and presented in the monolingual medium of English. Further, this same corpus of Hopi oral literature seems to have been bowdlerized of nearly every conceivable 'unprintable' words or actions, with two notable exceptions: one a rather obscene tale collected by Stephen,[4] and one recorded by Titiev concerning the hunch-back figure of *Kookopölö*.[5] In the latter the reader comes across such words as "penis" and "vagina."

The resulting sterile and often emasculated picture of Hopi culture that transpires in most available translated Hopi literature amounts to a rather one-sided view. Hopi society's everyday reality is actually impregnated with a good dose of earthy humor anchored primarily in the sexual and the scatological. One who is intimately familiar with the gregarious and communal Hopi knows that their way of life does not foster an atmosphere that is conducive to prudery or censorship of the spoken language. In a community founded on the extended family principle, where parents and children sleep in the same room, and several generations of kindred are concentrated in rather close quarters, it would be unnatural for attitudes and practices of this sort to develop; still, outside pressure in the form of Anglo missionaries, school superintendents, and other representatives of the American government and administration, as well as general acculturation have brought about definite, and sometimes, drastic changes in many behavioral patterns of Hopi life.

Two examples at extreme poles of the spectrum of change are worthy of mention. First, young children do not roam the villages naked any more, and, second, religious practices involving fertility acts with phallic symbols and performances have grown extinct. Nevertheless, there still exists a frank sexual component in many aspects of the Hopi cultural fabric. One need only point to the sexual "mimesis" in the antics of Hopi clowns; the erotic byplay in certain kin relationships that are based on teasing; and the sexual overtones that tinge Hopi verbal humor, which consists to a large extent of punning.

The two latter insights can, naturally, be best experienced by one versed in the Hopi language. Familiarity with the vernacular is also the prerequisite necessary to rectify the distorted impression of Hopi "asexual" literature. There hardly is an original tale that will not at one point or another evoke laughter in the listening audience through some reference to what is considered pornographic or obscene in Anglo culture. Many an instance in this author's bilingual collection of Hopi stories bears witness to this. Further, Hopi narrators do not differentiate between sexual or scatological elements in tale-plots on the one hand, and violence, death, seduction, etc., on the other. All of these elements are taken in stride. Sexual topics are vital and functional factors in a natural context of spontaneous narration. If they are left out intentionally, much of the spontaneity of the narratives is destroyed. "Clean," expurgated literature simply cannot reflect the ordinary life situation.

The Hopi tale presented here bilingually is a good example of sexual folk-literature. As Legman has pointed out, this genre "always has the air of being humorous." He is aware, however, that more is at stake. "Actually it concerns some of the most pressing fears and most destructive life problems of the people who tell the jokes and sing the songs . . . They are projecting the endemic sexual fears and problems, and defeats of their culture—in which there are very few victories for anyone—on certain standard comedy figures and situations, such as cuckoldry, seduction, impotence, homosexuality, castration, and disease, which are obviously not humorous at all."[6]

The central theme of the story of the *Tsimonmamant* or Jimson Weed Girls revolves around the psychologically deep-rooted motif of the *vagina dentata*. Commonly associated with its related motif of the *penis captivus* it is less frequently known as *cunnus dentata*. As a rule, it is translated as "toothed vagina" or "dentate vulva." The motif of the *vagina dentata* is prominent in many accounts of North American Indian mythology, and is traditionally narrated with straightforward simplicity. Legman mentions a characteristic ingredient of many such stories—the appearance of the "tooth-breaker." This person figures in cultures where stories tell "of a race of Amazonian women . . . who have actual teeth in their vagina, which must be broken by the culture-hero 'so that women will be harmless to men.'"[7] Thompson has surveyed the distribution of the motif among North American Indians[8] and lists occurrences from other parts of the world in his *Motif-Index of Folk-Literature*.[9]

Psychoanalytically, the strange and menacing concept of the *vagina dentata* usually is interpreted as a projection of the unconscious anxiety of castration and is associated with male impotence. Bonaparte, in elaborating a remark by Freud, points to the equation of mouth and vagina and considers the notion of the *vagina dentata* and its accompanying threat as "a factor with roots deep in infantile experience."[10] At first it was the infant who displayed aggressive, i.e., occasionally biting behavior towards his mother's breast. Later it is the adult who, due to a sense of guilt stemming from his infantile behavior, feels threatened by a mother who intends to castrate him.[11]

Newman has shown that the symbolism of the toothed vagina with its destructive and lethal consequences is truly archetypal and has universal distribution.[12] This image of the teeth-studded womb is also encountered in different form in the marine monster Scylla; the terrifying female creature Gorgo, who was equipped with fanged snakes instead of teeth; and many other mythological dragon monsters with female attributes.[13]

How wide the vaginal teeth motif was distributed in the Southwest culture area is difficult to ascertain. Thompson lists only one reference to it, in conjunction with literature from the San Carlos Apache.[14] Benedict records one Zuni story that features the motif in a rather subordinate role. It appears only in the story's conclusion where the oversexed Crazy Woman who pursues the young hunter turns out to be Toothed Vagina Woman.[15] The only Navajo reference to this motif, of which this author is aware, occurs in Dyk's Navajo autobiography *Son of Old Man Hat*. In it the protagonist is warned by his mother not to bother with girls:

"The girls will sometimes take your c—— out and bite it off." Her admonition equally pertains to women: "All the women have teeth where their c——s are."[16] Whether the Navajos borrowed this notion from Hopi mythology, as they did with so many other elements (including the idea of an emergence from the womb of the earth), need not trouble us here. As we were able to show above, its distribution is practically universal.

What really heightens the formidability of the *vagina dentata* motif in the present tale is made more so by its association with the Jimson weed plant. This showy herb (also known as Sacred Datura, a name that is partially based on its scientific term of *Datura meteloides*) is easily spotted when in bloom due to its large, trumpet-shaped white flowers. Widely branching and rank-smelling, its dry fruit capsule, according to McDougall, possesses prickles ranging from 5 to 12mm in length.[17] Being a member of the *Solanaceae* or Nightshade family, its botanic properties are well known to the Hopi. They consider the root and other parts of the plant, especially the seeds, medicinally beneficial, and also destructive. The poisonous qualities of the powerful narcotic stramonium contained in Jimson weed far outweigh the drug's potential benefits.[18] As one of my Hopi informants put it, "Jimson weed acts as a painkiller in that it keeps the mind off the pain." Generally, the herb is feared, due to the hallucinations that may be caused by just a slight overdose. My most knowledgeable Hopi informant in this matter, who also is consulted as a medicine-man, described the plant as *nukurtusaqa* or "evil grass," and its medicinal value as *honaqngahu* or "crazy medicine." He specifically referred to its white root, which when eaten produces a craziness sometimes associated with fatal consequences. He claimed that even touching the plant makes it necessary to wash one's hands, and he protested its use as a medicine.

Whiting reports that "Datura was sometimes given to a person 'who is mean,' apparently with the idea of curing him of his 'meanness.'"[19] He also claims "that the root may be chewed to induce vision by the medicine man while making a diagnosis."[20] None of my informants were able to confirm this. Knowing the Hopis' general disinclination if not aversion to experiment with hallucinogenic potions, I would suggest only that the above-mentioned practices cannot have been very widespread.

The abstinence from Jimson weed is not, however, found among all cultures in the Southwest. The Luiseño Indians in southern California, for example, integrated the drinking of Jimson weed into their male initiation rites. This custom is reputed to have been instituted by the god Chinigchinix.[21] The decoction of the narcotic drug had a stupefying effect on the initiate and induced the seeing of visions.[22] Moriarty believes to have discovered new evidence that Jimson weed also played a role during the female adolescent rites of the Chinigchinix religious movement, and, of significance here, that there was a direct connection between these rites and *vagina dentata* configurations.[23]

It now becomes apparent why this Hopi story combines the dreadful concept of the toothed vagina with the Jimson herb. The Hopi term *tsimona*, imbued with connotations of narcotic powers that derange the mind and are usually fatal, is equated or coalesces with sexual aberration, which must be considered equally dangerous and devastating. This association is acted out here by the *Tsimonmamant* or "Jimson Weed Girls," who are anthropomorphized Jimson weed plants that represent oversexed unmarried girls and women. In addition, the dreadful fear of castration by a toothed vagina, a fear lodged deep in the subconscious, is dramatized here in the capture of a young man by a horde of oversexed females whose genitals are toothed. The physical link to this motif is clearly established in the prickly or spiny capsule of the plant, which actually contains the seeds responsible for the physical and mental abnormality depicted in the story.

It is also evident that neither the destructive effect of the narcotic derived from the *tsimona* plant, nor the destructive behavior displayed by the sexually aberrant *Tsimonmamant,* can be tolerated by a society that attempts to remain intact and live in harmony with nature. This motivates the climactic revenge scene in the tale. The offending vaginal teeth of the *Tsimonmamant* are broken and worn down by artificial cottonwood penises, and then the girls and women resorting to such treacherous devices during intercourse are actually "copulated to death" in a denouement that brings about a solution that may truly be termed cathartic.

Interestingly, no such cleansing of the emotions and no such sense of restored order results from a variant of this story collected by Stephen in the 1880s.[24] The general mood of Stephen's tale is much more erotic, and some of its details much more obscene if compared with this version, even though Stephen generally avoided Anglo-Saxon terms and resorted to latinisms throughout his rendition. Also, while the protagonist here survives the compulsory ordeal of copulation relatively unharmed, Stephen's hero loses his penis: "The last one to copulate was a maid and as she finished the act, with her vulva, she bit off, and ate with her vulva, the penis of the youth."[25] The man survives. The revenge, however, that is organized can only be described as anticlimactic compared to the finale in our story. The men in Stephen's version also use artificial penises, filled with sour sumac seeds in this case, "that took off the edge of the vulva teeth."[26] The visit of the men to the "Jamestown weed maids," as Stephen refers to them, only leads to promiscuous copulation that "was maintained. . . . until all the women were completely exhausted."[27] Did the narrator shy away from a more drastic ending in the presence of the white ethnologist, or did the translator fail to convey the exact meaning of the final scene? To one familiar with typical Hopi story endings, this finale seems thoroughly un-Hopi.

This also is evidenced in a third variant of this tale-plot, that was recorded by Armin Geertz in the Hotevilla vernacular.[28] In this variant men from Oraibi are lured to the kiva abode of the *Tsimonmamant* and murdered during intercourse by means of the vaginal teeth. The hero survives the ordeal with the assistance of Spider Woman, and revenges the death of his fellow villagers by turning the Jimson weed creatures into stone. He achieves this by making use of a magic medicine supplied to him by Spider Woman, and once again the evil force is destroyed. Such an ending is in line with the Hopi philosophy of revenge as it transpires in oral literature.

Folklore is a powerful catalyst with a therapeutic impact, but hardly a functional facet in the cultural web of Western society. In a society that is print-oriented and has succumbed to the mass media of radio and television, oral literature no longer has a real place. Ironically, the verbal arts still seem to flourish in those societies which are often labeled illiterate. As Burling points out, "illiteracy has never implied a lack of verbal skill, and oral verbal skills may even tend to develop in inverse proportion to written verbal skills."[29]

Unfortunately, Hopi narrative tradition does not thrive as much as it did a generation or two ago. The tradition also has given way to the deadening impact of premanufactured television entertainment and has become moribund. Every effort should be made, therefore, to salvage what still is viable of this oral tradition. Every effort also should be made to collect these oral artifacts in the vernacular. Their accompanying translations should be presented without embellishments or expurgated passages. Only then will folk-literature permit us to gain true insights into the psyche of a folk; insights that can be found nowhere else.

THE JIMSON WEED GIRLS

1   *Aliksa'i.*[30] *They were living in Oraibi. Among the people living there long ago was a youth who still had both his parents. In those days it was customary for boys and men to spend a great deal of time in the kivas. This youth, too, would sometimes join the others in the kiva, but then again, when he was not in the mood, he would busy himself at home.*

2   *One day, when his family was eating supper, there was a public announcement. An outing to gather herbs was going to take place; the youth, however, took no interest in things of this sort. He asked his parents whether they were planning to go along, but they were not sure. Then, in turn, his parents asked him if he would join the others.*

3   *"I don't know what I'll do," he replied.*

4   *"Well," they said, "why don't you go along for once. Be grateful that you are still an unmarried man." This is what his parents said to him.*

5   *Early the next day some of the young men and girls began to leave. They were headed down to the south side of Oraibi. The youth was still not at all sure whether he wanted to join the party. But finally he got the urge to go and said to his parents, "I suppose I'll go after them."*

6   *"Very well," his parents replied.*

7   *So he, too, started out. When he reached the southern edge of the mesa, no one was there anymore. He now had second thoughts about going, but then he said,*

"Well, I guess I'll go after them," and started downhill. He had nearly reached the bottom when he saw someone else ahead of him. When he caught up with that person, it turned out to be a beautiful girl. Though he did not know her, he greeted her, "I see you're also on your way."

8   "Yes," she answered, "I almost didn't want to go, but then I changed my mind, so here I am. And so are you."

9   "Well, yes, I did the same as you and that's why I am late." This is what he said to her.

10   The girl suggested, "Let's go together."

11   "That's fine with me. We may catch up with the others somewhere."

12   From there on they walked together until they did come up to the rest. And so they joined the group in collecting herbs and edible greens. When it was noontime, the young man and the girl went along with the others to the place where they were going to have lunch and ate with them. Then the group began to head back.

13   But the youth and the girl again followed quite a bit later and kept lagging behind them. The youth picked a lot of greens, so the girl had a good load to carry on her back. By and by they caught up with the rest at the foot of the mesa. There the girl said to him, "I'm very tired. Why don't we rest for a while."

14   He agreed. "Yes, all right."

15   So they rested there while all the others continued on up to the top. The two chatted with each other until the girl said, "I suppose we should go up, too. The others left quite a while ago." So the two set out. They were about to start the ascent to the high plateau of Oraibi when the girl said, "Let's go this way," and turned off toward the foot of the mesa.

16   "Why?" he asked.

17   "I live here; so come along."

18   They headed toward the terrace. At the foot was a big overhang and inside along the base an abundance of Jimson weed was growing. Right in the midst of the flowers was a kiva. That was the place she was taking him to. When they arrived she said, "This is where I'm at home. Come on in." She went ahead and he followed her. After he had entered, he noticed that some other people were living there who were strangers to him. They welcomed him and made him feel at home.

19   On taking a closer look at them, though, he realized that all of them were girls; also, they were very beautiful. Evidently only girls were living there. They spread

some food out for him and he ate. At the same time the girls beside him were talking to one another. They all wanted him and were arguing, "I'll sleep with him first."

20 *"No, it'll be me."*

21 *Finally the girl who had brought him said, "I can assure you it's going to be me. I'll be the first to sleep with him."*

22 *When the young man was full he got up and said, "Thank you for the food. I'll move on now."*

23 *"You can't go anywhere," they replied. "You still have to sleep with us here. Tomorrow you can go home." This is what the girls said.*

24 *He now tried to leave but he could not find a door anywhere; there was no way out of this house. He was forced to stay whether he wanted to or not. It was not long before the girls began making the beds. "We'll be going to bed now," they were saying. He didn't know what to do. He wanted to get out but had no idea how. He couldn't find a door. So there the girls were preparing a bed for him. Then they said, "You can sleep here, you must be tired. Tomorrow at daylight you can go home."*

25 *He resigned himself to his situation and lay down. Since he was quite exhausted he fell asleep at once. It was some time later when something touched him and he awoke. It turned out to be the girl that had lured him here. She said to him, "I'm going to sleep with you," and lay down next to him.*

26 *He, however, lay there without stirring. The girl began to urge him, "Please, fuck me," she pleaded. But he did not make a move. So she climbed on him herself and made love to him. After that she withdrew.*

27 *It did not take long before another girl appeared. Again she kept urging him until he finally had to consent. This time he fucked her. After she had departed, another approached him; in this manner all of them dealt with him.*

28 *In the meantime he had reached a point where he almost didn't know where he was. The cunts of the girls seemed to have teeth. His penis hurt considerably by now. He got to his feet and went to the girl who had led him to this place. "Please, let me out, I think I'm going to pass out." This is what he said.*

29 *"You can fuck me first and then I'll let you out."*

30 *"But I'm nearly out of my mind."*

31 *"If you want to leave, you fuck me once more and then I'll let you go."*

32   Thereupon he had to sleep with her again. When he was through she said, "I'll let you out now."

33   "All right," he replied, and then he asked, "Who are you anyway?"

34   "We are the Jimson Weed Girls," was her response.

35   They now went to the eastern base of the wall. There was a door which he had not spotted before. When he walked out, the sun was about to rise.

36   Just when the sun came up he reached home. His parents were eating breakfast and said to him, "Here, have a seat and help yourself. We are eating." So he sat down. He had barely started eating when his parents asked, "Did you come home yesterday?"

37   "Yes, I did, but I went straight to the kiva to spend the night there. I returned somewhat tired."

38   "So that's why you didn't show up last night," they responded.

39   When they were full the youth said, "I'll go to the kiva and will stay there with the others."

40   He left and went to the kiva, but not a soul was there yet. After some time they began arriving, boys and men. When a great many of them had gathered, he addressed them as follows: "I have something to say to you. As you recall, people went to pick greens yesterday, and I was one of them. On the way I met a girl. She invited me to her house in the evening. There, she and a bunch of other girls caused me a great deal of suffering. It is my hope that you will go there to revenge me. I'll tell you later where they live. To begin with, however, you should carve some penises for yourselves. Carve them out of cottonwood root. When you're done, I'll give you further instructions." This is what he said to them.

41   The boys and men were elated about this undertaking. Everywhere they were working on their penises. Finally, they were all finished. The penises had been made in various sizes and lengths.

42   The youth spoke to them again: "I guess all of you are done. Tonight you can go down here to the south side to visit these girls and revenge me. You only have to descend a little distance and then there, at the north base, you'll spot a large patch of Jimson weed plants. Right in their midst is a kiva which houses those girls. That's the place you can go tonight and get even with them for me. The girls there are obsessed with fucking, but their cunts have teeth. So I suggest you first use the things you just carved. Later, if someone wants to fuck without it, he can do that too." These were his instructions to the men.

43 *They were looking forward to the evening, but it seemed as if time was standing still. Finally darkness fell; they left the kiva and were on their way. Sure enough, when they reached their destination, there was a kiva. They entered and the girls greeted them happily. They all wanted to have the men for themselves. The excitement was enormous.*

44 *Soon the girls began making the beds and then they went to it. There were just as many men as there were girls. At first they fucked them with their cottonwood penises. For it was true: the girls' cunts were simply grinding away on their cottonwood stalks. The creatures just couldn't get enough. So the men kept fucking them there. Finally the time came when the teeth of their vaginas were worn down. Now the men used their real penises.*

45 *Eventually the girls became bored. So the men resorted to their cottonwood stalks once more and fucked them all night long. In this manner they killed all of them. Whenever someone had fucked his girl to death, he stopped. When all of the girls were dead, the men went home. They had really enjoyed themselves.*

46 *The following day the youth came to the kiva again. All of those who were members of the kiva were present. The youth asked them, "Did you take revenge on the girls for me?"*

47 *"Yes, we did; we enjoyed ourselves. We destroyed them all."*

48 *Thereupon he expressed his gratitude to them. "Thank you for revenging me. That's the way I wanted it."*

49 *This is how the men wreaked vengeance upon the Jimson Weed Girls on behalf of this youth. They probably still have their cottonwood stalks stashed away somewhere. And here the story ends.*

TSIMONMAMANT

1 *Aliksa'i. Yaw Orayve yeesiwa. Noq yaw hak pep tiyo kiy'ta. Paas yaw naat yumuy'ta. Noq pay pi hisat tootim, taataqt sutsep kya pi kivaapa yesngwu. Noq pay yaw pam ephaqam nuutum kivaapeningwu. Pu' yaw pay ephaqam kya pi piw qa pan unangway'te' pay kiy ep hiita hintsakngwu.*

2 *Noq yaw hisat puma tapkiqw noonovaqw yaw tsa'lawu, niiqe yaw kur nevenwehekniqat tsa'lawu. Noq pay i' tiyo yaw qa pas hiita ningwu. Niiqe pu' yaw yumuy tuuvingta sen pi yaw puma nuutumniqat, noq pay yaw qa pas suyan hingqawu. Noq pu' yaw put yumat tuwat tuuvingta sen pi yaw nuutumniqat.*

3 *"Pay pi nu' hin pi hintini," yaw amumi kita.*

4   *"Paapu um suushaqam nuutumni. Tsangaw pi naat um tiyo," kita yaw aw
     yumatu.*

5   *Noq pu' yaw oovi qavongvaqw iits pay yaw peetu nöönganta, tootim, mamant.
     Aqw Orayviy tatkyaqöymiq yaw hanta. Noq pay yaw pam qa hin pas suyan
     nuutumniqay anta, nit pu' yaw hisatniqw pam pan unangwti, niiqe pu' yaw
     pam yumuy aw pangqawu. "Pay pi kur nu' amungkni," yaw kita.*

6   *"Ta'ay," pay yaw yumat aw kita.*

7   *Pu' yaw oovi pam pangqw tuwat nakwsu. Pam yaw aqw taatöq tumpoq pituqw
     pay yaw qa hak haqam. Pu' yaw as paasat pay pam piw qeeqe'ti, nit pu' pay yaw
     pangqawu, "Pay pi nu' amungkni." Kitaaqe pu' yaw pam hawto. Pas pay yaw
     pam oovi soosok hawniniqw, piw yaw hak apyeve'. Noq yaw pam angk pituqw,
     piw yaw hak lomamana. Yaw pam hakiy qa tuwiy'ta. Pu' yaw pam aw
     pangqawu, "Um pu' tuwat yangqe'?"*

8   *"Owi," yaw put aw kita, "nu' pay as pas qe'ninit, pu' nu' pay piw hinwattiqe pu'
     oovi yang'a. Piw pi oovi um'i."*

9   *"Hep owi, pay nu' piw unhaqam hintiqe oovi qa iitsi," yaw pam aw kita.*

10   *"Himu tur pay itam naamani," yaw maana put aw kita.*

11   *"Ta'ay, pay pi antsa itam naamani, pay pi kya as itam haqami amungk
     pituni."*

12   *Kitaaqe pu' yaw puma paapiy naama'. Panmakyangw pu' yaw puma antsa
     haqami amungk pitu. Paasat pu' yaw puma nuutum neevennuma. Noq pu' yaw
     kur taawanasapti. Pu' yaw pay puma nuutum haqam nöönösaniqat panso'.
     Pep yaw oovi puma nuutum nöösa. Pantotit pu' yaw kur pay pangqw ahoyyani.*

13   *Oovi yaw ahoyyaqw, pu' yaw pay ima piw qa iits pas amungk nakwsu. Pay yaw
     oovi puma pangqaqw amungk hinma. Noq pay i' tiyo yaw wuuhaq nepna, noq
     oovi pay yaw maana wuuhaq iikwiwta. Panmakyangw pu' yaw puma tupo
     amungk pitu. Pep pu' yaw maana put aw pangqawu, "Pas nu' maangu'i," yaw
     kita, "itam as hiisavo naasungwnat pu'ni."*

14   *Pu' yaw pay pam nakwha. "Ta'ay," yaw aw kita.*

15   *Pu' yaw oovi puma pephaqam naasungwniy'taqw yaw pay mimawat soosoyam
     aapiy yayva. Pu' yaw pay puma pep hiita naami yu'a'ata, noq pu' hisatniqw pu'
     yaw maana piw pangqawu, "Pay pi itam tuwat wuptoni. Pay pi se'elhaq
     mimawat aqwhaqamiya." Paasat pu' yaw oovi puma tuwat pangqaqw nakwsu.
     Panmakyangw pu' yaw puma pas pay Oraymiq wupniniqw pu' yaw maana put
     aw pangqawu, "Itam pewni," yaw aw kita. Pu' yaw pay angqw tupo laasi.*

16 *"Ya hintoq oovi'oy?" yaw pam aw kita.*

17 *"Pay nu' yep kiy'ta, noq oovi um pewni."*

18 *Pu' yaw puma angqw tupo, noq pep tup yaw kur wukotuusöy'ta, noq pep put tuusöt ang tupkye' yaw a'ni tsimona kuyta. Noq put yaw su'aasonvehaqam yaw kur kiva. Noq panso yaw kur pam put wiiki. Pu' yaw puma aw pituqw pam yaw aw pangqawu, "Yep nu' kiy'ta, um oovi peqw pakini." Aw yaw kitat pu' yaw aqw paki. Paasat pu' yaw pam angk aqw paki. Yaw pam aqw pakiqw, piw yaw hakim epeq yeese, niiqe yaw put aw haalaytoti. Pu' yaw paas put taviya.*

19 *Noq pas yaw pam paasat pu' amuupa paas taatayqw pas yaw kur mamantsaya. Pas pi yaw piw lomamamantsa kur pepehaq kiy'yungwa. Pu' yaw oovi put aw tunösvongyaatota. Noq pu' yaw oovi pam tuumoyta. Oovi yaw pam tuumoytaqw pu' yaw tuwat aqle' mamant naanaapa hingqaqwa. Yaw put naanaqasya niiqe yaw pangqaqwa, "Nu' hapi mooti amum puwni."*

20 *"So'ni, songqa nu'ni."*

21 *Paasat i' maana wikvaqa pu' yaw pangqawu, "Son pi qa nu' mooti amum puwni."*

22 *Pu' yaw pam oovi öyqe pu' wunuptu. Pu' yaw pam amumi pangqawu, "Kwakwhay, nu' nöösa, niiqe oovi nu' pay hoytani," yaw kita.*

23 *"Pay um son haqamini," yaw aw kitota, "pay um naat yepeq itamum puwni. Ason um qaavo pu' nimani," kitota yaw awi'.*

24 *Pu' yaw pam as antsa yamakniniqw yaw qa haqam hötsiwa. Yan pu' yaw pay kur pam hin pangqw yamakni. Pu' yaw pay pam oovi nawus huruuti. Noq pay yaw qa wuuyavotiqw pay yaw mamant aapalalwa. "Itam pay tokni," yaw kitikyaakyangw. Pu' yaw kur pam hintini. Yaw as pam hin pangqw yamaknikyangw kur hinni. Yaw pam hötsiwat qa tuwa. Pu' yaw paasat put engem haqe' aapatota, pu' yaw aw pangqaqwa, "Yang um puwni, son um qa mangu'iwta. Ason um qaavo taalawvaqw pu' nimani," kitota yaw awi'.*

25 *Pu' pay pi yaw kur pam hintiqe pu' yaw pam nawus wa'ö. Noq pay pi yaw antsa pam mangu'iwtaqe pay yaw kur pam suupuwva. Pu' yaw hisatniqw put aw himu hintsakqw pam taatayi. Noq yaw kur maana put wikvaqa. Pam yaw kura'. Pu' yaw aw pangqawu, "Nu' umum puwni," yaw aw kita. Pu' yaw pay put aqlavaqe wa'ö.*

26 *Pu' yaw pay pam sun yanta. Paasat pu' yaw maana put aw öqalti, "Um as nuy tsopni," yaw aw kita. Noq pay yaw pam pas qa poniniyku. Noq pay yaw naap atsmi wuuvi. Pu' yaw oovi pay pam maana put tsoova. Paasat pu' yaw aapiyo'.*

27   *Pay yaw qa wuuyavotiqw pay yaw piw suukya aw pitu. Pu' yaw piw tuwat aw
ö'qala. Pu' yaw pam pay nawus nakwha. Pu' yaw pam put tsoova. Pu' yaw piw
aapiyo'. Piw pay yaw suukya aw pitu. Pu' pay yaw puma pepehaq put aw
pantsatskya.*

28   *Nungwu yaw pay paapu pam pas hin unangwti. Pas pi yaw piw mamantuy
löwa'am suupan tamay'yungwa. Pas yaw put kwasi'at nungwu a'ni tuyva.
Paasat pu' yaw pam qatuptuqe pu' angqw mantuway awi'. Pu' yaw aw
pangqawu, "Um as nuy horoknani, pas nu' hin unangwti," yaw aw kita.*

29   *"Um tur ason nuy mooti tsopq pu' nu' ung horoknani."*

30   *"Hep pas nu' hin unangwti."*

31   *"Pay pi um yamakniqay naawakne' nuy tsopq, pu' nu' ung horoknani."*

32   *Paasat pu' yaw pam nawus piw put tsopta. Pas yaw oovi pantiqw pu' yaw put aw
pangqawu, "Nu' hapi ung horoknani."*

33   *"Ta'ay," pam yaw aw kitat pu' yaw pam tuuvingta, "Ya uma hakimu?" yaw
aw kita.*

35   *Paasat pu' yaw angqw puma hoopoq tupoq. Pang yaw kur hötsiwaniqw pam put
qa tuwa. Paasatniqw pu' yaw pam pangqaqw yama. Pay yaw kur pas pay taawa
yamakni.*

36   *Pu' yaw pam oovi su'aw kiy aw pituqw yaw taawa yama. Noq pay yaw yu'at
puma tuumoyta. Pu' yaw put aw pangqawu, "Yangqö, itam tuumoyta." Pu'
yaw oovi pam aw qatuptu. Naat yaw oovi pam pu' tuumoyvaqw, pu' yaw yu'at
puma tuuvingta, "Ya um taavok pay as pitu?"*

37   *"Owi, pay nu' as pitut pay yuumosa kivami puwto. Pay nu' pas hihin
mangu'iwvaqe oovi'o."*

38   *"Oovi um tooki qa pitu," yaw aw kita.*

39   *Pu' yaw oovi puma öö'öya. Paasat pu' yaw i' tiyo pangqawu, "Nu' kur pay
kivamini," yaw kita, "pay nu' kur pu' nuutum pep qatuni."*

40   *Pu' yaw oovi pam pangqw yamakt pu' kivami'. Pay yaw qa hak pas naat epe'.
Hisatniqw pu' yaw ökiwta, tootim, taataqt. Yaw oovi wuuhaqniiqam tsovaltiqw
pu' yaw pam amumi pangqawu, "Nu' kur umumi hingqawni. Ura taavok
yangqw sinom nevenwehekqw nu' nuutumay," yaw kita, "nit nu' hakiy maanat
aw pitu. Pam nuy tapkiqw kiy aw wiiki, noq puma pep amum kiy'yungqam pas
nuy okiwsasnaqw, uma as inungem aqw naa'oywisniy," yaw amumi kita. "Pay
nu' ason umuy aa'awnani haqam kiy'yungq'ö. Niikyangw uma mooti neegem*

kwasit yukuutotani, pay uma paakot angqw put yukuutotani. Ason uma pantotiqw pu' nu' piw umumi hinwat tutaptani," kita yaw amumi'.

41   *Paasat pu' yaw tootim, taataqt kwangwtapnaya. Pu' yaw naanaqle' neengem kwasit yuykuya. Hisatniqw pu' yaw kur soosoyam yukuya. Naap hiisakw pu' piw naap hiisavat yaw hak yukungwu.*

42   *Paasat pu' yaw pam piw amumi pangqawu, "Pay kya uma soosoyam yukuya. Uma hapi pu' tapkiqw yukyiq tatkyaqöymiq imuy mamantuy amumi inungem naa'oywisni. Pay hak panis aw hiisavo atkyami hawqw, pep kwiniwi tupo tsimona a'ni kuytaqw, put aasonve kiva. Pep puma mamant kiy'yungwa. Noq pansoq uma tapkiqye' uma pepeq pumuy amumi inungem naa'oyyani. Pas puma pepeq mamant natsophooyamu. Noq piw pas löwa'am tamay'yungqw oovi uma ason it yukuutotaniqay, put mooti akwyani. Pu' pay pi ason piw qa put akwniqa pay pi qa put akwni." Yanhaqam yaw pam pumuy amumi tutapta.*

43   *Pu' yaw oovi puma tapkimi kwangwtotoya, noq pas pi yaw suupan paasat taawa qa hoyta. Hisatniqw pu' yaw tapki. Pu' yaw puma pangqw kivangaqw aqwya. Antsa yaw puma aqw ökiqw pay yaw kur pas antsa pephaqam kiva. Pu' yaw puma aqw yungya. Pas pi yaw mamant haalaytoti, pu' yaw pumuy naanaqasya. Pas pi yaw hin unangwa.*

44   *Pay yaw paasat mamant aapativaya. Paasat pu' yaw puma aw pitsinaya. Pas pi yaw puma amuptsiwta. Pu' yaw oovi puma pay mooti pakokwasit akw pumuy tsoptota. Noq pas pi yaw antsa mamantuy löwa'am paysoq pakokwasiyamuy nguriritota. Pas yaw hiitu qa öönatotingwu. Pepehaq yaw puma pumuy tsoplalwa. Hisatniqw pu' yaw kur löwayamuy tama'am tsakwamti. Paasat pu' yaw pas puma qa atsat kwasiy akw pepehaq pumuy tsoplalwa.*

45   *Pu' yaw pay tuwat mamant hisatniqw öönatoti. Paasat pu' yaw puma pay pakokwasit akw pumuy pepehaq tookyep tsoplalwa. Pantsakkyaakyangw pay yaw puma pumuy pas qöqya. Pay yaw himuwa mantuway tsovinine' pu' yaw qe'tingwu. Yaw oovi puma soosoyam mantuwmuy qöqyat pu' pangqaqw ninma. Pas pi yaw puma kwangwa'ewtota.*

46   *Qavongvaqw pu' yaw i' tiyo piw kivami', noq pay yaw ep soosoyam kivay'yungqam yeese. Paasat pu' yaw pam pumuy tuuvingta, "Ya uma inungem amumi naa'o'ya?" yaw amumi kita.*

47   *"Owi, pas itam kwangwa'ewtota. Pay itam pas pumuy qöqya."*

48   *Paasat pu' yaw pam amumi haalayti. "Kwakwhay, uma inungem amumi naa'o'ya. Pan pi nu' naawakna," kita yaw pam amumi'.*

49   *Yanhaqam yaw puma put engem tsimonmamantuy aw naa'o'ya. Naat kya oovi haqam pakokwasiy songqe oyiy'yungwa. Pay yuk pölö.*

NOTES

[1] For additional elaboration of the term "prehuman flux" see Karl Luckert, *The Navajo Hunter Tradition* (Tucson: University of Arizona Press, 1975), p. 133. There he defines it as referring "to man's primeval kinship with all creatures of the living world."

[2] In my translation I have tried to stay close to the Hopi original. However, I am aware that any translation constitutes a distorting filter that detracts from the original. I am also painfully aware that the occurring four-letter words are much too loaded with emotional associations in our society to qualify as approximate equivalents of the Hopi terms. For a simple and honest narrative as the one presented here, I did think, though, that Anglo-Saxon words were in general preferable to pompous Latinisms and pretentious euphemisms. The translator's dilemma is a genuine one that fortunately does not exist for the Hopi narrator.

[3] See Fred Eggan's foreword to G. M. Mullett, *Spider Woman Stories: Legends of the Hopi Indians* (Tucson: University of Arizona Press, 1979), pp. ix–xiv.

[4] Alexander M. Stephen, "Hopi Tales," *Journal of American Folklore* 42 (1929): 28–30.

[5] Mischa Titiev, "The Story of Kokopele," *American Anthropologist* 41 (1939): 91–98.

[6] G. Legman, *The Horn Book: Studies in Erotic Folklore and Bibliography* (New Hyde Park, New York: University Books, 1963), pp. 245–46.

[7] G. Legman, *Rationale of the Dirty Joke: An Analysis of Sexual Humor* (2nd series, Wharton, New York: Breaking Point, 1975), p. 429.

[8] Stith Thompson, *Tales of the North American Indians* (1929; rpt. Bloomington, Indiana: Indiana University Press, 1966), p. 309.

[9] Stith Thompson, *Motif-Index of Folk-Literature* (rev. and enl. ed. Bloomington, Indiana: Indiana University Press, 1955), p. 164.

[10] Marie Bonaparte, *Female Sexuality,* trans. John Rodker (New York: International Universities Press, 1953), p. 218.

[11] See Lo Duca, ed., *Moderne Enzyklopädie der Erotik,* (München, Wien, and Basel: Desch Verlag, 1963), p. 727.

[12] Erich Neumann, *Die grosse Mutter: Der Archetyp des grossen Weiblichen* (Zürich: Rhein-Verlag, 1956), pp. 165–69.

[13] Jacques Schnier, "Dragon Lady," *American Imago* 4 (1947): 80–83.

[14] Thompson, *Tales,* p. 309.

[15] Ruth Benedict, *Zuni Mythology,* Columbia University Contributions to Anthropology, No. 21 (1935; rpt. New York: AMS Press, 1969), I: 169.

[16] Walter Dyk, *Son of Old Man Hat: A Navaho Autobiography,* 3rd Bison printing (Lincoln: University of Nebraska Press, 1938), p. 45.

[17] W. B. McDougall, *Seed Plants of Northern Arizona* (Flagstaff: Museum of Northern Arizona Press, 1973), p. 428.

[18] Alfred F. Whiting, *Ethnobotany of the Hopi* (1939; rpt. Flagstaff: Northland Press, 1966), p. 89.

[19] Ibid.

[20] Ibid.

[21] James R. Moriarty, *Chinigchinix: An Indigenous California Indian Religion.* Hodge Fund Publication, vol. 10, (Los Angeles: Southwest Museum, 1969), p. 22.

[22]Maria Leach, gen. ed., *Standard Dictionary of Folklore, Mythology, and Legend* (New York: Funk and Wagnalls, 1972), p. 552.

[23]Personal communication, April 24, 1979.

[24]Stephen, "Hopi Tales," pp. 28–36.

[25]Ibid., p. 28.

[26]Ibid., p. 30.

[27]Ibid.

[28]The story was tape-recorded in December 1978 and was narrated by an elderly woman from the Third Mesa village of Hotevilla.

[29]Robbins Burling, *English in Black and White* (New York: Holt, Rinehart and Winston, 1973), p. 78.

[30]*Aliksa'i* is the traditional story opener which, in the Hopi dialect area of Third Mesa, serves as a signal to an audience that the storyteller is about to begin his narrative.

BIBLIOGRAPHY

Albert, Roy, Tom Mootzka, and Charlie Talawepi. *Coyote Tales.* Eighteen bilingual booklet sets. Flagstaff: Northern Arizona Supplementary Education Center, 1968.

Benedict, Ruth. *Zuni Mythology,* 2 vols. Columbia University Contributions to Anthropology, No. 21; 1935; rpt. New York: AMS Press, 1969.

Bonaparte, Marie. *Female Sexuality.* Trans. John Rodker. New York: International Universities Press, 1953.

Burling, Robbins. *English in Black and White.* New York: Holt, Rinehart and Winston, 1973.

Dyk, Walter. *Son of Old Man Hat: A Navaho Autobiography.* 3rd Bison Book printing, Lincoln: University of Nebraska Press, 1938.

Fewkes, Jesse Walter. "Tusayan Migration Traditions." Smithsonian Institution, *Bureau of American Ethnology, Annual Report* 19, pt. 2 (1897): 573–633.

Kennard, Edward, and Albert Yava. *Field Mouse Goes to War. Tusan Homichi Tuwvöta.* Washington: Education Division, Bureau of Indian Affairs, 1944.

Leach, Maria, gen. ed. *Standard Dictionary of Folklore, Mythology, and Legend.* New York: Funk and Wagnalls, 1972.

Legman, G. *The Horn Book: Studies in Erotic Folklore and Bibliography.* New Hyde Park, New York: University Books, 1963.

————. *Rationale of the Dirty Joke: An Analysis of Sexual Humor.* Second series. Wharton, New York: Breaking Point, 1975.

Lo Duca, ed. *Moderne Enzyklopädie der Erotik.* München, Wien, and Basel: Desch Verlag, 1963.

Luckert, Karl W. *The Navajo Hunter Tradition.* Tucson: University of Arizona Press, 1975.

Malotki, Ekkehart. *Hopitutuwutsi. Hopi Tales: A Bilingual Collection of Hopi Indian Stories.* Flagstaff: Museum of Northern Arizona Press, 1978.

McDougall, W. B. *Seed Plants of Northern Arizona.* Flagstaff: Museum of Northern Arizona Press, 1973.

Mindeleff, Victor. "A Story of Pueblo Architecture, Tusayan and Cibola." Smithsonian Institution, *Bureau of American Ethnology, Annual Report* 8 (1886): 3–228.

Moriarty, James R. *Chinigchinix: An Indigenous California Indian Religion*. Hodge Fund Publication, vol. 10, Los Angeles: Southwest Museum, 1969.

Mullett, G.M. *Spider Woman Stories: Legends of the Hopi Indians*. Tucson: University of Arizona Press, 1979.

Neumann, Erich. *Die grosse Mutter: Der Archetyp des grossen Weiblichen*. Zürich: Rhein-Verlag, 1956.

Schnier, Jacques. "Dragon Lady." *American Imago* 4 (1947): 78–97.

Stephen, Alexander M. "Hopi Tales." *Journal of American Folklore* 42 (1929): 1–72.

Thompson, Stith. *Tales of the North American Indians*. 1929; rpt. Bloomington, Indiana: Indiana University Press, 1966.

———. *Motif-Index of Folk-Literature*. rev. and enl. ed. Bloomington, Indiana; Indiana University Press, 1955.

Titiev, Mischa. "The Story of Kokopele." *American Anthropologist* 41 (1939): 91–98.

Voth, Henry R. *The Traditions of the Hopi*. Field Columbian Museum, Anthropological Series, vol. 8. Chicago, 1905.

Wallis, Wilson D. "Folk Tales from Shumopovi, Second Mesa." *Journal of American Folklore* 49 (1936): 1–68.

Whiting, Alfred F. *Ethnobotany of the Hopi*. 1939; rpt. Flagstaff: Northland Press, 1966.

ACKNOWLEDGEMENTS

I wish to express my sincere gratitude to the narrator of the story, Herschel Talashoma from Bakabi. His excellent memory is truly admirable. In addition, I need to thank Michael Lomatewama from Hotevilla for checking the Hopi transcription, E. Nicholas Genovese for improving my English translation, Robert Breunig, Richard Sims, and Paul Trotta for making stylistic suggestions on the introductory essay. I am indebted to Paul Zolbrod for mentioning my interest in Hopi literature to Brian Swann. Armin Geertz was kind enough to let me have his tape-recorded version of the *Tsimonmamant*.

Paul G. Zolbrod: POETRY AND CULTURE: THE NAVAJO EXAMPLE

After spending three years among the Navajos in the early eighteen-fifties, Dr. Jonathan Letherman, an army surgeon, had this to say: "Of their religion little or nothing is known, as indeed, all inquiries tend to show that they have none." He called their singing "a succession of grunts . . . anything but agreeable." And, professing that he found a "lack of tradition" among them, he insisted that "they have no knowledge of their origin or of the history of the tribe." He concluded with a glibness that had already become familiar among white officials that the Navajos "are neither . . . industrious, moral, nor civilized."[1]

But less than fifty years later, Dr. Washington Matthews, another army surgeon serving in the Southwest, gave an entirely different report. Observing the same gatherings that Letherman had dismissed as meaningless, Matthews declared that they were actually ceremonials which "might vie in allegory, symbolism, and intricacy of ritual with the ceremonies of any people. . . ." These so-called heathens, he said, actually "possessed lengthy myths and traditions—so numerous that one can never hope to collect them all, a pantheon as well stocked with gods and heroes as that of the ancient Greeks. . . ."[2]

Today, of course, with the improved perspective that time sometimes allows, we are likely to be more sympathetic to the attitude implicit in Matthews' observations. But that sympathy is, we must remember, inimical to what was believed a century ago. Letherman's paper appeared in 1856, in the *Tenth Annual Smithsonian Report,* and I have the clear impression that it circulated widely among government officials for the next thirty years or so more or less as the official rationale behind the Government's Indian policy.[3] Meanwhile, what Matthews wrote received attention only among a fairly small, relatively uninfluential circle of ethnographers, folklorists and naturalists. While he enjoyed high status among members of the scientific community during the second half of his lifetime, he seems to have made little impact in official Washington. So that while the Letherman report testifies to the thinking that resulted in such events as Kit Carson's exploits against the Navajos, Matthews' writings survive only to indicate that another point of view did exist. Ironically, Letherman spent only several years in the southwest; his report indicates, too, that he studied the terrain and the climate more carefully than he observed the culture.

Matthews, on the other hand, actually lived in Navajo Country for eight years and spent an additional ten years travelling back and forth between Washington, D.C. and the reservation to do additional research.[4] He had an abiding scholarly interest in the Navajos, and much of what he wrote about their culture remains valuable. Yet somehow Letherman's point of view still prevails, albeit in a more subtle fashion.

To be sure, we don't shoot Indians any more, and we have even stopped making movies in which they are the bad guys. Yet the effects of our early racism still linger. Physicians and social workers are sent to treat them with little or no training in ethnography. The teachers who educate them assume that they should be trained to participate in middle class white society with no sense of the great cultural leap involved. If ceremonial gatherings are no longer regarded by whites as disagreeable grunts, they are now viewed thoughtlessly as amusing tourist attractions suggestive of a quaint, lingering primitivism in the popular, misunderstood sense of that term. Native American artifacts are solemnly encased in museum displays with no attempt to explain them fully in terms of the cultural context wherein they function. Or else they fetch high prices in a marketplace dominated by white middlemen. During the last century warfare against the Indians has gradually given way to a superficial, fawning sympathy, which is really another kind of oppression.

The enduring effects of our early racism can likewise be detected in the continued obscurity of Washington Matthews, who really deserves to be better known. Although today a handful of scholars recognize the value of his even-handed, objective observations and admire him as a pioneer anthropologist, his works are largely out of print and many details of his life remain sketchy. Those who do know of his accomplishments have not succeeded in broadcasting them very widely. Which is too bad, particularly in the case of one of his all-too-obscure volumes. Titled *Navaho Legends,* it contains, in addition to two shorter narratives, one of the earliest English renditions of the Navajo creation story, a cycle of closely related tales fundamental to the entire culture. This cycle tells of the emergence of insect people from a primal domain deep within the present earth. It describes how they gradually made their way to the surface of the present world, where they evolved into *Nihokáá dine'é* or Earth Surface People and then into an aggregate of human clans ready to form an intricate society.

The central theme of the story is *hózhǫ,* a fairly untranslatable term which can only be approximated in English by combining terms like beauty, balance and harmony.[5] As the people grow more complex biologically, psychologically, spiritually and socially, they learn how to mitigate evil with good by developing a relationship with the supernaturals and among themselves. The pivotal element in achieving that intricate set of relationships is the fundamental relationship between male and female, represented first by *Áłtsé hastiin* or First Man and *Áłtsé asdzą́ą́* or First Woman, and later by *Asdzą́ą́ nadleehé* or Changing Woman and *Jóhónaa'éí* the Sun. The inability of the former two to get along causes evil by bringing about the birth of the *bináá' yee* or alien giants. The union of the latter couple represents the first step leading to the destruction of the evil monsters, but full harmony cannot be achieved until Changing Woman and the Sun achieve a fully equitable relationship; and not until then does the creation of the Navajo people occur. So that everything that happens throughout the story relates directly or indirectly to the notion of delicate balance between male and female.[6]

Representing narrative poetry at its richest, the cycle displays an awareness of human complexity different from anything in our own literature. While we are aware of them as virtually abstract prototypes of male and female, we identify in First Woman and First Man easily recognizable impulses fundamental to being female and male respectively. Their initial conflict is both sexual and egocentric, and it is difficult to think of any literary passage where man and woman embroil themselves in such a conflict, caused equally by hurt and anger, wounded pride and foolish obstinacy, and tragic blindness combined with comical stubbornness. Because of their origin as ears of corn, they remain as basic as germinating seeds; but since they develop distinct psyches of their own, they also assume proportions that can easily be associated with the quintessent human spirit. The whole story, then, occurs in a setting that combines the real and the earthly with the mystical and the cosmic, where spirits and humans interact in a way duplicated nowhere in our own familiar western literature. Reflected is a poetic intricacy that would certainly surprise many of us, because whether we realize it or not, we have actually inherited Letherman's assumptions that Indians do not have a high culture so-called, in spite of our current fashion of professing sympathy for them.

To the best of my knowledge, the Matthews translation of the Navajo creation story remains the most comprehensive English edition of any extended Native American narrative.[7] For all of its flaws and obscurities, it provides an index of the range and depth of Native American oral tradition. Any authentic Indian artifact should be viewed closely in its full relationship with the culture and the tradition it represents. Looked at that way, Matthews' rendition of this narrative demonstrates that he had an instinct for recognizing a capacity for literature among the Navajos, even if his own prose does not immediately yield a sense of the poetry intrinsic to the Navajo prototype.

How Matthews actually acquired this material is not entirely clear. I have gone through the set of his notes and papers deposited in the Wheelwright Museum in Santa Fe, and still have no sure sense of how he proceeded. Among the Matthews material in the Wheelwright I have found copious notations on the language, including make-shift word-lists in various notebooks along with index cards full of linguistic notations. I have also found hand-written glosses of Navajo songs indicating that he could translate Navajo into English quite well. It is obvious that he took great pains to translate songs and prayers accurately, and those translations still are highly regarded. But I have found no transcriptions in the Navajo script he employed of any portion of the creation story. In fact, among his field notes and notebooks there is no full-length, hand-written manuscript version of what ultimately appears as the printed version of *The Navaho Origin Legend*, the title he gives the Navajo creation story in *Navaho Legends*. There are only two fragments among the papers in the Wheelwright that seem at all related to what appears in the book. One is an unbound set of small, unlined pages that summarize parts of the story and that obviously provided the basis for an account of the creation story he had published earlier.[8] The other is a set of entries in a bound, lined notebook that seem to have some bearing on parts of the story which he ultimately recorded in *Navaho Legends*. However, there are some discrepancies between what that notebook contains and what ultimately found its way into print in the final volume.

I suspect that what appears in *The Navajo Origin Legend* is a synthesis that Matthews prepared while he was living in Washington after leaving the Southwest. He may have worked partly from notes, partly from memory, and perhaps partly from impressions he carried away with him after subsequent visits to the reservation. I do not consider it likely that he recorded the entire story or any part of it in his own makeshift Navajo script. The language is too difficult for any non-native speaker to transcribe straight away in the field. Nor do I consider it very likely that he heard portions of it in the original Navajo and immediately transcribed it in English translation. While it may have been possible for him to do so, the differences between the two languages create such complications that even an expert in Navajo could not easily listen in one language and swiftly record in the other.

Given the evidence presently available, we may never know exactly what procedure Matthews used in assembling his English text of *The Navaho Origin Legend*. I believe that he may have listened simultaneously to a native-speaker while an English-speaking Navajo translated for him. There may also have been occasions when he listened exclusively to a Navajo reciting portions of the story in English. Some of the surviving notes that were obviously incorporated into the text were written hastily in the field: there are frequent misspellings, crude abbreviations, obvious lapses in handwriting and punctuation. Some sheets contain smudge marks. Others are not easily legible. All told, the evidence suggests that he recorded a great deal of information where the lighting was bad or where he had to write without the benefit of a table to rest his notepad or a conventional chair to sit in. Perhaps he even compiled some of his field notes surreptitiously, since there are indications among his various notebooks that many Navajos objected to his presence at night-long ceremonials where he displayed the white man's foreign habits of writing things down.

In any case, he almost certainly gathered his material piecemeal, perhaps over a span of a dozen years or more. He first arrived in Fort Wingate, New Mexico, in 1880, having already published a monograph on one Indian tribe, the Hidatsa.[9] He remained there until 1884, when he was transferred to Washington, by then having published several articles on Navajo culture and on his experiences among the Navajos. While stationed in Washington, he continued writing about them, making an unspecified number of trips back to the Fort Wingate region at the southeast edge of the Navajo reservation, where he was able to do additional field research. Then, in 1890, he was transferred back to Fort Wingate, where he remained until shortly after suffering a paralytic stroke in 1892. He was then summoned back to

Washington for medical discharge. Not until then, it seems, did he begin preparing the manuscript for *Navaho Legends*.

Thus, the work is probably a synthesis worked out from notes originally acquired in fragments, from memory, from a sense both of the language and of the overall story that grew familiar to him over the years as he made one foray after another to attend Navajo ceremonies and to compile additional data. He speaks in occasional letters of Navajo friends and acquaintances, sometimes with fondness and always with respect that apparently resulted from his unopinionated, objective observations. He never romanticizes the way someone like Schoolcraft does, and his painstakingly acquired knowledge of the Navajo language becomes more and more apparent when his notes and letters are read chronologically. By the time he left Fort Wingate at the end of his second tour of duty there, he could well have become a fluent conversationalist in that language, perhaps even with a sense of the nuances of its puns and its peculiarities, and of the characteristic style of its songs and prayers. His published and unpublished writings alike indicate that he had a special gift for observing minute details, while his letters suggest that he also had a very good memory. So it is likely indeed that what finally appears in print as *The Navaho Origin Legend* represents a retrospective synthesis of notes and recollections carefully assembled as a unified text and edited intentionally to demonstrate to an English-speaking audience that the Navajos did indeed have poetic traditions comparable to that of the Greeks.

All the same, his version is not fully representative of the poetic effects intrinsic to Navajo oral recitations.[10] Matthews appears to have grown partially deaf before he finished recording all that he transcribed, for one thing. Yet he was struggling to master a complex tonal, holophrastic language with particles of tense and mode having no precise counterparts in any Indo-European language that he knew. Furthermore, he managed to learn Navajo without any of the formal linguistic training he might get today and with none of the instruments now available to anyone who wishes to gather linguistic data.

For another thing, he was schooled to think of poetry primarily as a printed art, very much the way we are. The assumption that all literature is composed alphabetically on a page is one so fully taken for granted that we seldom if ever question it. For him —as for us today—the long prose passage was a basic typographical unit. Only when it is designated by the deliberate arrangement of type or handwritten script on a page do we have something that can be called poetry. Conditioned to accept such a tacitly fixed bias, Matthews does not seem to have listened to Navajo informants recite narrative as attentively as he might have. What he heard them say, then, he wrote as prose. Or else he composed his final manuscript as prose, seeing no reason to do otherwise, which makes his version of the creation story seem dense and distinctly unpoetic. Not fully sensitive to the immediate difference between the printed word and the spoken, he assumed that the sound of a narrator's voice should in all respects be subordinated to print. To prove to members of a highly print-oriented culture that the Navajos did in fact have a "literary" tradition he had to do no more than that. Missing, then, from Matthews' text is the full effect of repetition as an important stylistic device, just as he failed to preserve other features of oral delivery such as the long pause, the abrupt phrase, the whispered statement, the delicate sense of timing a storyteller brings to an audience to establish a certain intimacy with it.

Ironically, Matthews thought of Navajo songs and prayers as poetry, and when he recorded examples of them he composed such material on the written page as verse. In one letter he acknowledges and admires the rhythm basic to those kinds of discourse. The lyrics he transcribed and translated stand today as some of the finest examples of Native American verse we now have. He may very well have been one of the first Americans to illustrate the poetic technique—common in the prayers, chants and songs of many Indian tribes—that Nellie Barnes calls "incremental repetition" in her pioneer investigation of Native American poetics. When he listened to a chant or a prayer, Matthews did not hesitate to duplicate its stylistic features by carefully arranging it in printed lines of fixed length enclosed in larger stanzaic units. But whenever he listened to a storyteller recite, he worked in conventional paragraph units, overlooking the more subtle patterns of pitch, stress and pause. It has been my experience that Navajo storytellers speak quietly and softly; they downplay their performances as a way of commanding careful attention, so that their technique of performance is subtle. Thus he overlooked the muted poetic devices employed by storytellers, especially after his hearing began to fail. And because he had such a strong influence on subsequent translators, the understated poetic features of Navajo storytelling have gone more or less unnoticed to this very day.

The Navajo Origin Legend remains an imperfect rendering for yet another reason. It appears that Matthews arbitrarily deleted passages dealing overtly with sex. The explicit sexuality in other versions I have found suggests that he must have encountered such allusions. Yet wherever such passages occur, they add to the understanding of the delicate balance between male and female intrinsic to the Navajo world-view. Sexual harmony is a central issue in Navajo thought. Directly or indirectly it is reflected not only in male-female relationships, but in the relationship between all sets of counterparts in the broad cosmic scheme: earth and sky, night and day, mortals and supernaturals, summer and winter. It is also reflected in relationships among humans and animals here on earth, and it predicates the way members of clans and individual families regard each other. Sexuality as it is understood in ideal human behavior among the Navajo reveals why certain events occur as they do in Matthews' account of the creation. The quarrel between First Man and First Woman which leads to their temporary separation acquires an added dimension of understanding in relation to a fragment, found elsewhere, that describes how First Woman created male and female genitals. She decides to make sex gratifying to both partners so that couples will stay together. Whether or not Matthews even heard such an account of the origin of the male penis and the female clitoris, he did not include it in his text. Likewise, when *Ma'ii* the Coyote wins *Asdzání shash nádleehé* the Changing Bear Maiden as his wife, he consummates his success by tricking her into having intercourse with him. I learned of the actual seduction in an unpublished version of that episode which Matthews either ignored or never heard.[12] In it their sexual relationship is very explicit, and we learn that she receives her evil power from him by allowing him to insert his penis in her. Sex, in fact, is a very important motif throughout the creation story; but sex is a subject Matthews explicitly shunned in what he wrote as much as he possibly could. Today that lapse may seem flagrant. Given what scholars have subsequently discovered in investigating Navajo culture, we know how much it matters in authentic storytelling. But Matthews, we must remember, published his work when so-called Victorian taste would scarcely sanction an English version of the Navajo creation story that would preserve the blunt sexual allusions that should be present in a fully authentic English version. Matthews was clearly a prude in what he wrote, but he was no more prudish than anyone else writing anything at that time.[13]

All told, then, *Navajo Legends* contains an imperfect rendering of the Navajo creation story, not easily recognized as a major Native American poetic work. But it is still a document worth noticing. To recognize its quality, however, we must fully come to terms with the relationship between an oral recitation in its cultural setting and what most of us have been conditioned to accept as literature.

The discovery that Native American oral discourse should be taken seriously as poetry has actually been slow in coming. Beginning in the late fifties while undertaking research among tribes in the Pacific Northwest, for example, Dell Hymes progressed toward the conclusion that what had been misconceived as casual tale-telling really could be accepted as poetry by the careful recognition of implicit semantic and rhetorical patterns.[14] Meanwhile, Robert A. George suggested in the late sixties that the overall setting of a performance has a bearing on the utterance of a storyteller not evident in ordinary prose, the printed medium conventionally employed by most translators.[15] Soon thereafter, De nis Tedlock, who had been translating Zuni narratives, demonstrated that what is often made to look like prose on the printed page and treated there as a quaint sort of data by earlier collectors actually has distinct poetic qualities. Poetry, he argued, exists in oral recitation by virtue of features as basic as the way a storyteller pauses.[16]

Thus, only recently have scholars recognized that there is a Native American poetic tradition of considerable proportions, and that poetry has a central prominence in American Indian cultures seldom seen in the familiar cultures that make up the aggregate we call Western civilization. But there is much to be learned before that reality can be widely accepted. The significant discoveries so far have been made for the most part by anthropologists and folklorists whose training had conditioned them to take preliterate cultures seriously and to study them objectively. One of the lingering effects of racism here in America, though, is that literary critics and trained literary scholars have not yet understood the important place poetry occupies among Indians. Because most of us have been trained to associate literature with print, we have dealt exclusively with what has been composed in writing. Thus, we unnecessarily limit the range of our appreciation or our understanding. Our own children are taught at the outset of their formal education to read and to write, while Indians have traditionally trained theirs to listen and to talk.

One manifestation of the resulting difference, which may be greater than we suppose, is that when we speak of literature we conventionally associate it with culture in a sense sharply unlike the way culture is accepted by tribal peoples or considered by ethnographers. For most of us, culture is capitalized, so to speak; it sits quite apart from ordinary activity. We look for it in books, in galleries, in concert halls, within the doors of theatres, under glass in museum displays. We do not expect to find it amidst the mundane everyday activities of unlettered people. In preliterate societies, though, culture is integral to ordinary, daily life. Its examples are found in the marketplace, at the workbench, in the fields, in the social gathering; it gives social groups their day-by-day identity, their dynamic capacity to function collectively, their ability to link the individual with the clan or the tribe. It functions within a social collectivity, not elevated above it in some sacrosanct way. In the last of the four distinct parts of Matthews' version of the Navajo creation story, where the Earth Surface People are created, we see them gathering from various places. They assemble as marginally organized bands, often subsisting on field mice, roots and wild berries. Only when they acquire an elaborate social structure as unified clans can they begin to exchange stories, teach one another to hunt large game, trade the various skills of sowing and planting, conduct ceremonies, and define a code of ethics. Because it contains little violence and conflict, this passage is in some ways the least spectacular part of the story. But in a very subtle way it is also the most moving. For here is where we watch individuals and small bands coalesce fully into an identifiable tribal unit by virtue of the cultural bonds they accept. The story itself, culminating as it does in the achievement of that unity, becomes a comprehensive statement about who the Navajo people are. Yet it was never actually written down until an outsider came along, listened to it with an openmindedness uncharacteristic of his race, and patiently assembled it as a unified printed text.

All of which might help to explain Jonathan Letherman's misunderstanding of Navajo civilization. Knowing nothing of their language, finding no printed works among them, no museums, no concert halls, no classrooms or displays, he assumed that they had no culture. Matthews, on the other hand, perceiving culture otherwise, looked for it not apart from the activities of the Navajo people but among them. He looked for it first of all in the utterances he heard as he learned their language. And instead of inspecting finished jewelry, he watched silversmiths at work. Instead of taking woven rugs aside, he observed weavers at their looms. Instead of looking for written texts, he listened to storytellers and chanters at gatherings. And if, in listening, he transformed what he heard awkwardly into the printed medium of prose, he at least made something of a transformation where Letherman simply made a dismal pronouncement.

I acknowledge the imperfection of *The Navaho Origin Legend,* to be sure. But what Matthews overlooked should be subordinated to what he attempted. He is singular for his willingness to find literature among a people dismissed by others as illiterates and hence savages without a tradition. Subsequent English versions of that Navajo creation story have been published, due largely to the pioneering force of Matthews' early influence in the fields of anthropology and folklore. Some of them have been richer in accounting for the details of a particular episode. Some have been more literally accurate in recasting one fragment or another in English prose. One or another might even be considered a more poetic rendering of at least some part of the story. Yet no other English version has the comprehensive sweep that Matthews attained in his version. And none is as evenhandedly unified; none functions quite as well as a tale complete in itself that satisfies the human appetite for storytelling well beyond its own cultural boundaries.

As such a tale, *The Navaho Origin Legend* deserves acceptance as one of the world's significant literary works, especially because it does so much to show that literature really is intrinsic to all societies, whether literate or preliterate. What is lacking in Matthews' translation of the Navajo creation story, though, is a poetic dimension he overlooked. And that is what I have attempted to provide, at least in part.

I have done so by learning as much Navajo as I could over the past twelve years, and by listening to storytellers wherever I could, not only among Native Americans but wherever it was possible to attend any sort of storytelling performance. I have also studied Navajo culture insofar as it was possible to do so, given the constraints of distance that allowed me less time on the reservation than I would have liked. But whatever I was able to do to acquire a thorough appreciation of the linguistic and cultural context of the creation story, I did. In particular, I studied transcriptions in English and Navajo of songs and prayers, so that I could acquire a precise sense of the poetics of the language insofar as that can be reflected in print. And, fully convinced of the poetic quality intrinsic to Navajo renditions of various parts of the creation cycle, I undertook to rewrite Matthews' version passage by passage, trying to correct its inaccuracies wherever I could and to replicate in written English something of the deliberate style of a native storyteller.

I have tried to improve on his work in three primary ways. First, to transfer at least something of the effect of the Navajo language, I have fused Navajo proper names with their English equivalents in identifying characters and places. And I have taken pains to insert repetitions that Matthews left out in his version, thinking that if something was said once in print it need not have been rewritten. The effect of doing that in his version was to destroy one of the principal elements of storytelling style and one of its most compelling effects. Where it is possible, I try to capture something of the rhythm of Navajo speech and song by maintaining the cadence of spoken English as it can sometimes be heard in a sermon or a political speech. Gladys Reichard agrees with Franz Boas that the rhythmic sense of preliterate discourse is "more highly developed than our own."[17] Navajo discourse is no exception, and it may even be particularly exemplary in the way rhythm permeates narratives, prayers, songs and speeches. Accordingly, I have tried to maintain such a sense of rhythm in my rendering, but without creating a tone of artificiality in the English I employ.

Second, I have fashioned a typographical arrangement of my own that is neither as compacted and dense as Matthews' own prose, which often makes the story read more like a discursive essay than a poetic rendering; nor as loose and as graphically variegated as Tedlocks' translations, which seem better suited to narratives that are shorter and less ceremonially recited than lengthy Navajo sacred narratives seem to be. I rely on small paragraph-like units that can be as short as a single line or as long as several sentences. Following the example of Dell Hymes to some extent, I attempt to compose these units each as a set of self-contained but parallel semantic components. Parallelism is another major stylistic element in Native American oral narrative. Like rhythm, it too enjoys a special prominence in Navajo examples. It may be the primary feature in Navajo storytelling, especially when sacred versions are recited. Parallel structure can be applied at many levels, starting with the smallest syntactic units such as holophrastic words which would translate into English as a simple combination of an unmodified noun and its coordinating verb, and extending to sets of as many as four or five independent clauses whose structure can be repeated in successive sets of independent clauses. In such constructions, syntax and semantics combine in carefully composed arrangements which create a slightly muted, chantlike, rhetorical effect. This device, when used by an expert storyteller, creates a certain intensity that generates suspense in listeners who may already know the plot of a story but who are being induced to hang their attention carefully upon what the performer is saying.[18]

Third, I have supplemented what Matthews originally wrote with several passages that I located in other sources. Principally, these additions compensate for the bowdlerizing that Matthews undoubtedly did in keeping with the prudish standards of the day. Likewise, I have expanded certain passages to place certain feelings and sentiments in sharper relief than Matthews provides. In dealing with strangers Navajos come across as taciturn, introverted people. Among themselves, though, and with close friends, they are more freely emotional. Furthermore, intense emotions and strong feelings are clearly displayed in their stories.[19] Matthews, perhaps because he sought to be objective in what he wrote, somehow loses that important emotional thrust in his translation. Where it seems appropriate to do so, I attempt to replace it by enlarging on what he provides. And I have expanded several other episodes—again relying on redoubtable sources to guarantee authenticity—where it seems that Matthews should have been more explicit in treating sexuality. Overall, I have tried to correct whatever inaccuracies I could find in his original text, and to alter his own prose idiom slightly to make it sound more like storytelling and less like a formal report.

I hope that my revision of Matthews' translation of this important Native American narrative will serve fairly to represent the poetic quality of Native American oral narrative. The work I have been doing, I am convinced, can help us all fathom the important relationship between oral traditions in preliterate cultures and good poetry. At the present time, not enough can be said in behalf of the discovery that has escaped widespread attention all too long: Native American traditions actually provide us with a rich poetic legacy. Considered as broadly as we ought to consider it, American civilization has features and contours that we have overlooked. The various North American tribes make ours a richer culture by far than we have supposed.

SAMPLE PASSAGES

I. After the animal-people commit a series of transgressions which anger the gods, First Man and First Woman are created to provide better examples of proper behavior.

It is said that late in the autumn of that year the newcomers heard a distant voice calling to them from far in the east.

They listened and waited, listened and waited. Until soon they heard the voice again, nearer and louder than before. They continued to listen and wait, listen and wait, until they heard the voice a third time, all the nearer and all the louder.

Continuing to listen, they heard the voice again, even louder than the last time, and so close now that it seemed directly upon them.

A moment later they found themselves standing among four mysterious beings. They had never seen such creatures anywhere before. For they were looking at those who would eventually become known as haashch'ééh dine'é.

In the language of Bilagáana *the White Man, that name means Holy People. For they are people unlike the Earth Surface People who come into the world today, live on the ground for a while, die at a ripe old age, and then move on.*

These are people who do not know the pain of being mortal. They are people who can travel far by following the path of the rainbow. And they can travel swiftly by following the path of the sunray. They can make the winds and the thunderbolts work for them so that the earth is theirs to control when they so wish.

The people who were then living on the surface of the fourth world were looking upon Bits'íís łigaii. *In the language of* Bilagáana *the White Man that name means White Body. He is the one that the Navajo people who now live in our own world would eventually call* Haashch'éélti'í, *which in today's language means Talking God.*

And they were looking upon Bits'íís dootł'izh. *In the language of* Bilagáana *that name means Blue Body. He is the one that the Navajo people in our own world would eventually come to know as* Tó ni'nilí *which in today's language means Water Sprinkler.*

And they were looking upon Bits'íís łitsoii. *In the language of the White Man that name means Yellow Body. He is the one that the Navajo people in our world would eventually call* Hashch'éoghan. *Nobody can be sure what that name means in today's language. Some say it means Calling God; some say it means House God.*

And they were looking upon Bits'íís łizhin. *In the White Man's language that name means Black Body. He is the one that the Navajo people would eventually come to know as* Haashch'ééshzhini, *which in today's language means Black God. Sometimes he is also called the God of Fire.*

Without speaking the Holy People made signs to the people, as if to give them instructions. But the exiles could not understand their gestures. So they stood by helplessly and watched.

And after the gods had left, the people talked about that mysterious visit for the rest of that day and all night long, trying to determine what it meant.

* * * *

As for the gods, they repeated their visit four days in a row. But on the fourth day, Bits'íís łizhin the Black Body remained after the other three departed. And when he was alone with the onlookers, he spoke to them in their own language. This is what he said:

"You do not seem to understand the Holy People," he said.

"So I will explain what they want you to know.

"They want more people to be created in this world.

"But they want them created in their likeness, not in yours.

"You have bodies like theirs, true enough.

"But you have the teeth of beasts!

"The mouths of beasts!

"The feet of beasts!

"The claws of beasts!

"The new creatures are to have hands like ours.

"Feet like ours.

"Mouths like ours.

"Teeth like ours.

"What is more, you are unclean!

"You smell bad.

"So you are instructed to cleanse yourselves before we return twelve days from now."

That is what Bits'íís łizhin *the Black Body said to the insect people who had emerged from the first world to the second, from the second world to the third, and from the third world to the fourth where they now lived.*

*   *   *   *

Accordingly, on the morning of the twelfth day the people bathed carefully. The women dried themselves with yellow corn meal. The men dried themselves with white corn meal.

Soon after they had bathed, they again heard the distant voice coming from far in the east.

They listened and waited as before, listened and waited. Until soon they heard the voice as before, nearer and louder this time. They continued to listen and wait, listen and wait, until they heard the voice a third time as before, all the nearer and all the louder.

Continuing to listen as before, they heard the voice again, even louder than the last time, and so close now that it seemed directly upon them, exactly as it had seemed before. And as before they found themselves standing among the same four Haashch'ééh dine'é, *or Holy People as* Bilagáana *the White Man might wish to call them.*

Bits'íís dootł'izh *the Blue Body and* Bits'íís łizhin *the Black Body each carried a sacred buckskin.* Bits'íís łigaii *the White Body carried two ears of corn.*

One ear of corn was yellow. The other ear was white. Each ear was completely covered at the end with grains, just as sacred ears of corn are covered in our own world now.

Proceeding silently, the gods lay one buckskin on the ground, careful that its head faced the west. Upon this skin they placed the two ears of corn, being just as careful that the tips of each pointed east. Over the corn they spread the other buckskin, making sure that its head faced east.

Under the white ear they put the feather of a white eagle.

And under the yellow ear they put the feather of a yellow eagle.

Then they told the onlooking people to stand at a distance.

So that the wind could enter.

Then, from the east, Niłch'i łigai *the White Wind blew between the buckskins. And while the wind thus blew, each of the Holy People came and walked four times around the objects they had placed so carefully on the ground.*

As they walked, the eagle feathers, whose tips protruded slightly from between the two buckskins, moved slightly.

Just slightly.

So that only those who watched carefully were able to notice.

And when the Holy People had finished walking, they lifted the topmost buckskin.

And lo! the ears of corn had disappeared.

In their place there lay a man and there lay a woman.

*   *   *   *

The white ear of corn had been transformed into our most ancient male ancestor. And the yellow ear of corn had been transformed into our most ancient female ancestor.

It was the wind that had given them life: the very wind that gives us our breath as we go about our daily affairs here in the world we ourselves live in!

When this wind ceases to blow inside of us, we become speechless. And then we die.

In the skin at the tips of our fingers, we can see the trail of that life-giving wind.

Look carefully at your own fingertips.

There you will see where the wind blew when it created your most ancient ancestors out of two ears of corn, it is said.

II. So that male and female would be attracted to each other as couples for life, First Woman creates male and female sex organs.

It is also said that while all of those things were happening, Áłtsé asdzą́ą́ the First Woman had continued to think about how she might strengthen the bond between men and women. And after considering the matter carefully, she came up with a plan.

Men and women should have the power to attract each other for a lifetime, thought she. So she fashioned a penis of turquoise. Then she rubbed loose cuticle from a woman's breast and mixed it with yucca fruit, which she put inside the turquoise penis. And she named the organ 'aziz.

Next she made a vagina of white shell. Into the vagina she placed a clitoris of red shell. Then she rubbed loose cuticle from a man's breast and mixed it with yucca fruit, which she placed in the clitoris. And she combined herbs with various kinds of water and placed that mixture deep inside the vagina. That way pregnancy would occur. She then named the organ ajóózh.

She placed the vagina on the ground. Next to it she placed the penis. Then she blew medicine upon both of them from her mouth. And she spoke these words to the penis:

"Now think!" she said to it.

"Think about the one to your left."

The penis did as it was told, and its mind extended a great distance. Whereupon Áłtsé asdzą́ą́ the First Woman said this to the vagina:

"You think, too!" she said to it.

"Think about the one to your right."

The vagina also extended. But it extended only half the distance that the penis had gone. Then it returned to the place where it first lay. That is why a woman's longing does not travel as far as a man's.

And to both of them Áłtsé asdzą́ą́ the First Woman said these words:

"Now shout!" she said to the two of them together.

"Shout, both of you.

"Penis, shout so that your partner can feel the might of your voice.

"Vagina, shout so that your partner can feel the touch of your voice."

Penis shouted very loud. But vagina had only a weak voice. So Áłtsé asdzą́ą́ the First Woman spoke to them again:

"Do it once more," she said to them again.

"Touch one another and shout once more.

"Penis, shout again so that your partner can feel it.

"Vagina, shout again so that your partner can feel it."

So they both tried again.

This time, though, penis could not shout as loudly as he had the first time.

Vagina, however, had a good voice this time.

Áłtsé asdzą́ą́ the First Woman was satisfied with her work. Now men and women would learn to care for each other. They would be eager to have children. They would

235

share the work to be done evenly between themselves. And they each would all the more willingly tend to the other's needs. So she commanded that upon reaching a certain age, every girl and every boy should be given such a vagina and such a penis as those she had fashioned.

* * * *

One day soon thereafter, while the elders were giving a penis to a boy who had come of age, and while they were giving a vagina to a girl who had come of age, the people saw the sky swooping down. It seemed to want to embrace the earth. And they saw the earth likewise looming up as if to meet the sky.

For a moment they came in contact. The sky touched the earth and the earth touched the sky. And just then, at exactly the spot where the sky and the earth had met, Mạ'ii the Coyote sprung out of the ground. And Nahashch'id the Badger sprung out of the ground.

It is our belief that Mạ'ii *the Coyote and* Nahashch'id *the Badger are children of the sky. Coyote came forth first, which leads us to suppose that he is Badger's older brother.*

Nahashch'id *the Badger began sniffing around the top of the hole that led down to the lower world. He finally disappeared into it and was not seen again for a long time.*

Mạ'ii *the Coyote saw at once that people lived nearby. So he came to their village right away. And he arrived among the people just as the boy was receiving his penis, and just as the girl was receiving her vagina.*

As the male organ was being placed, Mạ'ii *the Coyote pulled some of his beard from his face and blew on it. Then he placed it between the legs of the boy. And this is what he had to say:*

"It looks pretty nice there," he said.

"But I can make it look nicer."

And as the female organ was being placed, Mạ'ii *the Coyote pulled more of his beard from his face and blew on it. Then he put it between the legs of the girl. This is what he said:*

"As nice as it looks there, it can look even nicer," he said.

"Watch, and see if you don't think so."

Everyone agreed that Coyote had made the boy and girl more attractive. But Áłtsé asdzą́ą́ the First Woman now feared that women and men would be too easily drawn to one another.

So she ordered the boy to cover himself at once. And she ordered the girl to cover herself likewise. She ordered them to dress that way in the company of others.

And she ordered all the people to likewise cover themselves in the company of others. Which is why the people have clad themselves modestly ever since then, it is said.

III. Having been created to exhibit leadership to the errant animal-people, First Man and First Woman quarrel between themselves.

It is also said that eight winters passed since the people had migrated from the third world. And for eight years they prospered doing nothing to create disorder.

Áłtsé hastiin *the First Man had become chief of all who lived in that world, except for the* Kiis'áanii. *And as chief he taught the people the names of the four mountains which rose in the distance and marked the four cardinal points.*

Dził naajiinii *lay to the east, he taught them. In the language of* Bilagáana *the White Man that mountain is called Dark Horizon Ridge.* Tsoodził *lay to the south, he taught them. In the language of* Bilagáana *that name means Blue Bead Mountain. To the west lay* Dook'o'oosłííd, *he taught them, which in the language of the White Man is given the name Abalone Shell Mountain. And to the north lay* Dibé nitsaa, *which in English means Place of Mountain Sheep.*

Those four names have been kept in the present Navajo world, too. And Áłtsé hastiin *the First Man taught the people that* Haashch'ééh dine'é *the Holy People lived in those mountains. He explained to them that they were different from the Wind Spirit People. For they could travel swiftly and they could travel far. They knew how to ride the sunbeam and the light ray and how to follow the path of the rainbow. They feel no pain, and nothing in any world can change the way they are.*

So it was that Áłtsé hastiin *the First Man taught the people the names of things and the ways of the gods. So it was that he taught them what to do and what not to do. So it was that the people grew to respect him. And so it was that they came to obey him.*

*   *   *   *

Áłtsé hastiin *the First Man became a great hunter in the fourth world. So he was able to provide his wife* Áłtsé asdzą́ą́ *the First Woman with plenty to eat.*

As a result, she grew very fat.

Now one day he brought home a fine, fleshy deer.

His wife boiled some of it, and together they had themselves a hearty meal. When she had finished eating, Áłtsé asdzą́ą́ *the First Woman wiped her greasy hands on her sheath.*

She belched deeply. And she had this to say:

"Thank you shi'ajóózh *my vagina," she said.*

"Thank you for that delicious dinner."

To which Áłtsé hastiin *the First Man replied this way:*

"Why do you say that?" he replied.

"Why not thank me?

"Was it not I who killed the deer whose flesh you have just feasted on?

"Was it not I who carried it here for you to eat?

"Who skinned it?

"Who made it ready for you to boil?

"Is ni'ajóózh *your vagina the great hunter, that you should thank it and not me?"*

To which Áłtsé asdzą́ą́ *offered this answer:*

"As a matter of fact, she is," offered she.

"In a manner of speaking it is ajóózh *the vagina who hunts.*

"Were it not for ajóózh *you would not have killed that deer.*

"You would not have carried it here.

"You would not have skinned it.

"Were it not for ajóózh *you lazy men would do nothing around here.*

"In truth, ajóózh *the vagina does all the work around here."*

To which Áłtsé hastiin *the First Man had this to say:*

"Then perhaps you women think you can live without us men," he said.

"Maybe you need only nihi'ajóózh *your vaginas:*

*"Nihi'ajóózh *the great huntresses:*

"Nihi'ajóózh *the tireless workers.*"

Quickly came this reply from Áłtsé asdzą́ą́ *the First Woman.*

"*We could live alone if we wanted to,*" *was her reply.*

"*We are the ones who till the fields, after all.*

"*We are the ones who gather food, after all.*

"*We can live on the crops that we grow. We can live on the seeds that we gather. We can live on the berries that we find and on the fruits that we bring.*

"*We have no need of you men.*"

On and on they argued that way, Áłtsé hastiin *the First Man permitting himself to grow angrier and angrier with each reply his wife made;* Áłtsé asdzą́ą́ *the First Woman permitting herself to grow more and more vexing with each reply she offered.*

Until at length he stalked out of the shelter where they had lived together as man and wife. Out he stalked and jumped across the fire in front of their home, where he remained all that night with only his anger to keep him company.

*   *   *   *

Early next morning he walked to the center of the village and called loudly so that everyone could hear:

"*All you men!*" *he called.*

"*Gather round me.*

"*I wish to speak to you.*

"*I wish to instruct you.*

"*As for the women, let them stay where they are.*

"*Not one woman do I wish to see.*

"*I have nothing to say to any woman around here.*"

Soon all the males were assembled around Áłtsé hastiin *the First Man. And he repeated to them what his wife had said the night before. Then he told the men this:*

"*They think they can live without us,*" *he told the men.*

"Well, let us see if they can.

"Let us see if they can hunt and till the fields, with only ajóózh *the vagina to help them. Let us see what sort of living they can make, with only* ajóózh *to assist them.*

"We will cross the stream and live apart from them. And from ajóózh.

"We will keep the raft with us on our side of the water so that even when they long for us they may not have us.

"If they seek companionship, let them seek it with ajóózh *the vagina.*

"And if ajóózh *wishes to shout, let her shout to herself.*

"Let us see what ajóózh *the vagina brings forth when she hears the sound of her own voice."*

*   *   *   *

So it was that all the men gathered at the river.

Áłtsé hastiin even summoned the twins nádleeh *who were neither entirely male nor entirely female. They were covered with meal when they arrived, for they had been grinding corn. This is what* Áłtsé hastiin *the First Man asked them:*

"What do you have that you have made all by yourselves?" he asked them.

"What is there that you have made without the help of any woman?"

Answered the twins nadlééh, *who were no more female than they were male:*

"We each have a set of grinding stones that we have made," they answered.

"We have cups and bowls. We have baskets and other utensils.

"We have made those things all by ourselves with the help of no woman."

To which Áłtsé hastiin *the First Man had this to say:*

"Go fetch those things and bring them here. For you must come with us.

"You are as much men as you are women. And you have made those things with no woman's help.

"Let the women learn what it means to live without the help of any men.

"Let them learn to live without anything that has been made by one who is even part of a man."

* * * *

So the men ferried across the river, taking the non-child-bearing twins nadlééh *with them. They crossed over to the north bank. And with them they carried their stone axes, their wooden scythes, their hoes of bone and the utensils that the twins had invented. They took everything else that they had made themselves.*

After they had crossed, they sent the raft downstream, inviting the men of the Kiis'áanii *to join them. And in fact six of their clans did join. They too had allowed their women to anger them.*

As some of the young men rode across the stream they wept at having to part with their wives. They had not been angered by anything the women had said. But they had become used to doing what Áltsé hastiin *had told them to do.*

The men left behind everything the women had made by themselves. And they left behind everything the women had helped them to make or to raise. They took only what they had produced without the help of any woman.

* * * *

Once they reached the north bank of the river, some of the men set out to hunt. For the young boys needed food. Others set to work cutting willows for huts. For the young boys also needed shelter.

It seems that they managed very well. Within four days they had plenty of food, and they built strong homes for themselves and the boys. Within four days they were sure that they could get along without the women.

They were sure that they would thrive without women to make them angry. And their spirits were high, at least at first, it is said.

NOTES

[1]Jonathan Letherman, "Sketch of the Navajo Tribe of Indians, Territory of New Mexico," *Tenth Annual Report of the Board of Regents of the Smithsonian Institution* (Washington, D.C., 1856), pp. 294–97.

[2]Washington Matthews, *Navajo Legends* (Boston: The American Folklore Society, 1897), p. 23.

[3]For one summary of the impact of the Letherman Report on federal policy toward Native Americans, see Frank Waters, *Masked Gods* (New York: Ballantine Books, 1970), pp. 62–79. See also, Raymond Friday Locke, *The Book of the Navajo* (Los Angeles: Mankind Books, 1976), pp. 3–7. For a summary account of the

impact of that policy specifically upon the Navajos, see Dee Brown, *Bury My Heart at Wounded Knee* (New York: Holt, Rinehart & Winston, 1971), pp. 13–36. For a thorough study of Anglo-European attitudes towards New World peoples in the broad context of Western intellectual tradition, see Roy Harvey Pearce, *Savagism and Civilization* (Baltimore: Johns Hopkins University Press, 1965). For a detailed survey of the earliest reactions of European explorers to the inhabitants discovered in the Americas, see Evelyn Page, *American Genesis: Pre-Colonial Writing in the North* (Boston: Gambit, 1973).

[4]There is no full-length biography of Matthews available that I know of. For what I know about him I have relied principally on Robert Marshall Poor, *Washington Matthews: An Intellectual Biography* (Reno: University of Nevada M.A. Thesis, 1975, University Microfilms number M-8323). In addition, I have used three brief sketches: "In Memoriam: Washington Matthews" *American Anthropologist* 7 (1905): 514–23, which includes a bibliography of his works; "In Memoriam: Washington Matthews," *Journal of American Folklore* 18 (1905): 245–47; and Margaret Schevill Link, "From the Desk of Washington Matthews," *Journal of American Folklore* 73 (1960): 317–25. The major portion of what survives from Matthews' letters and papers is deposited at the Wheelwright Museum in Santa Fe. I have also consulted these.

[5]The importance of the term is demonstrated and its meaning thoroughly discussed in Gary Witherspoon, *Language and Art in the Navajo Universe* (Ann Arbor: The University of Michigan Press, 1977), pp. 23–34.

[6]See Witherspoon's summary discussion of gender in *Language and Art in the Navajo Universe,* pp. 140–44. See, too, his discussion of male-female solidarity in his analysis of kinship in the context of Navajo culture in *Navajo Kinship and Marriage* (Chicago: The University of Chicago Press, 1975), pp. 3–66. One good example of how sexual balance permeates Navajo mythology and ceremonialism appears in Father Berard Haile, *Love-Magic and Butterfly People* (Flagstaff, Arizona: Museum of Northern Arizona Press, 1978). See especially, the introductory statement, pp. 1–2.

[7]Other versions and fragments thereof of the Navajo creation story exist in various sources. For an annotated bibliographical guide to these texts, see Katherine Spencer, *Reflections of Social Life in the Navajo Origin Myth* (Albuquerque: University of New Mexico Press, 1947), pp. 12–30. Subsequently published versions of the creation story include Jeff King, Maud Oakes and Joseph Campbell, *Where the Two Came to Their Father* (New York: Pantheon Books, 1948); Margaret Schevill Link, *The Pollen Path* (Palo Alto: Stanford University Press, 1956); Stanley A. Fishler, *In the Beginning: A Navajo Creation Myth* (Salt Lake City: University of Utah Anthropological Paper No. 13, 1953); Aileen O'Bryan, *The Dine: Origin Myths of the Navajo Indians* (Washington, D.C. Bureau of American Ethnology Bulletin 163, 1956); Franc Johnson Newcomb, *Navajo Folk Tales* (Santa Fe: Museum of Navajo Ceremonial Art, 1967); and Ethelou Yazzie, *Navajo History* (Many Farms, Arizona: Navajo Community College Press, 1971). See also the monumental volume edited by Leland C. Wyman, *Blessingway* (Tucson: The University of Arizona Press, 1970), which contains a set of corollary tales that demonstrate the philosophical underpinnings of the Navajo creation cycle.

[8]"A Part of the Navajo Mythology," *American Antiquarian* 5 (1883): 207–24.

[9]*Ethnography and Philology of the Hidatsa Indians,* U.S. Geological Survey Miscellaneous Publication No. 7 (Washington, D.C.: 1877).

[10]Without going into detail, Gladys Reichard—the only scholar who has attempted to analyze Navajo poetic style thoroughly and systematically—agrees that Matthews did not go far enough in replicating the poetry intrinsic to spoken prototypes. See "Individualism and Mythological Style," *Journal of American Folklore* 57 (1944): 16–25. Reichard's study of aesthetic effects of Navajo prayers is, in my estimation, an unrecognized landmark in Native American poetics. See in particular, *Prayer: The Compulsive Word* (New York: J.J. Augustin, 1944).

[11]*American Indian Verse: Characteristics of Style,* Bulletin of the University of Kansas, vol. 22, no. 18 (Lawrence: 1922). For a more general statement, see Franz Boas, "Stylistic Aspects of Primitive Poetry," *Journal of American Fo klore* 35 (1925): 329–34.

[12]Father Berard Haile, *Changing Bear Maiden,* unpublished manuscript, Museum of Northern Arizona, MS pp. 63–7, 63–8.

[13]Poor documents Matthews' "reticence on sexual matters" on p. 13, and again on p. 32.

[14]See, "Linguistic Features Peculiar to Chinookan Myths," *International Journal of American Linguistics* 24 (1958): 253–57. See also, "Louis Simpson's 'The Deserted Boy,'" *Poetics* 5 (1976): 119–55; "Breakthrough Into Performance," Dan Ben-Amos and Kenneth Goldstein, eds. (The Hague: Mouton, 1975), pp. 11–74; and "Folklore's Nature and the Sun's Myth," *Journal of American Folklore* 88 (1975): 345–69.

[15]"Toward an Understanding of Storytelling Events," *Journal of American Folklore* 82 (1969), 313–28.

[16]"On the Translation of Style in Oral Narrative," *Journal of American Folklore* 84, (1971): 114–33 (reprinted in this volume); "Pueblo Literature: Style and Verisimilitude," *New Perspectives on the Pueblos,* Alfonso Ortiz, ed. (Albuquerque: University of New Mexico Press, 1972), pp. 220–47; and *Finding the Center* (New York: Dial, 1972; reprinted by the University of Nebraska Press as a Bison Book, 1978).

[17]Reichard, *Prayer: The Compulsive Word,* p. 35. See also, Franz Boas, *Primitive Art* (Cambridge: Harvard University Press, 1927), pp. 310–11.

[18]The stylistic device I am trying to describe all too briefly is one I hope to be able to write about more comprehensively in the future. My primary exposure to it, in addition to what I have read in published works, comes from some two dozen unpublished transcriptions in Navajo script along with English translations compiled by Father Berard Haile and Gladys Reichard. These manuscripts are stored at the Museum of Northern Arizona in Flagstaff. I was made more sensitive to their ultimate rhetorical effect by discussing them with Mr. Danny Blackgoat, a native speaker of Navajo who helped me translate selected passages particle by particle. The reader who seeks to inspect parallelism in Navajo narrative closely in the full context of a complete story-cycle can find such an example in Haile, *Love Magic and Butterfly People,* previously cited in note 6 above. There a full English translation is aligned with corresponding Navajo script. In addition to the general discussions of this aspect of style listed in note 15, see how Gladys Reichard deals with it in the discussion of Navajo performance in *Social Life of the Navajo Indians,* Columbia University Contributions to Anthropology, vol. 7 (New York: 1928), pp. 9–10. See,

too, Clyde Kluckhohn, "Patterning As Exemplified in Navaho Culture," *Language, Culture and Personality: Essays in Memory of Edward Sapir,* Leslie Spier, ed. (Menasha, Wisconsin, 1941), pp. 109–30.

[19]Reichard, for one, confirms the presence of the emotional element and indicates that Matthews did not deal with it adequately in "Individualism and Mythological Style," p. 17.

Galen Buller: COMANCHE AND COYOTE, THE CULTURE MAKER

THE "TRICKSTER"
AS CONCEPT

Kiowus, the coyote, of all the many colorful characters found in Comanche literature, perhaps best fictionalizes the self-conception the Comanches hold as a people. It is Coyote who has lasted throughout the generations, and his antics are the ones Comanches still like best to relate. While many of the other characters have been reduced in importance, or have been neglected altogether, by modern storytellers, Coyote has taken on new dimensions in the technocratic age for which the modern storyteller must accommodate.

Because the Comanche storytellers have been, for the most part, lost to time and transition, it is mandatory that the student of Comanche literature look to Shoshone versions of the creation to trace properly the character of Coyote as a mirror of the Comanche people and their culture. According to Clark:

> Coyote was the culture-hero and trickster for the Shoshone people. . . . Wolf, his elder and benevolent brother, tried to make life pleasant and easy for people but Coyote thought that they should work hard for their living. . . . Because of Coyote's impudence toward the Creator, death was brought into the World.[1]

Again, in a creation myth told by the Lemhi Shoshone and recorded by Clark:

> Coyote was the father of all the Indians and the special guardian of his tribe. When he washed the first Shoshonis, his new-born babies, he said to them "You are my children. I am going to stay with you. . . ." But because their mothers had washed the babies that became the other Indians, the other tribes were always fighting the Shoshonis.[2]

Hoebel, in *Comanches: Lords of the South Plains,* agrees that the Wolf was a wholly beneficent creator—the creator of a Utopian world in which all things were perfect and good, but not human. He sees Coyote as a cultural transformer. Coyote transforms that Utopian world created by his elder brother, the Wolf, into a human or "cultural" world. He transforms the natural order into a cultural one. Originally, this was done in a spiritual way, inasmuch as the stories relate Coyote's activities, but later Coyote's purpose became less sacred though no less necessary.

Hoebel equates Coyote with

> *. . . the mischievous Til Eulenspiegel of Shoshonean folklore, who was the spoiler of all things. . . . His was the role of the transformer who undid the good works of his big brother. He brought hardship, travail, and effort into the lives of men. He represented the force of Evil as we conceive it—and yet the Shoshones in no way thought of him in his relationship to Wolf as a conflict of good and evil. Coyote was not bad; he was no more than wantonly mischievous.*[3]

Hoebel goes on, though, to suggest that amongst the Comanche storytellers, nearly all vestiges of Coyote as a cultural transformer have disappeared.[4]

C.G. Jung has written perhaps as well as any on the subject of the trickster character as a cultural transformer. In his comments on the Winnebago Trickster Cycle titled "On the Psychology of the Trickster Figure," Jung suggests that the trickster

> *. . . is a forerunner of the savior, and, like him, God, man, and animal at once. He is both subhuman and superhuman, a bestial and divine being, whose chief and most alarming characteristic is his unconsciousness.*

> *The trickster is a primitive "cosmic" being of* divine-animal *nature, on the one hand superior to man because of superhuman qualities, and on the other hand inferior to him because of his unreason and unconsciousness.*[5]

Jung continues by suggesting that the Trickster is really no match for animals either, because of his lack of functional animal instinct. This is because of his human nature which has moved out of the natural environment and into the somewhat artificial world of culture.[6]

As a result, the Trickster, or Coyote in the case of the Comanches, serves a therapeutic purpose. We can laugh at his frailties, though we can't when the same situation occurs to us, consciously or unconsciously, in our real world. Paul Radin illustrates, in his book, *The Trickster,* a cycle of Winnebago Trickster stories in which the Trickster moves from a period of unconsciousness through a kind of civilizing process. Jung sees this as the primary function of the trickster stories.[7] If man can laugh at his primitive self as illustrated by the Trickster, then he can cope with being civilized man as well. The myths, according to Jung, hold "the earlier low intellectual and moral level before the eyes of the more highly developed individual, so that he shall not forget how things looked yesterday."[8] Jung continues by quoting Radin's *The World of Primitive Man*. "Viewed psychologically, it might be contended that the history of civilization is largely the account of the attempts of man to forget his transformation from an animal into a human being."[9] Outwardly, his attempt to forget may be successful. Inwardly, however, he is committed to retaining a knowledge of his past. Outwardly, he considers himself "civilized," but inwardly he still is primitive. According to Jung, "the trickster is a collective shadow figure, an epitome of all inferior traits of character in individuals. And since the individual shadow is never absent as a component of personality, the collective figure can construct itself out of it continually."[10] The shadow remains hidden from our consciousness, because the reality the shadow attempts to hide represents more "truth" than man's conscious can deal with. If, however, recognition of the realities of man's psychological makeup are uncovered, the trickster-myth cycle takes on a new dimension. It moves beyond the representation of the "collective shadow," and, because the shadow is brought to light, the Trickster becomes, or at least exhibits a tendency to become, a savior. Such is the case in the Winnebago trickster cycle and Jung says of it: "If, at the end of the trickster myth, the savior is hinted at, this comforting premonition or hope means that some calamity or other has happened and been consciously understood. Only out of disaster can the longing for the savior arise—in other words, the recognition and unavoidable integration of the shadow create such a harrowing situation that nobody but a savior can undo the tangled web of fate."[11]

Jung goes on, in *Man and His Symbols,* to identify the four stages in the evolution of human identity as represented by the Winnebago Trickster Cycles. They are: identity as biological man, identity as ordinary man on the street, identity as hero, and identity as spiritual man, conscious of both his inner and outer nature.[12]

It is through the Trickster characters that Man can mythologize the real struggles he has in the search for these four stages of identity. They represent, in essence, a move from the purely natural man (the biological awareness of one's self), through culture, and beyond to the supernatural (the religious).[13] The Comanche Coyote assists the Comanche in that he fictionalizes all aspects of the question, "What part of me is animal (natural) and what part of me is human (cultural) and, for that matter, what constitutes those parts of our lives we classify as being supernatural?"

FROM CHAOS TO ORDER: THE COYOTE AS CULTURE CREATOR

What then, is it to be Kiowus, the cultural transformer? Basically, it is a fictionalizing of the movement from a biological world, one in which the bodily functions control the man, and where the external problems are nonexistent (these are best symbolized in the early Shoshone stories of the world of perfect order created by Coyote's older brother, Wolf, and comparable to the life of a small baby as Radin suggested in The Trickster), to a world which is essentially man-controlled—a "cultural" world— with all of its problems in coping with a social life, and, to put it into a twentieth century context, the technocratic problems of a world moving outward from the closed Comanche community. As the Shoshones put it, Coyote undoes the Wolf's Utopian society in the name of culture. The Edenic world is not one for man—the fall of man must occur for man to be what he is and do what he must do.

Thus, Kiowus is a teacher. More than this, he is a Promethean Giver, and ultimately, Savior. On the other side of the same coin, however, he is a bungler. He offers the Comanche listeners comic relief from the harshness of this world which surrounds them daily. The audience laughs at his attempts to become what he is not, or to do what he should not do, but through the laughter, the story's listener sees, through his unconscious eye, a movement from chaos to order.

Because Coyote doesn't always live within his limits, physically or psychologically, his misfortunes tend often to be short lessons in the morality of being one's self. This is especially important within the context of the Comanche culture where medicine (*puha*) plays such an important role in the way a person reacts to his own environment. It is important for the Comanche to obtain and understand his *puha* early in his adult life and then conform to the criterion that particular *puha* determines. To live outside of the limitations established by the power of a particular medicine would be to invite danger and tragedy. Coyote fails time and again to live within the limits of his own *puha*, but because he is superhuman and bungler both, his mistakes are not as irretrievable as the same mistake would be for man.

The tragicomedy spawned by Trickster's behavior again allows the listener an opportunity for comic relief, but he is always conscious of the ramifications of such behavior were he to do it himself. The Comanches had paid the price for leaving Wolf's Edenic paradise. This life was a hard one, but the *puha* given them by the Spirits living all around them provided a way of dealing with the problems, and Coyote tended, from time to time, to be a handy scapegoat for problems which are probably inevitable for all cultures worldwide.

To begin with the stories which most clearly display Coyote's culture-creating characteristics, the earliest versions of the Coyote Trickster stories exhibit most clearly Kiowus as the cultural transformer. In the tale, "Coyote and Regulations of the Seasons; Origin of Death," the Comanche notion of the order of Nature is shown. According to the tale, although seasons seem to exist, the people are dissatisfied with the way the seasons are arranged. Nature exists in an order of her own, but to the people this order is not satisfactory. It is Coyote who suggests to the people that an alternative situation might be arranged:

> *Coyote called all the people together to decide how many winter months and how many summer months there ought to be. They set up a large council lodge. Coyote sat down in the centre* (sic) *on the west side.*[14]

Because Coyote sat on the West side, in the center—the position of the "head man"—there is no doubt that he is considered a leader by these people. His intentions, however, are not as honorable as they may seem. Coyote argues:

> *"Six cold months would be too much, we should suffer from cold. Ten summer months would be good. . . ." Coyote was in favor of ten hot months because he wished to play a trick on them.*[15]

He uses a situation in which the people are dissatisfied with the existing order of nature as an opportunity to once again play the role of Trickster. It is here that his superhuman-subhuman characteristics are best exhibited. Because he is, in part, divine, he is capable of calling a meeting such as this and to do something about the problem. And, because he is subhuman, he is incapable of seeing the implications of such action simply for the benefit of the people. He is nearsighted—he only wants to play a trick on them. The results of this action, though, are that Coyote, in his own bungling way develops an opportunity for the people to bring a beneficent order to their universe. Coyote's argument for ten hot months is overruled in favor of Snow-Bird's suggestion that there be six hot months and six cold months.

According to an old Bannock chief, Gray Wolf, the creator "had the power to change all animal and plant life into other forms. . . . Some that were very good, he made into birds with beautiful feathers; to some he gave the power to sing."[16] Snow-Bird seems to be a representative of this ideal. His logic is sound and his intentions are to help his people. He sings songs which are beautiful to his people. Coyote sets up the opportunity but loses control, thus bungling his part in the play. But he is the Trickster/Transformer, and the transformation into a world order as the Comanches now perceive it does come about.

Another similar situation occurs in the second part of the tale. The order of Nature, though predictable, is abnormal. And again Coyote blunders into this situation opening an opportunity for the transformation to Nature as Comanche people now know it.

> After the council was over, Coyote said, "Now do all of you go over there; I shall join you, and we will decide whether our dead should return after the lapse of four days. Long ago that was our way. Today I object to our dead coming back."[17]

In the Comanche world-view, the Spirits of the dead are to be avoided. They are perceived as being frightening and disruptive to the Comanche community.[18] Therefore, Coyote's suggestion is of value to Comanche culture. Although there is no indication here of Coyote's desire to trick the people, his intentions do seem selfish. It is not necessarily his intention to be a savior for the people. Rather, he seems a bit irritated at the fact that the dead are returning and he wants to alleviate this situation. But, again, the result is one of transformation from one sense of Nature to another more familiar one.

This concept of Coyote as the vehicle in establishing a natural situation out of an abnormal, though ordered, universe is perhaps best exhibited in the tale, "Coyote and the Liberation of the Buffalo." In one version of the story, the buffalo are corralled and held captive by an older woman and her young cousin:

> Long ago two persons owned all the buffalo. They were an old woman and her young cousin. They kept them penned up in the mountains, so that they could not get out.[19]

And in another version the buffalo are kept by the Coyote himself:

> There was once a Coyote, who lived with his wife and son off by themselves. The Coyote had the buffalo corralled in a large cave.[20]

In both cases the buffalo are in an abnormal situation in that they are held captive—not allowed to roam free—in an indifferent universe which, though well defined, is not beneficent to the people. In the second version of the story we find that "the people were very hungry, for they had no buffalo." This is a world the Comanche people are incapable of relating to; it is Nature without Culture.

In both versions of the tale, the Coyote is instrumental in the people's ultimate victory and in the establishment of "Nature" as the people today are used to seeing it. In the first version, it is Coyote who thinks of a plan to steal the buffalo away from the old woman—perhaps the personification of earth—and her little cousin. In the second version, Coyote plays the role of the Old Woman, and, because of Coyote's carelessness, the buffalo are taken away from his cave. Coyote can be exchanged with the Old Woman in these tales, I believe, because the importance in the tale lies not so much in who plans the scheme, but in the results of the scheme. And as long as Coyote functions in a superhuman-subhuman capacity, the same mythological function is achieved.

In the first version, the last sentence is perhaps the most telling. It says, "Coyote was a great schemer."[21] Put into the context of the other Kiowus stories, this suggests that his intentions are more oriented towards his playing a trick on the old woman and her young cousin, than they are towards his helping the people obtain their buffalo. His scheme is successful and as a result the buffalo are freed. As a result of his ministrations, a Nature is formed which, in turn, can lend itself to the formation of a culture. In the second version we again find Coyote in a superhuman-subhuman role. He is capable of starving the people by controlling the buffalo, but he is careless enough to let them escape. His trick (of keeping the buffalo) remains effective only as long as he is actively controlling the situation. When he turns his back, the trick backfires on him and the buffalo are freed. As a result, the buffalo form the beginnings of movement by the people toward a culture-creating process, one which ultimately leads to their own distinctive version of the Plains Buffalo Culture.

The remaining Coyote stories deal with the Nature/Culture theme, but in a less obvious way. The four most common types of Coyote stories are those which deal with Coyote and his attempts to imitate other animals, his relationships with people, his predicaments in an adaptive situation dealing with White people, and his efforts in dealing with twentieth century problems. These stories, if read in a series, indicate a movement in Coyote's personality, from bungler and imitator, to leader—a character in control of his environment.

THE PRE-MAN TRICKSTER: COYOTE AS ANIMAL

In the first group of stories—those in which Coyote tries to be like other animals—there seems to be an unconscious attempt on the part of the storytellers to categorize. The categorization is centered around the individual animal species' medicine power (*puha*), and results in structures which deal essentially with self-awareness. (According to Jung, one of the functions the Trickster character fulfills is to allow man to identify his own biological, social, and psychological self.) The Comanches have fictionalized Trickster's function of defining man's humanness by allowing a wide variety of animals, acting in relation to Coyote, to act out symbolically the process of defining what a creature-surrogate for man, Coyote, cannot be. Though I intend to speak more extensively of the *puha* elsewhere, there are some aspects of it, having to do with Trickster's character, which must be observed now, if a serious attempt to define Kiowus is to be made.

The tale, "Coyote and the Kingfisher," serves as a good example of Coyote's problems in this series of tales. In the story, Coyote finds he has a problem:

> *A long time ago, it is said, Kingfisher and Coyote were friends. Coyote was very hungry, so he said, "I will go to my friend's home."*[22]

Two problems are indicated by this excerpt. The first is that Coyote is hungry, thus not in control of his environment; and the second is that rather than try to solve his problem through his own initiative, he goes to another animal. Kingfisher, better equipped for hunting food in what are presumably hard times, has no problem in furnishing some fish for both Coyote and himself. Kingfisher says:

> *"Somewhere near, I will get some food for us." So Kingfisher flew over the water, then dove into the water, and came up carrying a fish. They ate a lot of food.*[23]

Coyote recognizes Kingfisher's ability to get food, but fails to recognize his own inability. He doesn't see himself as he really is. Thoughtlessly, he invites Kingfisher to come eat with him when it gets cold. When winter comes, Kingfisher has trouble finding food, and, remembering Coyote's invitation, makes the trip over to his friend's house.

> *Kingfisher said, "I am going to eat with you, friend." Then Coyote said, "Sit down, my friend, I will get some food for us."*[24]

Coyote, quite unequipped for the task ahead of him, sits by the water and barks. "The water was frozen. He jumped in it and broke his hip."[25] Kingfisher ultimately had to come and find food for both of them.

Coyote's basic problem in the story is that he fails to rely on himself for the solution of his own problem. Although he has his own medicine (*puha*), it is as though it is too much bother for him to understand himself. Rather, he "borrows" a hunting methodology—medicine in itself—from Kingfisher. In the first place, this way of hunting for food is not suitable for a coyote, and, beyond that, it is unsuitable for even a Kingfisher if the hunting plunge is a plunge into frozen water. Clearly, Coyote is not in charge of his environment. His attempts to borrow the *puha* of another animal, without proper training, would surely be recognized by the Comanche listener as sheer folly. We all try these silly things as we educate ourselves, but such tricks are particularly foolish in a world where each animal and man has his own *puha*. In Coyote's folly, we see our own shortcomings and release the tension this creates by laughing.

The unifying characteristic in each of all of these types of stories is found in Coyote's lack of recognition of a deficiency in himself, which is perceived clearly by the listener. By the same token, in each of these stories Coyote does recognize a need. The search for a remedy to a felt need is human and tragic. Our observance of some characteristic deficiency in Coyote's personality, comic in itself, also leads us, as listeners, unconsciously through a search for identity. To carry this one step further, we must recognize that to understand our "primitive" self, as Jung puts it, we must look at our real self.

Why Coyote has selected these particular animals—kingfishers, geese, bears, beaver, owls, opposum, and yellow-birds, to name a few—is an intriguing question. Lévi-Strauss suggests, in *The Savage Mind,* that it is not uncommon for a culture to select animals for mythic structure which they find easy to anthropomorphize.[26] In the Comanche stories, then, it may be people-surrogates (or at least *puha* offered by other animals which could lead ultimately to a culture-creating process) that Coyote wants to imitate. At another level, each of the animals which is used in these stories has a unique medicine (i.e., bears had power to cure wounds, cf. next section). If Coyote's primary function is, as previously stated, to form a movement from Nature to Culture, from Chaos to Order and Control, then is it not understandable that in the Comanche unconscious the animals best suited to represent that movement would be those perceived as most anthropomorphic? Although there was little ethnographical data available to support this notion, aside from tales such as "The Woman Who Married the Bear," the existence of such tales does suggest that the animals which we have named are a "transitional" station between culture and nature.

The symbolism moves on to more complex meanings. At the very least, the animal characteristics Coyote tries to imitate symbolize a moral or cultural trait. In the most complex of the stories, the characters hold the key to the "truths beyond the shadows" of which Jung speaks. These "truths," deeply hidden in man's unconscious, are probably most painlessly released with the symbolic help of anthropomorphic animal characters.[27]

COYOTE AS THE TRICKY TRICKSTER

The stories most loved by the storytellers are those in which the emphasis is on Coyote's attempts at trickery. I have recognized in these stories two types: those in which Coyote tricks other animals and those in which he tricks people. Perhaps the best two examples of Coyote's tricking other animals are in the tales, "The Coyote Steals the Possum's Persimmons," and "Coyote and the Hoodwinked Dancers." There are surprisingly few stories in which Coyote attempts to trick other animals, and even fewer in which he is successful. Even in the first of these two stories, Coyote is only moderately successful, and in some versions of the second story he is actually outtricked. These stories seem to be transitional in that, although Coyote is in more control than he was in his early attempts at imitations, he is not as successful as he is depicted to be later when he tricks White people and almost never loses.

The trickery stories seem to represent a searching Coyote. He is trying to exert some influence over his environment and is experiencing moderate success. To use Jung's stages of Trickster's development as a guideline for discussion, we can say that Coyote is beyond the search for the identity of his biological self. He is not the same Coyote that he was, for instance, when he wanted to eat his leg because the quail had scared him by flying at him ("Coyote and the Quail"). This is, rather, a Coyote with whom the Comanche people can identify. He is not perfect; he still falls victim to a variety of traps. And there still is a search, but now that search is for an internal identity—for control. In his encounter with Possum, the question is not, "How does Possum find persimmons while I go hungry?" but, rather, "How can I trick Possum out of her persimmons without having to do any of the work?" And even though Coyote falls into the trap, it is because he is the leader. He falls in of his own accord. Furthermore, he is embarrassed by it, something which would never have occurred in the earlier stories.

> Coyote was in front and Possum was following him. All of a sudden he fell out of sight. She was right behind him and she fell out of sight too. "Now our children will starve," she said. Coyote was not talking.[28]

This short segment pretty much explains who is who in the story. The maternal possum is living by instinct (Nature). She is uncreative, a follower. Coyote, on the other hand, is angry about his predicament. The sentence, "Coyote was not talking," is exactly what a Comanche person might say about a person in an embarrassing situation.

In "Coyote and the Hoodwinked Dancers," Coyote is "knocking about the prairie" when he stumbles onto a prairie dog village. Immediately upon his arrival, Coyote springs into action with a plan to trick and eat the prairie dogs. His scheme is simple, but effective. He has them dance with their eyes closed, and as they are dancing unprotected he snatches up a few for his dinner. The ostensible moral of this tale (which is quite common throughout the Plains area) is that in a hostile world one should protect himself at all times, and not succumb to the many traps which may beset the unsuspecting. But a look at another version of this story may add depth to what the more complex meaning of this story might be.

A second version begins like this:

> Coyote met a skunk. "Halloo, brother! I am very hungry. Let us work some scheme to get something to eat! I will lead the way, do you follow."—"Well, I will do whatever you propose."[29]

Again, if we are to believe the version of the creation story in which Gray Wolf changes the animals, then, as the old Bannock chief has said:

When they, animal and plant life, were very bad he changed them into skunks.[30]

Together with this skunk, the lowest of all the creatures—and also a bit of a schemer himself—Coyote makes plans to trick the prairie dogs. The scheme is much the same as it was in the other version, but there is more to this story. Coyote proposes to Skunk, following their mutual victory over the prairie dogs, a winner-take-all race for the spoils with the skunk. In this case, Coyote runs a fair race, but is cheated by Skunk, who, as a result, gets all but two of the prairie dogs. The humor, of course, lies in the fact that Coyote may have a stronger medicine than do the prairie dogs, but that doesn't mean he has the power to be successful all of the time. The intrinsically evil Skunk, who, it is said, possesses great power, here shows Coyote his shortcomings.

In a third version of this story the same procedure is followed, but in the end Coyote and the polecat divide the spoils and then Coyote is tricked out of his spoils by a crippled coyote who cheats much like Skunk had in the second version. What these three stories hold in common with each other, in addition to the obvious aspects of the story line, is that in each of these stories, when Coyote plans his trickery he is successful, but when pride and quick decisions are introduced into his thinking, he is unsuccessful. And, ultimately, Coyote's folly is our own. In the Red Horn series of the Winnebago Trickster Cycle which Jung uses for his analysis we find a basic theme, which according to Jung, "raises, in effect, the vital question: How long can human beings be successful without falling victims to their own pride, or in mythological terms, to the jealousy of the gods?"[31]

Essentially, this is the problem Coyote finds himself grappling with. He has found a strength—a *puha*—which enables him to exert some control over his environment, but, as a bungler, he destroys this new found order by overdoing it. He falls by pride.

This same pattern is developed in those stories in which Coyote tries to trick people. Sometimes, as in the tale, "Fox's Medicine," or "Coyote Cheats Some People Out of Pecans," he is successful. Other times, such as in the tale "The Old Lady and the Coyote," he overdoes it and loses in the long run. The third of these three tales is indicative of the general pattern which develops when Coyote tricks Indian people. In this tale Coyote overhears the lonely old lady talking to herself, and what he hears whets his palate:

> *A long time ago an old lady lived by herself. She wanted to find some Indians. "Now I will go to hunt for some Indians," she said. "I am going to pound my meat." After pounding her meat, she put it in a sack. Coyote heard her. . . .*[32]

Coyote's concern is not for the reintegration of an ostracized woman back into her tribe. His interest is only in getting some meat from that old woman. At another level this story can be read for additional meaning. If the Old Woman, for instance, is the same old woman—a personification of the earth—who held captive the buffalo, then perhaps her search for Indians is representative of an integration of

Nature with Culture. Again, Coyote, as a spoiler of this kind of synthesis, shows no interest in this attempt at integration. He thinks only of himself. Although his first attempts at tricking the Old Woman are quite successful, his over-indulgence in trickery ultimately leads to his demise by the domination of the Old Woman over the Coyote. The story ends:

> *The old woman saw her meat between his teeth. "Coyote!" she said. Getting a stick she beat him. For that reason the coyote is always afraid of a woman.*[33]

COYOTE AND THE WHITE MAN: THE NEWEST FUNCTION

The most commonly told stories presently are those in which Coyote is forced, for one reason or another, to grapple with the transition brought on by White intrusion. These tales range from those in which Coyote has to deal with a foreign and embarrassing situation, as in "Coyote and the Camp Meeting," to those in which Coyote tricks White people, especially the carriers of White culture, such as "Coyote Cheats the Preacher" and "Coyote and the Soldiers."[34]

In the tale "Coyote and the Camp Meeting," Coyote happens upon an early twentieth century phenomenon of the Southern Oklahoma Plains—the camp meeting. Historically, it was the camp meeting situation which the early missionaries to the Comanche/Kiowa areas found most successful in their evangelization and enculturation program. No wonder that the church camp meeting, with all its appeal and unfamiliarity, found its way into the body of Comanche trickster tales.

The appeal of the camp meeting came, perhaps, mostly because it centered around singing, a favorite Comanche pasttime. What must have seemed strange to them, however, was the ever-present collection plate. In traditional Comanche fashion, the sponsor of an event—such as a Pow-Wow—would show his gratitude by give-aways. But here, at these camp meetings, the sponsors asked for money and had collection plates handy. The collection plates, then, served as a symbol for the awkwardness of cultural differences. No doubt, many of the early Comanches made embarrassing mistakes of protocol at those meetings—especially the first time they attended. So, what better scapegoat than Trickster to laugh at in order to overcome their own embarrassment. In this story, Coyote does what must have been a temptation for many of the people; he takes back some change from the collection plate:

> *One time some people were having a camp meeting and Coyote was just wandering around. His wife was at home. He came up to where the big crowd was, and they were having a camp meeting. Coyote's wild and so he sat way back in the last seat. When it was over and they were passing the plate around, he had only a dime, so he took it out of his pocket and put that dime in the plate and got a nickle back.*[35]

His only reward for his effort is a shameful scolding from his wife. Coyote was, no doubt, not the first Comanche to suffer through such a scolding.

Many of the other problems endured as a result of the acculturation process were far more serious, though. The White intrusion into a strong and stable Comanche culture must have thoroughly traumatized the people, giving them a somewhat pessimistic world-view. Something had to be done to build up emotional self-confidence after White culture had so completely engulfed them. What better way than to allow Coyote, the worst bungler of them all, to trick the two most common agents of White culture—the soldier and the preacher. In "Coyote Cheats the Preacher" Kiowus shows that he is capable of fighting fire with fire. The preacher didn't force a new culture on the Comanche people, but, once entrenched, his messages continually stripped away the last remaining vestiges of a community which had developed a moral and ethical value system of its own. He kept preaching, and, little by little, eventually he wore down and eliminated what little was left. Then when these pillars had been removed, he rebuilt the shattered community on new principles—those he had brought with him from another religion, another culture. And he was quite successful at his task.

Coyote gets even by stripping not the moral, but the physical man. He tricks the preacher out of his clothes. The preacher has already heard about Coyote's power upon their first meeting. He says to Coyote, "Hi, fellow. I heard that you were a big joker and cheater." The preacher ought to know better than to deal with Coyote, but he seemingly can't resist. The result is that Coyote tricks him out of his horse, cap, coat, trousers, and shoes. Coyote is completely successful, and the preacher is left in the cold, stripped and embarrassed.

This same theme is carried through to another Coyote story, "Coyote and the Soldiers." In this story, Coyote has to fight a powerful medicine—the gun—with another powerful medicine, i.e., his own ability to trick. In those stories in which Coyote deals with White people, he shows much more maturity and ability than he ever did in his earlier encounters. As a matter of fact, not once, in all the stories I was able to collect, did I find a case in which Coyote's medicine failed him or in which he fell to pride while he was dealing with White people. His medicine had become very powerful.

There are several versions of the story "Coyote and the Soldiers," but in each the soldiers seem to initially present a threat to Coyote. One begins, "Coyote was thinking how he might get some money. A great many soldiers were following his trail."[36] And another begins, "One time the army was going by and they wanted to see why Coyote didn't run."[37] A natural opposition is indicated and in this second version, Coyote's failure to fear the army arouses the soldiers' interest.

The trick Coyote plays on these soldiers is a simple one. He hides the fire under a cave and boils water in a kettle above the cave. The soldiers cannot see the fire. They are impressed that Coyote can boil water without fire. It has to be a magic kettle he is using. So Coyote uses their greed against them. If they want something for nothing, they are going to have to pay Coyote for the opportunity. He teases them for a while until he finally gets their best horse.

In one version, the story ends when the soldiers camped and began to prepare their meat:

> They camped . . . and they made the ground the way he (Coyote) had it. Those boys
> put a lot of meat in it, then they left. When they came back it hadn't done a thing.
> The meat was still all raw, and the head man was mad.[38]

It is easy to see the kind of emotional release a story like this might have offered the Comanche who every day saw the soldier in a position of complete dominance. Here, the soldiers make a stupid mistake, lose their best horse and are made fools of by the Comanche's biggest bungler. The ending of another version of the story provides an interesting twist:

> When they camped, they set the kettle down, poured in water, and sat watching to
> see it boil. They had to wait a very long time. "Evidently Coyote has got the better of
> us," they said. From that time on, the Whites have always traded with the Indians.
> Coyote taught us to do so.[39]

In this version, not only does Coyote embarrass the White soldiers, but he performs an act which establishes a cultural pattern. He has made accommodations in his own world for White intruders—on his own terms. The Comanche unconscious must also have realized that these White soldiers were here to stay and they would have to be integrated into the Comanche's world-view. This did not mean, however, that they would be integrated at an equal level. Coyote shows them how these intruders could be dealt with, and, as a teacher, he shows them that trading with Whites can be both entertaining and advantageous. Coyote teaches Comanches not only how to trade with Whites, but how to take advantage, at least emotionally and psychologically. At last, Coyote has become, for the Comanche people, a savior; a way of escaping emotionally from the trauma of White intrusion.

NOTES

[1] Ella E. Clark, *Indian Legends from the Northern Rockies* (Norman, Oklahoma: University of Oklahoma Press, 1966), p. 169.

[2] Ibid., p. 170.

[3] Ernest Wallace and E. Adamson Hoebel, *The Comanches: Lords of the South Plains* (Norman, Oklahoma: University of Oklahoma Press, 1952), pp. 193–94.

[4] Ibid., p. 194.

[5] C.G. Jung, "On the Psychology of the Trickster Figure," in Paul Radin, *The Trickster: A Study in American Indian Mythology* (1956; rpt. New York: Schocken Books, 1972), pp. 203–4.

[6] Ibid., p. 204.

[7] Ibid.

[8] Ibid., p. 207.

[9] Ibid., p. 207–8.

[10] Ibid., p. 209.

[11] Ibid., p. 211.

[12] C.J. Jung, *Man and His Symbols* (1964; rpt. New York: Dell, 1968), pp. 101–7.

[13] Ibid.

[14] H.H. St. Clair, 2d., "Shoshone and Comanche Tales," *Journal of American Folklore* 22 (1909): 279.

[15] Ibid.

[16] Ella E. Clark, *Indian Legends*, p. 169.

[17] St. Clair, "Shoshone and Comanche Tales," p. 279.

[18] Elliott Canonge, in *Comanche Texts* (Norman, Oklahoma: Summer Institute of Linguistics of the University of Oklahoma, 1958), has included a variety of stories dealing with ghosts and life after death.

[19] St. Clair, "Shoshone and Comanche Tales," p. 280.

[20] Edward S. Curtis, *The North American Indians,* 19 (Norwood, Massachusetts: The Plimpton Press, 1930).

[21] St. Clair, "Shoshone and Comanche Tales," p. 279.

[22] Elliot Canonge, Unpublished Texts. Used by permission of Mrs. Viola (Canonge) Frew.

[23] Ibid.

[24] Ibid.

[25] Ibid.

[26] Claude Lévi-Strauss, *The Savage Mind* (Chicago: University of Chicago Press, 1966).

[27] Jung, "On the Psychology of the Trickster," pp. 202ff.

[28] Canonge, Unpublished Texts.

[29] St. Clair, "Shoshone and Comanche Tales," p. 281.

[30] Clark, *Indian Legends,* p. 169.

[31] Jung, *Man and His Symbols, p.* 22.

[32] Canonge, Unpublished Texts.

[33] Ibid.

[34] These can be found in St. Clair's collection.

[35] Lillie Asee, interviewed July 1976, Elgin, Oklahoma.

[36] St. Clair, "Shoshone and Comanche Tales," p. 282.

[37] Ibid., 283.

[38] Ibid.

[39] Ibid., p. 282.

Part Four: NATIVE AMERICAN CULTURE
AND THE
'DOMINANT' CULTURE

Arnold Krupat: THE INDIAN AUTOBIOGRAPHY: ORIGINS, TYPE, AND FUNCTION

The interesting group of texts I propose to treat as a genre and call the Indian autobiography has almost entirely been ignored by students of American literature. This may be because Indian autobiographies have been presented by the whites who have written them as more nearly "scientific" documents of the historical or ethnographic type than as "literary" works. In any case, no Indian autobiography conforms to the definition of autobiography "we all know," as James Cox states it, "a narrative of a person's life written by himself."[1]

"Autobiography" as a particular form of self-written life is a European invention of comparatively recent date. Southey is credited with coining the word in English in 1809, and the earliest American book title I have discovered to use it is from 1832. Great labor has recently been expended in the effort to define "autobiography" as a genre. For our purposes, we may note only that the autobiographical project, as we usually understand it, is marked by egocentric individualism, historicism, and writing. These are all present in European and Euramerican culture after the revolutionary last quarter of the eighteenth century. But none has ever characterized the native cultures of the present-day United States.

Although the Indian's sense of personal freedom, worth, and responsibility became legendary, the "autonomy of the [male] individual" was always subordinated to communal and collective requirements.[2] That egocentric individualism associated with the names of Byron or Rousseau, the cultivation of originality and differentness, was never legitimated by native cultures, to which celebration of the hero-as-solitary would have been incomprehensible.

Neither is the post-Napoleonic sense of progressive, linear history at all like the historical sense found among Indian cultures. (A strict account would require noting many variations.) The Sioux have a well-known proverb to the effect that, "A people without history is like wind on the buffalo grass." But the understanding of "history" at issue here, if European analogues may be invoked, is more nearly Hellenic than Hebraic. Or, somewhat more precisely, "history" is not evolutionary, teleological, or progressive. Means for preserving tribal memory were developed in all "culture areas," but these did not privilege the dimensions of causality and uniqueness which mark the "modern" forms of Euramerican historicism.

Further, while no culture is possible without "writing" in some very broad sense, no Indian culture developed the phonetic alphabet which Lewis Henry Morgan isolated as the distinctive feature of "civilized" culture. Patterns worked in wampum belts, tattoos, pictographs painted on animal skins or in sand may all be considered forms of "writing." But the black-on-white which distinguishes scription from diction for the Euramerican, the letter and the book, were not found among native cultures in the pre-contact period. Even later—after John Eliot had transcribed the Bible into a Massachusetts dialect of the Algonquin language in the seventeenth century; after Sequoyah, in the early nineteenth century, had devised a Cherokee syllabary; or the Dakota language, by the late nineteenth century, had become available for inscription—the presence of the grapheme still signified for the Indian the cultural Other, the track of the Indo-European snake in the American garden.

Strictly speaking, therefore, *Indian autobiography* is a contradiction in terms. Indian autobiographies are collaborative efforts, jointly produced by some white who translates, transcribes, compiles, edits, interprets, polishes, and ultimately determines the "form" of the text in writing, and by an Indian who is its "subject" and whose "life" becomes the "content" of the "autobiography" whose title may bear his "name." Although they are unfortunate, these quotation marks are necessary to indicate the problematic status of the terms they enclose. I may now state the principle constituting the Indian autobiography as a genre as the principle of bi-cultural composite authorship. Although there will always be debatable cases, it should be possible to demonstrate this complex origination for any work claimed for the genre.[3] To this extent I follow Todorov, who has written: "When we examine works of literature from the perspective of genre, we engage in a very particular enterprise: we discover a principle operative in a number of texts, rather than what is specific about each of them."[4] But to work in this way turns us back to that question with which we began, how far it is proper to treat works conceived of as contributions to "history" or "anthropology" as "works of literature."

Texts bound by the real insist upon an epistemological status different from works of the imagination in which the real is more nearly hypothetical. Yet no text can offer a neutral presentation of "the order of things"; rather, works of "science" as well as "literature" can only re-present the world, filtering it through the orders of language. In spite of the "narrative" dimension all texts have been shown to share, there are nonetheless important differences between "historical/scientific" and "literary" texts and the differences in type bear upon differences in function.

Briefly, then, I would justify a "literary" typing for the Indian autobiography by reference to the genre's constituting principle of bi-cultural composite authorship. There is an actual doubling of the "sender" and of the cultural "code" in Indian autobiography, and this complication in the production of the signifier serves to complicate the relationship of signifier to signified in just those ways we associate with the "literary" use of language.

The principle of bi-cultural composite authorship provides not only the key to the Indian autobiography's discursive type but to its discursive function as well, its purposive dimension as an act of power and will. For to see the Indian autobiography as a ground on which two cultures meet is to see it as the textual equivalent of the "frontier." Here, the "frontier" does not only mean the furthest line of points to which "civilization" has extended itself; rather, to adopt the systemic view of the contemporary ethnohistorian, the "frontier" also signifies "the reciprocal relationship between two cultures in contact."[5] But, however much it may have been "reciprocal," the "relationship" between native Americans and Euramericans was never—with the exception, perhaps, of moments during the eighteenth century—one between equals. For the whites, the "advance" of the "frontier" always meant domination and appropriation, and the movement westward was achieved not only with the power of the sword but of the pen as well. To "win" the continent required not only troops and technology but a discourse of what Foucault would call *assujetissement*, of (in Edward Said's description) "the subjugation of individuals in societies [or of whole societies] to some suprapersonal discipline or authority."[6]

During the nineteenth century, part of that "discipline" was the idea of progressive "history" as a "scientific" determinism or "law" which authorized the doctrine of cultural evolution, the belief that "civilization" must everywhere replace "savagery." This was the official sanction for the "removal" of the eastern tribes west of the Mississippi in the 1830's as it was the unofficial sanction for the enormous body of writing about Indians that appeared in these same years. Along with novels, poems, plays, and "histories" of Indians, the decade of Indian Removal saw the production of a new form of writing "by" as well as about Indians, the Indian autobiography. Following native defeat in the Black Hawk "War," J.B. Patterson, in 1833, published the first Indian autobiography, the *Life of Ma-Ka-tai-me-she-kia-kiak or Black Hawk*. As Black Hawk had submitted to Euramerican military and political forms, so he now submitted to Euramerican discursive form. But the form of writing proposed to this Indian who could not write was not the standard "Life and Times" biography; instead, it was the newer form of personal "history," the autobiography. Produced as an acknowledgement of Indian defeat in the service of progressivist ideology, the book made by Patterson and Black Hawk, by admitting an Indian to the ranks of the self-represented, also questioned progressivist ideology. Unlike Indian biographies, Indian autobiographies require "contact" with living Indians, for it is the central convention of autobiography that the subject speaks for himself. And it is in its presentation of an Indian voice as not "vanished" but still living and able to speak for itself that the oppositional potential of Indian autobiography resides.

The Indian autobiography flourished as a genre, however, only in the twentieth century in the discourse of the "new" anthropological "science" founded by Franz Boas, a "science" which, if it was "historical," was nonetheless decidedly anti-evolutionary. I shall not pursue the progress of the genre this far in the present paper. Instead, I limit myself in what follows to an attempt to describe the origins of the Indian autobiography in "history" and the nineteenth century, with some further comment on its discursive type and function.

During the first stages of the "invasion of America," the East itself was West, and the towns of the "frontier" were named Plimoth, Jamestown, and Boston.[7] "Contact" between the Euramerican invader-settlers and native Americans led to conflict; the most common "reciprocal relationships" were conquest and capitivity, and it should come as no surprise that the first two indigenous forms of "history" writing developed in the New World were the Indian War Narrative and the Indian Captivity Narrative.

Recognizing the insatiable colonial appetite for land, Indians—for the most part—chose the "wrong" side in the American Revolution and suffered the consequences of British defeat. By the end of the eighteenth century, the American invasion had pushed forward into the Ohio valley and Daniel Boone's "dark and bloody ground" of Kentucky where the by-now traditional "frontier" relations of battle and bondage were re-established. Indians fought Americans once more in 1812 and once more lost. After the Treaty of Ghent in 1815, the natives could no longer hope for European support to check the further advance of the new American nation. Jackson's election to the presidency, signalling the "rise" of the West, signalled also the fall of the Red Man, for Indian Removal now became a national, not merely a local priority.

"Indian-haters" avid to appropriate and "improve" native holdings, and "Indian-lovers" avid to protect the "noble" Red Man from white drink, disease, and depredation, joined in supporting the Indian Removal Bill which, after fierce debate in Congress, was passed into law on May 28, 1830. The opposition included Davey Crockett, a western rival of Jackson, and John Quincy Adams, quintessential easterner. For the decade of the 1830's, response to the plight of the Indian was of paramount importance to American thought about "history" and "science."

The forcible removal of the eastern tribes into the "Great American Desert" west of the Mississippi was generally viewed—sadly or gladly—as the inevitable consequence of the advance of "civilization." Not white cupidity, but the "scientific" "law" of cultural evolution, popularly equated with the "doctrine of progress," determined the disappearance of the natives, giving an odor of sanctity to the most violent acts of exploitation and authorizing the wholesale destruction of Indian culture.

Or, rather, authorizing the accession of "nature" to "culture." For, as Pearce showed some time ago, in nineteenth-century American discourse, Indian "savages" had no "culture." The "customs" of "savagery" could not be dignified as a different form of culture than Euramerican "civilization" nor even a different stage of culture; rather, they were to be seen as the antithesis of culture, its zero degree.[8] In the '70s and '80s, after Morgan had defined "savagery" as an evolutionary stage prior to "barbarism" (the category into which most American Indians actually fell), which was itself but a stage prior to "civilization," "Friends of the Indian" succeeded in their fight to declare the Indian indeed civilizable. But for the 1830s and forties, the "savage" remained the one who could never be civilized. As the "Jew" is to the anti-semite, in Sartre's analysis, or the "Oriental" to the European in Edward Said's analysis, so was the "savage," to the "civilized" American of the nineteenth century, the term for radical alterity, a condition of being which no act could contradict.

Because the Indian "savage" could not himself be "civilized," "civilization" could not help but supplant him. The "aborigines," "Persons of little worth found cumbering the soil," in Ambrose Bierce's unsentimental definition, "soon cease to cumber; they fertilize."[9] As American troops removed Indians to the West in the 1830s, there arose an enormous interest in this material for fertilizer, and a great deal of writing about the "vanishing American" began to appear. New Captivity Narratives, authentic and apocryphal, were rushed to press while older Captivities, along with Indian War Narratives, were reprinted. Cooper's fiction reached the height of its popularity in this period, and gave voice to the typical eastern sadness at the passing of a primitive-but-noble race. Not sadness but satisfaction was the attitude more usual to the westerner (or southerner), and expressed in the Indian fiction of Robert Bird and William Gilmore Simms, novelists whose knowledge of Indians, unlike Cooper's, was derived not only from the library but from "contact" as well.

Painters as well as writers became Indian "historians," setting themselves the task of representing Indian life before it was gone forever. George Catlin, still the best known of the Indian-painters, left Pennsylvania for the West in 1830, the year of the Removal Act; his task, he wrote, was to rescue "from oblivion the looks and customs of the vanishing races of native man in America."[10] In every case, as A.D. Coleman has only recently written of the photographer Edward Curtis, a later "historian" of the still-vanishing Indian, all those who took the Indian as their "subject" sought "to document all aspects of a marvelous culture which was being inexorably [!] destroyed, in such a way as to retain the spirit of the culture and keep it alive."[11] Only the "spirit" of Indian culture might be kept "alive"; no intervention in "history" was believed possible to save it materially from "inexorable" destruction. And even that "spirit" would have to be kept "alive" by those who were destroying it: for only they possessed the means of documentation and representation. The Indian himself did not paint things as they "really were"; the Indian could not "write." His part was to pose—and disappear.

The West saw the destruction of the Indians not only as inevitable but just as well; but the East, which did not doubt the inevitability of it all, nonetheless questioned its justice. Considering the deeds of their own forebears, ministers in Boston protested Jackson's Indian policy, concerned that the "mistakes of the Puritan founders," their "historical blunders," not be repeated on the "frontier."[12] Urging that we learn from the past, these easterners provided a powerful impetus for the writing of Puritan history. But there was other writing to be undertaken as well, "an act of mere justice to the fame and the memories of many wise, brilliant, brave and generous men—patriots, orators, warriors and statesmen,—who ruled over barbarian communities, and were indeed themselves barbarians," as B.B. Thatcher explained in the "Preface" to his *Indian Biography* which, along with Samuel G. Drake's *Indian Biography* . . ., was published in Boston in 1832. "We owe, and our Fathers owed, too much to the Indians . . . to deny them the poor restitution of historical justice at least," Thatcher continued, adding darkly, "however the issue may have been or may be with themselves."[13]

The form Thatcher and Drake chose for "restitution" was the "Life and Times" form of eighteenth-century biography. Their Indians are represented as eminent men in the neoclassic mold but they are not yet conceived of as "heroes." Biography writing in the West, on the other hand, was very much engaged with the heroic and produced not only lives of that nearly-legendary, Indian-like white hero, Daniel Boone, but in time, of Indians as well.

In view of Slotkin's influential work on the Boone material which privileges the explanatory categories of "myth" and "archetype," it seems important to point out that the search for an American "hero" was rooted not only in some universal human longing, but in some very specific nineteenth-century ideas about "history," "science," and "law."[14] Interest in the *heldensleben* in mid-nineteenth-century America was spurred by a concern to discover an individual author of events and to locate "historical" beginnings—rather than absolute origins, in Said's useful distinction—in personal action. We need only think of Carlyle, the contemporary of these American hero-seekers, to recall how great an explanatory force the belief in "great men" once had. Carlyle's dictum that "history" is "the essence of innumerable biographies,"—an opinion shared on these shores by Emerson and Thoreau—is the "essence" of the nineteenth-century "romantic" reaction against neo-classic "Universal History," which, as Louis Mink has written, simply "never made room for . . . the uniqueness, vividness, and intrinsic value of *individuals*. . . ."[15] What is curious to note is that the reaction against "Universal History" does not prevent its simultaneous survival, as Mink also notes, in the guise of the doctrine of progress. In this context, autobiography, the self-written narrative of the "hero's" life, will become available both to support this "suprapersonal discipline" yet also potentially to oppose it.

For the decade of Indian Removal was also the decade when a conjunction of historicism and egocentric individualism first brought autobiography as a term and a type of writing to America. In Boston, in the same year that Thatcher and Drake issued their Indian biographies, the seventeenth-century "personal narrative" of Thomas Sheperd was published as an "autobiography"; *The Autobiography of Thomas Sheperd, the Celebrated Minister of Cambridge, New England* is the first American book I have found to use the term "autobiography" in its title. The following year, Asa Greene became the first American to apply the term to a "narrative of [his] life written by himself," when he published, in New York, *A Yankee Among the Nullifiers, an Auto-Biography,* under the pseudonym Elnathan Elmwood.

Although Elnathan Elmwood has lapsed into obscurity, we still think of autobiography as a "yankee" affair. Those we usually place in the great tradition of "personal narrative" or autobiography in America—Jonathan Edwards in the colonial period, Benjamin Franklin in the revolutionary period, Henry Thoreau in the period preceding the Civil War—are all easterners. So, too, are Henry Adams, the next major figure in this tradition, and, to step firmly into the twentieth century, Gertrude Stein, as well. From the first days of settlement until the end of the nineteenth century, the American self has tended to locate its peculiar national distinctiveness in relation to the perceived opposition between the European, the "man of culture," and the Indian, the "child of nature." And, for the writers I have named, the European polarity was decisive. The works of eastern autobiography from Edwards through Stein are old-world oriented and self-consciously literary. (Edwards, Franklin, and Thoreau, however, wrote extensively about Indians.) These autobiographers were conscious of themselves as writers where it was writing that precisely distinguished the European "man of culture" from "nature's child," the Indian—who did not "write." The classic eastern autobiographies include scenes of writing (and reading) as important to self-definition. Only with Thoreau, formed in the Jacksonian era of the "rise" of the West and intense concern with Indians, did the "natural" polarity enter into the autobiographical project. Thoreau's movement from the study to the woods and back was an exemplary journey as fact and as metaphor for Americans of the 1830s and forties. (It is interesting, too, to note that pencil-making and surveying were Thoreau's only regular sources of income throughout his life.)

But there is another tradition of autobiography in America for which the Indian polarity was definitive. In this tradition, we have the autobiographies of Daniel Boone, Davey Crockett, Kit Carson, Jim Beckwourth, and Sam Houston.[16] Unlike "yankee" autobiography, the western tradition is restless, and, reflecting the split between "high" and "low" culture already hardening in the age of Jackson, explicitly anti-literary. The subjects of western autobiography are all "world-historical" chiefs whose public reputations, like that of Andrew Jackson himself, were first established by Indian-fighting. Yet these men, in comparison to the European or the easterner, seemed themselves to be "Indians," men of action not letters, hunters and warriors, not preachers or farmers, neither book-keepers nor book-writers. Nearly or wholly illiterate, they rejected the fall into writing and "civilization," and balked at cultivating either the field or the page. Defined by Indian War and voluntary or involuntary Indian Captivity, these western autobiographers did not settle down long enough to establish their texts in writing, which, as an act, they largely scorned. Invoking the "natural," oral tradition of the Indian, telling *coup* stories or tall tales, the western autobiographer lived his life apart from writing, going so far as to entrust its actual inscription to another.

Although the "real" Daniel Boone at least once carried a copy of Gulliver with him, as the story of the naming of Lulbegrud Creek attests, he was not, himself, interested in writing. If he kept notes for a story of his life, as he was urged, they have not survived. Fairly consistent in signing correspondence "your omble Sarvent," Boone, it would seem, attempted to pass "naturally" from diction to scription.[17] His was exactly the orthographical and grammatological theory Colonel Davey Crockett espoused in the "Preface" to his "Autobiography": "I despise this way of spelling contrary to nature. And as for grammar, it's pretty much a thing of nothing at last, after all the fuss that's made about it. . . ."[18]

But even Crockett had to acknowledge, as Boone before him had done in collaborating with John Filson, that the book of a man's life cannot be made strictly according to "nature." In Louis Renza's phrase, "Autobiography. . . transforms empirical facts into *art*ifacts."[19] Thus the western autobiographer encountered a problem different from any faced by his eastern counterpart. For, when the eastern autobiographer looked to Europe for a model of the self, he also found a formal model for his book. But, if the western autobiographer, looking to the Indian, found a valuable experiential model, he found no textual model whatever. The solution to this problem turned out to be submission to varying degrees of collaborative composition, where the "empirical," "natural," and "historical" "facts" of a man's life were the contribution of the nominal "subject" of the autobiographical book, while its "artifactuality," its "grammar," and "writing" were the contribution of one credentialled as the culture-bearer: the journalist-editor, or, in Crockett's scornful term, the "critic," ". . . a sort of vermin," finally, the book's "author" in the strictly etymological sense (*augere*) of one who augments as well as originates.[20]

Boone's "autobiography," the first of this western line, was actually written by John Filson, a Pennsylvania schoolmaster saturated in eighteenth-century biographical conventions. Crockett insisted of his "autobiography" that "the whole book is my own, and every sentiment and sentence in it." Yet he "would not be such a fool, or knave either, as to deny that I have had it hastily run over by a friend or so, and that some little alterations have been made in the spelling and grammar." Perhaps the book "is the worse of even that"; still, there is no avoiding "a little correcting of the spelling and the grammar to make them fit for use."[21] To make the book of Kit Carson's life "fit for use" took very nearly an absolute division of compositional labor, for Carson could neither read nor write. Approaching the Indian in incomprehensibility, Carson spoke a language "markedly" different, according to M.M. Quaife, "from ordinary literary [sic] English," and expressed his "sentiments" in a "patois" common to mountain men.[22] Sam Houston's autobiography required the mediation of C.E. Lester to be achieved; and James Beckwourth, born of mixed black and white parentage, who rose to the status of War Chief of the Crow, returning to Euramerican ways and to autobiography, required the aid of T.D. Bonner for the book of his life. Thus Eastern Indian biography with its orientation to "historical justice" through the textual representation of individual Indian lives provided the motive force for Indian autobiography, while western autobiography with its discovery of composite authorship provided the solution to its formal problem.

After the passage of the Indian Removal Act, William Hagan writes,

> *Most of the tribes were prevailed upon to remove by the routine methods of persuasion or bribery or threats, or some combination of these. The three exceptions were a band of confederated Sacs and Foxes, the Creeks, and the Seminoles. Back in 1804 the Sacs and Foxes had signed a treaty under suspicious circumstances at the request of Governor Harrison. It provided for a cession of their lands east of the Mississippi, but did not require removal until the line of settlement reached them. Most of the tribesmen were ignorant of their situation until in the late 1820s peremptory demands were made on them to move. Then a faction led by old war chief Black Hawk, who had opposed the Americans in the War of 1812 and had subsequently plagued government agents by his conservative policies, denied the validity of the 1804 treaty.*[23]

Eventually, in April of 1832, the Black Hawk "War" broke out, a fifteen-week affair in which large numbers of Illinois militia (among them the young Abraham Lincoln), together with detachments of federal troops, decimated and demoralized Black Hawk's band sufficiently to induce the chief's surrender. Following months of imprisonment at Jefferson Barracks (where Catlin among others came to preserve him on canvas), Black Hawk was brought before his contemporary, the Great War Chief of the whites, Old Hickory, Andrew Jackson. After their meeting, apparently unaware of the partial coincidence of their routes, the two warriors set out on a tour of the East where both Black Hawk and the President received, to borrow Davey Crockett's phrase, "much custom." Black Hawk was briefly detained at Fortress Monroe, and then returned to his people on the Rock River. It was at this time, according to Antoine LeClair, the government interpreter for the Sacs and Foxes, that Black Hawk approached him and did "express a great desire to have a History of his Life written and published."[24]

Although he was highly regarded by both Indians and whites as an interpreter, and reputedly competent in some dozen native languages, LeClair did not speak English as his own first language. For this (or some other) reason, he engaged the assistance of young J.B. Patterson, editor of the Galena, Illinois *Galenian*. And it was Patterson, in the role of Black Hawk's "Editor" and "amanuensis," who actually "wrote" the "History" of Black Hawk's "Life" from LeClair's translation of Black Hawk's dictation.

In a prefatory "Advertisement" from the "Editor," Patterson writes, "It is presumed no apology will be required for presenting to the public, the life of a Hero who has lately taken such high rank among the distinguished individuals of America." The first part of this is entirely conventional and parallels Thatcher's opening statement: "The Author does not propose an elaborate explanation, nor an apology of any kind, for the benefit of the following work."[25] But the proposal of Black Hawk's life as a "Hero's" life goes beyond Thatcher whose Indians, "remarkable characters,"— as his title page puts it,—though they may have been, are not yet "heros." Moreover, although they are "individuals who have been distinguished among the North American natives," this is not necessarily to give them "high rank among the distinguished individuals of America" as a whole. Patterson goes beyond Thatcher not only in permitting Black Hawk the context of heroism and national distinction, but also in relinquishing his claim to the full authority of the "Author" for the more limited power of editorship. Thus, on the title page of each Indian autobiography there appears that fraternal couple so frequently invoked by the American imagination, the White Man and the Indian—Natty Bumppo and Chingachgook, Ishmael and Queequeg, the Lone Ranger and Tonto—but with a difference. For the claim of Indian autobiography is that the white man is silent while the Indian, no longer a mute or monosyllabic figure, speaks for himself.

Patterson's relation to Black Hawk replicates Filson's relation to Boone, and it is indicative of the West's "literary reconciliation to identification with the Indian" that there is extended the graphological supplement, the distinctive property of "civilization," not only to the Indian-like white frontiersman but to Indian "nature" itself.[26] In this way, Black Hawk, no less than the great Boone himself, may speak his "life" in "writing."

The formal similarity of western autobiography and Indian autobiography may be extended to a functional similarity, as well—but only to a point. Both, that is, function to affirm the central authority of American progressivist ideology, offering testimony to the inevitable replacement of "savagery" by "civilization." Filson's Boone concludes his "autobiography," saying:

> . . . I now live in peace and safety, enjoying the sweets of liberty, and the bounties of Providence, with my once fellow-sufferers, in this delightful country, which I have seen purchased with a vast expence of blood and treasure, delighting in the prospect of its being, in a short time, one of the most opulent and powerful states on the continent of North-America; which with the love and gratitude of my country-men, I esteem a sufficient reward for all my toil and dangers.[27]

Boone's life and his book are evidence that the long knife and long rifle are adequate to the work of "civilization," driving the "savage" out and transforming the "wilderness" into "one of the most opulent and powerful states on the continent of North-America." Black Hawk concludes his "autobiography" with the assurance that "the white man will always be welcome in our village or camps, as a brother. . . and may the watch-word between Americans and Sacs and Foxes, ever be—'Friendship'!" (153–54) But these are not the words of a man basking in success and looking forward to glory; rather, as Black Hawk has announced in the "Dedication" of his book to Brigadier General H. Atkinson, his "conqueror," they are the words of one who is "now an obscure member of a nation, that formerly honored and respected [his] opinions . . .," one who hopes "you may never experience the humility that the power of the American government has reduced me to. . . ." Admitting "the power of the American government," Indian autobiography takes its place beside western autobiography in a discourse of *assujetissement*.

Whereas victory is the enabling condition of western autobiography, defeat is the enabling condition of Indian autobiography. The narrative of the life of the western hero follows the "emplotment" of American "history" as the nineteenth century conceived it, and is figured as "comedy," the just progression to a "happy ending" in which the redskinned "blocking characters" are overcome. "The society emerging at the conclusion of comedy," as Frye has written, "represents . . . a kind of moral norm, or pragmatically free society."[28] And so it is in *The Autobiography of Daniel Boone*. Its structure is not only determined by the "facts" of Boone's "life," nor even strictly—in Hayden White's terms—by the pregeneric figural preferences of John Filson, but by the authority and discipline of discourse. In the same way, the narrative of the "life" of the Indian "hero" can only be structured in a manner consistent with the "tragic" mythos of decline-and-fall (which proposes the curiosity of the *heldensleben* as prisoner-of-war narrative). For it is only when the Indian "subject" of an "autobiography" acknowledges his defeat, when he becomes what Patterson calls a "State-prisoner," that he can appear as a "hero." Even as a

"State-prisoner," Patterson writes, in his "Advertisement," "in every situation [Black Hawk] is still the Chief of his Band [but he has been superceded by Keokuk], asserting their rights with dignity, fairness, and courage." Perhaps; yet it is only as a "State-prisoner" that he can "assert" anything at all, or be "allowed to make known to the world the injuries his people have received from the whites. . . ." Thus the narrative, in Patterson's final determination of it, confirms the inevitability of Indian defeat in the manner of western autobiography: but it also strongly questions its "justice" in the manner of eastern Indian biography. According to Patterson, Black Hawk "thinks justice is not done to himself or nation" in hitherto-published accounts of the "War" (although Black Hawk could not actually have read them), and part of the motive force behind the Black Hawk- (LeClair-) Patterson collaboration is the performance of an act of textual "justice." Patterson includes many instances of the "injuries" done to Black Hawk and his people, and, speaking in his own voice, he explicitly criticizes the Treaty of 1804. Patterson also draws back from full responsibility for anything in the book that may seem to the "whites" too-strong criticism of their behavior. The concluding paragraph of his "Advertisement" announces that "The Editor has written this work according to the dictation of Black Hawk, through the United States Interpreter, at the Sac and Fox Agency of Rock Island. He does not, therefore, consider himself responsible for any of the facts or views, contained in it. . . ."

Rather than weakening the oppositional force of this first Indian autobiography, Patterson's disclaimer may, instead, point to its very essence, the unprecedented instance of an Indian speaking for himself. Unlike the eastern Indian-biographer, Patterson did not make his book from the safe distance of Boston or New York, nor was his "subject" the "Life and Times" of some bygone noble barbarian. Patterson was an Illinoisian, who wrote from Rock Island only a year after the Black Hawk "War." In just five more years, even a western Indian-biographer could echo Thatcher and the ministers of Boston on the Indians; in a biography of Black Hawk published in Cincinnati in 1838, Benjamin Drake wrote, "Have we not more frequently met [the Indians] in bad faith than in a Christian spirit?" And Drake accepted full responsibility for his book's purpose, "to awaken the public mind to a sense of the wrongs inflicted on the Indians."[29]

I would not minimize the efforts of Samuel Drake, B.B. Thatcher, or Benjamin Drake to do "justice" to the Indian in writing. Yet unlike Patterson, these men adopted the biographical, not the autobiographical form which, whatever its author's intentions, cannot help but function in support of the belief that the "savage" has no intelligible voice of his own, that the "civilized" man of letters must speak for him if he is to be heard at all. The Indian biographer, master of books and writing, required no "contact" with his "subject"; he had no need to enter into a "reciprocal relationship" with him. According to Samuel Drake, his *Indian Biography* takes "much of" its material "from manuscripts never before published"; its title page is adorned with a verse from Byron, and, interestingly, a verse of Isaiah from what it calls the "Indian Bible," no native product but the white man's gift to the red.[30] Appropriately, Drake's book is published by "Josiah Drake at the Antiquarian

Bookstore," first established in 1830, the year of the Indian Removal Bill. Thatcher, too, is almost entirely indebted to the "archive" for his work, like Drake exploiting the resources of the Antiquarian Bookstore, as well as materials from the Harvard Library, and other collections.

Turning to books not to Indians, Drake and Thatcher retained their "exteriority" and kept the full author-ity of the author not as augmentor but as originator. Although the Indian biographer approached the *impensé*, the epistemic unthinkable of the period, when he suggested that Indians "must" "vanish" only if the constant "wrongs inflicted" on them forced them to "vanish," he never went so far as to grant the Indian the right to speak for himself. Whatever injustices and injuries he protested, he was not yet able to protest in the actual form of his work what DeLeuze has called the indignity of speaking for others. With all his sympathy for the Indian, the Indian biographer still defined him as he would be defined by Robert Frost's murderous Miller, in "The Vanishing Red," as "one who had no right to be heard from."

But it is the central convention of autobiography that its "subject" speaks for himself. Black Hawk may speak in Patterson's presence, but "The Editor," as we have noted, "does not . . . consider himself responsible" for what is said. As discursive equivalent of the "frontier," the textual ground on which two cultures meet, the Indian autobiography requires "contact" between its "subject-author" and its "editor-author," and a relationship which, if it is unequal, is nonetheless genuinely reciprocal. Only by submitting to the Euramerican form of "autobiography" could Black Hawk speak to the whites at all; only by accepting the graphematic supplement of the "editor" and the fall into "writing" and "culture" could Black Hawk achieve the book of his life, whose final form was not his to determine. Yet an Indian autobiography could be achieved by no white alone; only by acknowledging reciprocity, reducing himself to the status of "editor," and entering into "contact" with Black Hawk could Patterson "write" the book of an Indian life: a book in which a still-living and formerly-unheard voice emerged to speak for itself, thus questioning the very discipline, authority, and form which enabled it to speak. And this Indian voice—translated, transcribed, edited, polished, interpreted, thoroughly mediated as it may be—had not sounded before either in western autobiography (hostile to it although indebted to it), or in eastern Indian biography (sympathetic to it, but formally indifferent to it).

Patterson's *Life of Black Hawk* was sufficiently popular to justify four more editions the following year in the East, and, after many years, an edition published in St. Louis in 1882.[31] For this, the last edition published in Patterson's lifetime, the "editor and sole proprietor," as he then called himself, provided some revisions of the text, expanding certain descriptions and elaborating the diction. For these changes, Patterson alone must be held responsible, Black Hawk having died in 1838. The 1882 edition also received a new title, for the "Life" now became *The Autobiography of Ma-Ka-Tai-Me-She-Kia-Kiak*. Subsequent editions have tended to use the 1882 title although reprinting the 1833 text as closer inevitably to Black Hawk's "own words." Despite this continued interest in Patterson's work, the remaining years of the nineteenth century present no other fully developed instance of Indian autobiography, a genre of American writing compositely author-ed, ambiguously authorized, complicatedly transmitted, dual in its discursive function, and problematic in its discursive type. Nonetheless, Patterson's *Black Hawk* offers a model for a very considerable number of Indian autobiographies, which, in the discourse of "history" and of "science," proliferate in the twentieth century.

NOTES

[1]James M. Cox, "Autobiography and America," in *Aspects of Narrative: Selected Papers from the English Institute*, ed. J. Hillis Miller (New York: Columbia University Press, 1971), p. 145.

[2]George and Louise Spindler, "American Indian Personality Types and their Sociocultural Roots," *Annals of the American Academy of Political and Social Science* 311 (1957), quoted by Harold E. Driver, *Indians of North America*, 2nd ed., rev. (Chicago: The University of Chicago Press, 1975), p. 434.

[3]In this way I intend to distinguish Indian autobiographies from autobiographies-by-Indians, in which, although a bi-cultural element is present, the element of composite composition is not. With the exception of Wolf-Killer's *Ploughed Under: the Story of an Indian Chief Told by Himself* (New York, 1881), the few nineteenth-century autobiographies-by-Indians are by avowedly Christian Indians. *Cf.*, William Apes, *A Son of the Forest* (New York, 1829), and George Copway, *The Life, History, and Travels of Kah-Ge-Ga-Gah-Bowh* (Philadelphia, 1847). See also the extraordinary *Sketch of the Life of Okah Tubbee, alias William Chubbee* by Laah Ceil Mannatoi Elaah Tubbee, his wife (Springfield, Massachusetts, 1848): this work, compositely authored but not bi-culturally, falls somewhere between Indian autobiography and autobiography-by-an-Indian, and might be listed among the "as-told-to" autobiographies.

In the twentieth century, autobiographies by "civilized" or Christian Indians include those by Dr. Charles Eastman (Ohiyesa), beginning with *Indian Boyhood* (Boston: McClure, Phillips, and Co., 1902); Joseph Griffis (Chief Tahan), *Tahan: Out of Savagery into Civilization* (New York: Doran, 1915); Chief Buffalo Child Long Lance, *Long Lance* (New York: Cosmopolitan Book Corporation, 1928); and Luther Standing Bear, *My Indian Boyhood* (Boston: Houghton, Mifflin, 1928). It is in relation to this substantial tradition of autobiography-by-Indians that recent work like N. Scott Momaday's *The Names: A Memoir* (New York: Harper and Row, 1974) needs to be examined. In spite of its pride in Indian culture and criticism of Euramerican culture, *The Names,* along with Momaday's earlier "autobiography," *The Way to Rainy Mountain* (Albuquerque: University of New Mexico Press, 1969) employs Euramerican forms. I see no difference in Momaday's attempt to find a "new" form for his experience from a long line of "modernist" experimentation. Autobiographies-by-Indians might also be considered as a genre of American writing whose problematics relate to those of the Indian autobiography.

The many "as-told-to" autobiographies which have appeared in the twentieth century I class among "autobiography-by-Indians" rather than Indian autobiographies because of the competence with written English of their subjects who take responsibility for the "form" of the work to a degree impossible to the Indian subjects of Indian autobiography. Here, because we face a difference of degree rather than kind, is where most of the debatable cases fall. Among "as-told-to" autobiographies are: Delphina Cuero: *The Autobiography of Delphina Cuero: A Diegueño Indian,* as told to Florence C. Shipek (Los Angeles: Dawson's Book Shop, 1968); Helen Sekaquaptewa, *Me and Mine: The Life Story of Helen Sekaquaptewa,* as told to Louise Udall (Tucson: University of Arizona Press, 1969); Carl Sweezy, *The Arapaho Way: A Memoir of an Indian Boyhood,* as told to Althea Bass (New York: Clarkson N. Potter, 1966); Elizabeth White (Polingaysi Qoyawayma), *No Turning Back,* as told to Vada D. Carlson (Albuquerque: University of New Mexico Press, 1964); and John (Fire) Lame Deer and Richard Erdoes, *Lame Deer, Seeker of Visions* (New York: Simon and Shuster, 1972).

Frank Linderman's portraits of Plenty-Coups (*American: The Life Story of a Great Indian, Plenty Coups, Chief of the Crows,* [New York: John Day, 1930]; rpt. *Plenty-Coups, Chief of the Crows* [Lincoln: The University of Nebraska Press, 1962]) and of Pretty-Shield (*Red Mother* [New York: John Day, 1932]; rpt. *Pretty-Shield: Medicine Woman of the Crows* [New York: John Day, 1972]) are a mixed form somewhere between Indian autobiographies and Indian biographies (see below, note 20). Linderman's "subjects" are Indians who speak for themselves but there is no pretense of white authorial absence. In the terms developed later in this paper, Linderman's books are "reciprocal" works which attempt to document "cultural contact" outside of the context of domination: domination, nonetheless, had already been achieved. L.V. McWhorter's fine *Yellow Wolf: His Own Story* (Caldwell, Idaho: Caxton Printers, 1940) belongs in this more nearly egalitarian category. More recently, see Vincent Crapanzano's *The Fifth World of Forster Bennet: Portrait of a Navaho* (New York: Viking-Compass, 1972), which, its "author" freely admits, "may reveal more of him than of the Navaho" (p. v).

[4]Tzvetan Todorov, *The Fantastic: A Structural Approach to a Literary Genre,* trans. Richard Howard (Ithaca, N.Y.: Cornell University Press, 1975), p. 3.

[5]James Axtell, "The Ethnohistory of Early America: A Review Essay," *The William and Mary Quarterly* 35, no. 1 (January, 1978): 116.

[6]Edward Said, "The Problem of Textuality: Two Exemplary Positions," *Critical Inquiry* 4, no. 4 (1978): 675 and 709n.

[7]*Cf.* Francis Jennings, *The Invasion of America: Indians, Colonialism, and the Cant of Conquest* (New York: Norton, 1976).

[8]*Cf.* Roy Harvey Pearce, *Savagism and Civilization* (Baltimore: The Johns Hopkins Press, 1967), originally published in 1953 as *The Savages of America: A Study of the Indian and the Idea of Civilization,* chapter four, "The Zero of Human Society: the Idea of the Savage."

[9]Ambrose Bierce, *The Devil's Dictionary* (New York: Dover, 1958), p. 7. Bierce wrote his definitions between 1881 and 1906.

[10]Quoted by Marjorie Halpin in her introduction to Catlin's *Letters and Notes on the Manners, Customs, and Conditions of North American Indians,* vol. 1 (New York: Dover, 1973), p. ix. Catlin's work was first published in London in 1844.

[11]A.D. Coleman in an introduction to Edward S. Curtis, *Portraits from North American Indian Life* (n.p.: A & W Visual library, 1972), p. v. Curtis' work was

originally published in a limited edition of five hundred sets (priced at three thousand dollars each) in 1907–8.

[12]William Fenton in his introduction to B.B. Thatcher's *Indian Biography* (Glorieta, N.M.: The Rio Grande Press, 1973), unpaged. This is a reprint of the New York edition of 1832; an edition appeared in Boston in the same year.

[13]Ibid. Further quotations from Thatcher are taken from this preface. Indian biography has a venerable tradition in American writing. I know of no systematic study of this genre and here I give only a sketch which others may expand. One might begin with Matthew Mayhew's *A Brief Narrative of the Success which the Gospel hath had, among the Indians of Martha's Vineyard (and the Places Adjacent) in New England* (Boston, 1694), and Daniel Gookin's frequently consulted *Historical Collections of the Indians in New England,* compiled in 1674 but not published until 1792. Focus on a single individual occurs with Samuel Moody's *A Summary Account of the Life and Death of Joseph Quasson, Indian* (Boston, 1726), and Samson Occom's brief "Life of Moses Paul," which concludes "A Sermon Preached at the Execution of Moses Paul, an Indian" (New London, 1772). In the eighteenth century there is also Experience Mayhew's *Indian Converts* (London, 1727). The first Indian biography of the nineteenth century is the *Memoir of Catherine Brown, a Christian Indian of the Cherokee Nation* by Rufus Anderson, A.M. (Boston, 1825). Near the end of the decade of Indian Removal, Indian biographies proliferate with Benjamin Drake's *Life of Black Hawk* (Cincinnati, 1838) cited in the text above, and his *Life of Tecumseh and of his brother the Prophet, with a historical sketch of the Shawanoe Indians* (Cincinnati, 1841). In the line of Samuel Drake and Thatcher is Samuel E. Goodrich's *Lives of Celebrated American Indians* (Boston, 1843). O.N. Matson recorded the life of Chief Shaubena of the Peoria and Galena Indians (who refused to join Black Hawk's rebellion) in 1836 but did not publish his book until more than forty years later: O.N. Matson, *Memories of Shaubena* (Chicago, 1878).

In the twentieth century, a listing of Indian biographies would be long indeed, all the great chiefs appearing in one or more accounts. Stanley Vestal, Mari Sandoz, and Grant Foreman are important Indian biographers, along with, more recently, Anthony Wallace on Teedyuscung and Handsome Lake. There are also a number of Indian biographies by Indians: see Arthur Parker's biography of his great-uncle, *The Life of General Ely S. Parker: Last Grand Sachem of the Iroquois and General Grant's Military Secretary,* Buffalo Historical Society Publications, vol. 23 (Buffalo, New York: Buffalo Historical Society, 1919), and of *Red Jacket: Last of the Senecas* (New York: McGraw, Hill, 1952); and John M. Oskison's *Tecumseh and his Times: The Story of a Great Indian* (New York: Putnam's, 1938).

[14]*Cf.* Richard Slotkin, *Regeneration Through Violence: The Mythology of the American Frontier, 1600–1860* (Middletown, Conn.: Wesleyan University Press, 1974), especially chapters 9 and 10.

[15]Louis O. Mink, "Narrative Form as a Cognitive Instrument," in *The Writing of History: Literary Form and Historical Understanding,* eds. R.H.Canary and Henry Kozicki (Madison: University of Wisconsin Press, 1978), p. 138.

[16]See John Filson, *The Discovery, Settlement and Present State of Kentucke* which includes as an appendix, "The Adventures of Colonel Daniel Boon, one of the first Settlers, etc." (Gloucester, Mass.: Peter Smith, 1975), originally published in Wil-

mington, Delaware in 1784; *A Narrative of the Life of David Crockett of the State of Tennessee, Written by Himself,* ed. Joseph J. Arpad (New Haven: College and University Press, 1972), originally published in Philadelphia in 1834; *Kit Carson's Autobiography,* ed. with an introduction by M.M. Quaife (Chicago: Lakeside Press, 1935; rpt. Lincoln: Bison Books-University of Nebraska Press, n.d.) originally published late 1858 or early 1859 in New York; *The Life of Sam Houston of Texas,* unsigned, by Charles Edwards Lester, under Houston's supervision (New York, 1855), also the *Life of General Sam Houston. A Short Autobiography* (Austin, Tex.: The Pemberton Press, 1964), originally published in 1855; and T.D. Bonner, *The Life and Adventures of James P. Beckwourth* (New York: Arno Press, 1969), originally published in New York in 1856.

[17]Quoted in John Bakeless, *Daniel Boone: Master of the Wilderness* (New York: William Morrow, 1939), *passim.*

[18]In the preface to Crockett, *Narrative,* p. 47.

[19]Louis P. Renza, "The Veto of the Imagination: A Theory of Autobiography," *New Literary History* 9, no. 1 (1977): 2. Renza's sentence concludes: autobiography "is definable as a form of 'prose fiction.'"

[20]Crockett, *Narrative,* p. 47.

[21]Ibid., pp. 47–48.

[22]In his introduction to *Kit Carson's Autobiography,* pp. xxvii–xxviii.

[23]William T. Hagan, *American Indians,* rev. edition (Chicago: University of Chicago Press, 1979), p. 72.

[24]Translator's preface to *Black Hawk, an autobiography,* ed. by Donald Jackson (Urbana: University of Illinois Press, 1964), unpaged. The full title of the original 1833 edition published at Cincinnati is the *Life of Ma-Ka-Tai-Me-She-Kia-Kiak or Black Hawk, embracing the Tradition of his Nation—Indian Wars in which he has been engaged—Cause of joining the British in their late War with America, and its History—Description of the Rock-River Village—Manners and Customs—Encroachments by the Whites, Contrary to Treaty—Removal from his Village in 1831. With an Account of the Cause and General History of the Late War, his Surrender and Confinement at Jefferson Barracks, and Travels through the United States. Dictated by Himself.* All quotations are from Jackson's edition in which the translator's preface, Black Hawk's dedication, and the editor's advertisement, are unpaged. Page references will be given in the text.

[25]Preface to Thatcher, *Indian Biography,* unpaged.

[26]Slotkin, *Regeneration,* p. 426.

[27]Filson, *State of Kentucke,* pp. 81–82.

[28]"Emplotment" is Hayden White's term for the large structures Frye would probably call "myths," as they appear in the narratives of "history." See Hayden White, *Metahistory: The Historical Imagination in Nineteenth-Century Europe* (Baltimore: the Johns Hopkins Press, 1973), and "The Historical Text as Literary Artifact," in Canary and Kozicki, eds., *The Writing of History.* The quotations from Frye are from the *Anatomy of Criticism* (New York: Atheneum, 1965), pp. 169ff.

[29]Benjamin F. Drake, *The Life and Adventures of Black Hawk* (Cincinnati, 1838), pp. 20–21.

[30]From the title page of the first edition, Boston, 1832.

[31]Two editions in Boston in 1834; one in Philadelphia in 1834, together with an

account of "a Lady who was taken prisoner by the Indians"; and one in New York in 1834. Other editions: London, 1836; Cooperstown, 1842; Boston, 1845; Leeuwarden, Netherlands, 1847 (this is listed in Sabin, *Bibliotheca Americana: Dictionary of Books Relating to America from its Discovery to the Present Time* [New York, 1868; rpt. New York: Mini-Print Corp., n.d.] under LeClair's pseudonym "R. Postumus"); Cincinnati, 1858; Chicago, 1916; and Iowa City, 1932.

BIBLIOGRAPHICAL APPENDIX

To aid further study of the Indian autobiography, I have put together the following brief bibliography of works constituted by the principle of bi-cultural composite composition. Black Hawk's *Life* is the paradigmatic instance in that its authorial division of labor is very nearly absolute: Black Hawk cannot "write" either English or a phonetic alphabet of his own language (he doesn't speak English either); and Patterson does not speak the Indian language. It might also be added that both Black Hawk and Patterson are "naive"—that is to say, un-self-conscious—representatives of their respective cultures, only newly marked by contact and so any reciprocal acculturation. But the rest of our Indian autobiographies were written in the twentieth century, and, in a large majority of cases, by professional anthropologists, some of whom did have a lesser or greater command of the native languages of their subjects. And many of the Indian subjects could both speak and write some English, even composing parts of the text of their autobiographies themselves. I have included these among Indian autobiographies when—as with several of the early Carlisle students like Jason Betzinez and Samuel Kenoi—there seems to be evidence that competence in English, particularly its written forms, is minimal so that white editorial responsibility persists in being of major importance to the final text. This is a judgment call; as I have indicated in the notes above, the line between as-told-to-autobiographies-by-Indians and Indian autobiographies is a fine one and criteria for establishing it are inexact. Indeed, the distinction has not seemed important to anthropological cataloguers of "life histories" in search of "scientific materials," as if these could be detached from the formal conditions of their textual existence. For the student of "literature," however, the distinction, although problematic, needs to be kept.

The Indian autobiographies I have listed are of different lengths but all offer a measure of detail about several aspects of the subject's life experience, e.g., birth and childhood, visions and dreams, war, work, love and marriage, travels, although they may develop no more than a couple of these. On the ground that it does not offer this kind of life experience, I have excluded the text now called (as it has been at least since 1907 when it appeared in *Northwestern Fights and Fighters,* by Cyrus Townsend Brady [The McClure Company: n.p., 1907; rpt. Cornerhouse Publishers, Williamstown, Mass., 1974]) "Chief Joseph's Own Story." There is not much in this of Joseph's own life or even of the life—the culture—of his people; rather, as the original title makes clear, this is "An Indian's Views of Indian Affairs" (*North American Review* 128 [1879]: 412–33), particularly the affairs leading to what is known in American history as the Flight of the Nez Perce. That earlier historical affair, the uprising of the Minnesota Sioux in 1862 gave rise to the "Narrative of Paul Mazakootemane" (*Minnesota Historical Society Collections* 3 [1870–80]: 82–90) and "A Sioux Story of the War" by Jerome Big Eagle (Wambde-Tonka) (*Minnesota Historical Society Collections* 6 [1894]: 382–400). Because, like Chief Joseph's story, these are focused almost exclusively on "history," they, too, have been excluded. Yet I have listed Samuel Kenoi's "A Chiricahua Apache's Account of the Geronimo Campaign of 1886" (*q.v.*) precisely because it does give what S.M. Barrett claimed for Geronimo's story of his life (*q.v.*) "an authentic record of the private life of the Apache Indians," and of Kenoi's own life both before and after the events of 1886. Paul Mazakootemane's "Narrative" is also excluded for the further reason that it is by an avidly Christian Indian, "a member and an office-bearer in [Christ's] church," who wrote specifically to "the American people who are my friends." As indicated in the notes above, I have considered works by Christian Indians autobiographies-by-Indians rather than Indian autobiographies. The listing which follows contains one exception, however. Gilbert Wilson's *Goodbird the Indian* (*q.v.*) is the story of a Christian Indian, with a pitch for salvation and civilization as part of its conclusion. Yet it seemed to me—as it had to earlier and more competent judges like Clyde Kluckhohn—that the bulk of Edward Goodbird's story conveyed quite an "authentic record" of a traditional Hidatsa life; in view, also, of Wilson's influence on the text, it seemed to have as good a claim to generic status among Indian autobiographies as among autobiographies-by-Indians.

One further explanation of an omission: I have not included Joseph White Bull's *The Warrior Who Killed Custer: The Personal Narrative of Chief Joseph White Bull,* ed. James H. Howard (The University of Nebraska Press: Lincoln, 1968) because, in the form we have the text, it does not comprise a continuous narrative. White Bull actually wrote his story (he also drew some of it) in the alphabet developed for Dakota by Bishop Riggs for his Dakota-English dictionary of 1890. Howard transcribed White Bull's writing page by page, reproduced the drawings, and provided an English translation together with commentary and notes between the pages, thus making it impossible to read White Bull's narrative consecutively— although also making clear what is White Bull's and what is Howard's. The status of notes and commentary less obtrusively but nonetheless firmly appended to many Indian autobiographies by their editors is interesting to consider in regard to our attempt to achieve the "literary" reading I have suggested as most appropriate to these works. I will only raise, but not pursue, this matter here.

I have worked from bibliographies compiled by Clyde Kluckhohn in *The Use of Personal Documents in History, Anthropology, and Sociology,* ed. Louis Gottschalk, Clyde Kluckhohn, and Robert Angell, Social Science Research Council, Bulletin no. 53, (1945); L.L. Langness in *The Life History in Anthropological Science* (Holt, Rinehart, and Winston: New York, 1965); Lynne Woods O'Brien in *Plains Indian Autobiographies,* Boise State College Western Writers Series, no. 10, (1973); L.H. Butterfield, Wilcomb E. Washburn, and William Fenton in *American Indian and White Relations to 1830: Needs and Opportunities for Study* (University of North Carolina Press: Chapel Hill, 1957); and used Arlene Hirschfelder's *American Indian and Eskimo Authors* (Association on American Indian Affairs: New York, 1973), and Jack Marken's *The American Indian: Language and Literature* (AHM Publishing Corporation: Arlington Heights, Ill., 1978), adding the very rare item I discovered that had slipped these bibliographers' notice (but passing over materials from

Alaska). *A Bibliography of Native American Writers: 1776–1924,* by Daniel Littlefield, Jr. and James W. Parins, (Scarecrow Press: Metuchen, N.J., 1981), and H. David Brumble's *An Annotated Bibliography of American Indian and Eskimo Autobiographies* (The University of Nebraska Press: Lincoln, 1981) appeared while my much more selective list was in press.

Bibliographical information appears under the name of the work's Indian subject, not its white editor: this decision must be acknowledged to rest on purely moral grounds, for the Indian autobiography requires both Native American and Euramerican participation and is precisely not possible except as the product of both. Yet it seemed more nearly just to do it this way.

Anonymous Acoma Indian. "Autobiography of an Acoma Indian." Edited by Leslie White. In *New Material from Acoma. Bureau of American Ethnology* Bulletin 136 (1943): 326–37.

Anonymous Arapaho Woman. "Narrative of an Arapaho Woman." Edited by Truman Michelson. *American Anthropologist* 35 (1933): 595–610.

Anonymous Cheyenne Old Man. "A Cheyenne Old Man," transcribed from a 1927 interview. In *Cheyenne and Sioux: The Reminiscences of Four Indians and a White Soldier,* compiled by Thomas B. Marquis. Edited by Ronald Limbaugh. Pacific Center for Western Historical Studies, *Monograph 3* (1973).

Anonymous Fox Woman. "The Autobiography of a Fox Woman." Edited by Truman Michelson. Bureau of American Ethnology, *Annual Report* 40: 1918–1919 (1925), 291–349.

Anonymous Southern Cheyenne Woman. "The Narrative of a Southern Cheyenne Woman." Edited by Truman Michelson. *Smithsonian Miscellaneous Collections,* 87: 5 (1932): 13.

Badger, Tom. "Reminiscences of a Chippewa Mide Priest." Edited by Victor Barnouw. *Wisconsin Archaeologist* 35: 4 (1954): 83–112.

Ball, Eve. See Kaywaykla.

Barnouw, Victor. See Badger.

Barrett, S.M. See Geronimo.

Betzinez, Jason, with Wilber S. Nye. *I Fought with Geronimo.* New York: Bonanza-Crown, 1959.

Black Eagle. "Xube, a Ponca Autobiography." Edited by William Whitman. *Journal of American Folklore* 52 (1939): 180–93.

Black Elk. *Black Elk Speaks, being the life story of a holy man of the Oglala Sioux,* as told to John G. Neihardt. New York: William Morrow, 1932; rpt. Lincoln: Bison-University of Nebraska Press, 1961. This edition changed "to" to "through" at the "author's request," and was re-issued New York: Pocket Books-Simon and Schuster, 1972. A further edition from Nebraska (1979) prints some new related material, and adds an introduction by Vine Deloria, Jr.

Black Hawk. *The Life of Ma-Ka-Tai-Me-She-Kia-Kiak, or Black Hawk.* Edited by J.B. Patterson. Cincinnati, 1833. Most recent edition: *Black Hawk, an autobiography.* Edited by Donald Jackson. Urbana: University of Illinois Press, 1964.

Bonnerjea, Biren. See Red Eagle.

Brant, Charles. See Whitewolf.

Chona, Maria. "Autobiography of a Papago Woman." Edited by Ruth Underhill. The American Anthropological Association, *Memoirs* 46 (1936): 64; rpt. New York: Kraus Reprint Corp., 1971.

Collins, June. See Fornsby.

Crashing Thunder. *Crashing Thunder: the autobiography of an American Indian.* Edited by Paul Radin. New York: Appleton, 1926. This is a revised and considerably expanded version of the work listed under S.B.

————. "Personal Reminiscences of a Winnebago Indian." Edited by Paul Radin. *Journal of American Folklore* 26 (1913): 293–318. Text in English and Winnebago.

Dyk, Walter. See Left-Handed, and Old Mexican.

Fools Crow, Frank. *Fools Crow.* Edited by Thomas E. Mails, assisted by Dallas Chief Eagle. New York: Discus-Avon-Doubleday, 1979.

Fornsby, John. "John Fornsby: The Personal Document of a Coast Salish Indian." Edited by June Collins. In *Indians of the Urban Northwest.* Edited by Marian W. Smith. *Columbia University Contributions to Anthropology* 36 (1949); rpt. New York: AMS Press, 1969.

Geronimo. *Geronimo's Story of his Life,* taken down and edited by S.M. Barrett. New York: Duffield, 1906; rpt. Williamstown, Mass.: Corner House Publishers, 1973. See also the slightly abridged paperback edition with an introduction and notes by Frederick W. Turner, III. New York: Ballantine-Random House, 1970.

Goodbird, Edward. *Goodbird, the Indian: His Story.* Edited by Gilbert L. Wilson. New York: Fleming H. Revell Co., 1914.

Good Shot, Oscar. "Oscar Good Shot, A Sioux Farmer." *Cheyenne and Sioux: The Reminiscences of Four Indians and a White Soldier,* compiled by Thomas B. Marquis. Edited by Ronald Limbaugh. Pacific Center for Western Historical Studies, *Monograph* 3, (1973). A condensed version appeared as "The Autobiography of a Sioux," in *Century Magazine* 113 (December, 1926): 182–88.

Iron Teeth. "Iron Teeth, A Cheyenne Old Woman. " *Cheyenne and Sioux: The Reminiscences of Four Indians and a White Soldier,* compiled by Thomas B. Marquis. Edited by Ronald Limbaugh. Pacific Center for Western Historical Studies, *Monograph* 3, (1973). A condensed version appeared as "Red Pipe's Squaw," in *Century Magazine* 118 (June, 1929): 201–9.

Kaywaykla, James. *In the Days of Victorio. Recollections of a Warm Springs Apache.* Edited by Eve Ball. Tucson: University of Arizona Press, 1970.

Kenoi, Samuel E. "A Chiricahua Apache's Account of the Geronimo Campaign of 1886." Edited by Morris E. Opler. *New Mexico Historical Review* 13 (1938): 360–86.

Kluckhohn, Clyde. See Mr. Moustache.

Left-Handed. *Son of Old Man Hat, A Navaho Autobiography.* Recorded by Walter Dyk, with an introduction by Edward Sapir. New York: Harcourt Brace, 1938; rpt. Lincoln: University of Nebraska Press, 1967.

Lowry, Annie. *Karnee: A Paiute Narrative.* Edited by Lalla Scott. Reno: University of Nevada Press, 1966.

Lurie, Nancy O. See Mountain Wolf Woman.

Mails, Thomas E. See Fools Crow.

Marquis, Thomas B. See Anonymous Cheyenne Old Man, Good Shot, Tangled Yellow Hair, Wooden Leg, Iron Teeth.

Michelson, Truman. See Anonymous Arapaho Woman, Anonymous Fox Woman, Anonymous Southern Cheyenne Woman.

Mountain Wolf Woman. *Mountain Wolf Woman: Sister of Crashing Thunder, The Autobiography of a Winnebago Indian.* Edited by Nancy O. Lurie. Ann Arbor: The University of Michigan Press, 1961.

Mr. Moustache. "A Navajo Personal Document with a Brief Paretian Analysis." Edited by Clyde Kluckhohn. *Southwestern Journal of Anthropology* 1 (1945): 260–83.

Murray, Edith V. A. See Young.

Nabokov, Peter. See Two-Leggings.

Neihardt, John G. See Black Elk.

Newland, Sam and Stewart, Jack. *Two Paiute Autobiographies,* as told to Julian H. Steward. University of California Publications in American Archaeology and Ethnology 33: 5 (1934): 423–38.

Nowell, Charles J. *Smoke from their Fires, the Life of a Kwakiutl Chief.* Edited by Clellan S. Ford. New Haven: Yale University Press, 1941; rpt. Hamden, Conn.: Archon Books, 1968.

Nye, Wilber S. See Betzinez.

Old Mexican. *Old Mexican, a Navajo Autobiography.* Edited by Walter Dyk. Viking Fund Publications in Anthropology, no. 8 (1947); rpt. New York: Johnson Reprint Corp., 1970.

Opler, Morris. See Kenoi.

Otterby, Thomas. See Red Eagle.

Patterson, J.B. See Black Hawk.

Radin, Paul. See Crashing Thunder, and S.B.

Red Eagle. "Reminiscences of a Cheyenne Indian." Edited by Biren Bonnerjea. *Journal de la Societé des Americanistes de Paris* 27 (1935): 129–43.

S.B. *The Autobiography of a Winnebago Indian.* Edited by Paul Radin. University of California Publications in American Archaeology and Ethnology, no. 16 (1920): 381–473. This is the Indian whose story Radin redoes as Crashing Thunder; he is the brother of the real Crashing Thunder, subject of Radin's 1913 "Personal Reniniscences of a Winnebago Indian."

Scott, Lalla. See Lowry.

Sewid, James. *Guests Never Leave Hungry: The Autobiography of James Sewid, A Kwakiutl Indian.* Edited by James P. Spradley. New Haven: Yale University Press, 1969.

Simmons, Leo. See Talayesva.

Spradley, James P. See Sewid.

Steward, Julian. See Newland, and Stewart.

Stewart, Jack and Newland, Sam. *Two Paiute Autobiographies,* as told to Julian H. Steward. University of California Publications in American Archaeology and Ethnology, vol. 33, no. 5 (1934): 424–38.

Tangled Yellow Hair, James. "James Tangled Yellow Hair, A Cheyenne Scout." *Cheyenne and Sioux: The Reminiscences of Four Indians and a White Soldier,* compiled by Thomas B. Marquis. Edited by Ronald Limbaugh, Pacific Center for Western Historical Studies, *Monograph* 3 (1973). From a 1927 interview.

Underhill, Ruth. See Chona.

Talayesva, Don. *Sun Chief: The Autobiography of a Hopi Indian.* Edited by Leo Simmons. New Haven: Yale University Press, 1942; rpt. Yale, 1970.

Two-Leggings. *Two Leggings: the Making of a Crow Warrior.* Edited by Peter Nabokov. New York: Thomas Crowell, 1967.

White, Leslie. See Anonymous Acoma Indian.

Whitewolf, Jim. *Jim Whitewolf: the Life of a Kiowa Apache.* Edited by Charles Brant. New York: Dover Books, 1969.

Whitman, William. See Black Eagle.

Wilson, Gilbert. See Goodbird.

Wooden Leg. *A Warrior Who Fought Custer.* Interpreted by Thomas B. Marquis. Minneapolis: The Midwest Co., 1931; rpt. Lincoln: The University of Nebraska Press, 1962.

Young, Lucy. "Out of the Past: A True Indian Story," as told to Edith V. A. Murray. *California Historical Society Quarterly* 20: 4 (December, 1941): 349–64.

H. David Brumble III: INDIAN SACRED MATERIALS: KROEBER, KROEBER, WATERS, AND MOMADAY

One of the threads that bind the bundle we are coming to call American Indian Literature is that of the Indian caught between two cultures; there are, to name but a few, Abel in Momaday's *House Made of Dawn,* Martiniano in Waters' *The Man Who Killed the Deer,* S.B. in Radin's *Autobiography of a Winnebago Indian,* and, in a muted way, the unnamed protagonist of Welch's *Winter in the Blood.* Probably this preoccupation with personal identity and the impingements of culture is one of the major reasons for the rising popularity of American Indian books in a country which is stirring its melting pot ever more gingerly. But as the protagonists of such books writhe about in the nets cultures weave, they might be comforted to know that their creators share some of their problems—that the nets are there for authors as well as for heroes.

One of the knottiest problems confronting these authors, Indian or white, is that of deciding upon which side of the culture line to take their narrative stance. Waters, for example, is one-quarter Indian, but, of course, white-educated. He is obviously in sympathy with the Hopis about whom he writes, but is he to write *as* an Indian, or *about* Indians? Waters is typical of many writers on Indian subjects in that he is fascinated by Indian religious and symbolic systems, but for many Indian peoples— certainly for Waters' Hopis—such matters are thought to be profaned by mere discussion, let alone commercial publication. Should one write on such subjects or not? If one does choose to write of the Indians' sacred things, what use is intended therefor? Why should the Indian lore be published at all? For preservation?—for whom? For entertainment? For moral instruction?—whose moral instruction? These are frequently obtrusive problems for authors who claim to be very much in sympathy with their Indian subjects.

I would like to discuss various responses to these problems, most particularly those of A.L. Kroeber, Frank Waters, Theodora Kroeber, and N. Scott Momaday. I hope that this will serve as an aid to the understanding and appreciation of these writers, of course; but, in suggesting a brief history of the attitudes toward the problems implicit in the use of Indian materials, the main purpose of this essay is the erection of one fragile framework upon which we can begin to piece together a coherent account of the development of American Indian literature in the twentieth century.

The earliest response to these problems could perhaps best be characterized as obliviousness. In 1907, for example, when J.W. Schultz wrote *My Life as an Indian*,[1] his account of his years among the pre-reservation Blackfeet, it did not occur to him that his sometime hosts might have had "rights of privacy" which could restrain him from telling about their ceremonies. Neither did it occur to Schultz, then, that he had in some way to justify his use of Indian materials. This non-apologetic use of Indian materials is, of course, typical of a great many such narratives. Indeed, examples of frankly exploitative, non-apologetic use of Indian materials abound to a degree that obviates further citation, but a passage from Theodora Kroeber's *Ishi in Two Worlds*[2] will, I think, prove helpful in establishing the habit of mind of such writers. In 1908, the year after the publication of Schultz's book, a surveying party was working in the foothills of Mt. Lassen, in California, when they happened upon the village of the last of the Yahi Indians, almost certainly the four last Stone Age people in the United States. Three of these Indians ran away, after covering up "the helpless old mother . . . that she might by chance go unnoticed." The response of the men of the surveying party to the tiny village could stand as a quintessential figure for the non-apologetic appropriation of Indian materials:

> *The surveying party searched the village. Under a pile of skins they found Ishi's mother. . . . As the strange man uncovered her, she trembled with fear. . . . The men looked farther. They found acorns and dried salmon in baskets in the storage room. In the cook house beside the small hearth there was a fire drill as well as the usual complement of Yahi cooking utensils, and in the other houses there were the arrow-flaking tools, a deer snare, bow, arrows, quivers, a two-pronged spear, baskets, moccasins, tanned hides, and a fur robe of wildcat pelts. The men gathered every movable possession, even the food, and for some unfathomably callous reason took it all with them as souvenirs.*

Kroeber's revulsion at such "callous" behavior is easy to understand, but the men's reasons for looting the village are hardly "unfathomable." Their attitude seems remarkably like that of delighted children who, full of the wonder of discovery, bring home birds' nests and unhatched eggs. Their assumption, like that of the children, seems to have been that the fascinating creatures they happened upon were so utterly unlike themselves that the rules which govern interhuman relations simply did not apply. This was, after all, the decade of Thomas Dixon's racist best-sellers, *The Leopard's Spots, The Sins of the Fathers,* and *The Clansman,* sensational literary expositions of the notions of black degeneracy and animality.

Non-apologetic use of Indian materials, however, was hardly confined to the racists. The anthropologists of the Boas school were not racist; indeed, Boas's environmentalist theories provided the intellectual underpinnings for a whole generation of racial liberals.[3] The Boasians were not racist, but they were avid collectors of Indian materials with few scruples about the possible sanctity—or otherwise taboo nature —of what they collected. And some of the Boasians were less than scrupulous about their informants' privacy, less than scrupulous as to the methods whereby they collected their materials. Paul Radin, for example, one of Boas's most prolific pupils, managed to convince his Winnebago informant, S.B., that as a convert to the Peyote Cult, he really ought to tell Radin all, "so that those who came after [S.B.] would not be deceived" by the lure of the old ways. The result of Radin's little deception was the altogether remarkable *Autobiography of a Winnebago Indian*.[4]

The work of A.L. Kroeber, Boas's most famous pupil, is an interesting example of the non-apologetic use of Indian materials. Off and on, throughout his long career, Kroeber had worked with the Mohave Indians of the lower Colorado basin. Late in his life he turned again to the Mohaves. In his introduction to the resultant *More Mohave Myths* he wrote: "I have long pondered to whom we owe the saving of human religious and aesthetic achievements as are recorded here. It is probably not to the group that produced them. Why should we preserve Mohave values when they themselves cannot preserve them, and their descendants are likely to be indifferent? It is the future of our own world culture that these values can enrich, and our ultimate understandings grow wider as well as deeper thereby."[5]

Kroeber, then, is like many anthropologists—both popularizing and professional anthropologists—in being content to glean Indian materials and put them to uses which have no relation to, which confer no benefit upon, "the group that produced them." This should not be misunderstood. By all accounts Kroeber developed warm relationships with individual Indians and with whole tribes. He certainly helped individual Indians and did his best in more than one arena to help groups of Indians.[6] But as he thinks about his work—and here it might be mentioned that virtually all of the artifacts taken from Ishi's village ended up in the museum at Berkeley which Kroeber superintended[7]—as he works out a rationale for his collection and publication of Indian materials, Kroeber does not imagine that his work will benefit the Indians themselves.

But if the "values" he describes and catalogues are no longer vital for the Mohave, how does Kroeber conceive of their use by twentieth-century readers, the participants in Kroeber's "world culture"? In what sense is our culture to be enriched? Is Kroeber presenting us with these values in the hope that we might be moved to adopt them? In the revised edition of his *Anthropology*,[8] Kroeber comes close to providing a direct answer. In a section entitled "The Death of Cultures" Kroeber talks about cultural survivals, about elements of Egyptian culture, for example, which survive today despite the "death" of the original culture matrix. Then he goes on to speculate about the possibility of an eventual "world culture"—all the people of the world adhering to the assumptions of a single culture. But what would happen, he worries, "When the exhausted, repetitive stage is reached, and there is no new rival culture to take over responsibility and opportunity and start fresh with new values in a different set of patterns—what then?"

Ideally, then, culture change, or "growth" to use Kroeber's normative term, is possible as long as the assumptions of one culture are open to challenges by the assumptions of "rival" cultures. Then Kroeber must be hoping that his Mohave values will become one of the hundreds of poles of a cultural dialectic around which modern man must create his syntheses.[9] Kroeber no more expects his studies of cultures to provide direct answers to problems of value than of metalurgy. Studies of cultures provide alternative sets of assumptions, our awareness of which forces us to question the assumptions of our own culture—and questioning will lead to new knowledge and "growth."[10]

Since Kroeber was one of the most influential anthropologists at work in the first half of this century, it is not surprising that Frank Waters reflects many of Kroeber's assumptions about the uses of the study of cultures. Waters' *The Man Who Killed the Deer,* filled as it is with the details of Tiwan life and religion (Waters' La Oreja is, of course, a thinly disguised Taos), is certainly not designed to convince us to become Tiwans. In fact, the book is a kind of dialogue between cultures, the Anglo, the Tiwan, the Spanish, the Peyote, the Navajo, the Apache each having their say.[11] In fact, the point of the book would seem to be that hide-bound insistence upon the forms of any single culture is wrong, is deadening. Waters writes, for example, of Palemon: "Palemon was a good man. Though he belonged to the old ways, he believed in the substance of life more than in the forms" (p. 59). Palemon is Tiwan and one of the novel's normative characters. And then there is Byers, the white trader, the "buyer," the trader in cultures, the cultural polymath, the man who takes from the Tiwan, the Anglo, the Spanish, enough to make his own roughshod, serviceable culture. With his Tiwan Indian proclivity for dirt, silence, and the mystic; with his Spanish wife and tableware and lace; and with his white rationality; with his insistence upon taking no culture whole; with all of this Byers is something like a fictional realization of Kroeber's ideal—but with a difference. Presented with the poles of a cultural dialectic, Byers does not ascend to synthesize (as Kroeber would have him do) he picks and chooses: a bit of rationality here, a bit of Spanish lace, a bit of mysticism there. . . .

Kroeber, as we have seen, did not assume that his readers should learn directly from his Mohave myths. Waters does want his readers to learn directly, to pick and choose after the fashion of Byers. Waters may not want us to become Tiwan, but he does urge us to espouse some of the most important aspects of Tiwan religion. We do not have to learn Tiwan dances; we do not have to send our sons off for kiva initiation; but we should learn that there is a kind of knowledge not available to our reasoning intellect, and we should cultivate within ourselves the source of that knowledge, as do Waters' Indians. Waters makes this clear in the introduction to his *Book of the Hopi,* a book which Waters claims is a veritable Hopi bible, compiled by himself with the aid of many elders of the Hopi nation: "That these Hopis have revealed their conceptual pattern to us now, for the first time, imparts to their gift a strangeness unique in our national experience. . . . They evoke old gods shaped by instincts we have long suppressed. They reassert a rhythm of life we have disastrously tried to ignore. They remind us we must attune ourselves to the need for inner change if we are to avert a cataclysmic rupture between our own minds and hearts. Now, if ever, is the time for them to talk, for us to listen."[12]

We can be saved, then, by Waters' exposition of a "world-view of life, deeply religious in nature, whose esoteric meaning they have kept inviolate for generations uncounted"—up until, that is, their collaboration with Waters. Waters argues that there really are self-validating truths in the system he describes, that he writes, that is to say, as a believer. I quote again from his introduction to *Book of the Hopi:* "To these doubts and denials of the professional anthropologist my only answer is that the book stems from a mythic and symbolic level far below the surface of anthropological and ethnological documentation. That it may not conform to rational conceptualization . . . does not detract from its own validity as a depth psychology different from our own" (p. xxiii).

In his attempt to straddle the line between his own "rational" culture and the instinct-dependent Pueblo cultures, Waters personifies a powerful tendency of modern Americans to see the Indian cultures as the obverse of our own, as lost Edens. Given this assumption it becomes one's duty to preach to the washed masses the gospel of Indian innocence. And especially one's duty to believe in the saving grace of Indian mysticism.[13] This is to be guilty of two errors at once. First, to assume, as Waters does, that the problems of twentieth-century America are the result of our collective refusal to listen to our hearts is a monumental oversimplification. Second, and potentially more damaging, is the notion that Indians are not rational, that they (and it is remarkable how easily we can lump "them"—all one kind of Indian) are essentially anti-rational,[14] which is next door to irrational. In this regard, though his books are less sensational, Waters is really not far from Carlos Castaneda's ever so earnestly intended hocus-pocus.

Waters is thus a kind of partial believer, and so he involves himself in problems Kroeber avoids. As a non-believer, Kroeber, like most anthropologists of his day, felt but little restrained by the taboos of cultures not his own. Waters, on the other hand, wants to have it both ways. He wants to write *from the perspective of the Pueblos,* but he also wants to publish all the details of the religious and symbolic system which he feels is so important to the "rational" culture which he so much wants to change. Meanwhile, the reader is hard put to distinguish between Waters' publication of sacred Hopi and Tiwan material and the anthropologist's publication of the "thin paper-backed booklet" which evoked such profound indignation among the Tiwan in *The Man Who Killed the Deer.* This booklet contained "a few photographs, a description of customs" and, much more seriously, a list of family names, an account of origin myths, descriptions of kiva ceremonies—all sacred matters: "It was not a question of how much or how little the contents of the book approximated the truth. . . . To them spoken words robbed a thought of its power, and printed words destroyed it entirely. They never looked at or pointed to an object or person being discussed; never spoke another's name . . . lest direct reference rob the one of this power" (pp. 168–70).

Waters quietly derides this booklet—Byers laughs at it (p. 170)—but how can Waters' own books be distinguished from the object of his derision? *The Book of the Hopi* contains photographs; *The Man Who Killed the Deer, Pumpkin Seed Point* (1973), and *Book of the Hopi* all contain descriptions of customs; the first section of *Book of the Hopi* is devoted to the Hopi origin myth; the kiva plays a prominent part in *The Man Who Killed the Deer*. I am certain that Waters considers his own accounts to be more accurate than those in "the booklet," but "it was not a question of how much or how little the contents of the book approximated the truth."

Waters responds directly to but one aspect of these problems in *The Man Who Killed the Deer*, namely, how can one print the ineffable? If there are, as the novel assumes, truths which can be known only to the heart and the instincts, if "spoken words robbed a thought of its power, and printed words destroyed it entirely," what is Waters to do? His solution is to distinguish typographically between two levels of communication: for the ineffable, for the silences that communicate, for the thoughts whose power utterance would weaken and printing would "destroy . . . entirely" there are italics. For normal speech and narration there is roman. For example:

Silence spoke, and it spoke the loudest of all.

There is no such thing as a simple thing. One drops a pebble into a pool, but the ripples travel far . . . nothing is simple and alone. We are not separate and alone . . . we are all one, indivisible. Nothing that any of us does but affects us all. [pp. 23–24]

This is, of course, no real solution. Even to afford the ineffable the benefit of italics is to dispute its ineffability. Whatever Waters may have felt in his heart, such sentiments on the printed page are but aphorisms. Even the device of italicization, however, is missing from such forthright presentations of religious matters as *Book of the Hopi* and *Masked Gods: Navaho and Pueblo Ceremonialism* (1970). Mind, I am not castigating Waters for his lack of piety. I am no believer. Nor is the question whether or not Waters is *really* a believer. The problem here is in the disjunction between Waters' profession on the one hand that there are truths of the "heart" which can be communicated only mystically, and, on the other hand, his printing of those supposed ineffables.

Given his stance as a partial believer, it is not surprising that Waters is not content with such a justification as Kroeber provided. Waters certainly hopes, with Kroeber, that the Indian materials he publishes will help to shape a "world culture," but in his ambivalence Waters evidently feels that no such justification can suffice. *Waters feels compelled to claim that what he writes he writes for the Indians themselves.* He makes this claim in his introduction to *Book of the Hopi*. Publication of materials previously jealously guarded is suddenly right and proper, Waters assures us, because each of his informants "regarded the compilation" of the book "as a sacred task." The book is to be "a monumental record that would give their children a complete history of their people and their religious belief" (p. xxi). The argument would seem to be that there is no profanation because, first, the Hopis themselves wrote the book, with Waters as a kind of amanuensis, and, second, that the book is really intended for the Hopis. It is the Hopis themselves who have allowed us to read the book over their shoulders, as it were.

There is evidence that no such collaboration as Waters describes ever took place. Albert Yava, a Tewa-Hopi, writes that "the old-timers around Oraibi" gave Waters'

Indian middleman "a lot of misinformation . . . just to get rid of him."[15] This is quite possible. In fact, Waters describes just such a peddling of misinformation in *The Man Who Killed the Deer*. But whatever the nature of Waters' collaboration with the Hopis may have been, Waters nowhere provides an explanation of why the culture he had described as so remarkably stable in *The Man Who Killed the Deer* should suddenly be so fearful of the continuance of its religion that its secrets must be entrusted to Waters and the Viking Press.

And again, the problem is not that Waters does not show proper respect for the sacred, or that he wants to publish sacred things. The problem is that he claims to regard it as sacred *and* he wants to publish it. His solution to the problem is to convince us that he really is doing it for the Indians themselves.

Now even among the most devoutly relativist of the professional anthropologists, there are few who ever seriously consider converting to whatever religious system they might study. Consequently, however much they may yearn for primitive innocence[16] they generally escape the kinds of self-contradictions which are the results of Waters' apologetic stance and partial conversion. When Cora DuBois did her research on the Ghost Dance, the fact that there was "everywhere . . . a deep-rooted fear of the risk incurred to one's health and well-being by speaking of one's personal dream experiences"[17] was an impediment to her work, but certainly no bar to publication. Isabel T. Kelly recalls the reluctance of her informants to speak on shamanism[18] as a research problem to be overcome, not as a source of personal embarrassment or guilt.

And there is a further difference between Waters and the anthropologists. Every one of the twenty-seven "spokesmen" whom Waters lists (p.xxi) "regarded the compilation" of Waters' *Book of the Hopi* "as a sacred task." When, on the other hand, the anthropologists tell about their informants' motives, we are presented with all the variety we would expect from hundreds of individuals from many different cultures. Some speak to the anthropologists because they are paid; some speak because they feel themselves to be competing with the anthropologists in their knowledge of their culture; some will not speak because they feel themselves to be competing with the anthropologist; some will not speak because they are embarrassed to have been associated with "crazy" movements; some will speak about games and baskets, but not about sacred matters; some simply will not speak; some want whiskey; at least one, as we have seen, was persuaded to speak in order to demonstrate to later generations the errors of the old ways; and some want to help to preserve their culture. One enterprising anthropologist even gets people talking by beginning as a census taker. One Hopi, Don Talayesva, informant to a whole generation of anthropologists and the hero of numberless Ph.D. dissertations, spoke for money—and for the prestige which his association with the anthropologists gained for him. He always insisted, however, when questioned by worried members of his tribe, that he never revealed tribal secrets.[19]

Given this diversity it is remarkable that, beginning around 1930, so many of the popular anthropologists, like Waters, seem to have so many informants whose only motive, crisply pure, is the preservation of their culture. I do not think that it is accidental that these remarkable informants allow the popular anthropologists to say: "True, I am in sympathy with my subjects; true, I write from their perspective, though I write of sacred matters; but they really wanted me to write it down. I do so in their behalf and at their behest." Neihardt's *Black Elk Speaks* provides a nice case in point. In his introduction to the 1961 Nebraska Press edition, Neihardt wrote that it was Black Elk who had urged upon Neihardt the writing of the book in order to "save his great vision for all men." The 1979 Nebraska Press edition, however, prints a letter from Neihardt to Black Elk. We read:

> *Now I have something to tell you that I hope and believe will interest you as much as it does me. . . . I feel that the whole story of your life ought to be written truthfully by somebody with the right feeling and understanding of your people. . . . I would, of course, expect to pay you well for all the time that you would give me.*[20]

It would seem, then, that there is some measure of fiction in Neihardt's description of himself as having played wedding guest to Black Elk's ancient mediciner.

Theodora Kroeber and Ishi provide another, and a fascinating, case in point. Kroeber's *Ishi in Two Worlds* is one of the most immediately affecting books I have ever read. It is a history of the Yahi Indians and of Ishi, literally the last of the Yahis, a Stone Age man who, after watching his people die around him, managed for years to live absolutely alone, out of sight of the white man. Finally in 1911 he was discovered, sick and still wearing the short hair of mourning, in a slaughterhouse cattle pen. Eventually he was brought to live in the museum at Berkeley under the watchful care of A.L. Krober (who was later to become Theodora's husband). Ishi was paid for his work as an assistant janitor, but, of course, he was a tremendous asset to the museum. Ishi gave demonstrations of arrow making, flint napping, spear making; worked as an informant for some of Berkeley's anthropologists; and was, in a word, something of a sensation in the Bay area.

One of the most appealing aspects of this book is the forthright way in which Theodora Kroeber confronts the eerie fact of Ishi's having been a kind of exhibit. She makes it clear that however pathetic it may seem to us that the last of the Yahi Indians should have spent his last four years in a museum, there really was no attractive alternative. Given the fact that he was utterly alone with what had become a private language, given the fact that there were people in the museum who were interested to learn to speak with Ishi, given the fact that he was not a young man when he came down from his mountain, given all this, his life in the museum provided him with a chance to be self-sufficient, to have real friends, and, evidently, to charm virtually everyone he met. However poignant the situation, Kroeber realizes that it was not the museum which had killed Ishi's people, that it was the museum which went to some trouble to make a home for the man. And, of course, he was in no way confined.

Now, all of this would have very little to do with our present discussion had Theodora Kroeber not written a second, a fictionalized account of Ishi, *Ishi, Last of*

His Tribe (New York, 1973 [1964]). Suddenly the marvellously forthright Kroeber is no more. Suddenly we have an account of all the matters concerning which the Ishi of her first book resolutely refused to speak; suddenly we find that Ishi's move to Berkeley was preordained and all neatly forecast for him in his power vision. Even A.L. Kroeber, Theodora's husband, has a place in that power vision. We find that Ishi and his family had been much concerned that their culture and its artifacts would "vanish after a few more moons of wind and rain" (p. 153). Needless to say, in this fictionalized account the museum becomes *for Ishi* the salvation of his culture. Kroeber actually has Ishi say that his people live on "in the notebooks"[21] of her anthropologist husband! Ishi's own work as an informant now becomes a way of "living the dream"; that is, of enacting his power vision. All of this is, of course, Kroeber's invention. Ishi, in fact, refused even to divulge his real name, let alone detail his power dream or speak of other taboo matters although he was willing, indeed evidently eager, to demonstrate bow making and arrow making and such like. This clear division is fair evidence that Ishi was quite willing to have die with him most of what his people had regarded as sacred or otherwise taboo.

A.L. Kroeber, as we have seen, finally decided that all of his work was not really for the Indians, most of whose "descendants are likely to be indifferent." He described himself quite frankly as working for what he called the "world culture." In his work with the Zuni, for example, Kroeber found that "the Zuni do not like to tell the names of their kinsmen." Kroeber wrote: "This reluctance of my friends made the work of compiling the table much slower than it would have been with the free use of names," but Kroeber "did not care to press their scruples"[22]—just as he seems to have done his best not to offend Ishi's Yahi sensibilities. But this respect for the Zuni *as individuals,* this respect for Ishi *as an individual* human being, certainly did not keep him from publishing what Zuni genealogy he had been able to collect.

Theodora Kroeber, on the other hand, is troubled in much the same way that Waters is troubled. Anthropologists take; anthropologists use. She feels driven to apologize for her husband's work in much the same way that Waters feels driven to apologize for his own taking and using. If Waters is preserving Hopi culture for the Hopis, then Theodora Kroeber's fictional Ishi is predestined by a happy Yahi providence to aid A.L. Kroeber in his preservation-salvation of the Yahis. In both cases the intrusions are "for their own good." This, ultimately, is the justification, the substance of the apology. By the way, even when we can believe the author who assures us that informants cooperated "in order to preserve their culture,"[23] we should remember that this has long been a favorite persuasive device of the fieldworker: "You really should tell me, whatever your feelings, because it will soon have vanished, and. . . ."

This is not to say that every Indian enthusiast who claims that his informants helped him in order to preserve their culture is necessarily a liar. I am saying that there are scruples which must be overcome in studying, especially at first hand, Indian cultures. It is easy to see field work as analogous to mining on Indian lands—much taken, little left behind; lots of government money for studies, very little of this money finding its way to the often hard-pressed people being studied.[24] Theodore Kroeber, Waters, Neihardt, and others convinced themselves that such work can be anti-exploitationist assumptions of the American civil rights movement began to be applied to the plight of the twentieth-century American Indian; as anti-paternalistic, anti-exploitationist assumptions began to be popularized by such persons as Vine Deloria and insisted upon by such forces as the American Indian Movement; as such assumptions gained currency, apologies like those of Waters and Theodora Kroeber and Neihardt began to ring ever more hollow, while the non-apologetic appropriation of Indian materials for the advancement of A.L. Kroeber's "world culture" became to many an embarrassment. As Indian informants became more and more recalcitrant, anthropologists began to speak more and more of the utility of their work, not in saving the Indians' culture for them, but rather in the achievement of much more immediate ends.

Weston La Barre provides an interesting example of just such a change. In his *The Peyote Cult,* a 1938 Yale Ph.D. dissertation done under the direction of the Boasian anthropologist Leslie Spier, La Barre describes (briefly) the prejudice against the Native American Church and the legal difficulties of the peyotists, but there is no indication that La Barre is writing with intent to aid the peyotists in their quest for freedom of religion. In the preface to the 1969 edition of the *same book,*however, things have changed: now La Barre makes explicit his feeling that the peyotists ought to be allowed freedom of religion, and he contends that his book has been and can continue to be an important document in pursuit of that freedom. He is, in a word, no longer content to be the pure Boasian solely intent upon collecting information on cultures (pp. xii-xiii).

Another anthropologist, J.G. Jorgenson, assures us that his work on *The Sun Dance Religion* (1972) was done for essentially the same reasons as La Barre adduces, the assumption again being that understanding breeds tolerance and compassion, that if the book's white audience can be made to understand the bases—economic, social, religious—of the Sun Dance, then white legislators, judges, and citizens generally will be more accepting of Sun Dance religionists, and more likely to act to correct the ills that afflict them. The claim is that the book has real and immediate utility for the Indians who are being studied, whose religion is being discussed. Jorgenson is also representative of a growing number of contemporary anthropologists who are explicitly unwilling to print any information which is considered by their informants to be too private or too sacred for publication.[25]

Yet another effect of these changes is the growing interest in the all-too-often nameless Indian "informants" upon whose memories the popular and professional anthropologists alike have so heavily depended. *American Indian Intellectuals* (1978),[26] edited by Margot Liberty, for example, provides no less than sixteen brief biographies of native historians going as far back as Ely S. Parker, a Seneca (1828–95). My own *Annotated Bibliography of American Indian and Eskimo Autobiographies*[27] includes accounts of close to five-hundred autobiographical narratives.

If there is a new respect for the Indians' rights to recognition and privacy among those who write about Indians, it is certainly due in part to the increasing likelihood that what gets written about Indians will be read by Indians—and responded to by Indians. See, for example, the cries of blasphemy which greeted Harper and Row's 1972 publication of Hyemeyohsts Storm's *Seven Arrows,* a lavishly illustrated book intended to impart the traditional wisdom of the Plains Indians by telling of tales, the explication of allegories, and the exposition of the Sun Dance, the Medicine Wheel, and so forth. The remarkably heated response of Rupert Costo, then president of the American Indian Historical Society, was typical. "The recent best-selling book *Chief Red Fox,* brought disgrace to McGraw-Hill. Its author was exposed as a fraud. This book, *Seven Arrows,* will bring disgrace to Harper and Row. . . . Its content falsifies and desecrates the traditions and religion of the Northern Cheyenne, which it purports to describe. . . . The color plates are a solid disaster. . . . to many Cheyenne people . . . the reaction to *Seven Arrows* was disbelief and anger."[28]

Now it is interesting to note that this book is really rather close in intent and execution to Waters' *Book of the Hopi*: both detail Indian religious and symbolic material; both books seek to move readers to adopt certain "Indian ways"; there are some errors in both books; each is, in fact, a deeply felt, non-professional account of traditional Indian materials colored and reshaped by the moral-aesthetic concerns of an Anglo-educated individual intelligence. The main difference is that Waters' book precedes Storm's by nearly ten years, and so Waters' errors are mentioned in obscure book reviews, and his "blasphemy" is mentioned not at all. Nine years later, on the other hand, the cries of the Cheyenne and their sympathizers, cries of Storm's "desecrations" and "falsifications" were sufficient to cause Harper and Row temporarily to cease distribution of *Seven Arrows*—a book which had otherwise been warmly received.

There is, then, a more and more widespread concern for the rights of privacy of Indians, more and more vocal unwillingness on the part of Indians to suffer violation of the sacred, and more and more concern that what is written about Indians have some more tangible effect than the preservation of culture.[29] In literature the effect, or at least the analogue, of these concerns is less emphasis on, less description of, traditional religious and symbolic systems. James Welch's *Winter in the Blood* (1974), for example, is very much concerned with the impingements of the old ways upon a contemporary Indian, the problems of achieving as an Indian, but there is virtually no explication of Blackfeet or Gros Ventre religious systems along the way. And, whatever else the book may be, it is certainly a plea for understanding and compassion.

N. Scott Momaday, however, provides the best example of a writer affected by these concerns, the best example because he is explicitly aware of such problems as have here detained us—and his style has, over the years, changed largely as a response to such problems. Let us begin with *House Made of Dawn,* Momaday's first book-length prose publication (1966).

At one point in *House Made of Dawn* Momaday introduces us to an Indian preacher, Tosamah, who delivers a sermon on St. John and The Word. The point of the sermon is that when St. John said that "In the beginning was the Word; he had provided an "instant of revelation, inspiration, Truth." But because John was a white man, he went on, trying to make his truth "bigger and better, but instead he only demeaned and encumbered it." John had spoken "the Truth, all right, but it was more than the Truth." By the time John had finished elaborating his moment of revelation "the Truth was overgrown with fat and the fat was . . . *John's* God," and it, this God-fat, stood between John and the Truth.

Then Tosamah tells his congregation about his Kiowa grandmother, a woman illiterate, but who nonetheless—or perhaps consequently—had learned "that in words and language, and there only, she could have consummate being." She told the child Tosamah stories. It was only much later that Tosamah came to realize the importance of that telling: "I was a child, and that old woman was asking me to come directly into the presence of her mind and spirit; she was taking hold of my imagination, giving me to share in the great fortune of her wonder and delight. *She was asking me to go with her to the confrontation of something that was sacred and eternal.*"[30]

The difference is clear. St. John had his moment of revelation, but then went on to cram the margins of his imagination with glosses, with attempts to make explicit all that was implicit in his imaginative moment. It is almost as though Momaday had Waters in mind, Waters, who imagines for himself ineffable truths in Tiwan silences, and who then elevates those truths to italics. Tosamah's grandmother, on the other hand, is content to commune with her imagination, and thereby bring herself and young Tosamah into touch with the "sacred and eternal." All of this would have been ruined had either she or Tosamah tried to say, "Yes, I see. The bear in the story represents the power of the universe, etc., etc." For Momaday, then *what* we see is ever holy. "And thus we see . . ." is ever taboo.

And this is at the heart of Momaday's style. Momaday provides us with descriptions of scenes and of events which, like the vastness of the valley early in *House Made of Dawn,* "make for illusion, a kind of illusion that comprehends reality" (p. 20). Event after event, each intended to awaken within us that same "instinctive will to wonder and regard" which fills Abel after he kills the evil albino (p. 78)—but each event without explication. Event after event, and each like the vision of the eagle "with its talons closed upon a snake," is "an awful, holy sight, full of magic and meaning" (p. 19).

Of course, it is not quite so simple. Of course, Momaday's literate, Anglo-educated, twentieth-century audience cannot simply experience stories as did nineteenth-century Kiowa participants in an oral culture. Another problem is that Momaday himself is no nineteenth-century preliterate Kiowa, however sophisticated may be his impersonation. Momaday may not provide the weight of explication that Waters rejoices to provide, but he does make use of some religious materials in the novel,[31] and he does feel compelled to explain (in Tosamah's sermon) something about what might be called preliterate habits of religious response, in order to allow his literate readers to respond to his novel in something like the way an Indian audience might have responded to oral tales.

Momaday seems to be well aware of the contradiction that all of this implies. This is quite clear if we see Tosamah as a kind of stand-in for Momaday. Like Momaday, Tosamah is a Kiowa, and Tosamah's account of his way to Rainy Mountain was later to appear, with very few changes, as a section of Momaday's autobiographical *The Way to Rainy Mountain*. Tosamah is at once an Indian Priest of the Sun and a preacher in the Anglo tradition; Momaday is an Indian story teller at a white university writing books for a literate audience. Further, Momaday's second Indian name, Tsotohah, or Red Bluff, allows him a deliciously self-deprecating pun, for there is a good deal of bluff in the Right Reverend *John* Big Bluff Tosamah as he goes on at such length to explicate his text from St. *John,* while the whole point of his explication is the inimical relationship between truth and explication. If there is wit here, elsewhere there is modest self-awareness. At one point Benally says: "He's always going on like that, Tosamah, talking crazy and showing off, but he doesn't understand. . . . He's educated. . . . he doesn't come from the reservation. He doesn't know how it is when you grow up out there someplace" (p. 137).

Elsewhere there is pathos, for Tosamah, and by implication Momaday, is torn in ways that Benally cannot imagine. If, for example, we look again at Tosamah's sermon on The Word, we find that at first it has nothing to do with explication. Tosamah begins, "*In principio erat Verbum,*" and then he goes on for a paragraph to describe such a scene, to tell such a story: "There were no mountains, no trees, no rocks, no rivers. . . . But there was a single sound . . . like a whisper of the wind," and so forth, an imagining of the scene of creation. This is the kind of thing, presumably, that Tosamah's and Momaday's storytelling grandmothers could have done. It is myth making. But "then a remarkable thing happened." Tosamah seems suddenly to remember that this mythic telling will not do for his congregation of inarticulate city Indians. He seems suddenly to remember that these city Indians can no longer respond to tales as their grandparents had done. "The Priest of the Sun seemed stricken; he let go of his audience and withdrew into himself. . . . His voice, which had been low and resonant, suddenly became harsh and flat; his shoulders sagged and his stomach protruded. . . . for a moment there was a look of amazement, then utter carelessness in his face. Conviction, caricature, callousness: the remainder of the sermon was a going back and forth among these" (pp. 85–86).

And so Tosamah launches into the explication of St. John that Momaday feels is necessary for us as well as Tosamah's congregation. This is, I think, Momaday's frank admission of the awkwardness, and something of the pain, of his own situation. He feels that he must explain to his audience how to respond to the stories that are so dear to him—to the confounding both of the story and of his conception of himself as a Kiowa teller of tales. He is like a stand-up comedian who must explain his every joke.

I think that it has been Momaday's goal as a writer to minimize the effects of these contradictions in his work. *The Way to Rainy Mountain* (1969) is more resolutely non-explicative than *House Made of Dawn* (1966). In *The Way to Rainy Mountain* Momaday simply juxtaposes thematically grouped events from the mythic past of his people, from the historic past of his people, and from his personal past. The juxtapositions at once enforce a sense of Momaday's participating in the mythic and the historic past of the Kiowas and a sense of the impingement of that past upon Momaday—his imagination, his pen, allows the past to live and that past forms him. He is the past's continuing creation, and the past is words. He is a "man made of words" as well as a man making words.[32]

In his latest prose work, *The Names* (1976), there is virtually no explication of religious notions, and there is more simplicity. The elaborate, Faulkerian narrative convolutions of *House Made of Dawn* are very little in evidence. Now, I am not saying that Momaday has invented the device of unexplained juxtaposition, to say nothing of the technique of straightforward narration. I am saying that, while Waters must provide an outline of Hopi religion in order to publish his message of the incompleteness of white rationality, Momaday is becoming more and more insistent that we take our Kiowa goods in much the same way as a Kiowa would have received them, as tales, simple tales, devoid of religious glosses, tales whose very starkness insists that the mind of the reader attach significances out of the well of that mind's own associations, own remembrances. Momaday does not want to introduce us to all of the intricacies, beauties, ineffabilities of Indian religious systems. He retains as a writer the respect he learned as a Kiowa child living among the Jemez pueblos: "And throughout the year there were ceremonies of many kinds, and some of these were secret dances, and on these holiest days . . . My parents and I kept then to ourselves . . . and in this way, through the tender of our respect and our belief we earned the trust of the Jemez people, and we were at home there" (p. 147).

The religious systems can take care of themselves. Momaday will not intrude. As he says on a frontispage of *The Names,* Momaday tried to "write in the same way, in the same spirit" as a traditional Kiowa storyteller. Insofar as he can write as the storytellers told, then his white readers can achieve some sense of what it is like to experience stories as a Kiowa would have done. Momaday wants there to be a small shared experience.

Momaday is, then, like Jorgenson in not being willing to reveal matters sacred to his Indians. He also is like Jorgenson and the later La Barre and many other post-civil-rights-movement anthropologists in his conception of his work's justification. At the 1970 convocation of American Indian Scholars Momaday made it clear that, while he does want to make "Indian values" available to other Americans, while he does want to preserve the fast-vanishing oral tradition of his people, he also is very much concerned to affect American attitudes toward the Indian. And he feels that, for example, the American Indian Literature Program which he instituted at Berkeley *is* a means of affecting attitudes.[33] I think that he would see his books in the same way: perhaps if he can make us share an experience with the Kiowas he will have affected our attitudes toward Indians.

In conclusion, it is possible to arrange chronologically three sets of assumptions about the use of Indian materials: 1) early in this century virtually all use of Indian materials was non-apologetic; 2) beginning mainly in the 1930s and 1940s some Indian enthusiasts began apologizing, began to assert that their collecting and publishing was really done on behalf of the Indians; 3) with the advent of the civil rights movement and Indian militancy we find more respect for Indian taboos, less emphasis upon Indian religious systems, more concern for Indian social problems.

Of course the civil rights movement did not signal the end of the apologetic use of Indian materials, or even the end of their non-apologetic use. Especially among the professional anthropologists non-apologetic use continues, though it is becoming increasingly difficult to get funding unless proposals either predict project-related benefits to Indians, or unless the proposal is in some way sanctioned by Indians.

Apologetic use continues as well. Storm's *Seven Arrows* was published in 1972, and Thomas Sanchez's *Rabbit Boss* is a good example of apologetic assumptions at work as late as 1973. In this gripping, often savage, portrayal of the extinction of the Washo nation, Sanchez is in sympathy with his Indian subjects. The reader, for example, is urged quite unambiguously to feel revulsion at the desecration by whites of certain Washo puberty rites—and yet Sanchez is quite willing to describe these and other sacred ceremonies in detail. His implied apology is that he is writing the book to an Indian audience, urging that audience to throw off the yoke of the white man, to fight back rather than suffer passively as did the Washo. One assumes that the lack of an outraged response to *Rabbit Boss* was more the result of the relative scarcity of educated, politically aware, vocal Washo than of any essential differences between *Rabbit Boss* and the much reviled *Seven Arrows*.

Finally, lest we decide too easily that the latest assumptions are the best assumptions, please allow me to quote "What the informant said to Franz Boas in 1920":

> *Long ago her mother*
> *had to sing this song and so*
> *she had to grind along with it*
> *the corn people have a song too*
> *it is very good*
> *I refuse to tell it.*[34]

Can anyone rejoice that Boas could not record this song of the corn people? What is so fragile as a fragment of an oral tradition? Even where it is maintained, such a song is amended over the years; with any gap it must perish utterly. Can anyone lament that Boas, Kroeber, Radin, and so many others collected as much as they did? And yet who, at least in this day, could lament the independence of the man who would not sing?

NOTES

[1]Most recent edition is by Fawcett, no date.

[2](Berkeley, 1971). The quotation that follows is from pp. 111–12.

[3]See George M. Fredrickson, *The Black Image in the White Mind* (New York, 1971), p. 330. See also Marvin Harris, *The Rise of Anthropological Theory* (New York, 1968), pp. 291–92.

[4](New York, 1963 [1920]).

[5]*Anthropological Records* (hereinafter *AR*) 27 (1972): xii.

[6]See, for example, Weston La Barre's account of "the first disposition against a Senate anti-peyote bill, made by La Barre, Boas, Kroeber and others in 1937," in his introduction to the first Schocken paperback edition of *The Peyote Cult* (New York, 1969), p. xii.

[7]Kroeber, *Ishi in Two Worlds,* p. 112.

[8](New York, 1948). The following quotation is from pp. 384–85.

[9]Kroeber did, in fact, incline toward such dialectic configurations. See, for example, "The Superorganic," *AR* 19 (1917): 163.

[10]There is a second use for these materials. We must study other cultures in order to discover the "principles that go into the shaping of human social life or civilization." We want to understand civilization "in the abstract or in form of generalizing principles if possible." See Kroeber, *Anthropology* (New York, 1923), p. 6. But it is well known that Kroeber deemed anthropology to be unprepared to make such generalizations. See Harris, pp. 319–42. Evidently Kroeber looked forward to a time when enough Boasian, particularist data would be collected and classified to allow for productive searches for laws and causes. See Kroeber, *Style and Civilization* (Ithaca, 1957), pp. 1–2.

[11]Not the Mexican, by the way. Waters perpetuates the curious assumption that the Mexicans are cultureless, because they are neither real Indians nor real Spaniards. See *The Man Who Killed the Deer* (Chicago, 1970 [1942]), pp. 153–57.

[12](New York, 1963), p. xviii. If Waters went no farther than a belief that the study of primitive peoples might curb "rational excesses" in our own culture, he would have a fair number of professional anthropologists alongside him. This is essentially the stance that Robin Horton calls "Romanticism." Horton finally includes himself, with important qualifications, in his catalog of anthropological Romantics. See "Levy-Bruhl, Durkheim and the Scientific Revolution," in Horton and Ruth Finnegan, eds., *Modes of Thought* (London, 1973), pp. 249–305.

[13]See, for example, Adolf Hungry Wolf, *The Blood People* (New York, 1977). "Hungry Wolf," one time white lad from the city, now one of The People, is fast becoming a pious adept in all the sacred lore of the Blood, and this he wants to pass along to us all. He includes pictures of the ceremony wherein the sacred weasel skin shirt is "passed on" to him.

[14]For the difficulties involved in making easy distinctions between non-rational-mystical primitives and the moderns, see Horton.

[15]Albert Yava, *Big Falling Snow* (New York, 1978), p. 80.

[16]See Horton, *Modes of Thought*, p. 305.

[17]"The 1870 Ghost Dance," *AR* 3, no. 1 (1939): v.

[18]"Southern Paiute Shamanism," *AR* 2, no. 4 (1939): 151.

[19]See Kelly, p. 151; DuBois, p. v; H.G. Barnett, "Culture Element Distributions: IX, Gulf of Georgia Salish," *AR* 1 (1939): 221–24; Omer Stewart, "Culture Element Distributions: XIV, Northern Paiute," *AR* 4 (1941): 362–65; H.E. Driver, "Culture Element Distributions: VI, Southern Sierra Nevada," *AR* 1 (1937): 56; Cora DuBois, "Study of Wintu Mythology," *Journal of American Folklore* 44 (1932): 375ff.; Mischa Titieu is the census taker, *The Hopi Indians of Old Oraibi* (Ann Arbor, 1972), p. 3; the Christian-peyote convert is Radin's S.B., p. 67; for Dan Talayesva see Leo W. Simmons, ed., *Sun Chief,* (New Haven, 1974 [1942]).

[20]*Black Elk Speaks* (Lincoln, 1979), Appendix 1, pp. 277–79. Thomas E. Mails, in *Fools Crow* (Garden City: Doubleday, 1979), an as-told-to autobiography of Fools Crow, a Teton Sioux (born c. 1891), seems to be quite self-consciously imitating Neihardt's claims. Mails assures us that Fools Crow had received word from Wakan-Tanka that "The time had come for him to tell certain things about himself and his Teton people to a person who would be made known to him" (p. 4). That person, needless to say, turns out to be Mails, whom Fools Crow "intuited" to be a writer. Mails could stop the rain at will, as though he really believed that Fools Crow had extrasensory powers, including the powers of prophecy. Further, when speaking of Fools Crow's relationship with his god, Mails speaks as one who participates in that belief: ". . . I was not certain [Fools Crow] knew how far Wakan-Tanka wanted him to go in exposing himself to the world" (p. 5). Mails even gives a blood-curdling account of the dangers of revealing the secrets of "divinely given power"—and yet he does urge Fools Crow to reveal these sacred matters, and he is delighted to print these revelations.

[21]P. 206. Not surprisingly, when NBC decided to produce a version for television (aired as *Ishi, Last of His Tribe,* 20 December 1978), they opted to follow Kroeber's fictionalized version—except, of course, where they chose to add the kinds of sentimentalization for which their medium is so well known.

[22]"Zuni Kin and Clan," *Anthropological Papers of the American Museum of Natural History* 18, no. 2 (1917): 51.

[23]See Joseph Epes-Brown, with whom Black Elk collaborated in order to preserve for his people the "greatness and truth" of Ogala traditions, in *The Sacred Pipe* (Baltimore, 1972), p. xx. See also Aileen O'Bryan, whose informant assured her that in times to come her "people will have forgotten their early ways of life unless they learn it from white men's books," in "The Dine: Origin Myths of the Navaho Indians," found in F.W. Turner III, ed., *The Portable North American Indian Reader,* (New York, 1973), p. 175.

[24]For one Indian's view of anthropological fieldwork see the chapter on "The Anthropologists" in Vine Deloria, *Custer Died for Your Sins* (New York, 1971).

[25]*The Sun Dance Religion* (Chicago, 1972), p. 178.

[26]1976 Proceedings of the American Ethnological Society (New York, 1978).

[27](Lincoln, Neb.) 1981.

[28]"*Seven Arrows* Desecrates Cheyenne," in Abraham Chapman, ed., *Literature of the American Indians* (New York, 1975) pp. 149–51. This review appeared originally in *The Indian Historian* 5 (1972). For further negative Indian responses to the book see "Northern Cheyenne Discuss Seven Arrows Book; Criticism is Expressed,"

Wassaja 2, no. 4 (1974): 12.

[29]Harper and Row, for example, went so far as to print the following on a frontispage of their first edition of Welch's *Winter in the Blood* (1974): "This book is the third in Harper and Row's Native American Publishing Program. All profits from this Program will be set aside in a special fund and used to support special projects designed to aid the Native American people." *Seven Arrows* was the first book in the series, and the idea of funding was part of Harper and Row's response to the criticism of Storm's book.

[30]*House Made of Dawn* (New York, 1969), pp. 86–88. Emphasis in final quotation is mine.

[31]See Lawrence J. Evers, "Words and Place: A Reading of *House Made of Dawn,*" *Western American Literature* 11 (1977): 297–320.

[32]See Momaday's "The Man Made of Words," in *Indian Voices* (San Francisco, 1970), pp. 49–62.

[33]See the panel discussion chaired by Momaday, *Indian Voices,* pp. 68–71.

[34]As found in Jerome Rothenberg's *Shaking the Pumpkin* (New York, 1972), p. 3.

William Nichols: 'Badger and Coyote Were Neighbors': Comic Reconciliation in a Clackamas Chinook Myth

Scattered examples of Native American speeches and myths are included in recent anthologies of American literature, but there is little evidence that the American literary canon has been truly reshaped to include Native American oral literature. One hurdle in the way of such change is no doubt the narrow literary education of most of us who teach American literature, but another problem may be sheer abundance. How are we to choose the best from among the great quantities of oral literature anthropologists and others have collected from hundreds of Native American societies?

Although I do not claim that the Clackamas Chinook myth "Badger and Coyote Were Neighbors" stands above other Native American works in style, beauty, complexity, or originality, I have chosen to discuss it for several reasons that seem important. First of all, Melville Jacobs has given us both a painstakingly careful translation of "Badger and Coyote" and a sustained analysis of it in *The Content and Style of an Oral Literature: Clackamas Chinook Myths and Tales*.[1] Secondly, perhaps because "Badger and Coyote" has interesting similarities with some modern fiction, it seems particularly accessible to undergraduates; and I have had good experiences with it in the classroom. In addition, the myth's complexity beneath a surface of apparent simplicity defies wonderfully some widely held views regarding the supposed "decadence" of the Native American societies of the lower Columbia River basin.[2] It is a good myth too for introducing the Coyote figure who moves in protean forms through much Native American literature. Finally, "Badger and Coyote" seems to show especially clearly how the study of Native American literature can illuminate the dominant American culture.

One

Melville Jacobs collected "Badger and Coyote" from Mrs. Victoria Howard sometime in 1929–30. My own rendering of the text, below, is based on Jacobs' translation; but I have abridged it considerably and tried to make its style somewhat more familiar to the western ear. In doing so, I have been influenced by Theodora Kroeber's beautiful translations of Native American oral literature in *The Inland Whale*.[3] My purpose was to provide a text which could fit comfortably within this brief essay and to suggest a version that might be used in a typical American literature course.

BADGER AND COYOTE WERE NEIGHBORS

This Coyote was the head man of a village, and he had five children, who were the swiftest runners in the village. The youngest, a daughter, was the swiftest of them all.

The five Coyote children were playing with the five Badger children, who were all boys, when they wandered together to the edge of a distant village. There they saw strangers playing a game with a ball as bright and lovely as the sun. Carved from wood and stained with a strange red dye, the ball was unlike any they had seen. The children soon decided that they must steal the beautiful ball, and they returned to their own village, talking of how proud their fathers would be when they had fooled the distant people.

The next day the children returned to the strange village with a plan. The oldest Coyote child buried himself in the field where the strangers played their game, and the other Coyote children buried themselves at points along the way to the forest. When the ball rolled near the first buried child, he took it and began to run toward the next one. But the people of the village ran swiftly, and they caught the oldest Coyote child just as he gave the ball to his younger brother. The villagers stopped only briefly to kill the oldest Coyote child, and soon they caught up with the younger brother, who threw the ball to another brother just as he too was about to be killed.

This chase continued until the swift young sister took the ball and ran to the place where the Badger children were watching. Then she too was finally caught. As she was about to die, she threw the ball to the Badgers and said, "Give the largest share to our father, for we have died because of the ball."

The Badger children began to stumble and fumble about with the ball in such a tumult that the villagers gathered around them in a circle and began to laugh. While the villagers were laughing, the children stirred up a great cloud of dust and escaped with the ball before the people could see again.

Then the Badger children returned to their own village and stood in the shadows of the trees, calling in voices like those of the Coyote children: "Oh, what sorrow! The children of Badger have been killed for stealing the ball from the distant village."

Hearing this sad news, Coyote went to Badger's lodge and said: "This terrible thing is your fault, for I told you your children could not do anything right."

While he spoke, the Badger children came into their father's lodge and told the truth about the Coyote children. At first Coyote was silent. Then he collapsed in sorrow. After a while, he threw himself into the river, but he could not drown. He threw himself into the fire, but he could not burn. He tried to hang himself from a tree and cut his throat with a knife, but he could not die. Then he stopped trying to kill himself and only wept.

Badger told his children to give Coyote half the ball, which they did. He took it to where his children used to play and cut it into little pieces.

Later, when the season was getting to be springtime, Coyote said, "I will go where my children are buried and bring back their bones." He set out with a large basket on his back.

When Coyote reached the place where the strange villagers had buried his children, he dug up their bones and placed them gently in the basket with many rhododendron leaves and blossoms. Then he set out for his home, walking very slowly so that he might not disturb the bones and stopping occasionally to put more leaves in the basket. Near the end of the first day, Coyote heard light whispers in his basket, and when he stopped for the night, he felt a tap of joy.

On the second day, Coyote moved even more slowly, and he could hear distinctly the voices of his children. They were no longer whispering. They were talking aloud, and the tapping had become louder, as though they were trying to walk. But in the evening Coyote saw a large centipede cross his path. "Sniff, sniff, sniff," the centipede said. "I smell the odor of death."

Coyote stopped and put his basket gently on the ground while he chased the centipede away. Then he slept through the night.

On the third day, the children began to sing, and the tapping grew louder, more joyful, as they began to dance. Coyote's heart was filled with gladness. But the large centipede crossed his path again, and this time Coyote became too angry. He did not set the basket down as gently as he had before, and it shook as he placed it on the ground. Suddenly there was silence, and when Coyote looked in the basket, there were only bones and wilted leaves and blossoms.

Then Coyote and Badger buried the bones of the children in the forest near Coyote's lodge, and Coyote spoke to the people of his village. "Now when people die," he said, "they will not return. Those who remain will grieve just ten days. Then they will do as they have done. They will hunt and sing and even gamble, and sometimes they will tell sweet stories."

Melville Jacobs has speculated brilliantly about the levels of meaning which the Clackamas Chinook probably found in this myth.[4] I want to take what seems to be the most important level, the myth's treatment of death, and try to link it to themes with which students of American literature are likely to be familiar. In its treatment of death "Badger and Coyote" achieves a complexity that is difficult to frame as a simple lesson, for Coyote comes to accept the deaths of his children and affirms the finality of death for all people; but he is most dramatically compelling as an actor in the myth when he is resisting the power of death. Coyote's final reconciliation with death gains dignity from his strong resistance.

Two

It is helpful, first of all, to compare the structure of the myth with a pattern found in some modern fiction. I have in mind the way in which conflict and human frailty are initially played out in comic scenes, and only after the audience has begun to enjoy the comic resolutions of conflict do death and violence intrude to shock and remind us that we have been laughing at situations which are finally grim indeed. It is the pattern associated with black comedy. Ken Kesey's *One Flew Over the Cuckoo's Nest,* both the novel and the movie version, provide good examples. When Kesey's protagonist, Randle P. McMurphy, first arrives at the mental hospital which is to be the setting for most of the action, his independence and shrewd assertiveness offer a wonderfully comic antidote to the dehumanizing poison at work in the institution. The story's comic dimension climaxes when McMurphy breaks out with several inmates, and they go deep-sea salmon fishing. Everything about the scene appears life-affirming—the successful escape, the sexuality, the fishing, the experience of the open sea on a beautiful day. But after the culminating comic idyl the story's grim undercurrent begins to dominate the action, and McMurphy's final trick leads to terrifying humiliation and death. The story, which begins by seeming to affirm the individual's control over his own destiny, ends in utter hopelessness, a pattern not uncommon in modern fiction.[5]

There are elements in the first part of "Badger and Coyote" that must have been humorous to the Clackamas—the Badger children's short legs, the Coyote children's burial tricks (which are also grimly ironic), the Badger children's clumsy, fumbling act, and even perhaps, as Jacobs suggests, Coyote's unsuccessful efforts to commit suicide. With the deaths of the Coyote children, however, the audience is reminded early in the story that there is no easy escape from harsh reality. If we often feel at the end of much modern comic fiction that we are somehow implicated in the horror for having laughed at its beginnings, there is no such trickery in "Badger and Coyote." The difference is partly a result of plot structure, but it has to do too with differences between oral literature, which assumes the audience knows what is going to happen, and Western literature, which does not.

Despite its concluding assertion of death as final, "Badger and Coyote" embodies a kind of affirmation that is rare in modern comic fiction: people need not be paralyzed by grief, the myth suggests, for it is possible to live with even the greatest sorrow. This is a modest claim when it is set against Coyote's struggle to overcome death itself, but it is a hard-earned acceptance of the world as it has been given to man. More than that, it suggests the possibility of salvaging some dignity in the face of loss and humiliation, for the pathetic bungler who cannot even kill himself becomes finally reconciled enough with his own limitations that he can help others comprehend their mortality.

The most dramatically compelling section of the myth is that in which Coyote attempts to bring his children back to life by carrying their remains slowly towards home in a pack basket. Here the story parallels the Orpheus motif in many Native American myths, including the powerful Nez Percé text "Coyote and the Shadow

People."[6] Coyote is not a comic trickster figure here; his patient and gentle struggle with death brings him already a measure of dignity. His ultimate loss of patience when the centipede persistently torments him with the thought of the finality of death is anything but trivial because the centipede obviously represents his own fear that his struggle against death will be futile. (Our society may be as well prepared as the Clackamas to feel the burden of this part of the myth, for we spend millions yearly on pesticides, and we are notable for having great difficulty in confronting death. There probably is a connection between our fears of death and our expensive, dangerous technological war against insects.) Finally, after Coyote loses patience and consequently fails to bring his children back to life, he offers this statement of reconciliation (the translation and interpolations are Jacobs'): "But now his [any mourner's] sorrow departs from him after ten days [of formal mourning]. Then he can go to anywhere where something [entertaining] is happening or they are gambling [and] he may [then shed his mourning and] watch on at it."[7] It is an affirmation of the power of ritual in overcoming grief, a promise that the mourner will be able to live fully once again, that the cycles of life will continue.

Coyote's losing struggle with death gives the myth much of its dramatic power, and this heroic effort to overcome a force greater than man is surely at the center of what we mean by the tragic vision. But Coyote's final submission to the everlasting cycle of birth and death, along with his bumbling frailty early in the story, is the essence of comedy.

Significantly, the final submission counselled by this Native American myth is profoundly "unAmerican." Our dominant culture's attitude toward death is well exemplified by a modern gerontologist's confession: "I really hate death." He goes on: "There is no principle in nature which dictates that individual living things, including men, cannot live for indefinitely long times in optimum health."[8] Such a combination of arrogance and innocence is undoubtedly linked to other American attitudes toward failure and human limitation. We cannot accept either with grace; Coyote accepts both. "When Coyote fails," Jacobs says, "it is as if he suddenly matures—in a manner which northwest Indians point up by his transition to a god-like enunciator of the future"; and Jacobs adds: "The myth appears to say that even the most deity-like personage was circumscribed in what he could do."[9] We are part of a society that tends to look contemptuously upon failure as self-induced and limits as self-imposed. This is the burden of what we call the American Dream, our vision of the self-made man. Not only do we want to believe as a society that people can succeed at whatever they want badly enough to do, but a seemingly corrolary faith is that our society itself can succeed at whatever it sets out to do. Indeed the view still is widely held that our society *must* continue to grow in power and influence in order to sustain the American Dream. Thus, while our society begins to convulse as we try to sustain a way of life dangerously wasteful of resources, our President tells us the first principles of our economy must be growth and expansion.

"Badger and Coyote," then, speaks directly to an important American confusion. As soon as we recognize that Coyote is no foolish cartoon figure, but an effort to imagine human being in the heroic dimensions of the Myth age, then it becomes easier to see how people achieve dignity while accepting failure, while living within the limits placed upon us all.

THREE

The American people see themselves marching through wilderness, drying up marshes, diverting rivers, peopling the wilds, and subduing nature. It is not just occasionally that their imagination catches a glimpse of this magnificent vision. [Alexis de Tocqueville, *Democracy in America*]

It is not too much to say that, despite the continuing power of the American Dream in American culture, the one characteristic which distinguishes today's undergraduates from those of other generations is a widely felt sense of being *circumscribed*, to use Jacobs' term for Coyote. Not only do our students see doors closing on their own futures, but many of them believe the prospects for mankind have nothing at all to do with the rhetoric of progress and success that continues to be part of our culture. It is possible to go a long way toward understanding the music, the religious groups, the lack of social and political activism, and even the humor of today's college students by considering their vision of a circumscribed future.

This sense of limits, of impending failure, is not simply morbid subjectivity. Indeed, in its inception it is probably closer to the realism of the child in "The Emperor's Clothes" who insists the emperor is naked despite all he has been told to the contrary. But it is a painful kind of realism, which can move young people quickly toward cynicism and despair when they lack the resources to affirm themselves within the limiting world they see. The crises and uncertainties in contemporary American education probably have more to do with the despair consequent upon this sense of limits than with diminished skills in mathematics and reading, for many of our students cannot see what is to be gained from the kind of disciplined study that is crucial to education at its best. Moreover, parents and teachers seem poorly prepared to help young people learn to live well in a world more obviously circumscribed than that in which we became adults.

Our strategies for dealing with the results of this despair are inadequate. Some of us repeat the litany of technological progress: there are no necessary limits; an expansive future only waits upon the invention of a new fuel, a better pesticide, or more effective managerial techniques. Others remind the young of what stronger generations accomplished, generations who fought their way out of the Depression or struggled for justice in the 1960s. Perhaps the most perverse explanation of all focuses on such data as falling SAT scores. Here the theme is often that we have produced a generation of slovenly youth, unwilling to apply themselves as others have to difficult intellectual problems. Out of this belief comes the call for getting back to "basics," whether they are understood as skills in mathematics and reading or traditional areas of study in general education, as though the diminished confidence of the young in their own futures were simply a matter of what they do not know.

But we are not able to convince young people that the "basics" are of consequence in the world of limits which they see, and this failure is closer to "Badger and Coyote" than it might seem. The Clackamas myth stresses precisely those values that allow people to live with dignity in a world they cannot control.

To set "Badger and Coyote" against a "classic" such as Thoreau's *Walden* is to see how far the Native American myth takes us from the American doctrine of success. Thoreau's intent in *Walden* is subversive of "success" in the sense that he works to undermine faith in material progress and the acquisition of wealth as authentic measures of success. In doing so, he offers a radical critique of American society. The argument which underlies *Walden,* the hypothesis which the Walden Pond experiment proves to Thoreau's satisfaction, is that the person who becomes an integral part of nature has succeeded in transcending society's categories for "success" so that even death itself becomes insignificant. The narrator of *Walden* has pushed life back to the "basics" which underlie civilization, achieving a selfhood that succeeds by virtue of its oneness with all nature. While this notion of selfhood sets some of the values of the dominant culture on their head, it is a success which requires disciplined self-reliance, a conscious striving toward a goal; and in that way it is consistent with our work ethic.

"Badger and Coyote," in contrast, suggests that people *are* a part of nature, or, as Jacobs puts it, "Clackamas hardly ventured upon a distinction between man and nature."[10] It is not necessary in "Badger and Coyote" to struggle to elude the falsities of society because the power of nature is what is given; in fact, Coyote turns to the traditional rituals of society, or perhaps establishes them, as a way of accepting death and thus controlling his grief. One might say that Thoreau is responding to what he takes to be too much civilization, an artificiality which cuts people off from nature and from their essential selves; and "Badger and Coyote," on the other hand, is told from the perspective of a small scale society in which nature retains all of its primeval force. But such logic can be misleading, as it was for a student from Chicago who commented while reading *Black Elk Speaks* that the Sioux were much more dependent on nature than he, because he lived some eighty floors above the ground in the John Hancock Building. It would be truer, of course, to say that the Sioux were more *aware* than the student of their dependence on nature. We are not, in fact, cut off from natural cycles, from death and decay, by even the most ingeniously contrived technologies, as we have perhaps begun to learn from our energy crisis. Even people who live eighty floors above the ground must ultimately grow old and die, and thus be reminded of the primacy of natural cycles, but because of the obvious limits to growth in our time, young people are feeling those cycles in their bones. Myths like "Badger and Coyote" can show how people have accepted that reality without surrendering to humiliating despair.

One might provide more extended comparative analyses of other works traditionally taught in American literature courses. "Badger and Coyote" might help to illuminate, for instance, the treatment of nature in several of Emerson's essays and poems, the apocalyptic dimensions in the ending of *Moby Dick,* the dark sense of entropy which haunts much of Robert Frost's poetry, and the haunting speculation about death in some of Emily Dickinson's finest poems. And such comparisons must surely throw light both ways. They will help us to begin to understand the values of cultures quite unlike our own and give us a new perspective on the values of the dominant culture.

In *Coyote Was Going There,* Jarold Ramsey has summed up well some of the values implicit in Native American literature of the Pacific Northwest: "unstinted hospitality, respect for elders, unceasing caution and alertness in all dealings with people and animals, the subordination (at least officially) of women to men, the superiority of one's own tribe or clan to all others, the adjustment of individual personality to the 'identity' of the tribe, the importance and dignity of work. . . ."[11] There is much to be said for engaging such a world from the inside, as one must do in studying the oral literature of Native American societies; and while it is true that the broad study of comparative literature offers many of the same advantages for those of us who study and teach in the area of American culture, the relationship between Native American culture and the dominant culture is so crucially important that the particular comparisons I have proposed seem especially significant. Just as we cannot understand American history apart from Afro-American history, we cannot come to grips fully with the American literary canon until it includes Native American literature.

NOTES

[1](Chicago: University of Chicago Press, 1959).

[2]I have tried to account for the very negative view of Columbia River tribes that has persisted since the time of the Expedition in an essay titled "Lewis and Clark Probe the Heart of Darkness," which appeared in *The American Scholar* (Winter 1979–80), pp. 94–101.

[3](Berkeley: University of California Press, 1959).

[4]Jacobs, *Content and Style,* pp. 29–36.

[5]One might argue that in *One Flew Over the Cuckoo's Nest* we are meant to find consolation in the escape of the Native American, who has been virtually resurrected by McMurphy; but here the contrast with "Badger and Coyote" is especially illuminating, for in the terms of Kesey's story, the Native American's escape is illusory, sentimental. In "Badger and Coyote" we are led to acknowledge a tragic reality and accept a comic resolution, but in *One Flew Over the Cuckoo's Nest,* we are invited to believe the Native American can survive by strength and integrity in a world so powerfully corrupt it has destroyed McMurphy despite his guile.

[6]Archie Phinney, *Nez Percé Texts,* Columbia University Contributions to Anthropology, vol. 25 (1934), pp. 283–85. It is collected also in Jarold Ramsey, ed., *Coyote Was Going There: Indian Literature of the Oregon Country* (Seattle: University of Washington Press, 1977), pp. 33–37.

[7]Jacobs, *Content and Style,* p. 29.

[8]Albert Rosenfeld, "The Longevity Seekers," *Saturday Review* (March 1973).

[9]Jacobs, *Content and Style,* pp. 35, 36.

[10]Ibid., p. 36.

[11]Ramsey, *Coyote Was Going There,* p. xxix.

Jarold Ramsey: 'THE HUNTER WHO HAD AN ELK FOR A GUARDIAN SPIRIT,' AND THE ECOLOGICAL IMAGINATION

ONE   It is altogether too easy to sentimentalize the American Indians and their traditional literature on the score of environmental widsom, as a glance at recent reviews of and dust-jacket blurbs about books by Indians and about native American culture will reveal. The Noble Savage stereotype, always an accurate mirror of our fears and guilts, is being re-cast nowadays as Aboriginal Ecologist, full of "PNW" (Profound Natural Wisdom)[1] and given to shedding silent tears on television over our botched landscapes, courtesy of the American Advertising Council and participating stations.

Yet our ecological crisis is diversely real, however we may misrepresent it, and we clearly need, as the saying goes, all the help we can get. In particular we need, beyond the political and economic incentives to clean up our land, air and water, to find ways to cultivate an *imaginative* awareness of man's beholden place in the natural order. Ecological science is not enough, I think, to bring us around to the simple but radical recognition that we belong to the biosphere more than it belongs to us; we must find ways to institutionalize the sense of that relationship in our very imaginations. And, all stereotypes and smarmy commercials aside, the American Indians *have* always had such ways to "reconcile/the people and the stones," as William Carlos Williams once put it ("A Sort of a Song"); and if there are sharp practical limits, given the enormous differences between the circumstances of their traditional world and ours today, to what we can learn from them on the basis of practices, we should nonetheless be looking closely at what Indians have done to inculcate in themselves the full awareness of ecological interdependence. Before the coming of the whites, at least, it was strictly a matter of daily life or death, this rapport with the rest of nature; and so, apocalyptically, it is becoming for us. "In imagination begins practicality;" we must imagine our survival on the earth.

TWO
Among Western Indian groups, the winter spirit-power ceremonials seem to have served (along with other purposes) to emphasize and renew the people's sense of participatory solidarity with the rest of creation. For example, the Wasco and Wishram Indians, closely-related Chinookan people who lived on both sides of the Columbia River near what is now The Dalles, Oregon, generally bestowed public

names on their young people in the winter season. The recipient was given the name of some long-dead but well-remembered tribesman, and in the course of the ceremony he would be identified as a named human being in the presence of the intermingled human, natural and supernatural communities of life. A ritual leader would speak to the assembly of family and tribesmen, and it would respond in unison:

> *This person will be [Spedis].*
> A-xi.
> *This name used to belong to [Spedis] a long time ago.*
> A-xi.
> *We want the mountains, creeks, rivers, bluffs, timber to know that this person is now named [Spedis].*
> A-xi.
> *We want to let the fishes, birds, winds, snow, rain, sun, moon, stars to know that [Spedis] has the same as become alive again. His name will be heard again when this person is called.*
> A-xi.[2]

Those who spoke *a-xi* on behalf of the child being named must have been sharply aware, once again, of their responsible human connections with the "mountains, rivers, timber, fishes, winds," and so on; in a special sense they and the ritual's leader were speaking *to* these entities. The same concern continues to this day in the seasonal "pre-harvest" festivals of the Wascos and Wishrams on the Warm Springs and Yakima Reservations. In the Warm Springs long-house, for example, the onset of the huckleberry season in late August is marked by several nights of ceremony, one highlight of which is an oration by a tribal leader, traditional in content and form, but delivered in English for the special benefit of children. Customarily the orator begins by observing how the people have once again met for "the dedication of a new food that's coming on this 198–," and goes on to stress how the lore of the huckleberry has been handed down since the beginning of time, according to the faith of the old people that each young generation would observe the traditional ways "as long as they are Indians."[3]

Similar ceremonies are currently observed (in some cases are being revived) in the Northwest and elsewhere on the occasion of a boy's first killing of a deer.[4] The emphasis in such rites is upon recognition of the hunter's new prowess in balance with traditional respect and gratitude for the deer and for the bounties of the land in general—bounties which, it is assumed, have a spiritual basis and are subject to human propitiation or (as the case may be) alienation and loss.

The spiritual basis of human survival in nature is widely and insistently dramatized, of course, in the traditional oral literatures of western Indians, as can be seen most clearly when one moves past sentimental Anglo re-tellings, and examines accurately transcribed and translated texts. In 1885, the pioneer ethnologist Jeremiah Curtin wintered on the Warm Springs Reservation, and, in the course of mastering the Wasco Chinook dialect, recorded a range of myths and tales from Charlie Pitt and

Donald McKay (the latter in temporary retirement as star of a Snake Oil troupe!). One of Curtin's tales, as edited by Edward Sapir and included in his *Wishram Texts* (1909)[5] is a small masterpiece of western Indian oral narrative art, marvelously concise and dramatic; and it imaginatively embodies the Indians' belief in the supreme importance of maintaining proper rapport with the rest of nature, better than any other narrative I know of. To identify the story as simply an "ecological fable" for our times would be a misrepresentation, given its considerable literary sophistication and the differences between the Wascos' "ecological" concerns, and ours—but even though we do not hunt for our daily meat, and tend to find our guardian spirits—if any—in the media, it is a story worth knowing, one to put an edge on the imagination.

The Hunter Who Had an Elk for a Guardian Spirit

There was a man at Dog River [Hood River] in days gone by, whose wife was with child. Pretty soon she gave birth to a boy. While she was sick, the man carried wood, and one day a piece of bark fell on his forehead and cut him. When the boy was large enough to shoot, he killed birds and squirrels; he was a good shot. One day, however, his father said to him, "You don't do as I used to. I am ashamed to own you. When I was of your age, I used to catch young elks. One day when I killed a young elk, the old one attacked me and made this scar you see on my forehead."

Then the boy had a visit from an elk, and the Elk said, "If you will serve me and hear what I say, I will be your master and will help you in every necessity. You must not be proud. You must not kill too many of any animal. I will be your guardian spirit."

So the young man became a great hunter, knew where every animal was—elk, bear, deer. He killed what he needed for himself, and no more. The old man, his father, said to him, "You are not doing enough. At your age I used to do much more." The young man was grieved at his father's scolding. The Elk, the young man's helper, was very angry at the old man. At last [he][6] helped the young man to kill five whole herds of elk. He killed all except his own spirit elk, though he tried without knowing it to kill even [that one]. This elk went to a lake and pretended to be dead; the young man went into the water to draw the elk out, but as soon as he touched it, both sank.

After touching bottom, the young man awoke as from a sleep, and saw bears, deer, and elk without number, and they were all persons. Those that he killed were there too, and they groaned. A voice called, "Draw him in." Each time the voice was heard, he was drawn nearer his master, the Elk, until he was at his side. Then the great Elk said, "Why did you go beyond what I commanded? Your father required more of you than he himself ever did. Do you see our people on both sides? These are they whom you have killed. You have inflicted many needless wounds on our people. Your father lied to you. He never saw my father, as he falsely told you, saying that my father had met him. He also told you that my father gave him a scar. That is not true; he was carrying fire-wood when you were born, and a piece of bark fell on him and cut him. Now I shall leave you, and never be your guardian spirit again."

When the Elk had finished, a voice was heard saying five times, "Cast him out." The young man went home. The old man was talking, feeling well. The young man told his wives to fix a bed for him. They did so. He lay there five days and nights, and then told his wives, "Heat water to wash me, also call my friends so that I may talk to them. Bring five elk-skins." All this was done. The people came together, and he told them, "My father was dissatisfied because, as he said, I did not do as he had done. What my father wanted grieved the guardian spirit which visited and aided me. My father deceived me. He said that he had been scarred on the head by a great elk while taking the young elk away. He said that I was a disgrace to him. He wanted me to kill more than was needed. He lied. The spirit has left me, and I die."

THREE

Even by the standards of Indian traditional literature, the story is strikingly compact; none of its details, it seems, is wasted, and none but contributes forcibly to the terse unity of the whole. For most Anglo readers it should be, overall, an *accessible* story—but it is well, nonetheless, to begin interpretation by aligning its elements with Chinookan ethnology.[7] Ethnographic commentary in this instance should provide, not so much revelations of esoteric meanings as a deepening of perceived meanings, and, at the same time, a set of valid limits to such perceptions.

The story centers its drama, then, on a major premise of Wasco-Chinookan culture: the highly-desirable acquisition of spirit-power, or *iyulmax,* and specifically the acquisition of a guardian-spirit.[8] Like most other western groups, the Wascos viewed their world animistically, and held that the shape and quality of an individual's life after childhood was largely determined, apart from family connections, by his secret personal commerce with animistic spirits. In particular, one was expected to go forth in childhood and adolescence in active quest for one or more guardian spirits; under conditions of physical and psychological duress (fatigue from a long solitary journey, fasting, isolation, etc.) a spirit might manifest itself to the quester, and offer, under certain conditions (notably secrecy and obedience) to serve as guardian and tutor for the rest of his life.

Occasionally the affinities between spirit and young candidate would be so strong and auspicious that the former would appear to the latter irrespective of the formal spirit quest—as, apparently, in the story at hand. But however attained, identification with a particular spirit meant that one's interests, aptitudes, and opportunities were accordingly channeled by the identification; to put it in socio-economic terms, there was a spirit-power "division of labor," such that, for example, those who received deer or elk guardians were in general supposed to be efficacious hunters, as in our story.

But, although an individual's kin and associates might infer his spiritual connection from his proclivities and accomplishments (and also from his singing and dancing during the mid-winter "power" festivities), it could not be more than a kind of "open secret" during life; and only at death, or under circumstances of mortal danger, was it to be openly revealed. So, in a historical memoir of a battle between

Wishrams and Northern Paiutes in the 1860s, when a Wishram man was wounded, apparently mortally, a wolf's backbone was displayed to represent his guardian spirit, and he revealed that, consequent to his boyhood wolf-vision, he saw certain strange weather signs which, if he were to recover now, would reappear. They did, and he recovered.[9] The display of the wolf's backbone on behalf of the dying soldier is analogous to the request on behalf of the young hunter in our story for "five elk skins" to be brought forward (*five* being, in Chinookan culture generally, the cult or spirit-pattern number, indicative of magical happenings). According to Spier and Sapir, the custom held that "the dying man called for some article connected with his spirit [and] told how he came by his power."[10]

To summarize: when a Chinookan anticipated imminent death, only then did he divulge "the greatest secret of his life,"[11] the implication being that through divulgence came release of the guardian, now no longer to be needed. What is special about our Wasco story, of course, is that the young hero dies *because* he has earlier alienated and lost his guardian spirit; what in normal circumstances would be a symptom of approaching death, the deliberate separation from one's guardian, here becomes under distressing circumstances the unwilled cause of death: "The spirit has left me, and I die." A terrible fate indeed, to be rejected by the very source of one's accustomed psychic vitality, well-being, and social identity—analogous in Christian terms to loss of the soul and in psychological terms to loss of ego.

The tensions and uncertainties of living according to the cultivation of acquired or conferred spirit-power are often neglected by ethnographers, but they are vividly manifested in traditional narratives like the Wasco story at hand. Melville Jacobs justly observes, in reference to a story from the closely related Clackamas Chinook, "The social function of the myth. . . . appears to be to reinforce in audience members their ideology of, acceptance of, and symbiotic ties with animistic super-naturals. For no greater security could be had in a precarious Chinook world than the certainties which people acquired when individual non-material helpers came and stayed through a lifetime." It is the negative of this security of spirit guardianship that is at stake in the Wasco story, and Jacobs' concluding remark points to the possibility of spiritual calamity as well as of spiritual success: "Tragedy befell when such helpers departed."[12]

Four

Now let's consider "The Hunter Who Had an Elk for a Guardian Spirit," not just as an ethnological vehicle, but as the structured and textured script of a story—as an imaginatively unified narrative. Curtin and his editor Sapir do not offer a Wasco-language text (although there is good evidence that Curtin transcribed from performances in Wasco);[13] hence it is impossible to examine and re-construct the text according to Dell Hymes' monumental discovery[14] that Chinookan narratives (as presented, for instance, prose-fashion in Sapir's dual-language *Wishram Texts*) are in reality elaborately "measured," that is, structured in terms of units of ascending scope: lines, verses, stanzas, scenes, and acts, as if in poetic drama. In fact, as numerous writers have suggested, poetic drama is the most serviceable analogy in western literature to traditional Indian narrative, given the tacit, inherently "dramatic," performable, and (it seems more and more clear) poetically measured qualities of the latter as well as the former.

Lacking the Chinookan-language text of the story, we can only approach it on the macro-structural level of "scenes" and "acts"—but I would hazard the guess that its five-paragraph translated form bears closely upon a "five-act" structure in the original. Certainly Curtin's paragraph-divisions correspond exactly to and mark off the chief movements of the narrative, as the following outline will show:

   I. The Father and the Son
       A. the boy's birth
       B. the father's injury
       C. the son's early success at hunting
       D. the father's lie about his scar
  II. The Son and the Elk Spirit
 III. The Son as a Hunter
       A. the son's success
       B. the father's censure
       C. the slaughter of the elks
       D. into the lake
 IV. The Elk's Revelations to the Son
       A. assembly of game animals
       B. censures, and revelation of father's lie
  V. The Son's Revelations to His People
       A. return to village
       B. preparation to die
       C. revelation to assembly of his spirit-guardian and of his father's lie

If this structure does correspond to the articulations of the original text (and according to Hymes' theory there would be verbal evidence, in the form of stock "marking" words and phrases), then the five-part format would presumably manifest to a Chinookan audience the sacramental power of the number *five*—warranting the story's hieratic significance. For us, adventitiously of course, such a five-part articulation may suggest tragic drama—and it is to an examination of the tragic elements of the narrative that I want now to turn.

From his boyhood on, the nameless young hero is caught up in a cruel conflict of allegiances, between his natural father and the Elk, his guardian spirit. One of the persistent impulses of traditional western Indian narrative is to dramatize and imaginatively mediate such polar oppositions between values or attitudes that in and of themselves are "good," but that may, in combination, lead a protagonist to evil consequences. In a much-discussed Clackamas story, "Seal and Her Younger Brother Lived There," for example, Seal's brother is murdered by a trickster disguised as his wife because Seal's instinct for social propriety overcomes her little daughter's acute perception that there is something suspicious about her brother's "wife."[15] In the Wasco story, of course, the father's attitudes and actions are not merely inappropriate, as Seal's are, but reprehensible. He is greedy, deceitful, exploitative, hypocritical, boastful, status-proud—yet he is the hunter's father, to whom the young man owes, as he poignantly recognizes throughout, filial obedience, even though obeying his father's demands for bigger and bigger kills means disobeying his guardian spirit's precepts.

The first act tersely reveals the father's shabby character. The fact that he received his scar while carrying wood during the period of his son's birth seems to be the fatal germ of the whole story: wood-gathering was generally women's work, analogous to men's hunting,[16] but whereas for normal husbands it would be nothing to be ashamed of, this one is compelled later, in the face of his son's initial success as a juvenile hunter, to memorialize his unheroic scar with an elaborate and evidently defensive lie about a heroic encounter with an elk. As the story unfolds, of course, the father's vicarious designs on his son's career are manifested all too clearly: it is to be assumed that he is benefitting both circumstantially (status, wealth) and psychologically from his deceitful exploitation of his son's ability, the spiritual basis of which he neither recognizes nor even considers as a possibility.

Over against the bad father, as if in compensation, comes the spirit-elk, with its noble and generous offer, apparently in response to the boy's own virtue ("he was a good shot"), of hunting prowess. The terms of the offer amount to a kind of shorthand paradigm, a code for hunters according to widespread Indian belief—to kill only what is needed, to practice humility in success, both before the animals one kills and before the human community that honors the killing, and above all to maintain grateful reverence towards the spiritual source of one's capabilities as a hunter ("serve me and hear what I say").

At first the hunter (now, significantly, the "young man") prospers according to these terms, but in the complication of Act Three his father recalls for him the lie of *his* much greater success at an equivalent age, and by scolding his son and urging him to kill more and more wantonly, he initiates the swift and continuous tragic actions of the last two acts.

Melville Jacobs has observed in his psychoanalytically-oriented studies of Clackamas and related Chinookan narratives that they reveal, to a striking degree, "an intensity of feelings about older persons, that is, about persons who possess control over others,"[17] in particular, Oedipal tensions between parents and maturing children. In particular, as Jacobs points out, there are numerous stories about "heavy," tyrannical fathers, whose attempts to control and/or exploit their children, especially sons, seem motivated by a kind of defensive and vicarious ambitiousness for their offspring. *Apropos* the ambitious father in our story, for example, there is the coyote in the Clackamas "Badger and Coyote Were Neighbors," who urges his children (four sons and a daughter) to take the lead in stealing a wonderful ball, with the result that they all are killed.[18] Another story, known to all Chinookans along the Columbia, is a veritable paradigm of the Oedipal conflict. A giant chief, with especially large feet, keeps many wives, and raises only daughters, killing all male offspring at birth. Finally some of his wives rebel, and save a boy-child by disguising it as a girl and eventually sending it away with its mother. The boy grows up, learns about his father, and after acquiring great spirit-powers, goes to the paternal "mansion" and matches his father's sexual prowess by sleeping with all of his wives in one night. The son then attacks his father on the Columbia River and (depending on the version in question), slays him and succeeds as chief, or spares him but seizes all his property and power. In either case the son "becomes" his father in approved Oedipal fashion.[19]

In still another tale bearing on the one under discussion, when a young man falls into a trance during a spirit-dancing episode, his father refuses to acknowledge that his son may be in communion with a guardian-spirit, and to prove his point places a glowing coal on the unconscious boy's hand—with the result that a hole is burned right through the hand! In terms of the focusing of our sympathies in a story like this one, or in "The Hunter Who Had an Elk for a Guardian Spirit," Jacobs' general remarks seem apt: "Paternal hostility to sons appears frequently in northwestern states myths," and "the fact of paternal initiation of Oedipal feelings seems to have been taken for granted. . . ."[20]

Another of Jacobs' ethnographic observations (specifically on a story from the Clackamas titled "Stick Drum Gambler and his older brother") serves to point out a particularly reprehensible aspect of the hunter's father. In that story, two boys receive hunting power (with eventual unhappy consequences) from their uncle "Stick Drum Gambler," who happens to be an incarnated spirit. Jacobs notes that "A person often received the supernatural of an older relative with whom he had been comparably intimate. The psychological mechanism of identification with a parent homologue is expressed as a kind of inheritance or acquisition of that homologue's spirit-power."[21] Later in the story, the two boys also manifest their father's power by turning into deer. If spirit power can then be communicated from older to younger kin, as from uncle to nephew or from father to son, or if at least the latter's acquisition of power can be facilitated by the former, then the Wasco father's lie appears as a cruel mockery of such kinship advantage, the implication in the lie being that the young hunter's prowess derives spiritually from his father's own, but does not measure up to it. And the peculiar detail in the lake-bottom revelation scene in Act Four, whereby the Elk engages the "plot" of the father's lie, in acknowledging that indeed he too had a father Elk who *might* have met the hunter's father under spirit-power circumstances—this detail now can be seen to suggest "what might have been," according to Chinookan belief, i.e., authentic transmission of spirit potency (or at least receptivity) from father to son in the human as well as the spirit world, a most auspicious interlocking of kinship relationships. Instead, the younger elk discloses, not only the father's deceit, but also his perversion of a rich spiritual possibility. "Your father lied to you. He never saw my father. . . ."

In these terms, the tragic interaction of familial and spiritual ties in the story, the terrible "double bind" of the hunter's predicament, is illuminated by and in turn extends one of Jacobs' observations on the Clackamas Chinook view of "fate"—

It is my impression that myths support the formulation that human life . . . is not affected by some ill-defined destiny; it is swayed concretely and decisively by family and more remote kin, and almost equally by spirit-powers, that is, by kin-like supernaturals with all their sharply-defined attributes.[22]

Is it not reasonable to assume that real-life conflicts occurred for young Chinookan men and their fathers and other elders upon the advent of spirit powers, realizing the potential antagonism between duty and obedience to elder kin, and the secret and imperative duties of a young man to his spirit guardian? Jacobs is right; in no way does our story suggest "some ill-defined destiny;" on the contrary it is axiomatically tragic in the way it mediates for the poor hunter between human kin and spirit kin. One wishes that Jacobs, with his unique and now irreplaceable wealth of ethnographic and literary knowledge about northwest Indians, had followed up the implications of his remarks here about "destiny."

What with his help we have found out about the hunter's fate is full of significance for the ecological understanding of the story, but before turning back, in conclusion, to that, I want to adduce two direct analogues to "The Hunter Who Had an Elk for a Guardian Spirit," from neighboring tribes, so as to set up what Dell Hymes, following Lévi-Strauss, calls a "semantic field," or "typology."[23]

First, there is in Sapir's *Wishram Texts* a rare, rather garbled Clackamas text collected by Franz Boas, titled "The Boy That Lied about His Scar."

She gave birth to a male (child), her son. Now he [the son] went to get wood, sticks he gathered. Then a stick ran into him right here [on the head]. Now his son became older. Then (his father) louses him on the head and finds his scar on his head. After they had given birth to him, a stick had run into him on his head (whence his scar). Then (his father) said to him: "How did you come to get this scar of yours?" Then he whipped his son. Then he said to him: "Where did you get to be so?"—"Once a deer struck me with its horns."—"Then bathe!" he said to his son. Then the boy bathed. Now he, the boy, became older, but elks never appeared to him (when he hunted, for he had falsely accused them of inflicting the scar upon him). Now then it is finished; he got to be old. Story, story.[24]

Clearly, for undetermined reasons, cultural priorities or simple garbling, the Wasco story has been radically transformed. There is no conflict of obedience between elder kin and spirit-guardian; the moral positions of the human actors have been reversed. Now it is the son who is a liar, and it is the father who, ignorant of his son's lie, appears to be scrupulous about spiritual observances and about truth-telling. The father does not urge impossible hunting exploits on his son, and the story offers neither a dramatic revelation in the spirit-world nor in the human realm. The ecological justice enacted is simple and private, compared to what happens in the Wasco tale—for the Clackamas boy it is a lifetime of failure at hunting, dramatized by the laconic statement "He got to be old," so different from the stark finality of the Wasco narrative.

The other text, too long to quote in full, is from the Sahaptin-speaking Klikitat of south-central Washington: "The Hunter Obtains a Deer-Hunting Power."[25] In content it is much closer to the Wasco narrative, but there are some illuminating differences. A one-legged man tells his son that he was once a great hunter, until an elk tore off his leg. "You may also encounter elk," he warns the son, "and it may do to you as it did to me." The son does not know that this is a lie, nor do we, until in the course of a hunt he encounters an "old man" who is really a Spirit Elk, and who tells the young man, "Your father (when out hunting) awakened, with only one leg. I did not do it, not I. He falsely deceived you. He was gathering wood, and there at that place he was hurt by a log. The log fell on him, and because of that his leg became that way."

The old man/elk goes on beyond this revelation (which seems to take place, as in the Wasco story, by or in a lake) with instructions that the son return to his father, expose him, and in effect supplant him—"When you return, speak to him in this manner. 'Here I am.' [Say] you saw me. 'You were no hunter of deer. I will be ruling. I see you, when you travel about, that you are a poor hunter. You should not just hunt and shoot deer. I will give it (game) to you. . . .'" The son then returns, catches his father in his persistent lie, exposes and upbraids him ("Then the old man was ashamed"), but instead of taking over his father's authority and duties, opts to return to the lake and the spirit-elk, where he "dies" (whether literally or through some sort of spiritual transformation—into an elk?—is not clear). The text ends, "That is how the old man no longer had a child."

What is important about the place this story occupies in our typological field is that the son does not act upon the father's compensatory lie about his injury until the elk's disclosure about it; then, in terms of the conflict of parental and spirit-guide obedience, he acts out of his new knowledge without hesitation in favor of the latter, and indeed eventually chooses to leave his father altogether and go back to the elk. The fact that we as audience do not know about the father's lie until the son learns about it, in itself structures a simplification of the son's predicament: contrast the Wasco narrative's declaration to us in Act One of the real origins of the father's scar, with its effect on us of an ironic foreshadowing that dramatically intensifies the father's villainy.

In terms of Lévi-Strauss's system of entabling and analyzing the permutations of bipolar oppositions in a "field" of cognate myths, we end up with the following set (in which "+" represents allegiance and "−" represents rejection in terms of the protagonist's relationship to father and spirit-guardian):

	Father	*Spirit-Guardian*
Wasco	+	−
Klikitat	−	+
Clackamas	−	−

(The Clackamas entry is conjectural—the lie the boy tells his father presumably expresses insensitivity to the possibility of spirit acquisition, and of course it costs him all hope of gaining hunting power.)

We are left, then, with an incomplete set—missing a "++" story, in which a young hunter would somehow maintain a proper measure of allegiance and obedience both to father and to spirit-guardian. It would be, clearly, a "hero" story, with idealized protagonists; such narratives exist in the western native literatures,[26] but as in our own tradition, Indian stories tend to dwell upon the *difficulties* of mediating a way between two conflicting goods, rather than upon the rewards of doing so.

Now, perhaps, this brief excursion in structuralist comparisons will allow us to see the Wasco text for the triumph of dramatic clarity and concentration it is, even in its transcribed and translated state. The narrative is so shaped from the outset that, in Acts Four and Five, the full tragic enormity of the son's predicament between two masters is dramatized in just a few details. The elk's crushing disclosure of fatherly perfidy in Act Four does not offer the son any hope of extenuation of his offense through ignorance of the father's crime; more than human justice is involved here, and the act of the crime, not the motive, will be decisive. Our sympathies notwithstanding, has not the young man in fact killed wastefully, and thus gone beyond what the Elk commanded?

As the hunter returns home to tell his secrets and die, we meet the father once more; in a marvelous ironic stroke, he is "talking, feeling well." Perhaps nothing in the story reveals more vividly how steady and whole is its imaginative view of what might seem, to Anglo readers at least, a relatively simple "ecological" issue, or, on Indian religious terms, chiefly a matter of concern between the hunter and his guardian spirit. The son's "crime," instead, is projected tragically across the whole spectrum of human life in all of its major categories—personal and psychological, familial (the father, the two wives), social ("call my friends"), economic (the hunter's evident wealth), spiritual. And, subsuming all these, in terms of what he has lost, there is what we in our mostly unimaginative way call "ecological"—but here meaning the *imaginative* perception, underscored by calamity, that our personal, familial, socio-economic, spiritual, and environmental obligations are precariously, that is to say organically, interrelated.

Five

If as a story-teller I *were* to try to appropriate "The Hunter Who Had an Elk for a Guardian Spirit" specifically for modern American purposes—in other words, make it out however reductively as "a fable for these times"—the effort would hinge, I think, on the conflict of generations in the story as in life. The Wasco father hides his inadequacies and failures behind a lie, and recklessly exploits his son's great gift and his very future by demanding more and more wasteful hunting. Is not our present environmental predicament (to say nothing of what is to come) premised on some such false and ruinous relationship between the "elder." members of our culture, and the "younger?" "Produce, produce; consume, consume; grow exponentially; do as we have done in our heroic careers, only bigger and better!" the elders of American capitalism seem to say, still, in actions if no longer so blatantly in words. And if I see this, resentfully, as a "son" of the elders of my culture, when I look in turn at my children, I find, helplessly it seems, that I am instilling some such ecological rapacity in them. The irreducible moral of the Wasco story in these terms—the bitter truth it might help us to imagine—is that in the ravaging of the natural order, it is the young who will suffer most.

"He wanted me to kill more than was needed. He lied. The spirit has left me, and I die."

NOTES

[1] I owe the sarcastic abbreviation to Karl Kroeber, who in turn got it from an Indian student of his.

[2] Leslie Spier and Edward Sapir, *Wishram Ethnography,* University of Washington Publications in Anthropology, vol. 3, no. 3 (May 1930), pp. 258–59. Reprinted in my *Coyote Was Going There: Indian Literature of the Oregon Country* (Seattle: University of Washington Press, 1977), pp. xxxiii; most of the other Chinookan texts mentioned here are likewise reprinted in this anthology.

[3] See "Coyote Made Everything" in Melville Jacobs, *The Content and Style of an Oral Literature* (New York: Wenner-Gren Foundation, 1959), pp. 59ff.: various spring-time foods say, in turn, "Were it not for me and my advent in this season, people would be unable to keep their breath."

[4] For example, see a Northern Paiute ethnographic text, "A Hunter's First Kill," in Ramsey, *Coyote Was Going There,* p. 257.

[5] Jeremiah Curtin, "Wasco Tales and Myths," in *Wishram Texts,* Edward Sapir, ed., Publications of the American Ethnological Society, vol. 2 (1909), pp. 257–59.

[6] Curtin's text appears to be slightly garbled here and in the next sentence; the guardian-elk is referred to as a female. I have restored the masculine references in keeping with the rest of the story.

[7] All who aim at a literary understanding and appreciation of traditional Indian literatures owe much to the heroic forty-years' work of Melville Jacobs as transcriber, translator, editor, and critical interpreter of Northwest repertories, and it is good to see the beginnings of a serious exploitation of his work. But on the question of accessibility, it must be noted with regret that Jacobs did *not* advance his or his subject's cause by persistently denying, in the dourest terms, that an untutored but literate "Euro-American" reader could ever enjoy and understand in the least degree native stories like those in his *Clackamas Chinook Texts*. The net effect of such pronouncements is to nullify unfairly what general readers can and do perceive in the stories as imaginative literature, incomplete and inadequate though these perceptions may be.

[8] See Spier and Sapir, *Wishram Ethnography,* pp. 238ff.; also Edward S. Curtis, *The North American Indian,* vol. 8 (Cambridge, Mass., 1911), pp. 100–106.

[9] Sapir, *Wishram Texts,* pp. 221–23, The narrator was Louis Simpson.

[10] Spier and Sapir, *Wishram Ethnography,* p. 238. The deathbed presentation of elk-skins may also, beyond the special circumstances of the story, have some connection with the fact that the Wishram and Wasco people danced their most sacred dances on elk-skins; hence the skins would have been inherently associated with spirit-power.

See Dell Hymes' analysis of Wishram guardian spirit-disclosures, based on materials in Spier and Sapir, in "Two Types of Linguistic Relativity," in *Socio-linguistics*, ed. William Bright (The Hague: Mouton, 1966), pp. 114–67, especially pp. 137–41. Hymes argues that for the Wishram people (and almost certainly for their trans-Columbia kin the Wasco), spirit-transactions, bestowal of names, and myth-recitations all partook of a linguistically-based pattern consisting of "a speaker as source, a speaker as addressor who repeats the words of the source, and an audience," (p. 150), and also a strict sense of timing. Space prevents a full discussion of this pattern in terms of the story under analysis here, but there does seem to have been an underlying formal connection between the story as a mythic narrative, and the guardian-spirit transactions it dramatized in performance. Hymes' essay helps to understand something that any Wishram or Wasco would have known by feeling: that two such "nodes" of their cultural system as spirit-power transactions and myth-tellings were organically related to one another, and together related to the other nodes of the system.

[11]Sapir, *Wishram Texts*, p. 289.

[12]Jacobs, *The People Are Coming Soon* (Seattle: University of Washington Press, 1960), p. 180.

[13]See *The Memoirs of Jeremiah Curtin*, Wisconsin Biography Series Vol. 2 (Madison, 1940), pp. 355, 360, *et seq.*

[14]Dell Hymes, "Discovering Oral Performance and Measured Verse in American Indian Narrative," *New Literary History* 8 (1976–1977): 431–57.

[15]See Hymes, "The 'Wife' Who 'Goes Out' Like a Man," in *Social Science Information* 7, no. 3 (1968): 173–99; and Jarold Ramsey, "The Wife Who Goes Out Like a Man, Comes Back as a Hero: The Art of Two Oregon Indian Narratives," *PMLA* 92, no. 1 (Jan. 1977): 9–18.

[16]In a Wishram tale in Curtin, *The American Indian*, vol. 8: 111–12, Coyote encounters a foolish Myth Age who is out gathering firewood because his wife is, they think, pregnant; he is carrying the wood between his feet, and it becomes clear that neither he nor his un-pregnant wife has any understanding of coitus! Lack of other evidence prevents the conclusion that "gathering firewood" during a wife's lying-in may have been a comic act, like our "boiling water" for nervous and useless husbands—but it is a possibility.

[17]Jacobs, *Content and Style*, p. 133.

[18]See text and commentary in Jacobs, *Content and Style*, 27–36; also commentary in Ramsey in "From 'Mythic' to 'Fictive' in a Nez Perce Orpheus Myth," *Western American Literature*, 13 no. 2 (Fall 1978): 19–31.

[19]Curtin, "Wasco Tales and Myths," in Sapir, *Wishram Texts*, pp. 248–52. There is a Clackamas version with commentary in Jacobs, *Content and Style*, pp. 108–16.

[20]Jacobs, *The People Are Coming Soon*, p. 52.

[21]Jacobs, *The People Are Coming Soon*, p. 176. In Charles Cultee's story about his great-grandfather's spirit-power accession, the young hero already has several powers, but is urged to seek *ut'unaqan*, "the female guardian spirit of your ancestors;" clearly a family spirit "connection" is meant. Franz Boas, *Chinook Texts*, UBAE 20 (1894): 214.

[22]Jacobs, *The People Are Coming Soon*, p. 179.

[23]Hymes, "The 'Wife' Who 'Goes Out' Like a Man," pp. 187ff.

[24]Sapir, *Wishram Texts,* p. 235. I have added bracketed clarifications to those in parentheses by Boas.

[25]Melville Jacobs, *Northwest Sahaptin Texts,* Columbia University Contributions to Anthropology (1934)19: 5–6.

[26]See for example, the Coos hero-tale, "The Revenge Against the Sky People," text and commentary in Ramsey, "The Wife Who Goes Out Like a Man, Comes Back as a Hero." I am indebted to Dell Hymes for suggesting, from the Lower Columbia Chinookan repertory, the story of "How Cultee's Great-Grandfather Acquired a Guardian Spirit" as a possible "++" hero story in these terms. The young hero manages to acquire the favor of the ancestral spirit *ut'unaqan,* as his father has ordered him to do, but upon his return he does not tell his father what he has accomplished, thereby preserving the secret basis of his power. See n. 21 above: Boas, *Chinook Texts,* pp. 213–14. In the same volume there is a story ("The Elk Hunter," pp. 236–67) in which a boy successfully acquires and employs elk-hunting power from a female spirit *because* he is an orphan; hence there is no conflict for him between human father and spirit-guardian, and the story stands outside our bipolar set.

Karl Kroeber: POEM, DREAM, AND THE CONSUMING OF CULTURE

For anyone trained in the study of Western literatures, the traditions of American Indian oral art are baffling. One discovers them to be radically different even from the oral literatures of Europe: Parry and his followers are of little use in North America.[1] Indian tales are confusing, but Indian poetry is often worse, seeming to be downright unpoetical. A common response has been to treat American Indian poetry with varying degrees of condescension—as "primitive." It seems to me, however, that "primitive" is exactly what it is not. It cannot accurately be described as an early or partially developed form of literature of which our own exemplifies advanced or perfected accomplishment. Indian poetry is radically different from ours, particularly in its cultural functions—a point that will be emphasized at the conclusion of this essay. Indian poetry becomes more interesting, as well as more valuable as a contrast to our art, the more we attend to differences, instead of depreciating it by creating spurious genetic orders and connections.

One fashion of highlighting distinctions is to consider how the "primitive" has been treated by poets in our own tradition. I begin, therefore, with a famous reference to "savage" thought, so as to establish a basis for subsequent examination of characteristics of Indian poetry. Almost any reference to "savages" in our literature is so far from historical fact as to be useful only for contrast with reality. But it happens that John Keats is a special case. He loved the ornate mythology of high classical antiquity, and the richly elaborated traditions of Western European poetry, especially as exploited by the great English poets of the Renaissance, Spenser, Shakespeare, Milton. Keats wasn't interested in "primitive" art, and he cared little even for the "folk" material becoming modish in his day. His longest poem after *Endymion* was *Hyperion,* to which, late in his brief career with the hand of death already on him, he returned, recasting it as *The Fall of Hyperion—A Dream.* Although perhaps more profoundly "Miltonic" than the original, the revision—reflecting a consistent evolution in Keats's art and the course of his life—focuses some of his most serious self-questionings and questionings of his aesthetic heritage. The introductory lines, significantly, carry us away from the European tradition:

Fanatics have their dreams, wherewith they weave
A paradise for a sect; the savage too

From forth the loftiest fashion of his sleep
Guesses at Heaven: pity these have not
Trac'd upon vellum or wild Indian leaf
The shadows of melodious utterance.
But bare of laurel they live, dream and die;
For Poesy alone can tell her dreams,
With the fine spell of words alone can save
Imagination from the sable charm
And dumb enchantment. Who alive can say
'Thou art no Poet; mayst not tell thy dreams'?
Since every man whose soul is not a clod
Hath visions, and would speak, if he had lov'd
And been well nurtured in his mother tongue
Whether the dream now purposed to rehearse
Be Poet's or Fanatic's will be known
When this warm scribe my hand is in the grave.[2]

At this point I am less interested in interpreting these lines than in making explicit *how* we read them, that we read by interpreting. We read, as we say, critically, because the poem is written to be read as a difficult text to be interpreted. That is the poetry's primary, effectively its sole, function. The contemporary critic Harold Bloom usefully exemplifies how and to what purpose we read Keats:

> . . . the Fall *is very nearly the archetypal Romantic poem. However Christian or classical some of his commentators might want him to be, Keats himself in the* Fall *chose to be a poet very much of the Shelleyan or Blakean kind, a vitalist of the imagination. Keats began the theme of the Titans as an attempt at epic, but found himself on the edge of composing an equivalent of the* Intimations *or* Dejection *odes, in concealed form. Having discovered this, he abandoned epic and turned to romance again, to a dream vision that could accommodate the great Romantic theme of the poet relating himself to the content of his own vision. The myth of the Titans and Olympians had to be made honestly representative of the poet's own state of mind.* The Fall of Hyperion *is a subjective version of the romance, just as* Childe Harold, Endymion, *and most of Shelley's major poems are psychologized versions of the ancient patterns of quest and alienation which typify the romance as a form. . . .*[3]

As will appear, I agree with some of this; but now I want to call attention to the self-contained, totally "literary" character of Bloom's criticism, which, whether one agrees or not with all details, responds appropriately to a "literary" quality in Keats's poetry. Bloom's interpretation, one notices, is sequential: "Keats began . . . found himself . . . having discovered . . . he . . . turned . . . again." Bloom consistently presents the poem as valuable for revealing patterns; specifically it is exemplary of the fashion in which a literary grouping, Romantics, modified pre-existent literary patterns. And the direction of the sequence is clear, consistent: the poet makes a pattern representative of his "own state of mind," which Bloom sees engaged in "relating himself to the content of his own vision." Traditional forms and themes are used by the Romantic poet to satisfy his particular psychic necessities. The criticism focuses our understanding on concealed processes of assimilating traditional modes to the needs of Keats's psyche, and so, presumably, satisfying analogous needs in us, the readers of Bloom's criticism. Quite simply, one "understands" Bloom's criticism very much in the same fashion that one understands Keats's poetry. The interpretation evoked by the poem calls upon mental energies in us like those Bloom finds in Keats.

What part can the illiterate poets to whom Keats refers have in all this? Keats, one must stress, knew nothing of Indians beyond what he may have read in Robertson. He was not really interested in "savages." And his style is about as remote from any "primitive" style as it is possible to be. So it is specially curious that in these introductory lines he links poetry, dream, and power in a fashion analogous to some American Indian cultures, which treat song as the telling of dreams manifesting great spiritual potency. Even Keats's suggestion that anyone might be such a poet accords with the "poetical democracy" of these cultures. The analogies are, of course, only superficial coincidences, but speculation about how they came about may be critically useful. The transposition of the "epic"—extensive, affirmative— *Hyperion* into *The Fall of Hyperion: A Dream* implies exactly the doubts and uncertainties which are stressed in the introductory eighteen lines. Equivalent dubieties continue throughout the revision Keats could not complete, in part at least because he could not reconcile into coherence the literary traditions to which he was committed and an antithetical personal experience. To put it bluntly, the dying poet found the heroic affirmations of the classical-Miltonic epic intolerable. Though the Dantesque dream-vision provided him a form for his bitter perspective on the tradition in which he had been working, Keats could not, as Bloom observes, accommodate the content of Dante's Christian vision to himself.

The root of this problem, as Stuart Sperry observes in the most judicious of recent analyses, is Keats's inability finally to discriminate (as he seems to intend) *vision* from *dream* and so to complete the "redemptive ascent" which should distinguish the visionary poet from the fanatic, idly selfish dreamer.[4] This "supreme expression of tragic irony in Keats's work" illuminates (as less tortured and less self-doubting works cannot) limits of our literary tradition. The fascination in the *Fall of Hyperion* lies in its unusual and unconventional questioning of the relation of poetry to dream, and its frustrated refusal to accept received definitions of that relation as a source of power. Sperry says that Keats not only had "come to see an important analogy between man's Original Sin and the primal act of poetic conception," but even to regard "the power of imagination . . . as something less than unqualified blessing" (p. 320). Certainly Keats, for whatever reasons, had come to agonized doubting of the whole religious/cultural structure upon which Western literature was founded. But that doubt is not shared by Bloom. The contemporary critic is surer than the Romantic poet of the absolute significance of the Western intellectual/ literary tradition—which may be why it is the poet who drags in savages.

In understanding Keats's confused awareness, an Indian, non-Western conception of the interrelation of dream to poetry as a source of power is helpful, since to do

Keats justice we need a view from outside the tradition with which he was engaged in such agonized self-debating. But it is difficult to get outside our own literary tradition, which powerfully insists upon its embodiment of universal aesthetic principles. Even the best-intentioned students of Indian literatures tend to assimilate them into our theory of art, thereby destroying their value as a counterforce to our habitual fashions of thinking about literary processes. An illustration is the claim in a recent popular anthology of American Indian literature by its editor, Frederick Turner III, that the following poem, translated from the Ojibwa, "will undoubtedly strike many readers as quintessentially modern with its anticipation of Gertrude Stein in the final line, its imagistic thingness/ineffability."

> *Whence does he spring*
> *the deer?*
> *Whence does he spring*
> *the deer, the deer, the deer?*[5]

So introduced and printed—Turner uses the version devised by John Bierhorst in an earlier anthology—the modern reader certainly will think of Gertrude Stein. But if we go back to Bierhorst's and Turner's source, our minds will probably take another direction. To this end it is worth looking at Frances Densmore's original presentation.[6]

SONG OF THE DEER DANCING

Ti - bi - wĕn - da - ba - no - gwĕn ai - ya - bĕ ti - bi - wĕn - da -

ba - no - gwĕm ai - ya - bĕ ai - ya - bĕ ai - ya - bĕ

Words:
ti´biwĕnda´banogwĕn´ . . . . *whence does he dawn?*
aiya´bĕ . . . . *the buck?*

Densmore calls the principal phrase a "common idiomatic phrase," which, though she translates it as "whence does he dawn," she says in a note "is not unlike the expression, 'Where did he spring from,'" the latter being perhaps the more accurate rendering. She translates *aiya'be* as "the buck," that is, referring specifically to male deer, which seems a worthwhile distinction in the light of the circumstances surrounding the original performance of the song. And, finally, one notices that her report of the Ojibwa song perhaps indicates less a Stein-like triple repetition than

This drawing by the nineteenth-century artist George Catlin of a Mandan Buffalo Dance illustrates a more formal ceremony than that of the Ojibwa "Song of the Deer Dancing." In both cases, however, the dancers represent both hunters and their quarry. (Photo courtesy of the Rare Book Division of the New York Public Library, Astor, Lenox, and Tilden Foundation.)

"line one" repetition and ending doublet. It seems clear that Bierhorst's and Turner's transformations of Densmore's original are unconscious efforts to make the Indian song conform to Western ideas of "the literary." But the song is primarily interesting precisely because it will not so conform. When we look into its origin and function, for example, we find something totally antagonistic to "imagistic" art:

> *Long ago an old man made a feast and invited all the men and women. He did not tell them why they were asked; he only said there would be a dance. When they were all assembled the old man who had asked them sang this song, which had come to him in a dream, and another old man led the dance, acting like a deer. The men followed him, acting like the buck deer and the women acted like the doe. In old times hunters had a dance like this in the evening and went out to hunt the deer the next morning.* [Densmore, p. 201]

It is worth being clear as to the sequence here. The singer Frances Densmore recorded more than half a century ago repeats the story of another's dream, the function of which "in old times" was to prepare for a hunt. The modern singer does not simply recollect the original old man's story of a dream, he verbally recreates part of it, just as in earlier times other Indians acted out, danced, the dream. The song, thus, gives us a glimpse into how unique experience can become, and has become, cultural tradition. Beginning in private dream, part of a personal gift, the song becomes available to others, finally, even to those, ourselves, beyond the culture from which it emerged. Because we receive the song "beyond" its originating culture, any comparison such as the one to Imagism is sure to be falsifying—and to that degree diminishing of the original's power to let us perceive our own art from a new perspective. For instance, the specific beginning of this Ojibwa traditional song is not exactly identified: it started with an anonymous "old man" sometime "long ago." The later singer participates in a tradition recreatively, rather than merely reciting a later "version" of some definitively placed original. The Indian tradition is not so purely genetic as our own; origination does not equate with primacy so neatly as in our art.

The point may usefully be pursued a little. How far the Ojibwa song is from imagistic or other poetic modes familiar to us is illustrated by the title Densmore uses, though it is understandably ignored by Turner and Bierhorst: "Song of the Deer Dancing." The title has the advantage of directing us away from any record of mere visual perception. It is a dance song, intended to engage its "audience" in reenactment of a private dream experience, the audience's performance leading to an increase in *their* power, namely success in hunting the next day. As Densmore notes, the rhythm of the song is "expressive of the dance and its pantomime." The song, in fact, is libretto and score for a dance drama. The invited audience acts like deer when the song is sung. And "when" is between dream-inspiration and actual hunt. This Indian dramatic lyric is a transactional event, a process by which dream power is realized as cultural potency. Without committing myself to the kind of exhaustive proof which ultimately would be required, I want to propose that the enactment, the dramatic dancing, of the "Song of the Deer Dancing" is typical of Ojibwa, and more generally of American Indian practices.

As a single example, one can cite a parallel brought forward by Densmore from another Ojibwa singer:

bi´jiki´wug	*the buffalo*
we´yaka´gabuwiwa´djin	*as they stand in a circle*
. . . .	
wa´doka´wagwa´nine	*I join with them*
be wa ni e wa ni e	
wa´doka´wagwa´nine	*I join with them*
. .	
ä bwi ä wi bi ä bwi ä	

In this example the first ellipsis indicates a three-measure musical phrase without words, the second a single wordless measure. Lines four and six are composed of "meaningless" vocables, though the structure of these "refrains" echoes the structure of the song as a whole.[7] One reason for citing this piece is that its origin lies in what we would normally call a vision rather than a dream, probably a more common source for Indian song than regular dreams:

A man who was fasting is said to have heard the buffalo sing and to have learned their song. As he was wandering about he heard sounds which seemed to come from some gathering of Indians. On going to the place he saw a herd of buffalo walking in a circle, knee-deep in mud, with swaying heads and lashing tails; all were singing as they walked around. The Indian joined the herd and thereupon became a buffalo. For this reason they gave him the song which they were singing. [Densmore, p. 202].

The fasting vigil to obtain visionary experience is a widespread feature of many American Indian cultures, and although there are important specific variations, the fundamental pattern illustrated by the Buffalo Song may be taken as representative. Although the accounts indicate that the Buffalo Song resulted from someone seeking visionary experience, whereas the Deer Dancing Song came unsought, in both cases dance/song reproduces an event of unusual psychic power, whereas in Keats's poem the words come after, are "telling" only. One should not be distracted by the intrinsic content of the Indian song, e.g., buffalo singing-dancing, which is not from the Ojibwa point of view as startling as it may be to us. Animals play virtually no part in Western poetry but are crucial to Indian literatures. And Indians usually regarded animals as superior to men, being impressed by animals' remarkable adaptations to the exigencies of natural existence. But more important than superiority or inferiority is the Indian attention to interactiveness between human and animal and their development of a rich, flexible imagining of animal beings.

Evidence of the interactivity is likely to impress us most in stories, such as those dealing with Coyote. These we find baffling because Coyote can be animal or man at any time and without any seeming consistency. This is a crucial imaginative point. The Indian imagination is not so rigidly tied as our own to given material forms and patterns. For us, to be "characters" animals have to be anthropomorphized. The Indian imagination recognizes Coyote as both animal and man, or either animal or man, the duality in fact making him "Coyote" rather than "just" the exceedingly interesting four-footed predator. The complexity of the Indian imagination is germane to the practical core of the hunting songs we are considering here. An Indian hunts to eat. He and his tribe survive so far as he and they understand effectively the nature of animals and their interrelations. Real hunting is entirely different from the random and gratuitous killing which members of the National Rifle Association *call* hunting. True hunting requires an intense, long-term, complexly reciprocal interaction between man and animals, an interaction that can be sustained only by active exercise of all man's powers, physical, mental, imaginative. The reciprocity can lead to profound understanding: as Farley Mowat discovered, the Eskimo have long known what we have only recently learned, that caribou need wolves hunting them, for the caribou are dependent on their predators to destroy the ill and feeble and thus sustain the genetic strength of the herd. Yet perception of ecosystem balances accompanies recognition of differentiation within the system—man and deer, more than wolf and caribou, are distinct. The Deer Dancing Song confirms human distinctness, as the dancers are the deer only pantomimically—"magically"—the differentiation making possible the reciprocity of activities which finally are most dramatically crystallized in the actual hunt when man's weapons kill deer. Preparatory and celebratory "dramatic" ceremonies for hunting are functional embodiments of the magical interdependence of diverse modes of being among natural creatures, including man. Culture, in the Indian view, has a distinctive role in the complex of processes constituting the natural world, and singing defines that role.

At this point one can begin to understand why so often, as in the Deer Dancing Song, Indian poems emerge from visionary states. It isn't here possible, of course, to indicate the variety of American Indian conceptions of "dream," nor the multitude of diverse significancies given by Indians to dreams, visions, and hallucinatory experiences.[8] It will suffice, however, to observe that a common element in the Indian dream or vision is a manifestation of power. Of course, power is dangerous: implicit in strength to heal is strength to infect. The danger of power threatens anyone, not just healer or shaman. This is why I have picked for a focal text a song associated with a person of no special sanctity, just an "old man." The most familiar European oral poetry depended upon professional singers, but for much Indian poetry no specialized bard, minstrel, or shaman is necessary. Again, the lack of specialization does not in itself make Indian song primitive, just different from ours, less alienated, more democratic.

But not without its peculiar tensions. One of these John Keats inadvertently pointed to in his muddled attempt toward discriminating vision from dream. As Sperry indicates, at issue is not a mere distinction between words but rather the question of finding a more than personal, a "visionary," significance for a totally personal, inner, "dream" experience. Keats's difficulty with "dream" and "vision" is symptomatic of his (and Western poets' generally) difficulty in making connections between experiences of interior psychic power and external, social efficacies.

An old Ojibwa had a dream. Why did he give a feast, invite others, and originate what then became a traditional hunting dance? He was old, that is, no longer a hunter. He apparently had dreamed of deer dancing. To the Ojibwa dreamer that dream made him a vessel of power for his tribe, his deer-hunting culture. Whatever pains or fears the dream may have caused the dreamer, wherever in his unconscious mind it may have taken shape, it provoked him to a sociocultural act, feast, dance, creation of ceremony. By inviting others to a feast and singing to them the song he had been taught in his dream as the basis for a dance (a repeatable ceremony, a ritual, if you will), he *transmitted* the power which had been given to him. Or perhaps we should say he purged himself of it, for there is no evidence that he enjoyed his dream experience. If anything, the suggestions are to the contrary, implying someone at the least awed by a power come unexpectedly upon him. But what had been inner experience was translated into external, transmissible cultural power.

The dance ceremony is a release of the power of the dream. By articulating his visionary experience so that it can be socially embodied, the dreamer frees himself from a burden of power while enhancing his tribal culture. The dance ceremony may legitimately be regarded as a kind of therapy, but not just for the dreamer. The tribe reenacts the individual's dream to possess that power which had possessed him. Crucial is the reenacting. The dancers act like deer, the men like bucks and the women like doe (how many of *us* can distinguish the movements of male and female deer?), because the song is not *about* the dream—as is Keats's *Fall of Hyperion*—but was *in* the dream. The song is dream material, not a report of it. The ceremony, therefore, culturally manifests private, psychic experience. Cultural form, the song-dance, makes possible retention for the strength of the group what originated in the recesses of the individual psyche, even during the isolation of sleep.

In the light of this Ojibwa example, Keats's suggestion that poetry is telling of dream takes on a specificity and intensity of meaning he could not consciously have intended, that he could not effectively develop. It appears that the painful circumstances of his life may have forced upon him a poignant intuition of his imaginative gift as a dangerous, even fatal, power. Keats had had enough medical training to know that he was a dying poet. If there are confusions in *The Fall of Hyperion* it may be because he felt obscurely that he was dying of poetry.

Yet even had Keats been aware of the Indian view I've described, the awareness could have done nothing more than further frustrate him. There was for him, as for all Western poets, no social outlet through which to discharge the dangerous potency within his psyche. Publication, admiring friends, even wide popularity are not effective substitutes for the Indian's tribe. The tribe consists not in listeners or audience merely, but of cultural supporters who can physically aid the poet by giving a social form to the power speaking through him. As the old man sings his dream, the dancers contribute to its recreation by acting like deer: they reproduce his dream for their tribe. The poem thus is means by which psychic energy flows into sociological structure, thence into practical activity, hunting, which makes the participants effective in the natural world, provides them with power.

Because the kind of contrast I've been drawing is to a degree arbitrary, it must be kept descriptive, not evaluative. While it is possible to suppress one's ethnocentric preferences, in so doing (since repression is not elimination), one may fall into a misleading nostalgia for some ideal of a "vanished primitive wholeness." I hope I've avoided that trap by keeping my contrast aimed at showing how American Indian poetry can aid us in understanding a particular poem and in clarifying fundamental problems of criticism, including that of what we call "literary history." The temporal indefiniteness of the Ojibwa song's origin, "long ago," is symptomatic of a wholly different concept of the history of art, as well as of history. Whereas we put stress upon particularized sequences of art works, the Indian, focusing on reenactment, regards specificity of genesis as less important than continuity of power-flow. Hence the repetitiveness *in* the poem is reflective of the performative repetitiveness which constitutes its persistence as a practical social force.

Or take the apparently simple matter of length. At first glance we would say that the passage from *The Fall of Hyperion* is longer than Deer Dancing Song, for it is our habit to equate length with physical size of text. But in each performance the Ojibwa poem is repeated. Danced out in this fashion, it will "last longer" than Keats's eighteen lines, which are not meant for repeating but for what we call *rereading*. Our criticism emphasizes, in fact, that each rereading should be a new experience. The nonrepetitive rereading seems to constitute the basis for our modern conception of a *text*, that is, the source for nonrepetitive reiterations. This difference, in turn, corresponds to differences in interior dynamics—the Keats passage can be briefer because it is so profoundly distilled. It is a condensation requiring a dramatically intricate verbal organization of polarized tensions. Every rhetorical and linguistic device to sustain self-implication, irony, metaphor, oxymoron, contrastive imagery, balancing of phonemes, and more, Keats deploys so carefully and rigorously that only the lengthiest and subtlest of critical analyses can reveal how much is locked within this dense verbal structuring—the kind of analysis adumbrated in the passage from Bloom quoted earlier. The Indian poem is fashioned otherwise. Its function is the transfer or utilization of tensions rather than their creation. It opens outward, away from itself, into ceremonial dance, into public activity, rather than concentrating into itself. *The Fall of Hyperion: A Dream* is characteristic of Western poetry, not just Keats's, in leading back into itself, returning us finally to the dreamer himself. And if Keats doesn't do the job properly, Bloom does it for him. Such return of desire upon its origin makes a kind of frustration inevitable. The Keatsian agony is to a significant degree the agony of all Western poetry. The articulation of the Ojibwa dream is a liberation of it from the dreamer's self. The contrast relates to the processes of energy-expenditure involved in the two works and characteristic of the two traditions.

Keats's poetry is energy-consuming. Response to it demands critical exertion which is absorbed into the poem, becomes subsumed in the strictly literary tradition of which criticism becomes itself a part, as modern critics like Bloom have demonstrated. Keats's poem in a real sense exists only in our criticism; it can only be read "critically." The Indian poem, however, is without critics. The tradition to which it belongs requires no criticism, just as it requires an "audience" only in a far more dynamic sense than that word connotes for us. Indeed, so far as the Indian song transfers energy rather than absorbing it, it is not part of any purely literary tradition at all: the flow of power is literal, dream producing dance which enables effectual hunting. So the song works to keep a balance of energy not just in literature, not just in culture, but throughout the world: life-power moves through dream to song to ceremony to the hunt sustaining life through death.

It is not at all easy for us imaginatively to appreciate this Indian conception, but at least it draws attention to the fact that any culture does depend on energy, and that our own energy-consumptive literature is in a profound and no paradoxical sense anti-cultural. It is not merely Romantic and post-Romantic poets and contemporary critics who have made our art energy-absorbing. Aesthetic piety tempts one to say the practice is as old at least as *The Aeneid,* but honesty compels one to go farther, all the way back to Homer. It is not easy to find any Western art that doesn't serve as a locus for collecting power to itself, rather than passing it on into socially productive activity. Hence the curious discontinuities in our literary traditions within cultural coherence. And it might be argued that Keats in *The Fall of Hyperion* marks the beginning of self-awareness of the problem of the anti-cultural thrust of our literature. Perhaps Keats's continuing appeal owes something to his naive confrontation of the entropic nature of poetry which so persistently would make an end of itself.

NOTES

[1]See *The Making of Homeric Verse: The Collected Papers of Milman Parry* (Oxford: Clarendon Press, 1971); also A. B. Lord, *The Singer of Tales* (Cambridge: Harvard Univ. Press, 1960).

[2]*The Poetical Works of John Keats,* ed. H.W. Garrod (Oxford: Clarendon Press, 1958, 2nd ed.), p. 509.

[3]Harold Bloom, *The Visionary Company* (Garden City: Anchor, 1963 [1961]), pp. 417–18.

[4]Stuart M. Sperry, *Keats the Poet* (Princeton: Princeton University Press, 1973), p. 334; the full discussion, pp. 310–35, richly repays attention.

[5]*The Portable North American Reader,* ed. Frederick W. Turner III (New York: Viking, 1974), p. 239, taken from *In the Trail of the Wind,* ed. John Bierhorst (New York: Farrar, Straus & Giroux, 1971).

[6]Frances Densmore, *Chippewa Music—II, Bureau of American Ethnology,* 53 (Washington, D.C. 1913): 201.

[7]Densmore, "Song of the Buffalo," p. 203. On the structure of such refrains, see Dell H. Hymes, "Some North Pacific Coast Poems: A Problem in Anthropological Philology," *American Anthropologist* 67 (1965): 316–41.

[8]Amongst the vast literature, two good starting places are Dorothy Eggan, "Hopi Dreams in Cultural Perspective," *The Dream and Human Societies,* ed. G. E. von Grunebaum and Roger Caillois (Berkeley and Los Angeles: University of California Press, 1966), pp. 237–63, and George Devereux, *Mohave Ethnopsychiatry and Suicide, Bureau of American Ethnology,* 175 (Washington, D.C. 1956). Here I wish to stress the simple, obvious point that dream is specially functional where preparatory (and celebratory) mimesis involves rehearsing not only the hunter's but also the quarry's role.

William Nichols: BLACK ELK'S TRUTH

In 1937, just six years after John G. Neihardt heard Black Elk recite the narrative of his life and visions which was published in 1932 as *Black Elk Speaks,* Erik H. Erikson visited the Pine Ridge Indian Reservation, where the important meeting between Neihardt and the Oglala Sioux holy man had taken place. Apparently, Erikson did not meet Black Elk, who moved around considerably in those years; but Erikson wrote a fascinating essay, "Hunters Across the Prairie," based primarily on his meetings with others among the Oglala Sioux. And more than three decades later Erikson published a brilliant study of another holy man who struggled to find a way to save his people from being engulfed by western society, *Gandhi's Truth.*

Erikson's efforts to understand modern Sioux culture and to uncover the roots of Gandhi's greatness offer help in grasping the thematic richness of *Black Elk Speaks,* which is the account of a lifelong struggle to lead the Sioux out of disaster and into the light of a vision which Black Elk experienced when he was nine years old. The text of *Black Elk Speaks* is infused with Sioux history and tradition, as well as Black Elk's complex inner life—with an approach to truth which parallels remarkably Gandhi's *Satyagraha,* his "truth force."

ONE

By 1890 and the massacre at Wounded Knee, Erikson says in "Hunters Across the Prairie," the Sioux world had essentially come to an end, the consequence of "an apocalyptic sequence of catastrophes, as if nature and history had united for a total war on their too manly offspring."[1] Erikson is not here asserting the savagist belief in the inevitable annihilation of the American Indian that Roy Harvey Pearce has analyzed in *Savagism and Civilization;*[2] instead, Erikson's emphasis is on the inner world. The key external event in the apocalypse was the killing of the buffalo, as Black Elk saw; and Erikson stresses the crisis in child training and leadership which this loss entailed.

Erikson's reminder of the cultural dimensions of these catastrophic decades for the Sioux is helpful as we consider *Black Elk Speaks* because there is a sad paradox in Black Elk's account of the period. He begins his story by insisting that he would not tell it if it were only his autobiography: "It is the story of all life that is holy and is good to tell, and of us two-leggeds sharing it with the four-leggeds and the wings of the air and all green things; for these are children of one mother and their father is one Spirit."[3] This is not simply a formula for modesty; it is what Black Elk truly believed about the world, as we shall see. It is at the center of his vision. Nevertheless —and this is the paradox—Black Elk's conclusion is deeply personal, as though the catastrophe were his responsibility alone.

At the same time that we honor Black Elk's sense of personal accountability, we must keep in mind the fact that it can be understood only in the context of the Sioux apocalypse. Like Henry Adams' "failure" in *The Education,* Black Elk's eludes the categories of success and failure as they are developed in much American autobiography. Both men set themselves against historical forces far more powerful than any single person. Moreover, Black Elk's story does not end with the sad conclusion of his narrative, for Neihardt tells us that, having finished the story, they made a trip to Harney Peak, where Black Elk called down rain from what had been a cloudless sky, and then he prayed: "O make my people live" (p. 234). Black Elk never seems to have given up entirely the hope that the power of his vision would redeem his people, and his decision to tell Neihardt his story can be understood as a desperate effort to give its healing power to the world beyond the Sioux.

Just how desperate this act must have seemed to Black Elk himself is perhaps suggested by the fact that his son, Benjamin Black Elk, who served as his interpreter, had heard only fragments of his father's great vision before Black Elk talked with Neihardt. The task of interpreting his vision in ways that would give meaning to his people's experience was arduous, and Black Elk was concerned throughout his life to be faithful to his visions, especially to the great vision which came to him when he was nine years old and near death. Indeed, his own powers as a warrior and a healer were wholly dependent on his vision, he believed; and if he were to misappropriate it in his efforts to share it with his people, he would lose his powers altogether. Thus, Black Elk's account of his long relationship with intensely remembered visionary experience tells of a tension-filled alternation of guardedness and sharing until he finally decided to share as much as he could put in words with Neihardt: "It has made me very sad to do this at last, and I have lain awake at night worrying and wondering if I was doing right; for I know I have given away my power when I have given away my vision, and maybe I cannot live very long now" (p. 174).

Erikson's view of the link between leadership and what he calls *generativity* offers a helpful way to think about Black Elk's decision to speak so fully to Neihardt. *Generativity,* a term for the individual's enlarging concern with projects and people beyond the self, typically dominates the middle years of the life cycle, in Erikson's view:

> I have said that in this stage a man and woman must have defined for themselves what and whom they have come to care for, what they care to do well, and how they plan to take care of what they have started and created. But it is clear that the great leader creates for himself and for many others new choices and new cares. These he derives from a mighty drivenness, an intense and yet flexible energy, a shocking

> *originality, and a capacity to impose on his time what most concerns him—which he does so convincingly that his time believes this concern to have emanated naturally from ripe necessities.*[4]

The impulse to care for his people developed early in Black Elk; it was a part of his vision. His decision to share the vision with Neihardt seems to have been a natural enlargement of that impulse. The "shocking originality" in Black Elk's narrative is not so much in what he did or said, but in what he meant to do—that is, share his vision with the world beyond the Sioux. He did not succeed in his lifetime, but *Black Elk Speaks* is built upon the "mighty drivenness" which Erikson associates with great leaders. If the tone of the narrative combines the irony of Henry Adams' *Education* with the religious humility of Gandhi's *Story of My Experiments with Truth* or Jonathan Edwards' *Personal Narrative,* the view of the self is closer to that in Walt Whitman's early poems. That is, Black Elk's sense of failure grows from his conviction that he was given the power to lead his people out of the nightmare brought upon them by the coming of the white man.

Two

> *Crazy Horse rides the circle of his people's sleep,*
>   *from Little Big Horn to Wounded Knee,*
> *Black Hills, their shadows are his only robe*
>   *dark breast feathers of a future storm.*
> [Peter Blue Cloud, "Crazy Horse Monument (to the sculptor)," 1973]

The early chapters of *Black Elk Speaks* say nothing about the need for a great leader. As Black Elk and his friends Fire Thunder and Standing Bear alternate in telling about the Fetterman Fight (December 21, 1866) and the Wagon Box Fight (August 2, 1867), they say little about the leadership of Chief Red Cloud. The chief calls the people together when they must fight, but the implicit message of Chaper II, "Early Boyhood," seems to be that Sioux children were so well-trained to deal with conflict that the people needed little direction when the time came to fight. Like jazz musicians who have subjected themselves so fully to a shared discipline that their separate improvisations ultimately merge, the Sioux warriors seemed to need no leader with a structured plan. This pattern of shared leadership is even more apparent in Chapter IV, "The Bison Hunt," where Black Elk and Standing Bear stress the ritualistic nature of the hunt. The strategy of the hunt is present in the traditions that surround it, and there is no need for a single leader to coordinate the actions of the people.

But as it becomes evident that in the seemingly endless stream of white men with their powerful technology, the *Wasichus,* the people are confronted with a threat which their traditions are not adequate to meet, then the theme of the great leader emerges. It first appears when some of the Oglalas, Black Elk's band, go to live near Fort Robinson in the winter of 1873. In an act similar to gestures of youthful defiance characteristic of the 1960s, one of the Sioux boys climbs the flagpole at the fort and chops off its top. The response, again reminiscent of the 1960s, is extravagantly military: the people are surrounded by soldiers with guns. Red Cloud stands unarmed in the middle and addresses the soldiers: "He said the boy who did it must be punished, and he told the Wasichus it was foolish for men to shoot grown people because little boys did foolish things in play; and he asked them if they ever did foolish things for fun when they were boys. So nothing happened" (p. 53). As usual, Black Elk understates the drama, but it seems clear that Red Cloud defused a situation which might have become a massacre. Significantly, however, Black Elk uses the event to say that Red Cloud's days as a leader were actually over when he made the courageous speech; and the account of his eloquence becomes the occasion for introducing the figure who dominates the middle section of the narrative: "Crazy Horse was an Oglala too, and I think he was the greatest chief of all" (p. 53).

Crazy Horse was a relative of Black Elk, and one of the first things Black Elk tells about him is that he was the first chief in their family. There had been holy men in the family but no chiefs, and although Black Elk tells of Crazy Horse's acts of courage, he emphasizes the power of the great man's vision. Indeed, Black Elk's childhood memory of Crazy Horse suggests he remembered him more as a holy man than as a warrior:

> All the Lakotas [Sioux] like to dance and sing; but he never joined a dance, and they say nobody ever heard him sing. But everybody liked him, and they would do anything he wanted or go anywhere he said. He was a small man among the Lakotas and he was slender and had a thin face and his eyes looked through things and he always seemed to be thinking hard about something. He never wanted to have many things for himself, and he did not have many ponies like a chief. They say that when game was scarce and the people were hungry, he would not eat at all. He was a queer man. Maybe he was always part way into that world of his vision. [p. 72]

Such a description tells as much about the collective mind of the Sioux during this terrible period in their history, and about Black Elk's conception of leadership, as it does about Crazy Horse. It did not seem wrong to the Sioux in 1874, or to Black Elk many years later, that their great leader should appear to be estranged from his own people and from their celebrations in dance and song. Crazy Horse was obviously struggling to find a new truth that would save his people.

When Erikson discusses the significance of identity in Gandhi's growing sense of himself as a leader, the terms help to illuminate Black Elk's description of Crazy Horse. *Identity,* Erikson has insisted, is a process which combines both "the core of the individual" and "the core of his communal culture":

> Great leaders know this definition instinctively, because they become great, and they become leaders, precisely because they themselves have experienced the identity struggle of their people in both a most personal and a most representative way. . . .
>
> Gandhi, in his development and in his emergence as a national leader, illustrates, because he lived every step of it, that each man, as a leader and as a follower, must

somehow integrate the irreversible facts of his development as a defined person within a given community in a particular geographic locus at a certain period of history so as to fulfill the potentialities of his existence.[5]

What Black Elk seems to have found in Crazy Horse was an embodiment of his people's condition. They were hungry and troubled, and Crazy Horse's physical appearance (similar to Gandhi's in important ways) affirmed those facts. Their traditions seemed somehow insufficient to meet a terrifying new reality, and Crazy Horse's estrangement from communal celebration acknowledged that as well. But Crazy Horse also had a sacred vision of "the real world that is behind this one." "It was this vision," Black Elk says, "that gave him his great power, for when he went into a fight, he had only to think of that world to be in it again, so that he could go through anything and not be hurt" (p. 71). When Crazy Horse had been killed, he continued to symbolize the power of visionary experience because he was not killed in battle but by duplicity. So Crazy Horse's greatness, as Black Elk saw it, appeared to be rooted in two paradoxes: he was estranged from his people at the same time that "everybody liked him" and he embodied their condition, and he fought bravely and skillfully in this world because of his commitment to the world of his vision.

THREE

Black Elk came to feel the power of those paradoxes in his own life, and in the years after Crazy Horse was killed he began to feel a sense of his own mission to the people: "I could feel them like a great burden upon me; but when I would go all through my vision again, I loved the burden and felt pity for my people" (p. 151). After years of feeling separated from his people by a vision he could not communicate, Black Elk was helped by Black Road and other medicine men to begin the task of sharing his vision. This process began when he was seventeen with the "horse dance," which was also Black Elk's ceremony of initiation into Sioux manhood. The horse dance brought momentary happiness to Black Elk and his people, and it raised his stature among the Sioux. But Black Elk found that the task of bringing the truth of his vision to his people was a formidable one, and he would be at it for the rest of his life.

In discussing this aspect of *Black Elk Speaks,* I will not say much about the substance of the great vision or Black Elk's subsequent lesser visions. They have been treated rather fully in a fine article by Robert F. Sayre, "Vision and Experience in *Black Elk Speaks.*"[6] Perhaps it is enough to say that the great vision, rich in traditional Sioux symbolism, is of *wholeness* finally triumphant. Past and future are joined; the Sioux nation is made whole and joined with other nations; all life is seen as interconnected; and Black Elk himself, physically cured during the time he experiences the vision, is given great spiritual powers. What I want to emphasize is the manner of Black Elk's commitment to his vision, his way of searching for truth. It involves what must seem to western readers yet another paradox, and Sayre has summed it up well: "He was a skeptical inquirer as well as a mystic or holy man, and his complete trust in his vision and its symbols was the basis of reason as well as faith."[7]

Black Elk's summary of his great vision takes more than twenty pages (pp. 18–39), and later he reminds Neihardt and his readers that "very much of it was not for words" (p. 174). But what seems crucially important about the vision, as I have said, is Black Elk's response, which continued to be tentative and searching throughout his life. It was tentative not in the sense that Black Elk doubted the importance of his vision; with the exception of a despairing time when he was fourteen, Black Elk had great confidence in the power of his vision. Although he does not put it quite this way, what he seems to have believed was that he had been allowed to glimpse as a child the wholeness of his people and their traditions, the spiritual foundations of their culture which they could build upon to remain whole despite the destructive forces that were moving in upon them. His response was tentative in the sense that he was never sure how best to interpret the vision to his people and help them act upon it. Consequently, he spent much of his adult life searching for ways to make the vision part of the living history of the Sioux.

This is the search which took Black Elk across the Atlantic for three years, beginning in 1866, a part of his life with which student readers of *Black Elk Speaks* are often impatient. How, they ask, could this holy man have expected to find sacred meaning in Buffalo Bill's western show? It sounds like foolishness when Black Elk says, "I thought I ought to go, because I might learn some secret of the Wasichu that would help my people somehow" (p. 182). Indeed, as he tells the story, Black Elk realizes that his stay in New York City should have taught him at once that there was nothing for his people in this other culture: "They had forgotten that the earth was their mother. This could not be better than the old ways of my people" (pp. 184–85). But Black Elk's journey to England and on into Europe makes good sense when one considers that part of him which Robert F. Sayre calls the "skeptical inquirer." Here was a people coming west, the Wasichu civilization, who combined an incomprehensible hunger for land, gold, and buffalo with a persistence and power that seemed irresistible. Was it so outrageous to think he might follow that power to its source and perhaps illuminate some part of his vision which still remained a mystery? Although he failed to find the illumination he was looking for, Black Elk saw enough of Queen Victoria and the dignified traditions of British monarchy to wonder if things might have gone better for his people under England (p. 189), a bit of speculation likely to make considerable sense to modern historians.

When Black Elk returned to his people in 1889, the Messiah movement had begun. Several tribes had accepted the belief, as he said, that "there was a sacred man among the Paiutes who had talked to the Great Spirit in a vision, and the Great Spirit had told him how to save the Indian peoples and make the Wasichus disappear and bring back all the bison and the people who were dead and how there would be a new earth." It was a vision far simpler than his own, with greater certitude; and Black Elk was skeptical. He worried that such belief might grow from despair, "just as a man who is starving may dream of plenty of everything good to eat" (p. 197). But during the year after his return, Black Elk began to recover the memory of his own vision, which had grown dim while he was abroad. Also, his brother and sister had died while he was away, and now his father died. In his grief, he felt increasingly the need to test the Messiah vision against his own, to find if possible some connection between the two that would allow him to believe in the Messiah. So when he heard the people were dancing on Wounded Knee Creek, he went to see the ghost dance. There his skepticism temporarily disappeared when he recognized important symbols from his great vision in the dance; and when he participated in the dances, he experienced what he came to view as lesser visions. Although he described this visionary experience in considerable detail, as though it were something he wished to preserve, by the time he spoke to Neihardt, Black Elk had come to view his participation in the Messiah movement as his "great mistake": "I had had a very great vision, and I should have depended only upon that to guide me to the good. But I followed the lesser visions that had come to me while dancing on Wounded Knee Creek" (p. 212).

It seems evident that Black Elk blamed himself for the massacre at Wounded Knee, which followed his participation in the ghost dances. He believed that in his failure to hold steadfastly to his great vision, he had failed to lead his people. Significantly, on the day of the massacre, December 29, 1890, when Black Elk went to Wounded Knee to try to help his people, he did not carry a gun because he was not sure enough of the Messiah religion to kill for it. He carried only a symbolic bow from his great vision. Having seen the slaughter of women and children, he no longer felt constrained; and in subsequent days he carried a gun as a warrior for the last time in his life. More importantly, in the days after Wounded Knee he was reminded once more of the power in his vision. When he could hold it in his mind, he was able to preserve himself and others from the guns of the soldiers. When he "awoke" for a moment from the vision, he was wounded. Like the power to heal the sick which his vision gave him, the power to fight was not enough. It was a fragment of something Black Elk believed he should have done to save his people, and when so many died at Wounded Knee, it was too late:

And I can see that something else died there in the bloody mud, and was buried in the blizzard. A people's dream died there. It was a beautiful dream.

And I, to whom so great a vision was given in my youth—you see me now a pitiful old man who has done nothing, for the nation's hope is broken and scattered. There is no center any longer, and the sacred tree is dead. [p. 230]

That is how Black Elk ended his account, but as I have said, his decision to speak of his vision to Neihardt and to make the trip to Harney Peak, as though to test the vision's power once more, suggest he entertained a hope, however faint, that his truth might still make a difference. He made such a hope explicit in 1947, when, at 85, he dictated to Joseph Epes Brown the text of *The Sacred Pipe*, an account of seven Sioux rituals: "I have wished to make this book through no other desire than to help my people in understanding the greatness and truth of our own tradition, and also to help in bringing peace upon the earth, not only among men, but within men and between the whole of creation."[8]

FOUR

Gandhi commits himself only to "the relative truth as I have conceived it," but he also clings firmly to the dictum that only insofar as we can commit ourselves on selected occasions "to the death" to the test of such truth in action—only to that extent can we be true to ourselves and to others, that is, to a joint humanity. This seems to call for an altogether rare mixture of detachment and commitment, and for an almost mystical conflux of inner voice and historical actuality. [Erikson, *Gandhi's Truth*]

Black Elk's truth is more than his great vision. It is the tentative, searching way he lived out his life in an effort to make the vision come alive among his people; and it is his faith in the vision, which transcended even his confidence in himself. Black Elk did not speak of "experiments in truth," as Gandhi did; but in *Black Elk Speaks* there is evident the same impulse to test the truth, an impulse that we associate more readily with science than with religious knowledge. If Black Elk's faith in his vision brought him little certitude about the changing world, it gave him a sense of hope and purpose in the face of the apocalypse that was the history of his people in his youth. What I want to suggest in conclusion, is that something like Black Elk's truth might work similarly for industrial societies which face the end of a world.

We face the end of a world that never existed—a world of limitless resources in which our ingenious technologies would solve any problem we could identify. That such a world was an illusion makes its end no easier to accept for those who find meaning and comfort in it; and in our efforts to preserve it, we are drawn to truths much simpler and more rigid than Black Elk's. We are drawn, for instance, to models like that of triage or Garret Hardin's lifeboat analogy as ways to understand our world. In the case of *triage,* we are told to view the world as though it were a great battlefield, where we must choose which of the wounded we can save. In the case of the lifeboat model, we must decide which nations in a world of poverty and famine we can assist without endangering our own survival.

Such models set aside the complex web of interrelationships that is the life we know on this planet, and they have been justly attacked. But it would be difficult to exaggerate the growing appeal of simple answers to our complex and frightening problems. Much activity that is called *contingency planning, futuristics,* and *simulation gaming* in universities, corporations, and governmental agencies can be linked to our modern faith in quantification and specialization as well, but the key is surely our desire to find meaning in a world that appears to be dying.

This desire is visible throughout our society. In addition to people committed professionally to imagining our future, or simulating it, others search for the fundamental, ultimately simple, explanation for human behavior. Both sociobiology and structuralism seem to be driven primarily by that impulse—the former to understand all life in terms of the gene, the latter to discover the underlying structures common to all human activity. And our students are drawn, understandably, toward these simplicities even when they do not like what sociobiology, for example, appears to say about altruism and the possibilities for true human community. But our students want answers now, as do others who turn to various kinds of self-improvement and individual therapy as ways of bringing some order to their world. It is as though the ideal of *parsimony* as it is understood in mathematics and physics, the delight in elegant simplicity, has come to dominate our approach to life itself.

Black Elk's truth can be an antidote to this desperate drive toward simple answers. It is not that Black Elk was uninterested in solutions to the terrible problems his people faced, but that he faithfully tested everything he found against a complex vision rich in mystery. Moreover, Black Elk's truth does not exist in isolation from other ways of affirming wholeness and peace in a fragmented world. Other American Indian literature approaches meaning in similar ways, and I have already pointed to important parallels between Black Elk's efforts to save his people and Gandhi's *Satyagraha*. Perhaps even more important for our own society are similarities between Black Elk's truth and the rise of ecology in modern science. Lynn White, Jr., a medieval historian, has commented on the fact that much criticism of modern science has come from people committed to ecological science—to a view of the world which stresses complex interdependencies among widely varying individual beings, places, and systems:

> *Modern science has been produced chiefly by two instruments: mathematics and the laboratory. Mathematics plays a part in ecological research, but conclusions rest on an almost aesthetic perception of the counterpoint among a vast array of qualitatively different quantities of both organic and inorganic beings. Ever since Galileo rolled balls down inclined planes, laboratories have been turning out some splendid results. But, whereas the laboratory method's power lies precisely in its isolation of the phenomenon to be studied, ecological science is, on principle, anti-isolationist. It is the science of totalities.*[9]

The conclusions of ecological science are likely to be tentative, not for lack of data but because of the complexity, even the mystery, of the interrelationships it tries to understand. The vision that undergirds ecology is of a biosphere greater than the sum of its parts because the relationships among the parts are crucial; the hope is that, beginning to understand this vast network of relationships, we might keep from doing irreparable harm to ourselves and our world.

My own hope is that ecological science will emerge as the dominant paradigm in modern science, and such a change, it seems to me, is related to making *Black Elk Speaks* and other native American literature integral parts of our tradition. Such literature encourages us to acknowledge the limits of what we know with certainty and to approach with humility the many aspects of our world that still remain a mystery. Such a shift in our thinking would not deny the importance of the restless search for knowledge that has been central to our intellectual history; indeed, it would affirm the kind of probing skepticism that was part of Black Elk's truth. But such a change would make us wary of simple answers and of turning knowledge too quickly into power.

NOTES

[1] Erik Erikson, *Childhood and Society* (New York: W. W. Norton, 1963), pp. 114–65.

[2] Roy Harvey Pearce, *Savagism and Civilization: A Study of the Indian and the American Mind* (Baltimore: The Johns Hopkins Press, 1965).

[3] John G. Neihardt, *Black Elk Speaks: Being the Life Story of a Holy Man of the Oglala Sioux* (New York: Pocket Books, 1972), p. 1. The page numbers for subsequent references to *Black Elk Speaks* will appear in parentheses following the quotations.

[4] Erik Erikson, *Gandhi's Truth: On the Origins of Militant Nonviolence* (New York: W. W. Norton, 1969), p. 395. Because I will be stressing similarities between their approaches to truth, it is probably important to acknowledge important differences between Gandhi and Black Elk. Gandhi became the powerful spiritual and political leader of millions in contrast to Black Elk, whose influence was probably felt in very limited ways even within the small-scale society of which he was a part. Gandhi made effective use of his own western education and was able to fuse ideas and customs from East and West. When Black Elk attempted a similar feat, he found little of use to his people. Gandhi was, in western terms, a success; Black Elk saw himself as an utter failure, although his decision to talk with Neihardt must complicate that assessment, as I will suggest.

[5] Erikson, *Gandhi's Truth,* pp. 265–67.

[6] *College English,* 32 (February 1971): 509–35.

[7] Ibid., p. 532.

[8] *The Sacred Pipe: Black Elk's Account of the Seven Rites of the Oglala Sioux,* ed. Joseph Epes Brown (Baltimore: Penguin Books, 1971), p. xx.

[9] Lynn White, jr., "The Ecology of Our Science," *Science 80,* 1 (November-December 1979): 72–76.

Part Five: REASONING TOGETHER

Reasoning Together

Karl Kroeber Writes: I wish to clarify and amplify issues raised in David Brumble's essay "Anthropologists, Novelists and Indian Sacred Material." I take this liberty because two of the authors he comments on were my father and mother, Alfred and Theodora Kroeber. Also I am editor of *Studies in American Indian Literatures,* the only scholarly journal devoted exclusively to Native American literatures, both contemporary and traditional, and the topics Brumble touches on are familiar to my readership. I hope I may help others to appreciate how complicated and significant are the nature and causes of changing attitudes (of both Indians and Whites) toward the religions of native peoples.

Since my personal relation is to the anthropologists Brumble speaks of, I'll comment only briefly on his presentation of Native American novelists. It is unfortunate that he concentrates on Frank Waters rather than better literary artists and important Indian figures. An obvious choice would be D'Arcy McNickle, especially because a comparison of his two superb novels *The Surrounded* (1936) and *Wind from an Enemy Sky* (1978), provides marvelous insight into the persistences and changes in both Indian and White attitudes toward the sacred core of Native American cultures, the thematic center of both novels.[1] Anyone seriously interested in either twentieth-century Native American literature or the leading Indian spokesmen and activists in the United States should attend to McNickle rather than Waters. In the 1950s, incidentally, McNickle published a book suitable for children, *Runner in the Sun,* which could illuminatingly be compared with Theodora Kroeber's children's version of the Ishi story, *Ishi, Last of His Tribe,* for both McNickle and my mother were conscious of the dangers, but not indifferent to the possibilities, of fictionalizing authentic Indian history, and, even trickier, authentic Indian imaginings.

Though it is understandable that Brumble concentrates on N. Scott Momaday among more recent artists, he oversimplifies Momaday's complex relation to his Kiowa heritage with statements such as "He is like a stand-up comedian who must explain his every joke." Two crucial issues for Native American writers Brumble overlooks are those of "the breed" and of cultural survival by change. The fine Native American poet Paula Gunn Allen has delineated the special intricacies of "full blood-half blood" definitions, which distinguish Indian ethnicity from that of

347

most other minorities in the United States. Leslie Marmon Silko from the Laguna Pueblo in her splendid novel *Ceremony* along with other excellences presents a subtly intelligent dramatization of how and why Indian cultures persist by changing.[2] Brumble's essay, inadvertently, gives an uninformed reader no sense of either the aesthetic richness of Native American literary accomplishments nor of the remarkable sophistication of contemporary Indian *self*-analyses.

A special warning needs to be sounded, however, about Brumble's casual dismissal of *Black Elk Speaks,* along with *Ishi in Two Worlds,* the best known and most influential book by or about Indians of the past fifty years. I can best illustrate why by quoting from the preface to a recent edition by Vine Deloria, Jr., himself a Sioux, and probably the leading Indian intellectual spokesman today. Of the part John Neihardt played in his editing of conversations with Black Elk, Deloria observes:

> *can it matter if we are talking with Black Elk or John Neihardt? . . . The very nature of great religious teachings is that they encompass everyone who understands them and personalities become indistinguishable from the transcendent truth which is expressed. So let it be with* Black Elk Speaks. *That it speaks to us with simple and compelling language about an aspect of human experience and encourages us to emphasize the best that dwells within us is sufficient.*

It should be noticed that Deloria does not equate the sacred significance of this work with "secrecy," but, to the contrary, with its general accessibility, noting that it "has become a North American bible of all tribes. They [young Indians of all tribes] look to it for spiritual guidance, for sociological identity, for political insight, and for affirmation of the continuing substance of Indian tribal life."[3]

All this does not, however, invalidate the importance of the questions Brumble poses:

> *If one does choose to write of the Indians' sacred things, what use is intended therefor? Why should the Indian lore be published at all? For preservation?—for whom? For entertainment? For moral instruction?—whose moral instruction?* [p. 32]

These are, indeed, questions which responsible Indian and White writers have long struggled with,[4] and which have engaged the attention of trained anthropologists in the United States since the origin of the profession. As to that, Alfred Kroeber was born in 1876, and Franz Boas, whose first student he was, about a generation earlier, in 1858. Professional anthropology in the United States thus came into being when official and popular attitudes were well represented by General Sherman's advice to troops in the West that every Indian killed this year was one less to be killed next year. Then as now, of course, every force had a counterforce. It is an oversimplification, for example, to say that obliviousness to Indian sensibilities toward the sacred characterized non-military Whites' dealings with Indians. Brumble cites J.L. Schulze (p. 32) as exemplary, but at the same time the more popular, influential, and still interesting books by Grinnell and McClintock—to mention only Whites who lived with and wrote about the Blackfoot—sensitively address the problems Schulze ignored.[5]

Brumble's selectivity in these matters seems to be representative of an historical and psychological naiveté characteristic of many modern scholars. He objects, for instance, to Theodora Kroeber's calling "unfathomably callous" men in a surveying party who discovered Ishi's crippled mother hidden in a cave and stole as "souvenirs" the utensils, implements of work and hunting, and the food upon which the woman's life clearly depended. To Brumble, however, their attitude is not unfathomable, because it is "like that of delighted children, who, full of the wonder of discovery, brings home birds' nests and unhatched eggs." The surveyors were adults with professional training, two of them deeply troubled by their actions,[6] and it is difficult to see how such "delighted children" are to be "explained," as Brumble then does, by associating them with the deliberate and systematic racist propaganda of Thomas Dixon. The muddle here seems, as I said, to derive from a naive, simplifying, pseudo-historicism, which produces psychological improbabilities.

An example is the assertion that Boasian anthropologists, though not racist, "were avid collectors of Indian materials with few scruples about the possible sanctity of what they collected, few scruples about the privacy of their informants."[7] So far as Boas and his most distinguished student, Alfred Kroeber, are concerned, the statement is as untrue as the later remark that Kroeber's respect for Ishi "did not extend to anything like hesitancy to collect, display, or publish items sacred to Ishi or to other Indians. He evidently felt that he could respect Ishi without respecting his taboos." I doubt that any person can fully respect another without having some respect for his attitudes toward what is sacred and profane. Certainly Alfred Kroeber could not.[8] Brumble can, of course, know nothing about Alfred Kroeber's "hesitancy" to collect or publish anything, and I know of no case of his publishing material he had reason to believe his sources wished kept private. While I cannot speak so authoritatively for Boas, I am certain the same is true for him, because, like my father, he had been reared in, and lived according to, a social code which respected profoundly, rather than abstractly, the privacy of others' beliefs and opinions.[9] Boas and Kroeber would not have published material that in Brumble's sense was "taboo;"[10] more important, Boas and Kroeber would not have published any material their sources did not want published *for whatever reason*. If one wants to understand the changing attitudes toward Native American sacred materials, one must recognize that the problem is not Boas' and Kroeber's lack of respect for what their Indian friends wished to keep private, for their respect on that score was complete. The problem is that most Indians with whom they (and many others) worked (their primary collecting in the field was done before 1920) were not only willing but often eager to recount and to have published matters which Indians today are reluctant to speak of and feel ought not to be published. Both attitudes make sense psychologically, if we understand in a more than superficial fashion their historical contexts.

Why around 1900 did Boasian anthropology so arouse young scholars to seek information from Indians, and why did the Indians so eagerly impart it? The most perceptive description of Boas' vision I know appears in my mother's book *Alfred Kroeber, A Personal Configuration:*

> *Kroeber stood . . . with Boas, who pointed out to him the land below, its shadowed parts and its sunny places alike virgin to the ethnologist. Virgin but fleeting—this was the urgency and the poetry of Boas' message. Everywhere over the land were virgin languages, brought to their polished and idiosyncratic perfection of grammar and syntax without benefit of a single recording scratch of stylus on papyrus or stone; living languages orally learned and transmitted and about to die with their last speakers. Everywhere there were to be discovered Ways of Life, many many ways. There were gods and created worlds unlike other gods and worlds, with extended relationships and values and ideals and dreams unlike anything known or imagined elsewhere, all soon to be forever lost—part of the human condition, part of the beautiful heartbreaking history of man. The time was late; the dark forces of invasion had almost done their ignorant work of annihilation. To the field then! With notebook and pencil, record, record, record. Rescue from historylessness all languages still living, all cultures. Each is precious, unique, irreplaceable, a people's ultimate expression and identity, which, being lost, the world is made poorer as surely as it was when a Praxitelean marble was broken and turned to dust.* [p. 51]

As I have pointed out, popular opinion and government policy alike in the last half of the nineteenth century favored destruction of the Indians. A basic fact about Ishi's people, the Yahi, is that they were deliberately and brutally exterminated. It was as a kind of counterforce that Boasians went into the field. There they met pitifully few survivors. Many of these were elderly, and they wished to save at least the memory of their cherished ways of life. Is it surprising that these victims of death marches and starvation "reservations" welcomed an opportunity to recount and thereby preserve the memory of their cultures, which seemed soon to be extinguished forever?

The condition of many American Indians today is intolerably wretched. But they are better off than Indians of seventy-five years ago. The American Indian population is growing, and some tribes are now estimated to be more populous than ever before. Indians have gained self-confidence and, understandably, they express this in hostility to intrusive anthropologists. Most intelligent people applaud their new attitude as a sign of the revivification of self-esteem. My own guess and hope is that in another couple of generations we will have Native Americans eager to tell Whites about their cultures in the pride of success, not out of the fear of extinction. In the meantime, it is comprehensible that some Indians resent even ethnologists of my father's or Boas' generations and think of them as having "stolen" by publishing stories and myths.

But to understand and respect this attitude is not necessarily to agree with it, and it is his failure to make such distinctions that leads Brumble to misunderstanding John Neihardt and Theodora Kroeber. Deloria's remarks, quoted above, sufficiently explain *Black Elk Speaks,* and *Ishi, Last of His Tribe* would have been an odd place to "apologize" for Alfred Kroeber's professional work, since the book was written for children. Brumble quotes from an unnamed 1973 edition; had he checked, he would have found that the first edition appeared in 1964, published by Parnassus Press in Berkeley, then exclusively a publisher of children's books. This work was written, reluctantly, by my mother only because after the first success of *Ishi in Two Worlds* several major publishers attacked her ("approached" would be too gentle) to let them bring out a children's version. One representative told her: "There is no copyrighting a person; we can get a ghost writer to do "Ishi;" if you won't do it, we will." To prevent this kind of exploitation (the nadir for her was, I think, a proposed tie-in with production of Ishi T-shirts) with considerable self-doubt she wrote the fictionalized version for Parnassus, then a local firm selling almost exclusively to children's libraries. Had it been possible later, my mother might have suppressed *Ishi, Last of His Tribe,* for I believe she was unsatisfied with her solutions to the problems of fictionalization I mentioned earlier. But the book was sold by Parnassus, and the ordinary paperback buyer (though not usually a literary scholar) may not realize he is buying children's fiction rather than factual history.

The crucial fact is that most buyers (apparently now including some scholars) without knowing the facts of the book's composition cannot distinguish a story intended for children from history intended for adults. Publishers understand this audience; the Oz books have recently been reissued as "adult fantasy." Any consideration of the change in attitudes toward Indian sacred material must take into account this quality of our culture's literary sensibility, even among those presumably trained to make intellectual discriminations. The Native Americans' resistance to ethnological exploitation is founded not alone on their growing self-confidence but also on their growing distaste for a society which makes best sellers out of trash like *Hanta Yo* and Castaneda's tripe.

Characteristic of such junk religiosity is a simple-minded identification of "sacred" and "secret." Some genuinely sacred matters are "secret," but many are not: there were the Eleusinian mysteries, and there are the Gospels. Reduction of sacred to secret is, I think, a pervasive disease of our time, which obscures the truly important problems involved in collecting religious materials from cultures other than the collector's own. These problems were of concern to Alfred Kroeber because he recognized the centrality of religion in most cultures. But "culture growth" was not, as Brumble says, a "normative" term for Kroeber; quite the contrary, it was a descriptive term. More than once he referred to his study of cultures as conducted in the manner of a natural historian. As deeply read in biology as in history, and having worked as an archaeologist, Alfred Kroeber was nearly as interested in dead cultures as in living ones. Indeed, he felt that one could not be fully understood without knowledge of the other. Theories of the "life" and "death" of cultures, especially as developed by Danilevsky, Spengler, Toynbee and Coulborn, focused several of his major papers. So his personal experience of the extinction of Indian peoples reinforced his most wide-ranging intellectual interests to direct his attention to the grim fact that cultures, like species, do cease to exist, and that the number now in existence is much smaller than the number we know to have become extinct. It is no wonder that he was pessimistic about Indians' ability to benefit from his preservation of their accomplishments. Nor does it take much imagination to realize the unique acuteness with which he must have felt the death of his friend Ishi as the final death of an entire people, that now Yahi artifacts must lie unused, unchanging in a museum.[11]

While it is not surprising, then, that Kroeber did not foresee the degree of Indian resurgence of the past few years, it is a complete misunderstanding of his (and Boasian anthropology) to represent him as *desiring* a single "world culture." He was at least as conscious as contemporary Native American writers that cultures continue, like living organisms, *only* through constant transformation—the questions of how and to what effect cultures change always fascinated him. The passage Brumble quotes as representative of Kroeber's thinking is not, as Brumble implies, assertive, but, as its final punctuation mark tells us, painfully interrogative, as Kroeber wonders how cultural change, and therefore cultural life, can continue in the conditions of a single "world culture": "When the exhausted, repetitive stage is reached, and there is no new rival culture to take over responsibility and opportunity and start fresh with new values in a different set of patterns—what then?" (p. 34).

This question rises from the center of Kroeber's personality and defines a bias of his professional studies, just as it reveals the affiliation of Boasian anthropology with Darwinian biology and its philosophic sources in Vico and Herder. Both the natural and human worlds delighted Kroeber because they were so diverse and unpredictable. This is why he sought out no sacred "secrets." He was deeply interested in different peoples' different religious beliefs and myths, practices and taboos, but he was as interested in their ways of weaving, cooking, playing games, philosophizing, dressing, defining kinship, counting, and so on. What people wished to keep secret he had no special urge to pry into, because there was so much else intriguing to be investigated and talked about. The "warm relationships" Brumble notices that Kroeber established with many Indians were based in part on his ability to arouse their interest in their own culture. The Boasian anthropology he practiced was a two-way transaction: the Indians with whom Kroeber and Boas worked extensively —George Hunt, Juan Dolores, Robert Spott—they regarded not as "informants" but as friends and colleagues. Not until I had grown up and left home did I learn the technical anthropological meaning of "informant." Although my father must have used the word in conversation, I cannot recall him doing so. And even today the idea of referring to Juan Dolores or Robert Spott as an "informant" turns my stomach. There are several appropriate names for someone who shares with you his knowledge and experience and dreams, but "informant" is not one.

The good Boasian fieldworker by his "insatiable curiosity" aroused the attention of Indians to features of their culture which they had taken for granted, as we all do with our culture. The Boasian fieldworker did not, like the structuralists of recent years, implicitly denigrate the significance of an individual "informant" by working from the assumption that *essential* features of a culture are "secret," hidden from the conscious awareness of individual participants in it. A Boasian anthropologist made life more interesting by giving everybody new insights to think about and talk over together. For such an anthropologist the vision of a unified, homogeneous world culture might seem inevitable, but it could be no ideal. Where there is only one way of doing things, when there are no more questions to ask about human diversity—what then?

H. DAVID BRUMBLE III, REPLIES:
In 1879 a group of ethnologists led by James and Matilda Cox Stevenson visited the Zuñi. These were difficult times. The Ute war was in progress over the border in Colorado, and the Apaches and Navajos were threatening war, according to Matilda Stevenson in *The Zuñi Indians: Their Mythology, Esoteric Fraternities, and Ceremonies*.[1] But fortunately, General Sherman —that same General Sherman whom Karl Kroeber regards as a counterforce to the Boasians—because of his "enthusiastic interest in ethnologic research," had directed his officers to give the Stevensons every possible assistance "in the way of transportation and otherwise." Matilda Stevenson was particularly interested in the ceremonials, but "while the priests and other high officials favored photographing the ceremonials . . . the populace were so opposed to having their masks and rituals 'carried away on paper,' that it was deemed prudent to make but few ceremonial pictures with the camera, and the altars and masks were sketched in color by the writer without the knowledge of the people."

Curiously—or do we here begin to sense what assistance General Sherman's army might have been willing to provide "otherwise"?—although the populace had so vigorously opposed the transportation of their masks "on paper," Stevenson reports no trouble at all when those masks, and a good deal more, were carried away on wagons: "The largest and most valuable collection, especially of fetishes and sacred vessels, ever secured from any of the pueblos was made at this time."

This amounted to many wagonloads of materials, so many that even "after securing all the available teams in the country," Stevenson still had to rely on General Sherman's army's wagons to haul the collection the fifty miles to the railhead at Las Vegas, New Mexico. Matilda Stevenson makes no mention at all, of course, of taking these wagonloads of fetishes and sacred vessels and stacks of field notes and pictures off to Washington in order to preserve them *for the Zuñi*. I quote again from Matilda Stevenson: "Two images of the saints and portions of the altar of the old Catholic church were obtained, the enamel finish on the face and limbs of the figures showing much artistic skill. . . . in order to determine whether they might be removed a council of religious and civil officers was held. It was finally decided that it would be well to have these objects go with the other Zuñi material to the

'great house' (National Museum) in Washington, where they might be preserved."
"It would be well"—the phrase fairly buzzes with Stevenson's unspoken assumptions
and the Zuñis' unmentioned feelings.

In 1886 Franz Boas travelled extensively among the Indians of the Northwest to
collect artifacts, myths, tales, descriptions of dances, songs, and more besides.
When he entered the northern reaches of Vancouver Island, wrote Boas, he could
see "the natives with their original customs and habits, and among them only one
white man!"[2] Whatever may have been Boas' private sense of the fragility of all that
he was seeing in that remote village, the appeal that he made to the Indians—and
their response— had nothing to do with preservation of their culture. Boas wrote
in a letter to his parents that before he could begin his collecting there he "had to
make a speech":

> So I arose and said: "My country is far from yours. . . . My people live far away and
> would like to know what people in distant lands do, and so . . . I went and I came
> here and I saw you eat and drink, sing and dance. And I shall go back and say: 'See,
> that is how the people there live. They were good to me and asked me to live with
> them.'" This beautiful speech, which fits their style of storytelling, was translated
> and caused great joy. . . . They were satisfied with this and promised to make a big
> celebration for me tomorrow. I think that I managed the affair quite well. . . .
>
> I gathered much material today. . . . I wonder how they will take it when they find
> that I want to buy the masks. [pp. 33–34]

These people were happy to have Boas witness their dances, not because they had
any idea that Boas would later "preserve" those dances by himself dancing before
the eye of a moving picture camera (as, in fact, he did), but rather because Boas was
willing to play the role of host as they understood it: "I held my own 'potlatch' to
pay for the dance held yesterday. . . . Gradually [the Indians] came and sat down on
the platform that extends around the house. A drum was brought, and while the
boy whom I had engaged as cook stirred the concoction the entire company sang
their songs. So far I have transcribed only one melody" (p. 37).

Boas planned to collect masks—especially those from secret societies—from these
people as well. For the Indians this was a matter of barter: "I was interrupted by
Herigon, who I had asked to bargain for me because I am supposed to be too aristo-
cratic to do any trading. In other words I would be cheated right and left" (p. 38).

In 1905, while he was a prisoner of war in Oklahoma, Geronimo agreed to tell the
story of his life.[3] Many years later his nephew Ace Daklugie had this to say:

> S.M. Barrett, Superintendent of Schools at Lawton, Oklahoma, wished to write a
> book about my uncle. And strangely, to me, Geronimo consented. Why . . . I still
> don't understand. . . . But my uncle wanted the book done, and he wanted me to
> act as his interpreter. . . .

There were many things to be considered. We were prisoners of war, and I believed that at any time a change in military command might mean a massacre for us. . . . There was a chance that Barrett was a spy. . . . As you know, Geronimo could foresee what would happen. I relied upon that and upon his habitual caution to keep us out of trouble.[4]

If his nephew and interpreter is uncertain as to Geronimo's reasons for cooperating with Barrett, we should move gingerly in suggesting what his motives might have been. It is clear, however, that he insisted upon being paid for his labors (p. 52), and it is clear that he tried to exert as much control as possible over the collaboration (p. 53). As one reads the autobiography, it seems fairly clear that Geronimo told the story of his life in order to correct the white man's conception of the Apache, in order to win understanding and leniency for his people, but of course we must remember that this was the reason for cooperation which Barrett had suggested to Geronimo. And Barrett did the editing.

In my "Anthropologists, Novelists and Indian Sacred Materials," I cited many more examples of Indian-anthropologist relationships which would tend to qualify Karl Kroeber's account of Indians' motivations in cooperating with anthropologists. And I could cite many more here; but, in fact, I am not at all certain whether Kroeber really disagrees with me on this point. I am, of course, aware that, as I put it, "some" Indians did "want to help preserve their culture" (p. 38). Does Kroeber simply want to substitute "most Indians" for my "some"? I used "some" intentionally; I find it difficult enough to determine what were the motivations of individual Indians, let alone the motivations of "most" of those who served as informants to A.L. Kroeber, Boas, and "many others." It is difficult enough to sort out the motives, say, of Don Talayesva[5]—about whom we know a great deal, and about whose relationship with the anthropologist Leo Simmons we know a great deal. But then it is perhaps because we know so much more about Talayesva's relationship with Simmons than we do about many other Indian-anthropologist relationships that the former seems so complex and the latter so simple.

Kroeber might, however, very well be right that "most" Indians who worked with anthropologists before the 1930s "welcomed an opportunity to recount and thereby preserve the memory of their cultures." But where is the evidence? Kroeber certainly is aware, for example, that A.L. Kroeber—like many other anthropologists in his and Boas' time—often worked through intermediaries, and so never even met many of the Indians whom he relied upon as informants. How can Kroeber be so certain as to how "most" of them felt? And even in those instances where it is clear that informants wanted to help preserve their culture, we must remember that this was a favorite persuasive device in the field: "You ought to tell me so that I can write it down, because in a few more years. . . ." As Kroeber puts it, A.L. Kroeber was often able to "arouse [Indians'] interest in their own culture." There is, of course, nothing wrong with arousing such interest, quite the contrary—but surely this must complicate Kroeber's sense that "most" would have "welcomed an opportunity to recount and thereby preserve the memory of their culture".

All this suggests that the long passage which Kroeber quotes from *Alfred Kroeber, A Personal Configuration,* the evocative account of the force that drove the Boasians, works much better as the explanation of the anthropologists' motivations which Theodora Kroeber intended it to be, than as the explanation of their informants' motivations which Karl Kroeber understands it to be.

On this point at least, I have the eerie feeling that Kroeber is actually arguing with someone other than me: Leslie Silko perhaps? She has written that ever since

> *white ethnologists like Boas and Swanton first intruded into Native American communities to "collect" prayers, songs and stories, a number of implicit racist assumptions about Native American culture and literature have flourished. . . .*
>
> *The second implicit racist assumption still abounding is that the prayers, chants, and stories weaseled out by the early white ethnographers, which are now collected in ethnological journals, are public property. Presently, a number of Native American communities are attempting to recover religious objects and other property taken from them in the early 1900s that are now placed in museums. Certainly the songs and stories which were taken by the ethnographers are no different.*[6]

Strong language. For Silko the anthropologists "intruded" and "weaseled"; their publication of stories and myths proceeded out of "racist" assumptions; and these published stories and myths are really stolen property which ought to be recovered by Indian peoples. For Kroeber, on the other hand, these same anthropologists met Indians who "welcomed an opportunity to record and thereby preserve the memory of their cultures". Not surprisingly, when we begin to look at individual Indian-anthropologist relationships, we find the truth scattered over a wide terrain between Silko's and Kroeber's positions. I have cited examples which must qualify Kroeber's generalization, but much of what he remembers for us about his father's work with such Indians as Robert Spott can serve in turn to qualify Silko's generalization. Spott eventually became so skilled—and so interested—an ethnographer that he published work under his own name and as co-author with A.L. Kroeber.[7] Those who still want to argue that it was theft, all theft, might look at A.L. Kroeber's *Fishing Among the Indians of Northwest California* to see the respect and credit given to Spott for his careful information.[8] Those still in doubt might look at Ruth Underhill's *Papago Woman,* the autobiography of Maria Chona.[9] I think that it would be very difficult to read this book cover to cover and come away with any sense that the collaboration between these two extraordinary women ought to be characterized in terms of "weaseling" rather than in terms of respect, interest, and friendship.

But in all of this Kroeber seems to miss my point. I wanted to contrast the sense of diversity we get when we read the anthropologists' accounts of their informants' motives with the supiciously uniform accounts of informants' motives we find in many popular books about Indians. Does Kroeber disagree with me here? Surely he too is suspicious of Frank Waters' claim that not most but *all* of his Hopi "spokesmen," some twenty-seven Hopi elders, regarded their work with Waters as a "sacred task." Surely Kroeber too is suspicious of Waters' claim that the Hopi regard his *Book of the Hopi*[10] as their "Bible." I can only assume, then, that Kroeber's suggestion that I ought to have discussed D'Arcy McNickle rather than Waters—like his suggestion that I ought to have dealt with such issues as "'the breed' and. . . . cultural survival by change"—proceeds out of the mistaken assumption that I thought that I was writing a history of American Indian literature.

Theodora Kroeber's *Ishi in Two Worlds* and *Ishi, Last of His Tribe* interested me in much the same way as Waters did: I was fascinated to see that part of what she chose to fictionalize in the second book was the motives of Ishi and A.L. Kroeber as they set about "preserving" Ishi's culture. There is nothing in the earlier, factual book to suggest that, as we read in the later version, Ishi was so eager that his culture might be preserved "in the notebooks" (p. 206) of A.L. Kroeber, that he was ever willing to divulge the details of something so private as his power vision—or even his own name. The fictionalized Ishi is wonderfully like Waters' twenty-seven Hopi elders: Ishi urges the work of preservation upon A.L. Kroeber, and we even find that Ishi's power vision had set for him this task of preserving his culture—with A.L. Kroeber, specifically, as his amanuensis. Neither is there anything in the factual version to suggest that A.L. Kroeber felt that he was working at the behest of the Indians. A.L. Kroeber himself, as I wrote, published accounts of his motives which explicitly contradict such a view. He was too forthright to pretend, as Waters did, that what he collected he collected for the Indians—although I think that no one would have been happier than A.L. Kroeber to realize how the ethnography to which he devoted his life would come to be studied by Indians interested in their history.

Kroeber's defense of Theodora Kroeber puzzles me. 1) I do not understand why he insists that I might have been duped, "like the ordinary paperback buyer," into thinking that *Ishi, Last of His Tribe* was factual history. I did first refer to the book as "a second, a fictionalized account of Ishi." 2) I do not understand why Kroeber feels that it is so important that the book was written "for children." He seems to want to have it both ways: Theodora Kroeber's account of informants' motivations is correct as we find it in *Ishi, Last of His Tribe,* and Brumble ought not to have discussed the book because it was written for children. In fact, I would have been every bit as interested in how Theodora Kroeber's tidying up of motives parallels that of Waters, whether she had been writing for pre-schoolers or the Book-of-the-Month Club. And by the bye, *Ishi, Last of His Tribe* is hardly "See Ishi go. Go Ishi, go." The book is 208 pages long, and according to its publisher, it is aimed at "the young adult." 3) I was surprised to find that Theodora Kroeber "might have suppressed" the book "had it been possible." If this is so, I find that my opinion of the book is higher than its author's own! I, for one, would have been much happier had it been possible to suppress NBC television's unintentionally comic "docu-drama," *Ishi, Last of His Tribe* (December 20, 1978).

Kroeber also is distressed at my characterization of A.L. Kroeber's and Boas' attitude toward Indian taboos—and he justly rebukes me for seeming to know what went on inside A.L. Kroeber's head: "Brumble can, of course, know nothing about Alfred Kroeber's 'hesitancy' to collect or publish anything, and I know of no case of his publishing material he had reason to believe his sources wished kept private." I am, of course, limited to published information. In A.L. Kroeber's *Zuñi Kin and Clan*[11] we find a Zuñi genealogy which goes back six generations. A.L. Kroeber wrote that "it would have been better to have more, but the Zuñi do not like to tell the names of their kinsmen; and while this is interesting in itself, it appears to have no direct bearing on relationship. This reluctance of my friends made the work of compiling the table much slower than it would have been with the free use of names, but I did not care to press their scruples, and while two or three would have been preferable to one, this seems sufficient to establish practically every trait in the system accurately."

This quotation is very helpful: 1) because it reflects A.L. Kroeber's sense of friendship for the people he studied; 2) because it makes clear that he was willing to transgress tribal taboos in the interest of science; 3) because it is also clear that he would have been quite moderate in so doing—more moderate, certainly, than some other early ethnologists. More moderate, I think, than Boas, whom we now rejoin after he has arrived at Cowichan (November, 1886). Boas wrote in his diary that the Indians here were "suspicious and unapproachable. . . . They evidently think I have come with some evil intent." At this point Kroeber's Boas would have sighed and politely moved on. The historical Boas, however, persevered. One Indian asked Boas to leave his property: "I replied just as quietly that I would leave when I felt like it." Another man refused to allow Boas to photograph his house. He also refused information because "he did not wish anyone to laugh at things that were their laws." Boas continues: "I could get nowhere with him, and, since I wanted something from this man, I did not insist. I said I cared nothing about the picture and spoke of other things. *In this way I learned a great deal by subterfuge.* A young man came with a stag and wanted me to take a picture of it. I placed it in front of the house I wished to photograph and so attained my end."[12] Boas seems very often to have had quite happy relations with his many, many Indian informants, but he also was quite capable of exercising his considerable pluck and ingenuity when he met opposition.

But part of my difference with Kroeber here is a result of my failure to distinguish, as I ought to have done, between respect for the feelings of an *individual* and compliance with a *society's* taboos. I am quite willing to believe that A.L. Kroeber (among others) respected the privacy of individuals. (This is, of course, why so many ethnographers' informants are known to us only by pseudonyms.) This he would have done, as Kroeber points out, because of the behests of his *own* culture.

There is also, evidently, some question as to A.L. Kroeber's attitudes toward cultures. Kroeber argues that I misunderstand A.L. Kroeber's talk about culture "growth," that this was not a normative term, but simply descriptive: cultures may develop, may evolve as plants evolve, but they do not get better. This, I take it, is an argument that A.L. Kroeber was a cultural relativist.

A *racial* relativist A.L. Kroeber certainly was, but not, I think, a cultural relativist—or at least this was the case in 1912 when he wrote about these issues in relation to Ishi:

> *The strange history of this survivor of the past seems to show that intelligence is not the monopoly of civilization. . . . Ishi has as good a head as the average American; but he is unspeakably ignorant. He knows nothing . . . of hours and years, of money and labor and pay, of government and authority, of newspapers and business, of the thousands of things that make up our life. In short, he has really lived in the stone age. . . . this does not involve a semi-animal . . . and inferior mental capacity. . . . What it does involve, is an almost inconceivable difference in education, in opportunity,* in a past of many centuries of achievement on which the present can build. . . . *in what his environment. . . . and* his puny native civilization *have made him,* he represents a stage which our ancestors passed through thousands of years ago.[13]

But I am no Indian and no anthropologist. Why should I be cluttering these pages with such meandering polemics? I do so because, however tangled these may be, they are vitally important issues to those who are interested in American Indian literature. Since so much of this literature comes to us via the ethnologists, if we hope to understand this literature in more than a casual way, we need to pay attention to the cultural and literary assumptions, the field methods, esthetics, translations, and editing procedures of individual ethnologists *as well as* to the cultural assumptions, esthetics, and narrative techniques of individual Indians. This is particularly important in the case of the longer narratives and especially in the autobiographies—in those cases where the editor-ethnologist has had most opportunity to influence the Indian's performance.

Attention to such matters in *Black Elk Speaks,* for example, has led us to realize that Neihardt's collaboration with Black Elk differed in some rather interesting ways from the account of the collaboration which we find in the book. Sally McClusky has shown that some important passages in the book are Neihardt's—including the oft-quoted passage about the death of the people's dream.[14] Michael Castro has shown that the emphasis on all the world's peoples, the book's pan-humanism, is largely Neihardt's. Castro has also shown that Neihardt diminished Black Elk's sense of his powers of destruction, that Neihardt imposed upon the book his own sense that Black Elk was a tragic figure, and that Neihardt exaggerated Black Elk's isolation and loneliness.[15] Furthermore, it was evidently Neihardt, not Black Elk, who decided that the autobiography was to end at Wounded Knee.[16]

It would seem, then, that *Black Elk Speaks*—whatever else it may be—is a working out of Neihardt's assumption that *real* Indians were very nearly gone from the face of the earth, the same assumption that led Charles Alexander Eastman, a Santee Sioux, to write on the frontispage of his intensely romantic *Indian Boyhood* that "the Indian no longer exists as a natural and free man. Those remnants which now dwell upon the reservations present only a fictitious copy of the past."[17] This notion has worked so much mischief that I am surprised that Vine Deloria and Kroeber would respond, "What can it matter?" when they find that Black Elk did not necessarily consider himself to be quite the "pitiful old man" we hear speaking at the end of the book. I find the knowledge bracing—even while I treasure the book just as Black Elk and Neihardt have given it to us.

Of course Castro and McClusky may be wrong. But I am surprised that Karl Kroeber, a scholar who has done so much in the way of careful interpretation and analysis of American Indian literature, would agree that it does not matter where Black Elk ends and Neihardt begins. Their book has, after all, been used as an important source of evidence by historians and anthropologists.

Careful attention to Indian-anthropologist relationships does not always lead to a diminished sense of the Indian's contribution. Paul Radin's *Crashing Thunder,* for example, is ripe for reevaluation. In 1961 Ruth Underhill wrote: "*Crashing Thunder* is not strictly an autobiography, although every word of it came out of the Indian's mouth. Rather it is a drama, centering around a religious experience. From the jumble of reminiscences which anyone pours out when talking about himself, one feels that the ethnologist has selected first, those bearing on religious education and myths, then the fall to drunkenness and murder, and finally, the salvation through peyote. . . . His vision achieved, Crashing Thunder's drama closes. . . . Here Radin was artist rather than ethnologist." [18]

Underhill evidently assumes that *Crashing Thunder* was the result of much the same kind of process which produced her own *Autobiography of a Papago Woman:* ethnologist leads informant to relate life history, asking questions along the way to guide informant and to insure adequate detail; ethnologist then edits this mass of (translated) material into something like chronological order, cutting repetitions and making the other changes necessary to transform a bundle of transcriptions into a single more or less continuous narrative—but *adding* nothing to the words of the Indian autobiographer. Underhill, however, did not structure her material in such a way as to turn it into a tightly unified drama; according to Underhill, Radin did. And anyone who has read *Crashing Thunder* will recognize the pattern of the book as Underhill describes it.

In fact, however, the book's pattern seems to be almost entirely the autobiographer's own. We must first remember that *Crashing Thunder* (1926) was based on an earlier book, *The Autobiography of a Winnebago Indian* (1920). Radin wrote of *The Autobiography*: "No attempt of any kind was made to influence [the autobiographer] in the selection of the particular facts of his life which he chose to present. So far as could be ascertained the Indian wrote the autobiography in two consecutive sessions in a syllabary now commonly in use among the Winnebago. The translation was made by the author on the basis of a rendition from his interpreter, Mr. Oliver Lamere" (p. 2).

Crashing Thunder is an expanded version of this *Autobiography*. Radin added more than a third again to its length by fitting in excerpts from material he had collected from Big Winnebago (Crashing Thunder was a pseudonym) over the years. Where, for example, Big Winnebago mentioned in the *Autobiography* that he had prayed at a certain time to the spirits, Radin interpolates in *Crashing Thunder* an appropriate prayer, which he had at some previous time taken down from Big Winnebago's dictation. Furthermore, the *Autobiography* had consisted of two parts, the first being the autobiography, the second being a separate description of traditional Winnebago teachings. In *Crashing Thunder* these teachings are interpolated at appropriate places along the way—but even in this new, expanded, popular version, the pattern of the book is the same as of the *Autobiography:* the old life, the fall, redemption by peyote.

How then can we reconcile the book's form—and it does read remarkably like a Winnebago version of Augustine's *Confessions* —with Radin's claims about his lack of interference? Quite simply, the confessional forms were well known to Big Winnebago because of his participation in the Peyote Cult, for the Peyote Cult which John Rave and Albert Hensley introduced among the Winnebago was heavily influenced by Christianity, and public confession was very much a part of the ritual.[19] There are published autobiographical conversion-confession narratives by both Rave and Hensley[20] and by Big Winnebago's brother.[21] These narratives, while brief, parallel Big Winnebago's sense of his life's pattern. As Rave summarized his life: "Throughout all the years that I had lived on earth, I now realized that I had never known anything holy. Now for the first time, I knew it. Would that some of the Winnebagoes might also know it!"[22]

Now Radin did suggest to Big Winnebago—as a way of moving him to cooperate —that he might want to describe the old ways in order to warn others of the dangers of those ways. But beyond this, I think, the pattern of *The Autobiography* is Big Winnebago's own. Having said this, there still is a good deal of work to be done with *Crashing Thunder* and *The Autobiography*—to say nothing of *Black Elk Speaks* and the many, many other as-told-to Indian autobiographies. Big Winnebago, for example, like his brother, says that he feels himself to be under a religious obligation to cooperate with Radin.[23] And so we have come full circle.

A concluding postscript: It probably ought to be noted that A.L. and Theodora Kroeber evidently did not share Karl Kroeber's distaste for the term "informant." Theodora Kroeber wrote: "I myself never saw Kroeber with an interpreter, since the informants who were also our friends happened also to be bilingual. . . . Juan Dolores [and] Robert Spott," among others.[24] And A.L. Kroeber could mention "Robert Spott, who is named as informant,"[25] just as he so mentioned hundreds of others who provided "information."

NOTES TO KROEBER
[1] D'Arcy McNickle, *The Surrounded* (New York: 1936; rpt. Albuquerque: 1978); *Wind From An Enemy Sky* (San Francisco: 1978).
[2] See Paula Gunn Allen, "A Stranger in My Own Life," *Newsletter of the Association for the Study of American Indian Literatures* 3 (1979), no. 1, pp. 1–10; no. 2, pp. 16–23; and Leslie Marmon Silko, *Ceremony* (New York: 1977).

[3]I quote from the preface to *Black Elk Speaks,* ed. John Neihardt (Lincoln, Neb.: 1979), pp. xiv and xiii.

[4]Indian writers as early as William Apes, *Indian Nullification* (1835), George Copway, *The Traditional History . . . of the Ojibway Nation* (1850), and Charles Eastman, *The Soul of an Indian* (1911), addressed these questions. Probably the best informed and most sensitive students of the sacred among contemporary anthropologists, surprisingly unmentioned by Brumble, are Dennis Tedlock and Clifford Geertz. The distinguished folklorists Richard Dorson and Barre Toelken have written perceptively on these matters.

[5]*James Bird Grinnell's Blackfoot Lodge Tales* (New York: 1892; 1920), and Walter McClintock's *The Old North Trail* (London: 1910), have both been reissued by Nebraska University Press, which also has begun (1980) publication of the texts collected by James R. Walker, *Lakota Belief and Ritual,* eds. Raymond J. DeMallie and Elaine A. Jahner. These important accounts of Oglala traditional religion were given to Walker by some of the most revered of the Sioux, because, as one said, "The Gods of the Oglala would be more pleased if the holy men told of them so that they might be kept in remembrance and all the world might know of them" (pp. xiii–xiv).

[6]It is worth quoting what Brumble omits from *Ishi in Two Worlds* (p.112): "Apperson came back to Bear's Hiding Place [where Ishi's mother had been] early the next morning; it was much on his mind that a terrible wrong had been done there . . . It should be said that not only was Apperson much troubled by the episode and its outcome, but Robert Hackley, one of the surveyors, wrote to Waterman on September 5, 1911, while the papers were full of the finding of Ishi and of retellings of this earlier discovery of the village. Said Hackley: 'The discredit of driving these harmless people from their home does not belong to the survey party altogether as some of the cattlemen [in the party] considered they had a grievance on account of stolen goods and proceeded to take matters off our hands.'"

[7]There are, or were, a lot of Boasians, and to the attitudes and practices of some Brumble's criticisms may be justly applied. Paul Radin, whom I cite because his work has been popular with *Kenyon Review* types playing with "primitive" literature, though a charming academic irregular, frequently distressed Boas and Kroeber. I find Radin's "literary" observations bothersome, because he so grossly imposes Western European patterns on Indian materials. But my concern is with Boas and Kroeber, because it is with them that one can define the central thrust of prestructuralist Boasian anthropology, so important to the history of the changing attitudes in which Brumble and I are interested.

[8]As is made clear in *Ishi in Two Worlds.* One portion of the book which has attracted much attention, for example, deals with my father's efforts to prevent an autopsy on Ishi's body, leading to his statement: "If there is any talk about the interests of science, say for me that science can go to hell. We propose to stand by our friends" (p. 234).

[9]A good description of the cultural milieu in which Alfred Kroeber grew up will be found in Theodora Kroeber, *Alfred Kroeber: A Personal Configuration* (Berkeley and Los Angeles: 1970), pp. 5–42, especially the section "19th Century Humanism," pp. 38–42.

[10]Both Kroeber and Boas were more circumspect than Brumble in using "taboo,"

in part because it means such opposite things, what is set aside because *either* sacred *or* profane.

[11]It should be remembered that Ishi was not the only "last informant" with whom my father worked, though the one with whom he developed the deepest emotional ties. Those interested in the detailed facts of Ishi's history should consult a book not mentioned by Brumble, *Ishi the Last Yahi: A Documentary History,* eds. Robert F. Heizer and Theodora Kroeber (Berkeley and Los Angeles: 1979).

NOTES TO BRUMBLE

[1]*23rd Annual Report of the Bureau of American Ethnology* (1904). All of the Stevenson quotations are from pp. 16–17.

[2]*The Ethnography of Franz Boas: Letters and Diaries of Franz Boas written on the Northwest Coast from 1886 to 1931,* ed. Ronald P. Rohner (Chicago, 1969), p. 34.

[3]S.M. Barrett, *Geronimo: His Own Story* (N.Y.: 1970 [1906]).

[4]As found in Eve Ball, *Indeh: An Apache Odyssey* (Provo, Utah: 1980), p. 173.

[5]Leo W. Simmons, *Sun Chief: The Autobiography of a Hopi Indian* (New Haven: 1942).

[6]"An Old-time Indian Attack in Two Parts: Part One: Imitation 'Indian' Poems," as found in *The Remembered Earth,* ed. Geary Hobson, (Albuquerque: 1979), pp. 211–12.

[7]See, e.g., Spott and Kroeber, "Yurok Narratives," *University of California Publications in Archaeology and Ethnology* 35 (1942): 143–256.

[8]*Anthropological Records* 21, no. 1 (1960), e.g., pp. 1, 76, 113.

[9]*Papago Woman* (New York: 1979). This is a republication—with a fascinating new introduction—of *The Autobiography of a Papago Woman,* Memoir 36 of the American Anthropological Association (1936).

Whether these Indian informants were exploited by their anthropologist is, I think, a more difficult question. If we ask, did the Indians *feel themselves* to be exploited, the answer is clearly *no* in some cases, clearly *yes* in some cases, and difficult or impossible to decide in other cases. But it is quite possible to argue that people can be exploited whether or not they feel themselves to be exploited. Marvin Harris, *Cultural Materialism* (New York: 1979), pp. 236–38, provides a brief introduction to these matters.

[10](New York: 1972 [1963]), p. xxi. I mentioned Albert Yava's skepticism about Waters' claims (p. 37); I might also have mentioned Alfonzo Ortiz, "An Indian Anthropologist's View on Anthropology," in *The American Indian Reader,* 1 (San Francisco: 1972), p. 12: The *Book of the Hopi* "has been repeatedly denounced as a fabrication . . . and several elders who were listed as collaborators in the preface were surprised to discover this."

In my discussion of Waters' *The Man Who Killed the Deer,* by the way, I stupidly spoke of Hopis, where I should have said Tiwas. My thanks to both Kay Sands and N. Scott Momaday for pointing this out to me.

[11]*Anthropological Papers of the American Museum of Natural History* 18, no. 2 (1917), p. 51.

[12]*The Ethnography of Franz Boas,* pp. 53–54. (Emphasis mine.)

[13] As found in *Ishi, the Last Yahi: A Documentary History,* eds. Robert F. Heizer and Theodora Kroeber (Berkeley: 1979), p. 123. (Emphasis mine.) This volume, unfortunately, did not appear until after my essay was in press.

[14] *"Black Elk Speaks,* and So Does John Neihardt," *Western American Literature* 6 (1972): 231–42.

[15] "Poetic License in *Black Elk Speaks,"* paper presented at a special session of the Modern Language Association devoted to American Indian autobiography (1979).

[16] See Neihardt's letter to Black Elk, wherein he suggests the idea of the book to Black Elk, Appendix I of the 1979 Nebraska Press edition of *Black Elk Speaks.*

[17] (Boston: 1922 [1902]). Eastman left his Sioux village at the age of fifteen, went on to medical school, and was the doctor in attendance upon the Indian survivors at Wounded Knee. The second volume of his autobiography, *From the Deep Woods to Civilization* (Lincoln, Neb.: 1977 [1916]), evinces a good deal more feeling for the plight of the reservation Indians.

[18] As found in Underhill's forward to Nancy O. Lurie, *Mountain Wolf Woman* (Ann Arbor, Mich.: 1971 [1966]), p. ix.

[19] See Weston La Barre, *The Peyote Cult* (New York: 1971 [1959]), p. 99; Radin, *The Winnebago Tribe* (Lincoln, Neb.: 1970 [1923]), p. 340.

[20] Radin, *The Winnebago,* pp. 341–52.

[21] Paul Radin, "Personal Reminiscences of a Winnebago Indian," *Journal of American Folklore* 27 (1913): 293–318. This brother's *real* name was Crashing Thunder. See Brumble, *An Annotated Bibliography of American Indian and Eskimo Autobiographies* (Lincoln, 1981), nos. 73, 74, 129, 349.

[22] Radin, *The Winnebago Tribe,* p. 343.

[23] Radin, *Autobiography,* p. 67.

[24] Foreword to A.L. Kroeber, *Yurok Myths* (Berkeley: 1976), p. xiv.

[25] "Fishing Among the Indians of Northwestern California", *Anthropological Records* 21, no. 1 (1960): 1.